Glimpses of the God-Man, Meher Baba

Books by Bal Natu

Glimpses of the God-Man, Meher Baba (1977)
Vol. I 1943-48

Glimpses of the God-Man, Meher Baba (1982)
Vol. III February 1952 - February 1953

Glimpses of the God-Man, Meher Baba (1984)
Vol. IV February - December 1953

Glimpses of the God-Man, Meher Baba (1987)
Vol. V January 1 - March 6 1954

Glimpses of the God-Man, Meher Baba (1994)
Vol. VI March 1954 - April 1955

The Samadhi: Star of Infinity (1997)

Showers of Grace (1984)

Our Constant Companion (1983)

When He Takes Over (1988)

Tales of Meher Baba's Love (2001)

Conversations with the Awakener (1991)

More Conversations with the Awakener (1993)

Intimate Conversations with the Awakener (1998)

Flowing Conversations with the Awakener (2004)

Intimate Times with Meher Baba - Glimpses of the God-Man at Guru Prasad (2018)

Avatar Meher Baba Bibliography, 1928 to February 1978 (1978)

AVATAR MEHER BABA
October 16, 1950
Mahabaeshwar
M.S. India

Glimpses
of the
God-Man,
Meher Baba

Volume II (Jan. 1949 – Jan. 1952)

Bal Natu

copyright © 1979, 2022 Avatar Meher Baba P. P. C. Trust, Ahmednagar, Maharashtra, India.

First book edition 1979 by R.J. Mistry, Meher House Publications, Bombay, India. 1979.

Print-on-demand edition by Companion Books, USA, 2022. A near-facsimile reprint of the 1979 Meher House Publications edition.

Photographs courtesy of MSI Collection.
All used by permission.

No part of this book may be reproduced, stored in a retrieval system, or transmitted in any form without prior written permission of the publisher, except by a reviewer who wishes to quote brief passages in connection with a review written for inclusion in a magazine, newspaper, or broadcast.

For information write:
Avatar Meher Baba P.P.C. Trust, Post Bag #31,
Ahmednagar 414001, Maharashtra State, India.
Or visit www.avatarmeherbabatrust.org.

ISBN: 978-0-9565530-5-8

*To the Loving and Abiding Presence
of the God-Man, Meher Baba*

Contents

Acknowledgments	ix
Preface	xi
1. Meher Baba at Mount Abu — 1949, Part I	1
2. Seclusion Preceding Meher Baba's New Life — 1949, Part II	30
3. Meetings Directing the New Life — 1949, Part III	57
4. Old Life Ends; New Life Begins — 1949, Part IV	90
5. Benares to Moradabad — 1949, Part V	128
6. Termination of the Gypsy Life — 1950, Part I	165
7. New Plans in the New Life — 1950, Part II	183
8. Stay at Motichur — 1950, Part III	200
9. Leaving Manjri Mafi — 1950, Part IV	227

10.	Headquarters at Satara — 1950, Part V	253
11.	Sermon on the Mount at Mahabaleshwar — 1950, Part VI	275
12.	Hundred Days' Seclusion — 1951, Part I	313
13.	*Manonash* Meeting at Hyderabad — 1951, Part II	329
14.	Beginning of the *Manonash* Phase — 1951, Part III	353
15.	Arriving at the Blessed Consummation — 1951, Part IV	372
	Glossary	402
	Bibliography	405

Acknowledgments

I gratefully acknowledge with thanks permission to reprint published material given to me by Adi K. Irani; The Universal Spiritual League in America, Inc.; Sufism Reoriented, Inc., Walnut Creek, CA.; Meher House Publications, Australia; Kitty Davy, Filis Frederick, Freiny Nalavala and Naosherwan Anzar. (see Bibliography). My special thanks to Pendu (A.R. Irani). one of Meher Baba's New Life companions whose diary enabled me to narrate the events of the *Manonash* phase.

Sincere thanks are due to my dear friend U. G. Parkhe, who untiringly typed the manuscripts of this Volume and also to May Lundquist for her help in typing. The picture on the cover page and those inside the book were taken by Padri, one of Meher Baba's closest disciples, and these with many others, covering different phases of Avatar Meher Baba's life are collected and copyrighted by Lawrence Reiter (Hermes). I am indebted to them both for their kind permission to use these pictures in *Glimpses of the God-Man, Meher Baba Vol. II*.

It was a happy coincidence that when Steve Klein visited India he offered his services for editing and preparing the final manuscript of this Volume, with the help of his wife Daphne. I owe thanks to them for their loving contributions.

I also feel greatly indebted to William Le Page of Meher Baba Foundation, Australia for his suggestions and encouragement; and my sincere thanks to Peter Booth for meticulously proof-reading the entire text.

I am especially grateful to Eruch Jessawala for his valuable guidance and suggestions throughout my writings.

With much love and gratitude in the Eternal Beloved, to all those who have helped me in various ways in this work.

BAL NATU

Meherazad
October 16, 1978

Preface

AVATAR MEHER BABA, who observed silence for over four decades, once conveyed through His graceful gestures to a large group of His followers:

> I am the only Beloved and you are all my lovers; or I am the only Lover and you are all my beloveds. I am the Ocean of Love.*

Meher Baba's life, lived as the Divine Beloved and Lover in one, is the theme of the two volumes of *Glimpses of the God-Man*. The first** narrates a part of His Old Life wherein He asserts Himself as the Beloved and the second mainly presents His New Life, the life of a lover.

The terms, Old Life and New Life, may sound strange to readers for they have not been used in the life story of any *Avatar* — the God-Man. So, instead of commenting on these two terms, I prefer to quote an excerpt from a message given by Meher Baba in October 1950 when He stepped into the Old Life for a few hours from the New Life. It reads:

> My Old Life places me on the altar of Absolute Godhood and Divine Perfection. My New Life makes me take the stand of a humble servant of God and His people. In my New Life, Perfect Divinity is replaced by Perfect Humility. In my New Life I am the Seeker, the Lover and the Friend. Both these aspects — Perfect Divinity and Perfect Humility — have been by God's Will and both are everlastingly linked with God's Eternal Life.

---

* C. B. Purdom, *The God-Man*, p. 299.
** *Glimpses*, Vol. I, published by Sufism Reoriented, Inc., Walnut Creek, Calif., USA, 1977.

To be frank, it is beyond my ability to explain, even remotely, the significance of these two terms. Nevertheless, I somehow feel that these two phases in the life of Meher Baba are not antithetical but complementary and it is only when they are taken together that the life of the God-Man as the Ocean of Love, in relation to His work for humanity, can be expressed. Based on this meager understanding, I have dared to "rush in" to narrate what I have gathered from various incidents and messages as well as explanations given by Meher Baba! My main intention, however, is to present a factual account of the New Life phase of Meher Baba, and the subtle implications can be judged or felt by the readers themselves.

As I commenced writing this particular account, time seemed to unfold backwards and the incredible stories I had heard from Meher Baba's companions — Eruch, Pendu, Adi and others — often flooded my memory, adding to the remembrance of the paltry part He allowed me to play in it. Arid intellectualism or cold-hearted mysticism will not help one to appreciate the profundity of the New Life led and lived by Meher Baba. Unless the mind, of its own volition, is completely silenced, its chattering will continue, and my mind is no exception to this. I presume that one of the ways of effacing one's mind is to share with others the *lilas** of the God-Man or to sing His praise. And who knows, this may lead to that blessed event of being struck by a glance of the Eternal Beloved, and at the opportune moment the awakened heart shall blossom into songs of His praise, eventually drowning all thoughts and words in the Infinite Silence; the drop merging in the Ocean of Love!

But until that time one has to find, maintain and enrich one's relationship with the One worthy of being served and loved. This may in a way appear simple, but

---

* *lilas*: The incidents revealing love and knowledge of the God-Man through the Divine Game He plays with Creation.

PREFACE

isn't it most difficult? Why? Avatar Meher Baba once stated:

> The humor of the Divine Love-Game is that the One who is sought is Himself the seeker.*

What fantastic fun! And in this incredible game, writing and reading can be one of the *Avatar's* infinite moves, to bring Him closer to Himself, in His Ocean of Love.

This book is a continuation of *Glimpses, Vol. I*. Those who begin reading *Glimpses* with this volume may not feel conversant with some of the non-English terms frequently used in this book; I request them to refer to the Glossary for their meaning. The opening chapter of Vol. II succintly introduces readers to the New Life phase of Meher Baba while continuing to narrate His work with the *masts*, the God-intoxicated souls.

The New Life of Meher Baba has no parallel in known spiritual history. However, there is some mention of God-absorbed souls in *Vedantic* and *Sufic* traditions. Such God-intoxicated souls, also known as *masts*, are spiritually advanced individuals overpowered with, and absorbed in, their love for God — the Beloved. In the 1940s, contact with the *masts*, in different parts of India and Pakistan, constituted one of Meher Baba's main external activities. He had clarified that these contacts had a spiritual purpose of recharging and raising the consciousness of the *masts*. *The Wayfarers* by William Donkin, with a profound foreword by Meher Baba, is a monumental work, the only one of its kind. In this book the different characteristics of the *masts*, experiencing sublime states of consciousness in which they are oblivious of the gross world, are recorded and their significance elucidated. Those who are interested in the study of inner realities of existence will be fascinated and enlightened by the material provided in

---

* Meher Baba, *The Everything and the Nothing*, p. 17.

that book. The *mast* contacts mentioned in Vol II, from 1950 onwards are not recorded in *The Wayfarers*.

Owing to these two intricate and puzzling subjects, I often thought of giving up totally the compilation of the inscrutable events and episodes mentioned in this volume. But, somehow, I don't know how, I summoned up courage and ventured to put on record through this volume the external features of the God-Man's life, led during the New Life phase.

In this narration of Meher Baba's life I have tried to create a pattern by shuttling back and forth often presenting an incident from the earlier years or quoting bits of messages given by Him during the later years. I have taken this liberty with the hope that in this way I might be able to weave a more comprehensive picture of His Life. A short life sketch of Meher Baba by His secretary-disciple, Adi K. Irani, forms the Introduction to the first volume of *Glimpses;* its reading will be helpful in arriving at a basic understanding of the life and work of Meher Baba — the *Avatar* of the age. To represent one of the common reactions regarding the role/mission of the *Avatar,* I intend to quote below a part of an interview which Meher Baba gave to a journalist at Nasik, India. The reporter was greatly impressed by Meher Baba's simple and profound replies on different subjects. But as he was not interested in the deeper aspects of life, he asked Meher Baba:

"What then is your philosophy about?"

"I have no philosophy."

"If you have no new philosophy to preach, what is your job?"

"My job," Baba answered, without wincing at the word, "is to awaken the feeling of Godliness in humanity."*

During one of His visits to the West, in reply to a question, "What is God's business?" Meher Baba, with His unique sense of humor stated:

---

* *The Awakener*, Vol. X, No. 2, (1964), p. 1.

PREFACE

God the everlasting and indivisible, transacts His universal illusory business of duality by playing His dual role of opposites simultaneously and eternally. Saints are God's assets and sinners are His liabilities. God, the infinite source of wisdom and justice, goes on eternally turning His liabilities into assets.*

And the Advent of God as the God-Man is to quicken this "business" through "the nobility of a life supremely lived, of a love unmixed with desire, of a power unused except for others, of a peace untroubled by ambition, of a knowledge undimmed by illusion."**

In other words, the *Avatar's* "business" is to awaken the heart of humanity, to the innermost presence of God. Meher Baba has often stated, "I have come not to teach but to awaken." The *Avatar* is the first, perfect miracle of the eternal awakening of God as God in Man, so He is known as the God-Man. In His unbounded love and compassion for humanity, age after age, the "first-born" assumes a human form and this is known as His Advent and as time is immeasurable He is also the Ancient One. In conclusion, I quote one of Meher Baba's messages declaring His divine status. He categorically stated:

> I was Rama, I was Krishna, I was this One, I was that One, and now I am Meher Baba. In this form of flesh and blood I am that same Ancient One who alone is eternally worshipped and ignored, ever remembered and forgotten.
>
> I am that Ancient One whose past is worshipped and remembered, whose present is ignored and forgotten and whose future (Advent) is anticipated with great fervour and longing.***

In the early years of my contact with Avatar Meher

---

* Meher Baba, *Life At its Best*, p. 11,
** Meher Baba, *Discourses*, Vol. 3, p. 16.
*** Meher Baba, *The Everything and the Nothing*, p. 48.

Baba, His overwhelming presence used to bother me a lot. The enormity of His Divinity would confuse me about the nature of my relationship with Him — the mighty, Infinite One. Sometimes I even feared that my weaknesses and drawbacks might take me away from Him! Then one day at Satara, as I was sitting in Meher Baba's presence, He asked me, "Any worry?" I said, though a bit shyly, "Baba, you are so Great and Infinite that I wonder whether I will hold on to you (to your *daaman*) till the very end." Baba looked at me with an expression conveying what a foolish question I had asked Him! He gestured that He is the Greatest and He is also the Smallest. Then He just smiled at me and it was a perfect answer. From this little event I gathered that whatever "great or small" is offered to Him in His loving remembrance pleases Him and takes one closer to Him. So in my own simple way, I am trying to please Beloved Avatar Meher Baba through *Glimpses*, and if others too feel pleased to some extent, glory be unto Him; it will be another joke of the Perfect Puppeteer!

I have tried to be accurate in the narration of Meher Baba's life and have quoted His statements and messages from authentic sources. In this important and responsible work, Eruch Jessawala, one of Meher Baba's closest disciples, greatly helped me by graciously going through the entire manuscript of *Glimpses, Vol. II*. His suggestions and corrections were most valuable and I feel greatly indebted to him for his loving guidance. If, however, a few errors have crept in, then I, as an amateur in this venture of writing, am responsible for them. However, when anyone sincerely tries to love the Eternal Beloved, Meher Baba, then a part of his heart becomes consecrated to Baba, to be used as He wishes. The lover's very being starts to become hollow as a reed. And when unaware of its "fluteness", Baba in His own time, plays a few good notes. If some lines from this writing appeal to anyone, the secret rests in the whim and pleasure of the Perfect Piper — Meher Baba.

PREFACE

As a drop of rain finds its way to the ocean—its source and goal — so also, I hope that this writing, a feeble response to Avatar Meher Baba's love, shall reach Him, the Ocean of Love.

BAL NATU

Meherazad
October 16, 1978

1

Meher Baba at Mount Abu

1949 — Part I

The Most Profound Phase

THE Advent of God as the God-Man is the perfect blending of the human and the Divine in one. So the life of the God-Man appears simple and appealing and yet mystical and puzzling as well; it cannot help being so. This quality manifested itself abundantly in the life of Avatar Meher Baba. Those who met Him, and especially those who lived with Him were amazed to watch Meher Baba's creative responses, so loving, so surprising! Countess Nadine Tolstoy, one of Meher Baba's disciples, has very aptly dealt with this aspect revealed through the life of the God-Man. She writes:

> Everything in him is a wonder, yet he is the most simple and selfless man that ever existed. His state of constant and unceasing oneness never changes under conditions of any kind. It is really beyond all human understanding. So marvellously human, he is obviously beyond the human plane, yet he is the Friend, the soul and the heart of everyone.... He is perpetual, universal life-activity, reaching to all planes and forms, constantly helping, ordering, raying its power and love — in all directions simultaneously. Never at rest, yet always divinely at rest — he is the motion in stillness and peace.... In applying to him our human terms, we can give him all names and definitions, but it will be only a part of the truth, and only so far as our perfections can go. He remains ever beyond the definitions of the human mind. Being a

super-conscious divine-man [God-Man], he is limitless, infinite, free and impersonal—"The Universal One."*

In the life of Avatar Meher Baba, the year 1949 will be especially remembered for ushering in the most human yet divine phase of His work. Its inauguration was veiled with unpredictability, and the mystery, which surrounded it for its duration, was not in the least dispelled at its termination. This phase which commenced on October 16, is known as the New Life. Meher Baba lived this New Life to its fullest extent, but rarely explained much about it. When asked by one of His companions if such a New Life had been undertaken by anyone in the past or if He was the first One to introduce it, He replied, "I do not know and therefore I cannot say anything more than this viz., 'This is it whatever it is.'" This answer clearly shows that He did not wish to disclose the significance of this phase through words. We know something of its external aspects and have a few explanations given by Baba during this period, but little do they help us understand the link between His Old and New Life. Once Meher Baba stated:

Although the New Life has emerged from me, I am not at all bound by it.... This New Life is endless, and even after my physical death will be kept alive by those who live the life of complete renunciation of falsehood, lies, hatred, anger, greed and lust; ... who do not let go the hand of Truth, and who, without being upset by calamities, bravely and whole-heartedly face all hardships with 100% cheerfulness, and give no importance to caste, creed and religious ceremonies.

This New Life will live by itself eternally, even if

---

* Countess Nadine Tolstoy, "Meher Baba and My Spiritual Path," *Meher Baba Journal,* September, 1941, pp. 621, 623.

there is no one to live it.*

From this it can be concluded that Meher Baba expected those who earnestly wished to know more about this phase to get into it boldly and that He would be their Eternal Companion. More about this profound phase as we come to that account in the latter part of the year — a most significant year!

A Special Circular

To begin with, on New Year's Day a special circular was sent to all the disciples and devotees of Meher Baba. The gist of some of the points mentioned therein is given below:

(1) Meher Baba hinted at an impending personal disaster.
(2) Meher Baba's close disciples were to be in readiness to face real tests and trials.
(3) All those who believed in Meher Baba were asked to observe complete silence for the month of July, 1949.
(4) From February 1, till the end of the year, the followers were not permitted to write letters to anyone, anywhere; however, for emergencies, telegrams were allowed.
(5) The year 1949 will mark the artificial end to an artificial beginning and the Real Beginning to the Real End.
(6) Although Baba is in everyone and in everything His work of spiritual awakening remains aloof from politics of any kind.

Everyone who received this circular was expected to acknowledge it. As regards communications, particularly those containing some instructions from Baba, He

---
* *Circular NL* 5, issued on 10-3-1950.

generally insisted on having signed acknowledgements. Perhaps He wished to ascertain that the offer of participating in His spiritual work had reached all His dear ones in time. In earlier days owing to this habit, a few even criticized Meher Baba by calling Him a "Circular-wala Baba!"

In January, Baba did not disclose to the people in Meherazad* (near Pimpalgaon — Malvi) or at Meherabad** (near Arangaon), the New Life phase of complete renunciation, though indirectly He frequently hinted at it. About the *ashrams* at these two places He often conveyed to the resident *mandali*,*** "I do not feel like caring for anything that is retained or given away. In spite of this, from now on, an immediate cut of 50% in all expenses should be effected." Did He wish to acclimate them to a harder life? He also instructed those who lived near Him to abstain from lust and greed of any kind. He advised the men to avoid even a formal handshake with women. Once Baba asked each of them whether he preferred to be buried, cremated or carried to the Tower of Silence in case he died! First and foremost, He expected them to remember Him whole-heartedly, while discharging their daily duties. In short, there was a remarkable change in Baba's attitude towards the closer ones as He was secretly preparing the ground to break the news to them at an opportune time about the New Life — "The Life of helplessness and hopelessness."

The God-Man Contacts the God-intoxicated

In the first week of January, 1949 Baba resumed His work with the spiritual wayfarers who were deeply and

---

* 15 kms. to the north of Ahmednagar (M.S.), a place where Meher Baba resided during His last years.
** 9 kms. to the south of Ahmednagar (M.S.). On a low hill is the Tomb of the Eternal Beloved, Meher Baba.
*** Meher Baba generally referred to the group of His close disciples as *mandali*.

madly in love with God, the Beloved. To begin with, the appropriate Sufi term that Baba used for such a person is *mast** meaning the God-intoxicated one. Just a few years after establishing Himself in the God-Man-State, in August, 1924, Meher Baba inaugurated this unique phase of His work of contacting the *masts*. It was at Pathri, a place a few kms. to the south of Hardwar. Here, Baba visited a recluse who was residing in a small hut by the roadside, which he rarely left. Baba later conveyed that this hermit was a high *mast* and added, "Any *mast* contacted before this one was incidental and anyone thereafter was purposely contacted." This particular and peculiar type of work gathered momentum as years passed by. In the 1940s it was in full swing. By 1965, a few years prior to the dropping of His body, this phase of Baba's work was practically over. The last outstanding *mast* contacted was Nilkanthwala from Rishikesh, who was especially brought to Meherazad.

There are hardly any references in the annals of religious and spiritual literature concerning the contacting, feeding and blessing, and bathing of God-intoxicated souls. Only in the *Ramayana* is it mentioned that Rama, the *Avatar*, visited the *ashrams* in the forest and, under some pretext, also visited many out of the way places to contact and guide the *masts*. But there is no account of it ever being done on the scale on which Baba did it. The *masts* whose hearts get drenched with "God's Wine" live far above the "bread-line". They not only perceive the Divine but live in It. In this immense, creative intoxication, they care little about outward cleanliness. *Masts* seem to overrule the laws of hygiene. Some of them dwelt in incredibly filthy surroundings. But love has that grace which no dirt can defile. The life of a *mast* is an honest expression of what he feels within. His involvement in the internal life is so profound that his external actions of body and speech appear enigmatic and puzzling. Being devoid of

---

* An Urdu word to be pronounced as "must".

social influence and selfish motives, he behaves to please the Divine Beloved. But this makes him a laughing stock and he is regarded as a mad person!

Meher Baba has explained* the subtle points of difference between ordinary madness and divine intoxication. He has also thrown some light on how the God-Man draws these souls out of their self-sufficiency and uses them as the media for relaying spiritual power and help to humanity at large. In the *Avataric* Age the number of such souls, it seems, increases considerably. Meher Baba journeyed to distant cities in undivided India from Peshawar (in the north of Pakistan) to Trivandrum (in the south of India) and also to far off mountainous regions to meet these souls.** He wanted to awaken in them the need to co-operate in His Game of awakening humanity by sharing the spiritual responsibilities of the higher "planes of consciousness" on which they were stationed.

In January, 1949 Ali Shah, known as Bapji, was brought to Meherazad for Baba's contact. He was a *mast* of the fifth plane. He was exceptionally responsive to shouldering his spiritual responsibilities and Baba regarded him as one of His "Five Favorites". After his first contact in 1943, Baba called him more than twenty times to stay with Him for both short and long visits. Bapji's smile was warm and inviting, his voice was quite pleasant but his speech was disconnected and repetitious. For the rest of January, 1949, Baba regularly fed him with His own hands and sat alone with Bapji in a room for solemn, speechless conferences. Sometimes, as Baba stepped out He looked very weary and the *mandali* gathered that the day's session had been rather tiring.

By the end of this month, one more *mast* named Mama who roamed about in Ahmednagar was brought to Baba for a few hours' contact. Mama was quite a bit

---

* See: William Donkin, *The Wayfarers.*
** See: Bal Natu, *Glimpses of the God-Man, Meher Baba,* Vol. I.

taller and heavier than Ali Shah. His body was well-shaped, but his shaved head, half-closed eyes and calm countenance distinguished him from others. Two decades later I chanced to see him in Ahmednagar. People told me that there was practically no change in his outward appearance, including his favorite dress of habitual red and white checkered garments. He would sit and rest anywhere he liked, whether on the dusty road or on the dung hill. Shams-e-Tabriz befittingly wrote, "The man of God is a treasure in a ruin."

A Move to Mount Abu

By the first week of March, Baba decided to shift to Mount Abu. This was to be His headquarters for three months. It is a small hill-station in the Aravali Hills, in Southern Rajasthan. Owing to the spiritual atmosphere vibrant with the associations of many saints and some Masters, Hindus and Jains regard this region as exceptionally holy. This particular area abounds in the bounty of nature. In the evening, the hill tops, aglow with the setting sun, look marvellous. In the memories of those who visited Abu such scenes continue to linger with unfading enchantment. Abu Road is the nearest railway station. A special bungalow for Baba and the women *mandali* was taken on lease. The men *mandali* accommodated themselves in the rooms near Bhisti Nullah. In March, Baba set out on two long trips, one to Ajmer, the other to Ahmedabad, and two short visits to nearby places, Oria and Dilwara.

On March 8, Baba was at Ajmer to contact dear old Chacha whom He first met in February, 1939. It was during this meeting that Baba coaxed him into having a bath which was long overdue! Believe it or not, those who know him during this period said that it was his first bath in 30 years! Nur Ali Shah Pathan, known as Chacha, hailed from Peshawar. He came to Ajmer to teach Arabic but his love for the Arabian Prophet invited Divine Grace and, thoroughly drenched in love, he became a Perfect *Majzoob*. In that divinely absorbed state, Baba told the *mandali* that he consciously experienced Unity with God and was completely oblivious of the world. Chacha's physical actions could be likened to the rotations of a switched off ceiling fan. His body lay in a squalid hovel while he was enjoying the infinite Bliss of the "I am God State."

Baba wished to sit with Chacha where they wouldn't be disturbed, so Chacha was taken to Taraghar, an old fortress that overlooked the holy city. He was carried there in a sedan chair and Baba sat alone with him continuously for eight hours, which was quite unusual. During this period, Baba plied Chacha, at intervals, with tea and cigarettes. At the close of this meeting, Baba presented him with a turban, a blanket and also a silken coat that He was wearing. Chacha was then sent back with great care to his original place. What spiritual transactions were carried out in and through such meetings we do not know; Baba was most reluctant to explain the details and the significance of these visits.

On the fortress at Taraghar about forty Muslim widows belonging to the Shia sect were brought together and Baba very sympathetically gave some money to each. About such "gifts" William Donkin writes, "It is a kind of catalyst by which Baba is able to bring out a certain spiritual reaction." After visiting Kishangarh, Baba reached Sojat where the famous *mast*, Nuru Baba stayed. This *mast* originally came from Punjab. One fine morning he came to Sojat which is in Rajasthan and started living on the veranda of someone's house. Nuru Baba was a born *mast* and wore no clothes. Who would welcome such a strange nude visitor? The *mast* was driven away. But he adamantly sat on a nearby slab of stone for days, in sun and rain. Owing to some striking experiences, the owner of the house finally felt compelled to request Nuru Baba to sit wherever he wished. It was on this veranda that Baba first met him in 1941. At that time the *mast* was surrounded by a band of dogs.

These details are recorded to indicate how unbelievable

are the life stories of the *masts*! A few Westerners may treat them as "Oriental nonsense" but they are true. Like the birds, the *masts* do not leave the footprints of their spiritual journey; it is for the physicians and psychologists to debate over the physiological and psychological issues involved in such incredible states. The inconceivable miracles which the *masts* have performed can provide them with another field for extensive investigation. The God-Man clearly knows the real worth of the spiritual states attained by the *masts* and their potentialities which can be used for His inner spiritual work. On the whole, Baba was happy to meet Nuru Baba in Sojat, on that memorable veranda. With reference to such *masts,* pointing at His fingers, where people generally wear rings, Baba used to gesture, "These are my gems." What an incredible Jeweller!

On the way back to Mount Abu the party stopped at Abu Road where after a lapse of eight years Baba again contacted Khuda Baksha. This *mast,* with steadfast devotion and with a vow of silence, had stayed in a shrine for many years. This time he offered Baba a *lungi* and Baba honored his gift of love by wearing it once. On March 11, He reached the headquarters.

The second tour of the month began with a visit to Ahmedabad. Baba was pleased to contact an old God-intoxicated person and offered him six cigars. After meeting Rehman and Bapu of Khambat, He returned to Mount Abu. For the rest of the month Baba met *sadhus* and *yogis* residing in nearby places. The two contacts worth noting were of Mattragiri Maharaj at Oria and Haridas Nirvan at Abu Road. Mattragiri greeted Baba warmly. He had penetrating, deep set eyes. In all seasons he wore only a loin cloth and ate whatever was offered to him. Hence he was also known as *aghori* — the indiscriminating one. He was tall and slim but his age was a subject of guess work. Some *yogis* have about them this quality of agelessness. Haridas Nirvan belonged to this category. He sat under a patched umbrella, its handle tied to a big stone. When he saw Baba he was overjoyed to see the *Avatar*; out of sheer joy, tears began to roll down his cheeks. Baba consolingly stroked him and helped him to compose himself. Baba was also happy to meet a good *yogi* who had been undergoing severe penance for forty years at Dilwara. He was known as Bengali Baba. With such loving and lively meetings with the advanced souls around Mount Abu, the month of March was over.

Baba Feeds a Love-hungry *Mast*

In the second week of April, 1949, Baba wished to visit Akola, one of the biggest cities in Maharashtra. Here He contacted a few God-intoxicated souls who were moving in the city like the dutiless doves and harnessed them to work as they played with the Divine Presence. Among these was Chamma Mai, a fat *mastani*. The carefree attitude of the wayfarers generally kept them healthy and sometimes made them chubby too.

On the way to Nagpur, the party reached Badnera where Baba learned about a very good *mast*—Badri Baba who had moved to a small village named Chandratara. News of a high *mast* would invariably make Baba impatient to meet him. It was evening but He was not willing to wait till the next morning. Baba's men made inquiries about transportation to the village. The road was very rough and the journey of 15 kms. was only possible by bullock cart. Baba readily agreed to this bone-shattering conveyance, so they all huddled into a bullock cart and started off. As it left the town the road deteriorated and the wooden wheels alternately lurched over the rocks in the path or slid into the well-worn ruts, causing the cart to jolt violently. About two hours later, during one such jolting, a bundle of currency notes worth seven hundred rupees slipped out of Eruch's well-buttoned coat; one of his shoes followed suit. When he became aware of this he told Baba about it, who gestured, "Don't think in the least about the money now. At present contacting the *mast* matters most." So the *mandali* continued the journey, without wasting time searching for the wallet.

The party reached Chandratara after midnight. This *mast*, Badri Baba, had a few peculiar habits. If he so wished, he would sleep or sit at any place not only for hours but even for a couple of days! Owing to the reverence that people had for him, no one would disturb him. After Baba's arrival the *mast* repeatedly cried aloud, "I am hungry. I am hungry." Was he asking for *prasad* at the hands of the God-Man? Baba was very particular in fulfilling the wishes of the *masts*. So Baba's men, even in the dead of night, secured a bowl of goat's milk, raw sugar and millet bread. Baba offered this to the *mast* and both felt very pleased. Baba picked this particular time to be with Badri Baba for a secluded contact. The meeting was not over until 2.30 in the morning and then the party started back. To light their way Chhagan walked ahead holding a torch in either hand. Luckily, after a few miles he spotted Eruch's shoe and then the bundle of notes intact. The *mandali* were very relieved to get the wallet back, not for the money it contained, but because it represented a sacred trust. Baba was very particular about the use of every paisa or cent offered to Him by His dear ones. In spite of the night's vigil Baba looked very cheerful. This was mostly due to His contact with Badri Baba. By dawn the party reached Badnera to prepare themselves for the next move.

The God-Man Invites Suffering!

On April 15, Baba reached Nagpur. One of his disciples named Jal Kerawala was working there as the Commissioner. He wished to offer his car to Baba for the *mast*-tour. To ensure that it would be in good working order he had specially sent it to a workshop for a check-up and necessary repairs, if any. In all journeys with Baba the *mandali* carried many pieces of luggage; they knew Baba's needs and always tried their best to provide Him with the things He might require in response to His inner spiritual work. So the luggage rack on the top of the car was overloaded with packages of all sizes. The car had to carry a complement of six — Baba, Kaka, Baidul, Eruch, Chhagan and Vishnu.

The same day Baba left for Seoni, a place 130 kms. to the north of Nagpur. After a drive of 40 kms. the party reached Ramtek. It was nine at night. By the side of the road there was a low hill about 230 meters high. At every stop Baba's disciples would ask people about the *masts* and saints residing in that area. Here they learned that in one of the huts on the hill, there lived a saintly personality. At Baba's instructions, two from the group left to confirm the news. The saint, who was perhaps engaged in his daily prayers and devotion, refused to open the door to meet Baba's men. The One whom he was worshipping had come to bless him, but unfortunately the saint missed this precious meeting! So it was ordained. What an irony! Didn't Baba know this in advance? The God-Man knew that His men would go up the hill and return unsuccessful, but as Man, in His mission of "doing good", Baba could not pass by without inquiring of the saint.

As the car sped on, things began to go wrong with it in quick succession. The car got two flats and was crippled. Patching them with a small repair kit they had with them they moved on. When they got 10 kms. from Seoni they got another flat and in addition the engine developed minor troubles. All patching, pumping and repairing failed. The car could go no further than a few yards at a time. It was 4 a.m. and the Baba-party was thus held up on a lonely road. Chhagan volunteered to walk the distance and get the necessary new parts from the town. In his haste however, he forgot to take money with him. Hence Vishnu had to follow him into town with the money. That same night there had been a robbery in Seoni. The police were milling around. When they spotted lanky, fatigued Chhagan they suspected that he was one of the bandits. This incident gives an idea of the arduous and awkward situations which the *mandali* had to endure in *mast*-tours. Chhagan managed finally to convince the police officer that he was not a burglar but a prospective customer on the way to buy necessary parts for a stranded car. Luckily he met Vishnu and the purchases were able to be made. By late morning Baba reached Seoni. The night's drive illustrates how the God-Man, in relation to His inner work, sometimes deliberately allows Himself to suffer, and those who accompany Him have to participate cheerfully in this *Avataric* Game!

In the 1930s Baba used to dictate letters to His close disciples and then add His signature, M. S. Irani. In one of these letters, pertaining to His relationship with the *mandali*, Baba wrote to William Donkin, "I am very strict with all the *mandali* and extract the last ounce from each. You will not find it always easy. It will be difficult at times but interesting. Still, if you love me then you will be prepared to face up to anything and obey implicitly. So, above all love me more and more. Only those who love can live near me." The type of tours mentioned above illustrate very well such statements of Baba. By the way, it may be stated that in the subsequent journey there was no further difficulty with the car. After contacting a *mast* at Seoni, Baba left for Jabalpur.

"I Take Nothing; I Give Nothing"

In 1939, Baba had opened a *mast ashram* in Jabalpur (M.P.). Baidul knew the lanes and streets where the *masts* dwelt or roamed about. One by one, the old-timers were contacted. One of them wandered in the city holding a long piece of bamboo in his hand; another carried a bundle of rags, while a *mastani* named Raji had a basket over her head with all sorts of junk in it. Various were the outward fancies of those who were intoxicated with the beatific visions on the Path. From skin to core they longed and lived only to see God. On the way to Katni, a fairly big town, the Baba-party reached Jumunia where an "adept pilgrim"* named Dada Thanthanpal stayed. His striking personality shone through his features. He was much revered by the people. They believed that his blessings brought them good luck in business and many other mundane affairs. Dada, however, often blurted out, "I don't take anything from anyone; I don't give anything to anyone. I don't care a fig for anyone and anything." But this very attitude of total indifference drew large crowds to him. Baba was happy to contact him and it seemed that his company gave Baba a genuine delight. Later, He conveyed to the *mandali*, "Dada is very loving and lovable as a 'lamb'." And then He added. "But he also radiates high spiritual power. If one were to sit near him longer one would feel that he were in the company of a [spiritual] 'tiger'." Dada Thanthanpal represented a rare blending of the *jamali* and *jalali* qualities.

The party proceeded to Mandla where Baba renewed His meeting with Dhaniram. Baba's presence flooded the heart of the *mast* with Divine love. Beholding the God-Man, the *mast* with eyes aflame, stared at Baba and spoke lovingly, "I know who You are!" Such spontaneous utterances from the spiritually advanced souls often disclosed Baba's divine status as the *Avatar* of the Age.

The Astounding Fact

Katni is about 160 kms. from Mandla. The Baba-party arrived in this city to contact the God-man and the God-intoxicated ones. It was learnt that years ago a *mast* had arrived here from Mandla, on horse-back. As soon as he got down, the horse galloped back to its owner. The name of the *mast* was Mehtab Shah. He lived with a tailor who accommodated him in his small shop. Another *mast* contacted wore on his arms and legs over twenty

---

* A spiritual wayfarer on the fifth or sixth plane of consciousness.

iron and brass rings. It seems that iron is a favourite metal with the *masts*.

The remarkable contact at this place was with Sobha, a *majzoob*-like *mast* of a high order. He was spotted at the back of a *dharmshala* — a free and charitable rest house. His seat was by the public latrines which were most unclean. Sobha was probably one of the filthiest *masts* contacted by Baba. Over a heap of refuse of every sort he continued to sit for hours and days. He was reluctant to leave his seat even to answer the calls of nature! Yet, he looked perfectly healthy. The hygienic laws of the gross world are nullified by the supervening laws of the spiritual planes. About the squalid and soiled surroundings in which the *masts* were found, Baba, a few months later explained at Poona:

> To live in dirty surroundings, such as in or near a latrine or urinal, is one way of utterly forgetting one's bodily existence. And the beauty of it is that when the body is utterly neglected or forgotten — because the consciousness is aware only of love for the Divine Beloved — it does not deteriorate but takes care of itself automatically. The minds of ordinary people are constantly busy looking after their bodies, but they find that, in spite of taking every kind of precaution and care, deterioration can never be avoided altogether. Kabir said,
>
> *Tan tajye tan rahe, tan rakhe tan jae;*
> *Yehi achamba hamne dekha, mada kalko khae.*
>
> Discard the body, it remains,
> Preserve the body, it goes;
> And so the astounding fact emerges
> That the [uncared for] corpse eats up death.*

---

* William Donkin, *The Work of Meher Baba with Advanced Souls, Sadhus, the Mad and the Poor*, p. 23. (San Francisco: Sufism Reoriented, Inc., 1969).

From Katni, Baba proceeded southeast to reach Rewah. Here a very advanced soul named Hafizi was contacted. Baba mentioned to the *mandali* that he too was an "adept pilgrim" like Dada Thanthanpal. With a *dhoti* — a piece of white cloth — Hafizi used to cover his whole body from shoulder to ankle. Though he was a centenarian he looked quite radiant. He was respected by Hindus and Muslims alike. He generally lived in a village named Maugnaj. The car sped on to Allahabad. In this holy city another *salik*-like person was contacted. He was an old Hindu Sufi, well-versed in Persian. Because of his knowledge of Sufism, some began to address him as *Inayat* Sain while he referred to himself as a *paramhansa*; Baba mentioned that he was a good *mast*. But what is there in a name or term whether Hindu, Muslim, Jew or Christian! It is the name of God and one's love for Him that leads the way.

Following Baba's instructions, Jal Kerawala sent his chauffeur to Allahabad and the car was taken back to Nagpur. Baba, nevertheless, wished to continue His *mast*-work. He proceeded by train to Gonda in Uttar Pradesh via Fyzabad. In 1942 He had visited these two places and most of the *masts* had the guiding touch of the God-Man. At that time in Gonda, a *mastani* named Nurjehan was contacted in a brothel. Baidul had entreated her to get ino a rickshaw with her mass of rags piled beside her seat. This time too, she was taken to the same place where Baba contacted her. No place is sacrilegious for the *Avatar* to meet the real lovers of God.

Effect of Refusing the God-Man's Gift

Baba reached Bahraih. A *mast* of this place was fascinated by the workings of the railway station. The changing of railway signals, the distant whistles and the clack-clack of the railway joints had a musical appeal for him. He roamed about, mostly on the railway premises. His additional fancy was for iron rings. Hence he was called Lohewala Baba (*loha* means iron). He did not immediately agree to accompany Baidul to his "Elder Brother", Baba. Instead he got into a railway engine and, like a locomotive inspector, watched the clocks and keys, expressed his satisfaction and got down. This was the right moment for Baidul to lead him to the waiting room where Baba was waiting for the *mast*.

Another God-intoxicated one passed most of his time in the compound of the Magistrate's Court. On the day of contact, Baba and Baidul saw him coming out of one of the court-rooms. He asked Baba for a *dhoti*. Baba had it purchased immediately, offered it to him and in addition gave him some sweets. Through this physical exchange, Baba seemed to have established the required contact. Perhaps it should be mentioned that, incredible as it seems, during those days in India it was often possible to find the "holy mads" even living in railway yards and courts.

The next contact was with a *majzoob*-like soul. In his state of *majzoobiyat*, he did not partake of the *prasad* given by Baba. To refuse the gift of the God-Man is to deny the operation of Universal Compassion. Such refusal by Divine Law, adversely affects the spiritual progress of the person concerned. So Baba felt rather sad at this. He sent His men, one by one to see whether the *mast* ate the *prasad* or not. Only after getting the news that the *mast* swallowed or nibbled all the eatables did Baba feel relieved and happy too. Baba worried not for Himself but for the good of the *mast*.

This reminds me of an incident in the later period known as the "Fiery Free Life". It was in this phase that Baba visited many places in the north and south of India to give *darshan* to the public. At a place in the district of Hamirpur (U.P.), a person running an orphanage asked Baba for some financial help. Baba assured him of a large sum but expressed a wish to wash the feet of the orphans. The person agreed to this, willingly. Accordingly, Baba commenced pouring water on the feet of the first boy. He was just about to place His forehead on them when the teenager, though unintentionally withdrew his feet. This made Baba extremely displeased and He became very serious. He left the place and conveyed to His people that He wished to cancel all the succeeding programs and return to Meherazad. At the request of His lovers in Hamirpur, He, however, suggested an alternative to counteract the adverse effect created by the boy's withdrawing his feet. He asked them to bring 14 boys, all fourteen years old, together next morning before sunrise for His contact. He wished to wash their feet and bow down to them. The frantic search in that illiterate area, where the parents did not know the years in which their children were born, was a story in itself. Suffice it to say that by dawn the Baba lovers had succeeded in this strange task entrusted to them. Baba felt happy and the programs were carried out as scheduled.

"Permitted and Allowed"

From Bahraih, on April 24, 1949, Baba reached Benares. During His short stay the meeting with Batwa Shah who was a renowned personality in Benares is worth recording. Born in a wealthy family, he could have easily continued to live the so-called good life. But his wallowing in luxuries came to a sudden end. Batwa Shah was blessed with God's gift of Love. Divine Love has a strange quality of reversing one's values completely. In his deep devotion and intoxication he would at times be in a *majzoob*-like state and then sometimes numberless lice would swarm around his body but he would remain unconcerned. On some occasions, when in a *salik*-like state, he seemed very affectionate and children looked upon him as their *chacha* (uncle). He was fond of carrying a few sheets of paper and a very long pencil. Sometimes he was engrossed in writing which was illegible. Baba has stated that this trait of scribbling, whether on paper or on roads, belongs to the *jamali* type of *masts*.

When the Baba-party approached this glorious personality, Baidul asked him to go into a nearby mosque where it would be convenient for Baba to meet him all alone. But Batwa Shah refused and replied, "I have left visiting any mosque!" He was then asked to go with them to some other secluded place but he was unwilling to leave his seat. Therefore, Baba left him and continued His work with the other *masts* in Benares. In the evening the party returned once again to this majestic *mast*. Baba instructed Eruch to plead with consummate skill and win him over. With Baba's help Eruch succeeded and Batwa Shah agreed to keep an appointment at 9 o'clock the same night.

When Baba arrived there were no people around Batwa Shah and he was lying on a *charpai* (Indian bed made by interweaving criss-cross ropes of coir). Baba sat by his side and His loving touch evoked the necessary response. The *mast* exchanged looks with Baba and commenced eating from a plate, lying on his bed. Soon he pushed it towards Baba, gesturing that He should partake of the rest of the food. To please the *mast* Baba gradually finished the leftovers. Just then another of Batwa Shah's devotees brought some food. He ate a few morsels and fortunately the rest of it was not offered to Baba but to the one who had handed it over to him.

After supper this *mast*—partly *salik*, partly Majzoob— had a peculiar whim. He asked Baba to scratch his back! Baba was well conversant in this art as His first Master, Hazarat Babajan, had often asked Him to scratch her back. Baba lovingly commenced this service. The *mast* did not feel satisfied till Baba had done it diligently for about an hour! Was not Baba's love and service for the *masts* matchless? At the close of this contact the *mast* most unexpectedly said in English, "Permitted and allowed." No one from the *mandali* expected Batwa Shah to speak in English, much less so correctly.

A few years earlier the *mandali* had a similar surprise when a *mast* in Mathura presented Baba with a new copy of *The Perfect Master* by C. B. Purdom, published in England, which he fished out of a heap of dirty rags over which he was sitting. The *masts* are not what they appear outwardly, and Batwa Shah's words indicated Baba's specific working on the inner plane of consciousness. With reference to this, William Donkin wrote, "The whole thing is a mystery as deep and insoluble as Life itself." However, those who accompanied Baba on His *mast*-tours, including William Donkin, intuitively believed and genuinely sensed that Baba was accomplishing great spiritual work by contacting the *masts* at different places.

From Benares the Baba-party journeyed on to Gaya which is regarded as one of the holy places in Bihar. A few *masts* and an "initiate pilgrim"* had the good fortune to have Baba's spiritual touch. By the end of April, Baba returned to His headquarters at Mount Abu.

A Strange Way of Maintaining Contact

In the first week of May, after a little rest, Baba resumed His work with the advanced souls on the Path who were residing near Mount Abu. Bengali Baba, Haridas Nirvan and Mattragiri Maharaj had been contacted a month ago; Baba revisited them. A few *sadhus* living in caves were also contacted. During this stay, Baba adopted a new method for maintaining contact with a certain *mast*. In Benares, Baba had met a person named Lakaria Baba. He was a middle-aged fat person. He used to give talismans to people to relieve them of their anxieties. Outwardly he looked like a well-fed, happy-go-lucky person. Baba, nevertheless, told the *mandali* that he was "an advanced pilgrim"** and asked Eruch to get his name and address. He also instructed Eruch to give it to Him after their return to the headquarters. At Mount Abu, Eruch gave that slip to Baba. He kept that piece of paper on a table by His bed for

---

* A spiritual wayfarer on the first or the second plane of consciousness.

** A spiritual wayfarer on the third or fourth plane of consciousness.

a few days. On May 4, He crumpled it into a small ball and asked Eruch to drop it into a certain well near Bhisti Nullah where the men *mandali* resided. The meaning behind this peculiar procedure Baba alone knew, for He sometimes gestured that His work with the God-intoxicated souls was a personal spiritual affair, and none need expect to know the why and wherefore of it.

On May 12, the Baba-party left for a long tour in the south. The first *mast* contacted during this tour was a *majzoob*-like person at Palanpur. It was a small state. The uncle of the *Nawab* had great regard for this *mast* named Amir Shah. He had built a special room for him. The *majzoob* dwelt there absorbed in and overpowered with the love of God. He was devoid of any artifice and never courted any reverence. People, however, brought food and placed it before him. But Amir Shah would often be so preoccupied with his esoteric ecstacies that goats and dogs would enter his room and leisurely munch the food, fruit or whatever was there. With a smile that was genuinely compassionate, Baba visited the *majzoob*. He was very pleased with this contact. The reason may be that through such *majzoobs*, life flows in its most pure and sublime expression, unhampered by self-conscious thoughts.

Concealing and Revealing Baba's Identity

From Palanpur, Baba proceeded for Gulbarga via Bombay. The journey was, as usual, by a train which was overcrowded. This particular station, Gulbarga, brings to mind an incident which illustrates one of Baba's typical ways of meeting those who yearned for His *darshan*. It was 1942 and Baba with a few of His *mandali* was travelling on this route. The Baba-party managed to accommodate themselves in the corner of a crowded compartment. At one of the stations an old bearded Mohammedan, with a five-year old boy, was trying to get in but was pushed back by the passengers. As the train was about to start he whole-heartedly appealed, "For God's sake, at least take the boy inside." And the God-Man was there to help him. In spite of the volley of protests from the other passengers, Baba asked His men to take the boy inside. Meanwhile the old man hung on to the handle bar of some other compartment. At every station the old man would get down and come by the window to have a look at his dear child. Seeing this, Baba suggested that His disciples also make room for the old man near them. It was again a difficult task. He had to be pulled inside through a window. Baba tucked His legs under Him and asked the old person to sit rather comfortably. The old man felt extremely relieved. He was going as far as Gulbarga.

Baba silently gestured to one of the *mandali* to ask him if he knew of any saintly or *mast*-like people living near Gulbarga. The venerable old man asked him, "What place do you belong to? May I know your intention in meeting such saintly personalities?" He was told that they were from around Poona. It was also made clear that they had no intention of reaping any material gains by contacting saints and *masts*. They revered them just for their love of God. At this the old man interjected, "You look like Parsees. You live near Poona. And Ahmednagar is quite close to your place. And yet you do not know about Meher Baba! What a pity!" Baba's men had to suppress a smile and to listen attentively to what the man was saying. He continued, "I had been to Ahmednagar twice, but unfortunately could not see Meher Baba. I am determined to visit Ahmednagar with my family to pay my respects to Him. So, dear brothers, instead of inquiring of other saints and Masters, I strongly recommend that you meet Meher Baba."

During *mast*-tours to conceal His identity, Baba generally wore a Kashmiri cap and dark glasses. After some time the old man thanked the Baba-party and got down at Gulbarga. A few minutes later Baba asked Eruch to go and find this aged gentleman and present him with a copy of the *Meher Baba Journal** which had a picture of Baba in it. Eruch was also to disclose to this person that he had been fortunate enough to sit in the compartment by Meher Baba's side and that he and his family had been blessed by Him. He no longer need visit Ahmednagar to see Baba in person.

Eruch found the old man just as he was about to get into a *tonga* (a horse carriage) and Baba's message was conveyed to him. The man was astonished and could not believe what had happened. He left the boy in the *tonga* and followed Eruch, who was making his way back to the train, "cursing" him all the way for not revealing Baba's identity sooner. He thought that young Eruch had deliberately concealed the secret to make fun of him. By the time Eruch got into the compartment the train whistled and started up. Just in time, Baba with the tender heavenly radiance that beautified His face, leaned out of the window. He had taken off the cap and the glasses and therefore the old man could easily recognize Him as Meher Baba. As the train pulled out Baba placed His healing hand on the old man's head and blessed him. As the man lifted up his face, the train was slowly leaving the platform. Wonderful are Baba's ways of concealing and revealing His identity!

A Marvellous Meeting

To get back to the account of 1949, Baba reached Gulbarga and proceeded for Khandal to meet a high *mast* named Guru Appaswami. Formerly, he went about completely naked, but lately he had started wearing clothes. *Masts*, in fact, need no footwear or headgear. In their madness to see and unite with the Infinite, they become "footless and headless". Appaswami at the beginning was reluctant to meet Baba. A few *masts*, at the outset, behave like naughty children but the God-Man is like the Divine Mother. Therefore, Baba sat

---

* A monthly devoted to Meher Baba (Nov., 1938 to Oct., 1942).

beside Appaswami and lovingly gazed at him. Baba's presence penetrated and enlightened the consciousness of the *mast* and this delighted him. There was a marked change in his manner and his unwillingness melted into co-operation. Baba offered him sweets. Like a child, this little favour mollified him and he became quite affectionate. He asked for tea and even asked Baba to have a little of it. In the end, Appaswami very affectionately embraced Baba. As a token of love Baba gave him a bed-sheet and a carpet as parting gifts. This "give and take" of things, whatever they may be, is a symbolic expression of communion on the inner planes of spiritual existence, where words have no access.

On Baba's return to the city, He contacted the *mast* Lal Mohammed known as *Buddhi* (meaning an old woman). Baba gave him some cigarettes. Later the same day, the Baba-party left for Hyderabad with a short break at Yadgiri, to meet Tilgur Swami, the *Jivanmukta** who stayed in a village called Tumkur. According to Meher Baba, Tilgur Swami was a God-realized soul in *Turiya Avastha* — the Divine Junction. When last contacted, he was fully dressed but this time he had no clothes on. He seemed to recognize Baba and very ardently embraced Him. A wonderful scene and a marvellous meeting of the two God-realized Ones. One, as *Jivanmukta*, had no spiritual duty, while the other, as the *Avatar*, was eternally duty-bound. About Tilgur Swami having given up the use of his clothes, Meher Baba explained, "Although a *Jivanmukta* does not himself change his habits, his habits, nevertheless change of their own accord."**

Mast Contacts at Hyderabad

Baba and the party reached Hyderabad by May 16,

---

* A Perfect One who has God-consciousness with Creation-consciousness. For details see: Meher Baba, *God Speaks*.
** William Donkin, *The Work of Meher Baba with Advanced Souls, Sadhus, the Mad and the Poor*, p. 28.

and stayed there for three days. On the first day three *masts* were contacted. One was an ex-serviceman and another was a policeman. Dina Shah, the one from the army, was very old. He carried three bamboo sticks with him wherever he went. These seemed indispensable to him. The other *mast* who was living in a mosque often cooked food and distributed it to the visitors. Nazir Ali, the third one, was very particular about collecting bits of paper. He felt that some pieces might have God's name printed on them. He wished to save people from committing the sin of trampling over the Holy Name. A good job and a worthy duty!

The second day's *mast*-work commenced with the contact of Amir Ahmed, a *wali* who was fond of *pan* (betel leaf). As was the case in 1945, Rajah Mastan was spotted while moving through the city. Baidul pleaded with him to get into a rickshaw and Baba had a secluded time with him in a room in a cemetery. At parting, Rajah gave Baba a lot of broken china. Baba asked Vishnu to count the pieces; there were 70. Vishnu was instructed to keep them safe till the party reached Mount Abu. Kale Khan had a good physique and he looked like a well-dressed gentleman; this was unusual in the case of a *mast*. When he passed by the road Baba recognized his spiritual worth and asked Baidul to get him. He was led to a restaurant where Baba fed him with His own hands. After a few more contacts in the city, the second day's work was over.

On the final day, in the early morning Baba visited Saiyid Moeinuddin. In 1945 he was contacted thrice. At the first meeting, Baba had to wait patiently for three hours to find him in a favourable mood. He loved sweets. These were offered to him but that did not dampen his hot temper. This time, despite all entreaties, he refused to be with Baba for a quiet contact. Some of the *masts*, anticipating that the *Avatar's* contact would mean their shouldering greater responsibility, tried to evade Him. Baba in His ineffable love and inimitable patience never contacted a *mast* against his wish. Hence, Moeinuddin was not contacted that day. Baba, however, might have felt that His spiritual work had to be shared by someone on the higher planes.

The *mandali*, therefore, tried to find some other *masts*. They were informed of Anand Swami who daily bathed at a certain tap. He had a peculiar habit of using dust to scrub his body. The party set out to meet him. On the way they unexpectedly noticed Shastri Bua. In his snuff-tinted and tea-stained dirty clothes no one could have guessed that once he was a *shastri* (a scholar) of great repute. But now he was a *mast* of the sixth plane and was not concerned with the scriptures at all. On the sixth plane, one sees the Beloved (God) face to face everywhere, continuously. The "finite" sees the Infinite; it is a strange stage! The bliss of seeing God and the agony of being separate from Him are simultaneously experienced. The final Union of the soul with the Oversoul needs the grace of the Perfect Master. Therefore, Meher Baba's contacts with those on the sixth plane had special significance. Baba had met this great *mast* on His last visit to Hyderabad. On this day he was taken to a *sarai* (a free rest-house), where Baba sat alone with him. After some time, Anand Swami too was seen near the tap. Baba was pleased to meet him. He conveyed that these two short meetings lifted the heavy spiritual burden that lay on Him. The same day Baba left Hyderabad. He reached Mount Abu on May 20, 1949.

Baba The Emperor

In the last week of May, Baba with all the *mandali* left Mount Abu for Meherazad. On the way He stopped for a day in Bombay as His heart went out in sympathy for His "dear children"— the *masts*. He met three of them. Bora was an old person. One easily felt in him the presence of a highly evolved soul. Under an awning made of cardboard and sack, he received Baba's divine touch. The name of the next *mast* is not known. The day he arrived in Bombay he started observing silence. People would see him sitting on Sandhurst Road, by the pavement of a cemetery, absorbed in communion with the Divine. In spite of his dirty clothes, his face shone all the more gracefully. At the time of contact the flashes in Baba's eyes must have conveyed many messages to this anonymous *mast* who had exceptional lustre in his eyes.

During Baba's visit to Dhamangaon, in 1944, He waded through muddy fields for three miles to contact "an adept pilgrim" named Mungsaji Maharaj. To one of Baba's men, he later conveyed that Meher Baba was the Emperor of *"masts and saints"*. It was learnt that he had come to stay at Churchgate, a suburb of Bombay. Baba paid a special visit to him. With these three contacts, Baba left Bombay for Meherazad, His permanent headquarters. Next day the *mandali* placed before Baba the gifts given by the *masts*. He instructed them to store "this treasure" neatly and safely in the boxes specially kept for this purpose. If Baba ever loved any material things, it would be these gifts from the *masts* which He regarded as His precious possessions!

On Baba's arrival, Adi sent Him the mail collected at Ahmednagar during Baba's tours. In spite of the ban on correspondence there were letters addressed to Him. These were mostly from those who had recently heard or read about Baba. He consented to hear the gist of each and Adi was asked to convey Baba's blessings and the necessary instructions, if any, to them. In reply to a letter to one of the old timers, Baba humorously spelt out, "No personal letters; and Babadas is not to send me even impersonal letters!" In this correspondence there was a telegram from one of His devotees in Gujarat, telling of the passing away of a dear one in the family. In reply Baba sent a message that the family should not mourn over the departed one's freedom from delusion and illusion. Among the foreign mail, Von Frankenberg and Gabriel Pascal had asked Baba for guidance in their lives and work. Frankenberg was the

Khalif — the leader of the Sufi movement in Australia. Pascal was a renowned Hollywood personality and he had a plan to produce a film of Baba's life.

The Saviour "Saved!"

In between the strenuous *mast*-tours from the headquarters at Mount Abu and the impending Great Seclusion that was to commence by the third week of June, Baba wished to rest for a short time by the sea; though for Baba, rest didn't differ much from work. Vengurla is a place to the south of Bombay in the district of Ratnagiri. The Government rest house, which in Maharashtra is called a *dak* bungalow, was reserved. Baba with a small group stayed here for a short while. During this period a rare event took place which for years even some of the resident *mandali* did not know about. After many years, Eruch casually referred to this incident.

One morning at Vengurla, Baba went out with the *mandali* to swim in the sea, and selected a far-off secluded beach for the purpose. All had a good time. Baba asked the *mandali* to continue swimming for a while and then to return to the rest house on foot. It was quite a long walk. Baba, however, decided to leave earlier with Eruch for He wanted to contact a certain *mast* before lunch. So He preferred to reach the town by taking a shorter route through a narrow creek.

There were some fishermen's children there, with a hollowed-out palm tree which served as a canoe, who offered to ferry them across. After admonishing them to be careful, Baba and Eruch got in, and the boys proceeded to paddle them across the creek. For awhile all went well. But then other boys, seeking to tease their friends, swam alongside and in their playful struggle with their friends, the canoe was inadvertantly tipped over. Baba and Eruch were flung headlong into the filthy water of the creek, but fortunately, as they sank Eruch was able to grasp Baba's arm and then, holding Baba with one hand, and the satchel, alphabet board, etc., with the other, he managed to swim to the shore, using his feet only. Both of them were thoroughly soiled. Baba told Eruch to run back to the rest house and obtain clean clothes for Him, so Eruch found a secluded spot under a tree behind an old building for Baba, and ran three-fourths of a mile to the rest house. The *mandali* had not returned to the rest house, and Eruch had to "break into" Baba's room through a bathroom.

On his return he found Baba sitting blissfully under a tree. Eruch recalled that as far as he knew, this had been the first time in many years that Baba had been left entirely alone in a town with no *mandali* nearby. Eruch obtained water from a well and helped Baba to wash Himself and to change His clothes. Eruch still looked filthy. They both, however, proceeded to the town and Baba contacted the *mast* of His choice. Baba was in an exceptionally happy mood and conveyed to Eruch, "As you rescued me today from the filthy water of the creek, so one day I will release you from the filth of Illusion!" An enviable promise!

2

Seclusion Preceding Meher Baba's New Life

1949 — Part II

About the Blue Bus at Meherazad

MEHER BABA's forty days' seclusion was to commence in the last week of June, 1949. He knew that He had to accomplish great and glorious spiritual work in that period. Immediately after His return from Vengurla where He had had a few days' rest and relaxation, Baba resumed His work with the *masts* on June 7, by inviting Ali Shah to stay at Meherazad. For eleven days Baba daily fed him, bathed him, and sat alone with him for an hour or two. Ali Shah, known as Bapji, with an innocent smile readily consented to Baba's wishes.

These God-intoxicated souls on the fifth or the sixth plane of consciousness were the media through which Baba channelled some of the divine power in the higher realms for its release in this world at an opportune time. Among those who co-operated with Baba in this task, Ali Shah was the foremost. With his heart set aflame with intense longing to see God as He should be seen, Ali Shah had established himself on the fifth plane. In a way he was also the luckiest to have the God-Man as the Guide to lead him on to Him — God, the Beloved.

Simultaneously, final preparations were being made for Baba's seclusion quarters. Baba chose the old body of the Blue Bus in which He, with His cosmopolitan group of disciples, had extensively travelled throughout India. The chassis was a Chevrolet model with a 29.5 HP engine. The body was specially designed and built at Bombay to accommodate His eastern and western disciples. For a small group of women who had been observing strict seclusion for years, a special compartment at the back of the driver's seat was made available. These women had to remain beyond the sight and sound of men. The body of the bus was painted in dark and pale blues; the curtains too were blue and hence it derived its name, "The Blue Bus".

With many bags and bed-rolls piled atop, this big bus looked like a hillock moving over the rough and narrow Indian roads. As it left Meherabad, on December 8, 1938, a few of Baba's men who knew the sort of load the bus had been designed for, feared that it would not even reach its first stop at Hyderabad safely. The bus, however, completed its journey throughout India, fairly well. Elizabeth (Patterson), Donkin and Eruch drove the bus. The entire itinerary provided a few unforgettable experiences to those who toured with Baba.

A few years later Baba wished to dispose of the bus. Someone suggested a raffle. Baba in a humorous mood agreed to this. The tickets, 100 rupees each, were purchased by Baba people. A Baba lover from Delhi was the fortunate one who won the Blue Bus. He, nevertheless, humbly requested Baba to keep the bus as a blessed monument to the unique, all-India itinerary. Baba consented, yet He temporarily gave it to Sarosh (Irani), one of His disciples, who owned an automobile shop in Ahmednagar. He overhauled the bus and later enlisted it as a public bus in the city. A few years passed and the coachwork became so battered that the bus was dumped in the garage.

In March, 1949, when Baba left for Mount Abu, He asked Sarosh to keep the engine and the wheels for himself and take the body of the bus to Meherazad to be used as Baba's seclusion cabin. The seats were removed and the body was placed on empty barrels. It was fixed in mortar, bricks and lime. By the time Baba returned from Mount Abu, in May, the old body of the bus with its bleached colors was transformed into a neat, clean, beautifully painted cabin. At present, the

Blue Bus stands well sheltered by the side of the *mandali's* hall, at Meherazad.

Reading of the Holy Books

Three sides of the bus faced the walls of the adjacent rooms. The remaining side was closed with bamboo matting. In the small enclosure there was a neem tree with its drooping branches swaying over the bus. According to the circular issued in January, Baba people were to observe silence for one full month — July 1949. Baba wished to commence His special spiritual work on June, 22. A day prior to this He invited the men devotees and disciples from Ahmednagar and Meherabad (Arangaon) to Meherazad (Pimpalgaon — Malvi). Kaka Baria, the manager of Meherazad, decorated the cabin enclosure with bunting to signify the day as a festive occasion. One of Baba's colored pictures was displayed on the bamboo matting and the seven-colored flag fluttered by its side.

The main program for this day was the reading of the Holy Books. Baba asked those present to listen attentively to the parts that would be read and the points He would explain. Kale Mama, one of Baba's old disciples, opened the session by reading the Ninth Discourse from the *Bhagavad Gita*, entitled "The Yoga of the Kingly Science and the Kingly Secret." At its beginning Lord Krishna says to Arjuna, "To thee I shall declare the profoundest secret which would free thee from Evil." Khaksaheb read the first twenty *aayat* of the Second *Sura* named Baqara from the *Koran*. Baba casually mentioned that the essence of Mohammed's teaching did not differ from Krishna's; he had, however, to adapt himself to the needs of the time.

Donkin read the Sermon on the Mount from the New Testament. It commenced: "And seeing the multitude, he went up into a mountain; and when he sat, his disciples came up to him, and he opened his mouth and taught them saying,

SECLUSION PRECEDING MEHER BABA'S NEW LIFE

Blessed are the poor in spirit: for theirs is the kingdom of heaven....
Our Father, which art in heaven, Hallowed be thy name. Thy kingdom come....
For thine is the kingdom, and the power, and the glory, for ever.... Amen.

As Donkin read from the Sermon, "Be ye therefore perfect, even as your Father which is in heaven is perfect," Baba conveyed that this was the *gol gol* (roundabout, indirect) way, Jesus used to tell people that God-realization is the goal of each individual and that everyone is potentially God. At the close of the Sermon, Baba spelt on the board, "My favorite." At the end Kaikobad read, *Hormaj Yest* from the *Avesta*. The gist of what Baba explained during the reading session was, "These Books represent different approaches to Truth. Any of the ways, if followed honestly and with love, leads one to God. The impending seclusion in which I am getting myself bound, voluntarily, is neither *tap* [penance] nor *chilla nashini* [austerities]. I have my own reasons for retiring in seclusion." In retrospect some of the *mandali* thought that the parts of the sacred texts read on that day had some close connection with Meher Baba's New Life phase which subsequently emerged. Possible!

After this solemn session there was a short break. When all gathered again Dr. Deshmukh performed a *kirtan*. It is a typically Indian way of explaining the divine truths with the help of stories from the lives of saints and Masters, interspersed with the singing of poems and songs, composed in praise of God and the God-Man. The main theme of Dr. Deshmukh's *kirtan* was the narration of the life of Shri Shankaracharya (686 A.D. to 718 A.D.) who is regarded as the founder of *advaitism* and *Mayawad*.

On a few occasions, Baba has explicitly mentioned that Shankaracharya was a Perfect Master. Baba liked the Sanskrit hymns composed by Shri Shankaracharya revealing the secrets of *Vedanta*. These compositions are exceptionally rhythmical and gracefully meaningful. Baba particularly liked the one ending with *"Shivoham, Shivoham."* The atmosphere during this gathering at Meherazad was vibrant with Baba's divine presence. As the performance was going on, He gave a look of love to each one; no one was overlooked. In this silent communion He touched the hearts of all. After *arti* Baba distributed *prasad* and the day's program was over.

Nine Days of Inconceivable Suffering

Next day Kaka was busy attending to the duty-charts and time-tables to be followed during the forty days. The persons concerned were asked to be very punctual and particular about their respective duties. Only four men disciples were to stay at Meherazad. They were Kaka, Nariman, Meherjee and Jal (Kerawala); Jal maintained a diary during this period. Kaka who was Baba's personal attendant had to be a jack of all trades, for no one else was allowed to enter the Blue Bus or the cabin enclosure, without Baba's permission. Among the westerners who stayed with the women disciples were Norina Matchabelli and Elizabeth Patterson.

On June 22, at 5.30 p.m., Baba entered the Blue Bus and thus inaugurated the period of seclusion and quietude at Meherazad. Four days later, 21 poor persons, not beggars, were taken to Meherazad. One by one, the group was led to the cabin enclosure where Baba washed the feet of each and gave ten rupees to everyone as *prasad*. On June 29, seven people, mostly mad and God-mad, were brought to Baba. He clipped their hair, bathed them, dressed them in new clothes and gave a packet of sweetmeats to each. Special phases of Baba's inner work generally commenced or concluded with the external activities of serving the poor, the mad and the God-intoxicated ones.

From July 1, Baba's work took a serious turn. That was the day when hundreds of His dear ones joined Him in observing fast and silence. The disciples at Meherazad, including Kaka who had to attend to Baba's personal needs, also observed silence. During the seclusion period Baba slept very little. On some nights He did not get even a wink of sleep. Till the end of June, Baba had only one meal a day and His regular tea. Referring to this period, the first nine days in July, Baba later stated, "Although infinite restlessness is my constant companion, I have never been so restless as from July 1, to July 9, [1949]. No one except myself and God knows what I went through during those days."

This reminds me of the "nine months",* mentioned by Baba (in one of the meetings) as a period of infinite, incredible suffering which He underwent after the final experience of God-realization in January 1914. Only the *Avatars* have to pass through such agonies. The "coming down" of the Infinite Consciousness from the eternal blissful seclusion of God-consciousness to Creation-consciousness, as the God-Man, is the cause of these agonies. What an infinitely incredible state! In this seclusion, the suffering referred to by Baba, if I might hazard a guess, was due to the inconceivable "stepping down" from the All-powerfulness of the Old Life to the hopelessness and helplessness of the forthcoming New Life!

Ratanshaw Ghyra owned a house in the adjacent field. Along with Meherjee and Nariman he too was on night watch for fixed hours. During this crucial nine day period Meherjee once heard the sound of heavy breathing in the bathroom, nearby the cabin enclosure. He opened it but there was no one inside. Instantaneously the sound ceased of itself and simultaneously, he began to hear the same type of sound from Baba's cabin. This continued for about three quarters of an hour. At the end, he heard heavy foot-steps, then he felt as if Baba were getting up from His bed and all became calm and quiet.

Jal Kerawala in his diary, has mentioned a few more instances of knocking and tapping, of light thumping and hissing noises at night, the origin of which could not be definitely located. On other occasions, over the

---

* Meher Baba, *Listen Humanity*, p. 245.

years, the close disciples had met with some similar uncommon happenings but Baba always insisted that they should not make much of these incidents. He often pointed out that in the natural course of His work, they just happen; that's all.

It was noticed that when Baba suffered severely He became more communicative. During the period of nine days He often sent messages about His health to the disciples through Kaka who also was observing silence. Baba would dictate the words on the board in Gujarati or express Himself through gestures; Kaka would hurriedly write down the contents on a slate. This slate or note was circulated among the resident people. The health report freely translated was as follows: "Today, I have taken butter-milk twice; yet there is burning, and water is not to be drunk!" The next note read: "Firstly, there are thoughts; secondly there are the sittings; thirdly the fast and along with it this burning!"

The following day the slate conveyed: "I eat nothing; thoughts continue running; I have my sittings; and at night I lie tossing. The cabin hits me in the head every day. Today, the part above the door hit me so hard that I began to feel giddy." A little later there was an addition. "Don't give these knocks against the low ceiling of the cabin any supernatural interpretations as our dear old Chanji* would have done out of his deep, undying love for me. These hard knocks on the skull show us how brave the real *yogis* must have been who lived in dark low-roofed caves, in remote wild jungles." In this way, while Baba was intensely working in the higher realms of consciousness, such indirect yet intimate gossiping with the disciples, perhaps helped Him to maintain the link with the physical plane.

During this seclusion period, Baba also composed some couplets in Gujarati which Kaka gathered from Baba's gestures. In the last stanza, out of His sense of

---

* F. H. Dadachanji known as Chanji was Meher Baba's very close disciple and secretary. He passed away at Srinagar (Kashmir) in August 1944.

humor, in addition to Gujarati, Baba used Marathi, Hindi, Urdu, Persian and even English words. The meaning conveyed through it was solemn and profound. I give below a free rendering of the first couplet: "People feel blessed to have a dip in the holy Ganges but the Ganges itself gets sanctified by 'bathing' in the tears shed by the lovers of God who love Him for the sake of Love. Such lovers become the objects of meditation even for God!"

Period of Partial Relaxation

After July 10, there followed a period of partial relaxation. Baba resumed taking solid food once a day. Mehera and Mani were allowed to see Him for a few minutes in the morning. As a change of pace in His work, Baba instructed His men to bring Ali Shah, the *mast* staying at Meherabad, to Meherazad. He was accommodated in a room by the Blue Bus. Baba sat alone with him everyday till the end of the seclusion. Gustadjee, one of His dear disciples, was also called to Meherazad to look after the needs of Ali Shah.

A few days earlier, a note had been sent to Donkin instructing him to mark out important passages in some books on Christian mysticism and to forward these books to Meherazad. He was specially asked to send the book of Friar Juniper. The other books were, *The Little Flower's Life* and *Mirror of Saint Francis, Classics of the Inner Life,* and *The Cloud of Unknowing*. From July 11, began the reading of the sacred books. Nariman read the passages marked by Donkin. The next day Meherjee read from the *Dasateer* — the holy book of the Zoroastrians — about the causes of suffering in this life and the importance of kindness towards all.

Jal Kerawala read the commentaries by Shankaracharya on *Brihadaranyaka Upanishad*, translated into English. In conclusion he read the Divine Theme by Meher Baba. I think this was rather significant, for the Theme indirectly represented the essence of all the spiritual explanations read. Nariman, Meherjee and Jal were allowed to break their silence during this hour of reading. They would sit by the door of the Blue Bus but were not allowed to have a direct look at Baba's face.

About this time, Baba wished to shift to some other place, preferably Poona, for a period of nine days. Eruch was given the duty of finding a provisional residence in Poona that would suit Baba's requirements. The villa had to be in a secluded place where Baba could have a stroll without being seen by outsiders. Eruch was about to send a telegram reporting his inability to secure such a solitary bungalow. Just then, by a stroke of luck, he heard about a place on the outskirts of Poona. It was on a chink-hill that overlooked the city. This property, on the Poona-Satara road, was known as Thube's Bungalow. Except for the noise caused by the monsoon winds and the adjacent telephone lines, the place fulfilled Baba's other requirements. The details were sent to Baba and He agreed to visit Poona.

In the morning on July 16, Adi drove his car near the cabin enclosure at Meherazad. Those not going with Baba got inside their rooms for they were not to have even a cursory glance at Baba during the forty days. The *mast*, Bapji, Gustadjee and Kaka accompanied Baba to Poona. Ghani, Jal S. (Baba's brother), and Eruch were asked to stay in Thube's Bungalow with Baba. They were to break their silence during Baba's stay in Poona.

On His arrival, Baba conveyed to the disciples that after the strenuous spiritual work at Meherazad, He wished to have some recreation and entertainment. His spiritual work, nevertheless, was not to be discontinued; so He wished to be by Himself for two hours each day. Two hours were to be devoted for *mast*-work and two hours were allotted for light talks, humorous stories and games. Time permitting, Baba wished to have long walks in unfrequented areas. This was a period of both work and relaxation. Therefore, Ghani and Jal S. entertained Baba with many jokes and funny stories. Eruch had to attend to out-door duties, of bringing *masts* to Baba.

SECLUSION PRECEDING MEHER BABA'S NEW LIFE

Beloved Seeks Union with Real Lovers

In the morning on July 17, Eruch and Jal went out in a jeep to bring a good *mast*. Meanwhile Ghani read some *ghazals* from *Divan-e-Arzoo* to Baba. Then Baba had a silent conference with Ali Shah. Eruch returned with a *mast* named Keshav who had radiant eyes and an innocent smile. Originally he was from north India and belonged to the class known as *Bhayya*. He was a noted personality in his locality. But where did he pass most of his time? It was near the public urinals of the filthiest type! These children of God somehow get attracted towards such places and it is surprising that their bodies are rendered immune to the dreadful and poisonous germs and bacteria. Theirs is a life lived in a different dimension!

After great persuasion Keshav consented to get into the jeep and off it sped to Thube's Bungalow. Baba was waiting near the bath-room to give Keshav a good bath. But the *mast* would not allow Baba either to touch his feet or bathe him. He repeatedly said, in Hindi, "Baba, I am like your son. How can I bear for you to touch my feet?" In this mood of reverence and humility, Keshav expressed a wish to get back to his seat. Baba asked Eruch to take him to the jeep. He got into the front seat but there the disciples repeatedly entreated him to let Baba bathe him. This pleading continued for an hour, Baba patiently waiting for the right moment.

At last, Keshav agreed that instead of touching his feet or bathing him, Baba could pour water on his feet, right in the jeep. This turned out to be an auspicious beginning and thereafter he submitted to Baba's wishes. He was offered tea and bread. Finding him in a good mood, the disciples disappeared from the scene so that Baba could be alone with him. In the end, the *mast* on his own asked for a coat and a rupee from Baba. This was a sign that Baba's work had been done to His satisfaction. It was noticed that Keshav was in raptures when he left Thube's Bungalow for his habitual seat near the public urinals.

Baba felt pleased with this first contact. Pointing at Ghani He gestured, "What is more difficult — to give up one's life or be resigned to it?" Ghani replied that the latter was definitely more difficult. Baba agreed and added that one could sacrifice one's life under the sudden impulse — noble or otherwise — but to resign oneself whole-heartedly to the Divine Will continuously, was possible only for the heroes like Keshav. Later in a short discourse He explained, "If I really like anything, I like two things — *masts* and children. I like *masts* for their strength and children for their helplessness. The fire of love is very terrible indeed, and *masts* present a challenge — of this terrible fire of love — to God, the Beloved."

Then Baba touched the subject of total resignation of the *masts* to the Will of God. "It is not given to everybody," continued Baba, "to be a lover of God. Such lovers are so consumed in the fire of love that they are not conscious of their stage of spiritual progress and they do not have any thought of union with God. They simply 'enjoy' the torture of love, and long for more and more of it. These lovers don't have any thoughts about their separation from the Beloved.... They are resigned to the state in which they find themselves, and when their resignation reaches its climax, it is the Beloved who seeks Union with them."*

After the discourse, Baba conveyed that, to Him, Keshav was endearingly lovable. Thus Baba's work in Poona had a favourable beginning. A few months after this contact, special photographs of Keshav were taken to be included in the Supplement to *The Wayfarers* by William Donkin. The next day the news was received that Keshav dropped his body to live eternally with the Beloved, far beyond the clean and the unclean of this dual world.

---

* William Donkin, *The Work of Meher Baba with Advanced Souls, Sadhus, the Mad and the Poor*, pp. 23, 24.

SECLUSION PRECEDING MEHER BABA'S NEW LIFE

Talkative Nannubhai and Silent Mounibaba

On July 18, during His morning walk Baba visited a nearby temple. He liked the place and wished to spend two hours in seclusion in its inner chamber. This was arranged the same day before lunch. During this time Baba's men kept watch so as to prevent anyone from entering the temple premises. Baba's disciples were asked to be alert but were not allowed to look towards the temple. After lunch Baba wished to play a game of table-tennis, but as the table could not be brought in such a short time, He played a game of cards.

The two people brought in the morning for Baba's contact were not on the spiritual Path. They were ordinary mad people. Eruch left again in the jeep to bring any God-intoxicated one for Baba's contact. He returned with an amazing fellow called Nannubhai, a *Bohari*. He too was not a *mast*. Baba referred to him as one with *hawa* — the one who is neither a *mast* nor a madman. He was not on the Path, but he was not far from it either. Baba bathed him and fed him like a *mast*.

This person had the capacity to quote Urdu couplets non-stop, in a sonorous voice. He was extremely talkative. In conversation he would freely mix couplets of the saintly people with lines from common Urdu songs in a funny way that would make the listeners fall into fits of laughter. To heighten this joviality, Baba gestured at Ghani to quote verses on different topics which served as starters. In response to them, Nannubhai, in his loud rather shrill voice, repeated line after line that made Baba laugh heartily. Baba's eyes lit up as He smiled and sometimes, as was His habit, He held His fingers over His eyelids.

In the end Baba signalled Eruch to ask Nannubhai, "Who is greater, Allah or Mohammed?" "Mohammed, of course," came Nannubhai's unhesitating and ear-splitting reply, "for God goes begging to Mohammed with outstretched hands — and by remembering Mohammed you will have a daughter by night and a son by day!"* A queer answer that reflected Nannubhai's psychological state. Anyway, Baba had a good time in his company, a few moments of real relaxation. For Nannubhai, that time spent with the God-Man might have resulted in leading him to the path as a *mast*.

In the afternoon, Baba indicated that He would not step out of the Bungalow for the next three days. He wished to be more by Himself in seclusion. Therefore, it was suggested that Baba should have a long drive that day, in Poona, towards the mango tree in the Bund Garden where *Hazrat* Babajan used to sit. Baba agreed. In the evening while passing by Wadia College, perhaps across from Guru Prasad, He pointed to a person in an ochre colored robe with a white flowing beard. It seems that Baba had a special fondness for old men with white beards.

At Baba's instruction Eruch got down and asked this man some questions. It turned out that he had been observing silence for the last seven years. In Poona he was staying in a room along the river, by the cremation ground. Kaka recalled that he was the same person named Mounibaba contacted at Hardwar. Baba wished to be alone with him. The person was asked to get into the car. Instead of the garden the car sped towards the Hindu cremation ground. Baba sat alone with Mounibaba in a small room. Even in a period of rest and relaxation Baba would not miss an opportunity to pass on His help to deserving aspirants. There are many incidents and interesting stories where Baba had incidentally pointed out some people and they turned out to be genuine seekers, observing spiritual disciplines.

Dnyani Mast, a Rare Type

From July 20, Baba commenced His three days' work in a vacant and secluded room on the first floor. When

---

* Ibid., p. 33.

He was working, the disciples had to maintain quiet in the entire bungalow. Baba had a cup of tea in the morning and one more by 10 a.m. By noon a *mast* named Ram was brought to Baba. He was staying near one of the Rama Temples in Poona. The real name of this person was not known. But as he stayed in the temple, repeating Rama's name, people began to address him as Ram Maharaj or Ram Mast. He was revered in the locality where he lived. He had a carefree look and he wore an unassuming, unfading smile. Unlike Keshav he did not resist being bathed or fed by Baba. This pleased Baba all the more. At Baba's indication Eruch asked him, "Where is Rama?" The *mast* replied, "Rama is here and is in everyone." The next question was, "Have you seen God?" Ram Mast answered, "I see God before my eyes and He is everywhere."

Baba classified this person under the category of *dnyani mast*. The gist of Baba's explanation about this type is given below:

Majzoob-e-Kamil of the seventh plane is merged in God. In his super-conscious state he asserts himself as "I am God." Generally a *mast* on the fifth or the sixth plane does not proclaim himself as God. Nevertheless there is a class of *masts* who, though not on the higher planes, honestly feel that they have become one with God. This is neither a fact nor a complete delusion. A *mast* who belongs to this category can be termed as *dnyani mast*. Here it should be noted that the term *dnyani mast* does not stand for one intoxicated with infinite Knowledge (*Dnyan*). But such a soul in his divine intoxication expresses himself as one who is God-realized.

In the course of light conversation about the contact with Ram Mast, Baba conveyed that when He was feeding this unique visitor a rare thing happened. The *mast* lovingly offered back to Baba half of the sweets. It was a coincidence that Baba too was feeling very hungry. But as He was fasting He could not have accepted food from anyone except a good *mast*. Thus with the *"prasad"* from a *dnyani mast* Baba's work with the God-intoxicated souls in Poona was satisfactorily concluded.

For the rest of Baba's stay in Poona no more *masts* were brought to Him. He, however, continued His contacts with Ali Shah each day. Baba seemed more absorbed in His work. He would not see the disciples till late noon. He would remain by Himself in the room on the first floor. At the close of His spiritual work in Poona, He went with His men to witness a cricket match between Fergusson College and Deccan College. This was a fine recreation for Him. On July 24, Baba left Poona for Meherazad. He arrived late in the evening. Getting down from the car He went straight to the Blue Bus and the atmosphere was once more vibrant with His silent yet dynamic presence.

Baba Comes Out of His Seclusion

During the last week of the seclusion, Baba seemed more and more occupied with His work. He started observing a fast on liquids and passed most of His time in the Blue Bus. His personal attendant, Kaka, was scarcely called. On the last day — July 31 — even the servants at Meherazad were asked to participate in that sanctifying silence. On August 1, Baba people staying at Ahmednagar and Meherabad who had observed silence for one month were called to Meherazad. They were to be present there before seven in the morning, without having tea or breakfast. They were instructed not to offer any homage to Baba, not even to fold their hands to Him. A special message was to be read out to this audience.

To quote Jal Kerawala, "When exactly at 7 a.m. Baba came out of the cabin enclosure, He appeared to be the very picture of freshness, radiance and health as if instead of forty days' privations He had just returned from a holiday trip." This brings to mind some occasions of people meeting Baba, especially after the two auto accidents. Those who stayed near Baba knew well how excruciating Baba's physical pain was. But when He met the groups of His lovers, He looked so cheerful and graceful that the veil of radiance baffled the visitors and they wondered what the circular meant which conveyed the news about Baba's intense suffering.

Those who read the passages from different Holy Books, on June 21, also read Baba's message on August 1, that was dictated earlier for this special occasion. The text in English was first read by Donkin. It is given below:

> May God whom the Muslims call *Allah*, whom the Zoroastrians call *Ahurmazd*, whom the Hindus call *Ishwar Paramatman* and whom many others call by many other names, may He whose union the lovers seek in self-annihilation, whom the seers see as the only Reality, and whom the knowers know as their own real Self, may this Supreme Conscious Being, this conscious Soul of souls who eternally manifests as *Avatar* and Perfect Masters, may He through His All-merciful act bestow on us His grace, and may He solve our difficulties by the end of this year, and may He decide everything for us by the end of this year, and may He according to Baba's Circular of 1949, finish everything by the end of this year, to enable Baba to break His silence in the beginning of the next year, to speak the one and the last Word of all-embracing Divinity.

The copy of the above was sent in advance to all those who observed one month's silence. They were instructed to read it at seven in the morning and then utter the sacred word Amen or *Amin* or *Tathastu* meaning "So be it." After reading the above message in four languages, all assembled near the Blue Bus and pronounced aloud one of the sacred words and broke the silence. Baba's physical presence transported all the visitors into a region of cheer and sunshine. Baba distributed *rava* (a sweet dish) as *prasad* and the programe ended.

The work in which Baba was engaged in this great seclusion is inconceivable. But it is believed that the *Avatar's* work for the betterment of humanity, particularly in relation to posterity, was worked out and directed during such periods. As we study Baba's life we notice that after every significant seclusion there emerged a new phase. It was after this period that Baba began to give out hints about the New Life. To me, the Blue Bus stands as a link between Baba's Old Life and New Life. As for the work accomplished during this particular seclusion, mostly in the Blue Bus, Baba later stated, "The work I have done at Meherazad, I have not done in any [other] part of the world."

"Dumb" Officer and Night-blind Orderly!

July 1949 was a memorable month for the Baba-followers in India who observed complete silence. When necessary they were allowed to communicate through gestures, signs and writing. Baba conveyed that the orders in the circular were quite clear and that no one should try to interpret them according to one's convenience; better they did not follow them at all. Some of Baba's followers were shop-keepers and businessmen. They used slates, paper and pencils to deal with the customers or to instruct the staff. This was unusual for the people. It provided an interesting news item for the local dailies. One of my friends who was a teacher in a high school secured permission from the headmaster to engage and to teach the class by conveying instructions through gestures or mainly by writing on the blackboard. The permission was granted! My friend managed to get through it all, fairly well. What the pupils thought about him and his ways, God knows!

SECLUSION PRECEDING MEHER BABA'S NEW LIFE

I had not this daring. I applied for leave but the headmaster hesitated to sanction a long leave. The managing body of the school, however, passed a resolution in my favour. For me this was a period of silent introspection, sometimes boring, sometimes very creative. This month of silence brought about eventful episodes for each one who participated in this discipline. Instead of narrating the experiences of many Baba-lovers (which is not practicable), I intend to relate as an illustration, the experience of one, Keshav Nigam from Hamirpur (U.P.) and the readers may well imagine the plight and delight of others who joined in this spiritual schooling!

At midnight on June 30, the members of the Cosmic Meher Family founded by Keshav Nigam, lovingly hailed aloud Baba's *Jai* and initiated one month's silence. Keshav had not yet met Baba in person. But so strong was his faith that the superior officers and the subordinate staff in the Secretariat where he worked at a high post, promised to co-operate so he could maintain his silence. In a way this made them think of Meher Baba more often. During this period, Keshav unexpectedly had to appear in court. He had received a summons from the Session Court to give evidence in a murder case; he could not refuse to attend. So he left Rewa (capital of former Vindhya Pradesh), for Datia, a district in the adjoining state. He left by train with an orderly named Brij Mohan. It was quite a long journey. After sunset they reached Manipur where they had to get down to catch the connecting train.

To save time the attendant got off the train by jumping through the window. Unfortunately he fell right over a pitcher of milk. It was night and he was night-blind. The milkman caught hold of Brij Mohan's neck and started a quarrel. Keshav got down, looked angrily at the milkman and gestured vigorously to set the servant free. What else could he do! His gestures somehow had the desired effect and the orderly was released. As they marched on Brij Mohan, for the second time, dashed against an old woman who staggered to the ground. Keshav had to console her through soft silent gestures. He now learnt that his orderly was night-blind but it was too late and Keshav was "dumb". The blind leading the dumb and the dumb guiding the blind, a good Baba joke!

In the train Brij Mohan could not understand completely what Keshav wanted him to do. It was an uncomfortable situation for Keshav. But to his great relief, because of his silence, a young girl in the compartment treated him with affection and reverence. She began to address him with respect and tried to see that he was not disturbed by others. By morning the train arrived at Jhansi. Here again they had to change trains to reach Datia. With sunrise the orderly's eyesight was restored but the troubles did not end. The orderly carried the luggage and the bedding to the train standing on the other platform without any mishap; Keshav felt relieved. He accommodated himself in the compartment and gave his purse, containing all the money he had, to Brij Mohan with a short note to the booking clerk explaining which tickets were required. The train whistled and steamed out of the station but Brij Mohan did not return. It was clear that either there had been a long queue for the tickets or this simpleton had not been able to find the booking office. This put Keshav in an awkward situation. On the one hand he dared not miss his appearance in court and on the other, he now found himself without a ticket or money. There was nothing for him to do but to continue the journey, remembering Baba all the more.

To his great surprise in the same compartment he soon met one of his close acquaintances from Hamirpur. He was the sub-inspector of police and was bound for Datia in connection with the same case. Most willingly he offered to assist Keshav not only in the train but also in the court at Datia. Keshav finally made it there where his attendance, as a special officer of the Vindhya Pradesh government, was required. However, his unusual conduct of maintaining silence in the Session Court became a widely discussed affair and because of it many people heard about Meher Baba.

By the time Brij Mohan arrived at the railway platform the train had left and so instead of proceeding to Datia by the next train he returned to Rewa. He told Keshav's wife who was also observing silence of his plight. This made Mrs. Nigam worry about how her husband would manage to return home with neither his money nor his companion. But Baba constantly accompanies each of His dear ones, especially when they are following His orders. Therefore it is not surprising that Keshav received help whenever he needed it and arrived in Rewa in a cheerful mood. Those who came in Baba's contact and sincerely tried to follow His instructions or those mentioned in circulars, often found that the embarrassing situations were seasoned with Baba's humor and compassion. Such sweet surprises in that "season of silence" — the month of July — were not uncommon.

Adding the "Sweet" to the "Bitter"

To resume the account I prefer to quote from Kitty Davy's article concerning Baba's meeting with the women disciples on August 1, at Meherazad. She writes:

> Mehera and Mani were to see Baba first at 6:30 in the morning. At 7:00 a.m. Baba would be with the men *mandali* and the women were to listen to the reading of Baba's message, to be read aloud by different members of the *mandali* in different languages. At the end of the last Urdu translation, all were to simultaneously say "Amen" or "Amin." ... Apart from saying "Amen" we, the women, were not to break silence till Baba came over to our side and gave the sign to speak. Baba then had *rava* and tea with us. We were then all dismissed and Norina and Elizabeth were called by Baba for a private interview and given final

instructions for his work regarding his forthcoming visit to the United States and his Center at Myrtle Beach, South Carolina. After a final embrace from Baba, they left by car for Bombay to board the plane for New York. They left with the promise that Baba would come to the West very soon.

Mehera and Mani, realizing the strain of this long seclusion and fast for Baba, had taken the opportunity to think out some surprise for him when the seclusion and fast ended. Amidst all her other work, this effort on Mani's part was really her *chef d'oeuvre*. It was a puppet show. Figures and dialogue were all her own creation.... Needless to say, Baba enjoyed it immensely, and we had no idea of the "bomb-shell" awaiting us all, later in the day. This performance with Baba in our midst was literally adding the "sweet" to the "bitter," a favourable device of Baba's. In short, Baba told us briefly what he had decided during his seclusion. We are prepared for changes. Seclusions always meant a new phase in Baba's changing activities. However, we were totally unprepared for the New Life phase. It was fortunate perhaps that it had such a numbing effect on us all, or we could not have carried on as we did.

Baba had decided to close all *ashrams*, dispose of all their contents and relinquish all properties in India. The majority of those living with Baba at the time were to be sent back into the world to work. A few disciples would form his "chosen companions" to accompany him in the New Life, starting October, 1949. Those agreeing to the severe conditions of the New Life (hence called "yes-wallas") had to be prepared to look upon themselves as already dead in the sense that the dead have no desires, concerns, attachments, questions or even provisions for the morrow.*

Accordingly, Norina and Elizabeth left Bombay by

---

* Kitty Davy, "Recollections Part II," *The Awakener*, Vol. VII.

TWA on August 3. Banjo, Elizabeth's pet dog, and a double-sized bed made from the best type of Indian wood, with proper length webbing for criss-crossing were booked in advance. The bed was meant for Baba's use, in His forthcoming visit to the United States. Later, during His stay in South Carolina at the Myrtle Beach Center that He regards as His Home in the West, this bed was used by Him and I hope it is still there. Through an oversight of the Postal Department, some necessary certificates of these two disciples were despatched to Ahmedabad in Gujarat instead of Ahmednagar in Maharashtra. This caused some inconvenience to them but at last the things were set in order. Perhaps by way of maintaining the link, till these two disciples returned to India, they received Baba's telegram at Bombay: "Give my love to my lovers in the West." This was promptly answered: "Shall deliver your message. All else you know." A cable dated August 6, conveyed their safe landing in the United States.

In Silver Oaks at Panchgani

In view of the New Life, Baba gave specific instructions to His closer ones and, maybe to grant them time to absorb this most unexpected change, He proposed to leave Meherazad to spend a few days at some hill station. It has also been observed that by the end of every important seclusion, Baba generally preferred a short change of scene. The inquiries were made and this time Panchgani, which is a hill station on the Poona-Mahabaleshwar Road, was chosen. Dr. Alu Khambata is one of Baba's dear ones. Some months earlier she had leased an estate with three cottages called Silver Oaks to lodge and board paying guests. Owing to her family's circumstances there was no one to look after this business and the cottages remained practically vacant. Alu felt herself very fortunate to be able to offer this place for Baba's use.

To digress for a moment, Alu Khambata had first

heard of Meher Baba during a visit she had made two decades earlier, to the Tiger Valley Cave at Panchgani, where one of Baba's disciples named Pleader used to stay. A few years later she became a doctor of medicine and opened a hospital in Bombay. The Dadachanjis — a group of Baba's most devoted family — were residing in the same building. About 1934 when Baba visited this family Alu first saw Him going upstairs. He wore a white turban which was rare for Him. She was much impressed by His regal gait and appearance. To her He appeared much like an Arab gem merchant, with a mystical aura about Him.

She felt drawn to Him but not with any spiritual intention. Later she expressed a desire to Mrs. Dadachanji, the mother of Arnavaz, to see Baba if that was conveniently possible. Later, when this request was brought to Baba's notice, He of His own unexpectedly visited Alu's hospital. He has that ancient habit of visiting His dear ones unawares! Alu felt happy but shy, delighted but confused, not knowing how to receive Him. She forgot even to greet Him formally or to offer Him a seat. Chanji, Baba's secretary, did that for her.

Baba expressed His happiness to meet her. He permitted her to ask Him whatever questions she had in mind. Although she was greatly interested in philosophy, theosophy and even spirituality, the idea of following someone as a spiritual Master was alien to her, so Baba's proposal put her in an embarrassing situation. At the time she was at a complete loss and couldn't think of any questions on any subject. As the talk opened, her voice quavered but subsequently became composed, one of her questions was whether she should visit England for a special medical course. Baba's prompt reply was, "Not now. I will let you know when." The moment the questions were over Baba left the room. He left the dispensary as suddenly as He had arrived. The *Avatar* is always in a hurry to meet his dear ones and also to withdraw His presence hurriedly!

SECLUSION PRECEDING MEHER BABA'S NEW LIFE

Some months later when Baba sent word that Alu should visit the United Kingdom there was a financial crisis in the family. But she tried to carry out His instructions and several times she received unexpected help from out of the blue. Things got adjusted and she sailed for England. Some time after her return from England, Baba asked her to discontinue her practice as a doctor, for her health's sake. Physician heal thyself! These do's and don'ts revealed to Alu different aspects of Baba's divine wisdom and compassion. Soon it turned out that thinking about Him was not a fleeting thought; it had resulted in an acute longing. This made her accept Baba as the Perfect Master — God in human form. Now she longed and waited for an opportunity to be of intimate service to Him. Baba's decision to visit Panchgani was a loving response to her patiently longed for, ardent aspiration. No wonder that she spared no pains to make Baba's stay as comfortable as He could wish. By the time He arrived at Silver Oaks, Alu managed to have the cottages clean, with garlands of sweet scented flowers decorating the doors and windows. It was a simple yet most devoted and delightful reception.

Eruch, Jal S. (Baba's brother), Mehera, Mani and Arnavaz were among those who accompanied Baba. Everyone felt at home with the loving arrangements made by Alu. During the stay one night Arnavaz and others heard a loud noise. It was as if a big stone had rolled onto the roof of Baba's room with a great thud, Arnavaz got out of bed, the clock struck twelve and again the spell of silence fell over the cottage. She did not dare make inquiries lest that might disturb Baba. Next morning in casual conversation, the women referred to this incident. With a look of surprise, Baba asked them what it could be. Alu said that one of the neighbors might have done it as a prank. Someone remarked that Baba might have released a spirit hovering in and around Silver Oaks. Baba smiled and made a sign that meant, "Quite possible!" and that ended the matter. He never expected that His dear ones should pay any extra or exclusive attention to such occurrences.

To those who lived and moved with Him this was nothing new. Baba in the earlier days had explained a little about such happenings. Sometimes "spirits" have tried to contact Baba with the intention of serving Him, particularly when He was resting at night. They knew that His blessings alone could liberate them from their "state of suspense". The presence of a human being — one of the men *mandali* who would invariably remain awake at night by Baba's side — prevented them from touching Baba's physical body. The one on night watch would also attend to Baba's needs who would be mostly engaged in His Spiritual work.

There were, however, rare occasions when Baba of Himself blessed a few "spirits". Kaka Baria once narrated that in July 1933, at Porto Fino — a village in Italy — the Baba-party was staying in Villa Altachiara overlooking the Mediterranean. One night Baba rushed out of His room, Kaka following Him. On His return Baba conveyed that a "spirit" had been set free from its most dismal state. Perhaps this meant that the obstacles barring this bodiless spirit from reincarnating as a human being were removed. Different kinds of events have occurred during Baba's night rest which outwardly indicate the depth of His inner spiritual work.

Baba, the Divine Humorist

The important decision about the New Life had been made by Baba and it seemed that at Panchgani, He was in a carefree holiday mood. He enjoyed long walks and drives. Sometimes, the intimate ones would play indoor games or charades. Baba would ask them to guess a number He had in mind and the winner would get some gift from Baba. During these informal sittings, with the help of the alphabet board, He sometimes referred to couplets in Marathi and Hindi, composed by the Perfect Masters of the past. His favorite poets were Tukaram and Kabir. About Tukaram He often gestured, "He is the chip of my Heart."

SECLUSION PRECEDING MEHER BABA'S NEW LIFE

Baba once quoted Tukaram's *abhang** with reference to the inborn nature of a person which mostly remains unchanged. Its meaning is: "Since his early age, Tukaram in the company of saints took great delight in singing the Name and Glory of God. Later, (with the grace of the *Sadguru*) he became One with God the Beloved — Pandurang. Yet, the innate inclination of singing *bhajans* continues; the original nature persists." Was Baba, through this quotation, hinting at His personal nature of playing the Divine Humorist? Once He stated, "Before I met my Beloved in Union — I lost everything. ego, mind and lower consciousness, but thank God, I did not lose my sense of humor."** On another occasion He cited a profound couplet of Kabir. The simple words of the Perfect Master are not born of intellectual inferences; they are the luminous flowers from the garden of spiritual wisdom. They have a perfume of deep unfading meaning. The original couplet is as follows:

Fikar sabko khagai, fikar sabka pir;
Fikar ki jo faki kare, uska nam Fakir.

Rendered freely in English it reads:

Worry wears out all, worry lords over all;
One, free from worry, is the *Fakir* amongst all.

One day in Silver Oaks, before going out for marketing, Arnavaz was whispering a song to herself. Baba called her and asked her to sing it out loudly. The song seemed to have two meanings, one apparent and one latent. The obvious meaning contained in the refrain of the song was: Oh traveller, be very vigilant and discreet as you pass by the road. Beware, there are many distractions on the way. The implied meaning of the song is: Oh wayfarer, the (spiritual) Path is very

---

* The name of a metre in Marathi poetry.
** *The Awakener*, Special Issue, Vol. 2, No. 3, 1955, p. 14.

slippery. May it not happen that you get enticed with the experiences in your journey. Baba listened to the whole song with a serious expression on His face. When the song was over, with a playful smile that flowed from His lips and glittered in His eyes, He gestured to Arnavaz, "Be careful as you pass by the road, be cautious in your dealings and return soon." Such instructions from Baba often indicated His humorous method of imparting spirituality; associating divine truths with our everyday affairs. And the *Avatar*'s Advent is the perfect association of the Divine with the human. He is God; He is man; He is the God-Man.

3

Meetings Directing the New Life

1949 — Part III

Raising the Curtain for the New Life

Now he entered his Great Seclusion of forty days — Curtain, in his divine Play, between the two Acts of Glory and Helplessness; and with the first act established in the hearts of the Audience in potentiality of being, stepped lightly onto the stage for Act II, inviting whoso to join him.*

— Francis Brabazon

FOLLOWING the seclusion in the Blue Bus, Baba with a small group, left for Panchgani in the district of Satara. Those at Meherabad and Meherazad were busy working on the drastic guidelines given by Baba. A few felt that it was just a test and that Baba might reconsider His decision to totally dispose of the two *ashrams* for good. But on His return, He expressly stated that from August 15, He would be holding meetings to disclose the details about His New Life.

I was at Kurduwadi and did not get wind of the fact that Act I (The Old Life) was to end so soon. The first bell, prior to the raising of the curtain for Act II (The New Life) chimed on August 1, but was audible only at a short range and to a very small group. Personally I had not met Baba since January 1949, and I was wholeheartedly looking forward to seeing Him. The previous year, in the summer, one of my friends named Mauni — the silent aspirant — had had an audience with Baba.

---

* Francis Brabazon, *Stay With God*, p. 137.

He was asked to visit the places of pilgrimage throughout India, for one year. He returned to Kurduwadi in July. I took this opportunity to inform Baba of his arrival and to express his ardent longing to meet Him. Baba graciously granted the request and I was asked to accompany him to Meherabad. The date of *darshan* was August 15.

Accordingly both of us were at Meherabad in a very cheerful mood, awaiting Baba's arrival. Dr. Daulat Singh, Minoo (Kharas) and a few others were specially called to see Baba. By 10 a.m. we were summoned inside the cabin facing the hall. Nilu, Vishnu and a few others were in the room. As Mauni was observing silence, I briefly related the main events of his itinerary of the past year, including the difficulties and temptations which he had had to face. Baba listened to the account with interest and conveyed, "What I have heard has made me happy. If Mauni is willing, I intend to ask him to observe a few more instructions." As soon as Mauni heard this he looked extremely happy. In fact he had had it in mind to ask Baba for some directions which he might devotedly follow for the rest of his life. Baba continued, "This time, I do not wish you to wander from place to place but to stay at one place for a period of six months. Now, go outside; discuss and decide with Bal the town or village that would suit you best. Then come again to see me in this cabin."

Six Months' *Sadhana* (Discipline)

We sat in the hall discussing some places in India that Mauni had visited. In the end he decided to stay in the vicinity of Hardwar-Rishikesh. In this area, free lodging in huts was easily available for aspirants. In addition to this, through religious and charitable institutions, each day food was served to *sadhus* and *sanyasis* without charge. Mauni seemed well-acquainted with the nooks and crannies of these twin centers of pilgrimage at the foot of the Himalayas. We returned to Baba's cabin and He gestured, "Which place?' I replied, "Hardwar-Rishikesh area." Pointing at Nilu, Baba conveyed to me, "A minute prior to your coming I told him that Mauni would choose this particular region." And He smiled, a knowing smile. Many times it had been revealed to those who stayed near Baba that He knew what they had in mind, before it was expressed in words.

Baba commenced giving instructions. They were: "Not to touch money; not to touch women; not to cook food but to beg for food. Once you decide to stay at a certain place do not change it for six months. Repeat daily the Divine Name — *Parabrahma* — ten thousand times. Don't repeat it loudly but it should just be audible to you. For the last seven days of this period no other liquid except water should be consumed. In consideration of the last instruction, to observe fast on water, you may, for that week, shift to some convenient place, if desired. During the period of fast do not repeat the Name audibly. After the completion of this *sadhana* come and see me." Mauni wrote on his slate, "Where will you be then, Baba?" Baba gestured, "I don't know! You find that out for yourself." As I had no idea about the forthcoming New Life, I wondered why Baba had given such a reply. Mauni, the silent devotee of the silent Master folded his hands and with a happy smile expressed his willingness to obey Baba.

Baba told Nilu to repeat the Divine Name — *Parabrahma* — in a very low voice and asked Mauni to hear the intonation and to say it in the same rhythm during the six months' period. He also asked Nilu to pray to God for Mauni's success in his *sadhana* and gave Mauni a few pieces of sweet cakes as *prasad*. He spelt on the board, "*Ho gaya*," meaning done or accomplished. The interview was over. We stood up to leave. As I looked at Baba, He incidentally asked me whether I was married. I replied, "No, Baba." He spelt on the board, "Good," and continued, "I have in mind to call you soon for an important meeting. Don't fail to come." I had not the least idea what that meeting would be about. Was it necessary to know? The propitious prospect of seeing the Glorious One within a few days was enough to fill my heart with joy. I folded my hands in gratitude for this unexpected appointment at Meherabad. What great significance lay in Baba's casual inquiry about my personal life I didn't realize then.

Both of us left the cabin with backward steps. It is an Indian custom that as far as possible one should not leave the Master's presence with one's back turned towards Him. As we came out I congratulated Mauni for his spontaneous response to Baba's instructions. In a jovial mood he brushed his fingers over his black beard and long hair and wrote on his slate, "Of what avail is this beard and wearing of long hair if I hesitate a bit to obey the Master!" Those staying at Meherabad knew a little about the impending change in Baba's activity but during our stay, no one referred to it even remotely. By the afternoon train we left Ahmednagar for Kurduwadi. Within a week, Mauni, with a few belongings but without carrying any money with him, left for Hardwar-Rishikesh, about sixteen hundred kms. to the north, near the holy Himalayas.

"You Will Join Baba in New Life"

After a week I received a registered letter from Adi, with postal acknowledgement for me to sign. This was not the usual procedure when receiving letters from Baba. The contents of that letter dated August 22, 1949 were as follows:

> Baba orders you to be at Meherabad on September 4, 1949 morning at 8 o'clock for one day without fail. You alone should come and if you don't come then you will never come.

I read the lines again and again and wondered what sort of meeting it would turn out to be and why the invitation had been sent by registered post. In all the previous letters some encouraging words from Baba along with His love and blessings would comfort me. But here was an ultimatum!

Some days later I happened to visit Poona on some private work. In the city bus I incidentally met one of my dear elderly friends — Baba's disciple, R. K. Gadekar. We used to call him Gadekar Saheb. Both of us were happy at this chance meeting. With an inquiring look he said, "Did you receive a call from Baba? I hope you have, and you must have decided to join Him in His New Life." "Yes, I received the invitation for the meeting," I replied. "But I don't understand what you mean by joining Baba in the New Life." Instead of answering the question he simply repeated, "You will join Him in the New Life." "Of course, I will feel myself most fortunate to be with Baba in any of His activities but for God's sake tell me what this New Life is about," I insisted.

He either did not know much about it or he somehow felt reluctant to talk further about it. Some minutes later we had to part and had no time to meet again. His words "The New Life" aroused my interest and I wondered about its nature. I deeply felt, however, that if a chance was ever offered in the meeting to go with Baba, I should jump at it no matter what. This decision was not the result of careful thought after weighing the pros and cons; it was just the unpremeditated response of the moment. As I first heard about the New Life, my decision to accompany Baba on it met no challenge from any corner of my mind.

Some Preliminary Meetings

The period from August 15 to August 31, was a very busy time for Baba. Practically everyday He visited Meherabad. He had instructed all the men disciples to be present in the hall at Meherabad in the morning when He would be specially discussing the points connected with the New Life. At the first meeting on August 15, a few members were late owing to a mistake in the typed notice displayed on the board. Baba nevertheless, informed all, "Even if I do not arrive from Meherabad, be in the hall by 7 a.m. " Baba was invariably present by 6.30 in the morning. He entrusted the work of noting down what transpired in the meetings to Feram Workingboxwala, a steno and long-standing disciple of Baba. He instructed him not to miss anything that He (Baba) would convey to anyone during these meetings.

On the first day of His arrival, He embraced Gustadjee and Kaikobad, the elderly members among His disciples. He seated Himself in the chair and the first general meeting about the New Life phase, with the closer ones, commenced. Here are the four main points that were discussed and decided during such preliminary meetings held on subsequent days.

(1) The persons who would decide to join Baba in His New Life would be entirely responsible before God for the decision. No one was to ask Baba's advice over this matter. Everyone who would wish to accompany Baba was expected to abide hundred per cent by the conditions that would be laid down by Baba.

(2) In the New Life, Baba would be absolutely helpless in the true and literal sense of the word.

(3) Meherabad and Meherazad *ashrams* were to be disbanded.*

(4) October 16, 1949 was the date fixed for the commencement of Baba's New Life.

On August 16, Baba had a meeting with the women

---

* Within a month and a half Meherjee Karkaria and Nariman Dadachanji, two of Baba's disciples became the owners of these two places. Yet, they both through their love for Baba kept these places entirely at the disposal of Baba and His disciples. Years later, in August 1968, Meherjee made the Gift Deed of Meherabad over in favor of the Avatar Meher Baba Trust, Ahmednagar. Meherazad is still owned by Nariman's wife, Arnavaz. Nariman died on July 2, 1974.

disciples in upper Meherabad.* Baba placed a four-point plan before them. He conveyed that if some of them wished to leave Meherabad and work independently for their living, He had no objection. Everyone was allowed to exercise her honest choice. The last alternative He offered was that they could leave everything to Baba accepting with full faith whatever decision He made for them. This proposal was unanimously accepted. All promised with pleasure and without the slightest demur to obey Baba. As a token of love and sincerity Baba asked each of them to kiss His hand. With a smiling face but retaining His dignity He gestured, "Let not this kiss be the kiss of Judas. Maintain it as the seal of your obedience to me."

Before continuing the discussion in the hall about the New Life on August 17, Baba asked Ghani to repeat the following prayer, "May God give *'buddhi'* [sense of discrimination] to the *mandali* and full *'shuddhi'* [perfect awareness] to Baba." He made it clear to each of His disciples that everyone was free to join Him or not, in His New Life. In spite of living with Baba for many years, if anyone so wished, he was allowed to live an independent life. But once one resolved to join Baba in His New Life phase, he had to obey Him in all matters. Baba agreed to give some guidelines to those who wished to stay behind.

Dying for Nothing

On August 18, morning, Baba asked four of His disciples to each bring the Holy Book of a different religion to the hall at Meherabad for a special reading. Kaikobad was the first to perform the *kusti*. It is a ceremony among the Zoroastrians that reminds them of the three principal precepts of Lord Zoroaster — good

---

* The premises on the hill comprising Meher Retreat, the Tomb, etc. were known as Upper Meherabad. The *ashram, dhuni,* etc. by the roadside were referred to as Lower Meherabad.

thoughts, good words and good deeds. Then he uttered some prayers from the *Avesta* — the prayer book of the Zoroastrians. Donkin read the Crucifixion of Jesus from the Gospel of St. Matthews. Khaksaheb offered *namaz* and solemnly but silently performed two *"Raqats* of *Nafil."* Kalemama opened the *Bhagavad Gita.* He read the Sanskrit verses from the tenth Discourse named the *Yoga* of Sovereignty or the Divine Glory. The gist of the last four verses of this Discourse present an all-inclusive vision of the *Avatar's* Divinity:

> O Arjuna, I am the Essence of all things. My divine manifestations are limitless. This world with its power, beauty, and glory is but a fraction of My Reality. Countless are these transient forms and needless is the knowledge of them. I alone exist and one spark of Myself sustains the Universe.

After each reading Baba asked for the Holy Book and kept it on His lap. At the close of this solemn ceremony He signalled all to stand up. He spread all the Books on a table and asked Ghani to place both hands on these Books and say aloud the prayer dictated by Him: "May God help Baba to make definitely this step, which He is taking, to give up everything and irrevocably to go away so that from October 16, when He enters the New Life there will be no turning back." About this incident Ramjoo wrote in *The New Phase,* "This was the first prayer of HELP ever before heard from Baba to God during the last 28 years and the *Mandali* were so taken aback and confused that no one could think of or dare say Amen!"

When all were seated Baba gave some additional points to Donkin. He was to prepare the final draft of the New Life conditions, with the help of Ghani. Baba was to approve the final text on August 21. Once, while referring to the tests and trials of the New Life, Baba casually gestured, "If you want to die for nothing, come with me!" The New Life as explained by Baba was an art or *yoga* of dying to the past completely and living in the present fully, without creating any future.

Touching the Feet and Twisting the Ear

I cannot leave out the following incident that happened on this day. It brought to the notice of the would-be companions the necessity of obeying Baba without any reservation or resistance. While dilating on the clauses and elucidating the qualities required to cope with the New Life, Baba incidentally admired Aloba's (Ali Akabar's) readiness to obey Him. In those days, Aloba was rather emotional; now he has considerably calmed down. On that day he was sitting quite close to Baba's seat. In response to Baba's words, out of deep gratitude, but quite unawares, he stretched out his hands and touched Baba's feet. This simple action changed the atmosphere of the meeting. Baba's standing injunction for the close ones was not to touch His feet as a gesture of reverence to Him. Even during the *darshan* programs when thousands were allowed to press their heads on His feet and unburden their *sanskaras* (impressions of thoughts and emotions), the intimate ones were not permitted to do so unless especially instructed. Hence, Baba became very displeased and appeared very serious. He decided to literally reciprocate the homage. He bade Aloba stand up and leaned down Himself to touch Aloba's feet.

All this was so unusual and unexpected that it was too much for Aloba to bear. He screamed and sprang up clean off the floor. To save him from falling on the stone floor and hurting himself, those nearby, as well as Baba, stretched out their hands to catch him. He was sobbing profusely and shedding tears. Baba, however, insisted that He must touch Aloba's feet and He did. The meeting continued. After some time Aloba calmed down. Baba used this occasion to clarify a few more conditions of the New Life. Baba conveyed, "In my New Life, I may ask anyone to spit on my face or slap me, the companion will have to act without the least hesitation."

After a little while Baba, the Master Psychologist, pointed at Aloba and in a very natural way asked him to twist His (Baba's) ear. Aloba silently got up and without any resentment was quick to act as ordered. Just then Jakkal, who was known in the *mandali* as Anna 104, raised his hand. When asked for the reason he said that he too was ready to twist Baba's ear! Hearing this, with a smile Baba gestured that if anyone wanted to pay off the old scores by pricking His ear He would gladly allow anyone to do so. But it was necessary to understand well that there was a world of difference between twisting His ear on one's own and doing it in response to Baba's order. In the ripples of laughter that followed the meeting was over.

Dr. Donkin and Dr. Nilu examined Baba's hand that bore the brunt of Aloba's body. The delicate muscles of Baba's fingers were strained and for some days Baba had to use a sling. The throbbing pain in the fingers caused Him many sleepless nights. After a week He could, though with great strain, put His signatures on important documents. Before leaving for the New Life, He did not wish to maintain anything in His name. As advised by the doctors, Baba had to hold a hard rubber ball in His palm and press it lightly; that was the exercise for the sprained hand. Baba's loving training, in helping His dear ones to obey Him, even at the cost of such physical suffering, stands unexcelled.

As Baba had instructed, Donkin was ready with the final write-up of the New Life conditions on August 21. Prior to its reading, on behalf of Baba, Ghani offered the following prayer, "May it please God to give His absolute strength to Baba to adhere to everything that is in his conditions, to the very end." With a few alterations and additions the draft was approved. At first, it was suggested that these conditions should be sent to all of Baba's followers. After a little discussion, however, it was decided that a list of over a thousand Baba lovers, men only, should be read out to Baba for selection. These were the people who, in one way or another, had in the past expressed their readiness to offer their services in Baba's cause. Excluding the Arrangement-wallas (those who were assigned certain duties in view of the New Life), Baba finally selected only 32 men, including the resident *mandali*. They were to have the choice of accompanying Baba in His New Life.

Baba's Decision about the Women Disciples

August 25 was the momentous day for the women disciples who had been staying with Baba for years. The bell rang. It was a call for the meeting with Baba in one of the rooms at Upper Meherabad. Baba looked radiant and happy and yet He appeared serious. In the previous meeting He had made it clear that though He would decide for each of them, nevertheless, everyone would be wholly responsible before God for whatever might happen to them after October 16. He told them that He might ask some to find jobs, some to remain celibate, and some to get married. All the statements made at this meeting were equally serious and grave as the women *mandali* waited to hear Baba's final instructions.

Baba was sitting on an iron cot with Mehera by His side. Mani was reading the board. Baba declared that Mehera, Mani, Mehru and Goher were to accompany Him in His New Life. Katie (Goher's sister), Naja (Pendu's sister), Masi, Khorshed, Rano and Kitty were to stay in Bombay. They were allowed to work and earn money if it were conveniently possible. At Bombay, Rano and Kitty later served as teachers for some months at Queen Mary High School. But all their earnings had to be spent in purchasing household necessities. No personal savings were allowed. They were allowed to go for outings but were not permitted to lunch or sup outside. They were not to accept anything as a gift from anyone. Nariman and Meherjee were to look after the necessary arrangements of their stay in Bombay. The women were not allowed to go to the movies for entertainment. In short, they had to lead an austere life.

Jerbai, wife of Kaikobad Dastur, with her three daughters and Mansari (Desai) were to reside on the hill at Upper Meherabad. Gulmai, Adi's mother, and Mehru (Eruch's sister) were to continue their stay in Ahmednagar. Baba asked them all to completely give up any hope of seeing Him again. He, however, advised them to carry out His orders with love and devotion. It was the best course open to them to share His New Life, though physically away from Him. In the end He added, "All the trouble is from hoping. . . . Where there is no hope there can follow no disappointment." A difficult lesson indeed!

Love Is Unconditional

Among the women *mandali*, Mani Desai was from Navsari and Mani Jessawala was from Nagpur. For the sake of convenience and with a sense of humor, Baba added the last letters of the places they came from to their names and nicknamed the former as Mansari and the latter as Manpur. For years, in accordance with Baba's instructions, Mansari has not crossed the railway lines that pass by the hill, except for medical reasons or under exceptional circumstances. Even after her death, her body, as instructed by Baba, will be buried on Upper Meherabad. In the above-mentioned meeting Mansari asked Baba to permit her to reside permanently on the Hill. There is an interesting story behind Mansari's simple request.

She first met Baba at Meherabad in 1927. The Desai family in Navsari revered Baba as a Perfect Master and most of its members were deeply devoted to Him. Mansari as a teenager was not drawn to Baba. Perhaps her mind was thoroughly occupied with a frightening skin disease which she had suffered from since she was five. There were boils and boils on her body and nobody could look at her without feeling a deep sympathy for her. After years of treatment the specialists declared that the disease was incurable. She was extremely miserable. It was April 1927 and as a matter of course — not with the longing to see Baba — she joined members of her family leaving for Meherabad. There must have been a special *darshan* program, for many had gathered there. The visitors formed a queue to offer their respects to Baba. Mansari was standing near a window staring at Baba with a blank mind. When she was unlacing her shoes, Baba beckoned her. At that soft casual glance her eyes glistened with tears. And unaware of them she let them fall down her face, some falling on her neck. This continued for a long time. She could not make out what had happened to her. It was a strange indefinable feeling.

Mansari joined the line of visitors and as she reached Baba's seat, she offered Him homage as one would offer to any saintly person or great personality. At this first meeting, Baba, with a face beaming with motherly love, embraced this tiny, thin, sickly girl and affectionately asked her to tell Him all about her disgusting disease. Hearing sympathetically all about the terrible tragedy, He conveyed, "Don't worry. You shall be cured." For Mansari it was too good to be true. Later Baba gave her some ash from the *dhuni* and instructed her, "Repeat my name and put a pinch of it in your mouth every morning before tea." Not with faith in Baba's divinity but merely out of respect she followed His counsel. And within a month, though unbelievable, Mansari was completely cured of her skin disease, declared incurable by the physicians of the day. Rarely did such miraculous cures occur in the lives of Baba people. And Baba strongly discourages those who follow Him from expecting such healings from Him or seeking them from others.

Anyway with this magic cure, Mansari felt strongly drawn to Baba. She intuitively felt that Baba was the Perfect Master, the Eternal One, for whom she should live and die. She sincerely longed to leave everything of the world to stay near Baba permanently. But she had to wait for about a decade. In 1930 she met Baba at Bombay at Kaka Baria's house and expressed her desire to join Him. Baba replied, "I wanted you since long ago but you have to wait till I call you." Later, on other occasions, whenever she put forth the same request, Baba's answer would be, "Wait till I call you."

Finally in July 1937, Baba granted her request and she was called bag and baggage to stay with Him as one of the resident women *mandali*.

At that time Baba was residing with a small group in the government rest house at Ahmednagar known as the Irrigation Bungalow. Jal, Baba's brother, was at the station to take her to this place. It was night when they arrived there and most of the members had gone to sleep, but Baba was awake. Mansari offered her respects to Him. He was happy and gestured, "I wanted you since long but this is the time that you had to come. Now that you are with me here, you have to do what I say." Mansari said, "Yes, Baba, surely everything except separation." To this Baba replied, "But, love is always unconditional and you are binding me!" Mansari responded, "Okay Baba. I will do whatever you say." It has been noticed that Baba never unduly emphasized the proximity of His personal presence but positively affirmed the importance of His impersonal Omnipresence; this is the basis for real understanding of spiritual life. Love for the God-Man may or may not bring occasions of being physically near Him but His loving remembrance will never fail to awaken the heart.

After several days Baba shifted His headquarters from Ahmednagar and Mansari, with the women *mandali*, commenced her stay on the hill. During that year whenever Baba visited Meherabad for His work, He found time to go up the hill and meet His disciples. Once, during His morning visit He asked Mansari to finish her breakfast and see Him. As she approached Baba, He held her by the wrist and strolled round the Retreat.

Through gestures Baba conveyed that the whole world belonged to Him. And pointing to the compound wall of the Meher Retreat He conveyed, "This is specially mine. Do you like this place?" Mansari answered, "Yes, Baba. I like it all the more because it is yours." Baba continued, "Will you then like to stay here if I go out on tour leaving you here, taking the rest of the women *mandali* with me?" After a little pause, He continued. "Of course, I will provide you with the necessities for a year." The very thought of separation brought tears to Mansari's eyes and she whispered, "I have not come here for that, Baba." Looking lovingly at her, Baba asked, "Are you crying? I don't like that. I just cracked a joke and it seems that you don't like my jokes." Mansari explained, "But Baba the joke was like a bomb exploding for me." Baba smiled ending the conversation by conveying, "Forget all about it. I won't crack any more jokes with you." However, through this first joke, it seems that He had planted the seed of her stay on the Meherabad Hill.

"Not Your Wish but My Will"

About 1944-45 Baba commenced staying in Meherazad (Pimpalgaon-Malvi). Whenever He visited Meherabad Mansari would say to Him, "When will you come back to Meherabad and stay here as before?" Baba's silent reply through gestures would be, "We'll see." Once He replied to her in a different way. He conveyed, "Instead of putting me the same old question again and again if you say, 'Baba, go anywhere you like, I will stay at Meherabad' it will make me happier." Was this an indication that Mansari had to stay there permanently?

In 1947 those staying at Upper Meherabad received a message from Baba about His special visit to the hill. Accordingly He was there by 9.30 a.m. All the women *mandali* were called. In the course of the meeting Baba conveyed, "Whosoever has any hope that I will come back and stay at Meherabad should think no more about it. Under these circumstances if any of you wants to leave Meherabad and go somewhere else, she may frankly inform me about it by 2.30 this afternoon. Such a decision will not displease me. On the other hand," Baba jokingly added, "I will pay for her ticket, garland the person concerned and arrange a lift to the railway station!" When this meeting was over Mansari was busy talking with the visitors from Poona. After awhile Baba called her and asked, "Have you decided?" "About what?" she asked. Baba gestured, "Don't you remember why I have called this meeting? What's your decision?" To this Mansari replied, "What's there to decide, Baba? It was already decided years ago. I will stay at Meherabad."

Baba looked very pleased. He referred to a line in Urdu, "*Jeena teri galime, marna teri galime* (I wish to live and to die in your lane O Beloved)," and added, "Are you really ready for this?" Mansari's spontaneous answer was, "Certainly, Baba." All these incidents spread over many years arrayed themselves before her and prompted Mansari on August 25, 1949 to put the above-mentioned request of permanently staying on the hill. Baba happily agreed but conveyed, "I am glad to hear this. You can stay here. But remember, you will be residing here not because of your wish but because of my Will." Mansari understood what Baba meant.

Response from the Women *Mandali*

Baba had already disclosed that He was going to disband the *ashrams* at Meherabad and Meherazad. He was to leave Ahmednagar on October 16 for good, so He wished to make provisions for the future requirements of those persons and families whom He had Himself made dependent upon Him. The women disciples responded whole-heartedly to this appeal by showing their readiness to sell their personal belongings to make the necessary arrangements. Kitty Davy was staying at Meherabad. She writes:

We too wanted to share. Chinese coats appeared from trunks that had lain there since our arrival in India in 1933. Jewellery rarely worn was brought out and other treasures. All displayed their "wares" on the beds and one morning Baba came up the Hill and went around systematically viewing what was laid out. He was deeply touched at our willingness to share in the spirit of the New Life, owning nothing but the barest necessities. Baba had made it clear that we could not dispose of anything that was really necessary. Not everything displayed was allowed to be sold. All I had of value was an amber necklace from Japan and a mandarine coat from China. I was fortunate. Baba allowed both to go "to the general fund."

Packing and dismantling, one *bhagulla* (saucepan) remained on the last day. From August 25th, in the midst of all this upheaval, Baba began coming up the Hill every afternoon at 3.00 to be with us. The time for departure was drawing near. Here was a test,— to forget the packing, play ping-pong, act charades, tell jokes, all with smiling faces and without tears!!*

In Spirituality Take Every Risk

August 21 was the day when Baba approved the final draft of the New Life conditions. It was a very busy day for Him from morning to evening. This was a red letter day for a small group of Baba lovers from Poona, anxiously waiting in Ahmednagar just to have a glimpse of Him. Half of the group had not met Baba before. This included Madhusudan Pund, one of Baba's favourite poet-singers of Hindi songs about Baba. On this day he met Baba just for a few minutes, but in the course of time Madhusudan was intimately linked with Him. Madhusudan's coming to Baba was more incidental

---

* Kitty Davy, "Recollections Part II," *The Awakener*, Vol. VII. No. 1 (1960), p. 12.

than planned. It was a Baba-coincidence. And every coincidence that draws a Baba lover closer to Him reveals a unique glimpse of the Divine Beloved, Baba.

Madhusudan was in his teens. His family's circumstances did not permit him to continue his education. In addition to this he was not keeping well and was passing through a phase of mental crisis. His love for music provided some consolation in life. This resulted in his friendship with Ramchandra Rao, a singer from north India. His rhythmical sweet voice so charmed Madhusudan that he started attending the different *bhajan* programs in Poona. This comradeship led him to participate in Meher Baba's birthday program, celebrated and arranged by Gadekar at his residence in Bhavani Peth, Poona. It was here that Madhusudan contacted the Baba people and gave a performance before Baba's picture. Unaware, at the time, that small incident not only brought him into Baba's fold but also introduced him to his sweetheart, Subhadra, whom he later married. A happy Baba-day!

Madhusudan was not very interested in lectures on Baba, but nevertheless he wished to continue his visits for the weekly *bhajans* at Gadekar's house. These programs gradually awakened in him a longing to see Baba in person. But there was a circular restricting *darshan* and even correspondence with Baba. Sule, who generally delivered talks at the meetings, convinced some of the youngsters to take the risk and have Baba's *darshan*. He told them that by imposing various restrictions, Baba was trying to create thirst in the hearts of His dear ones to see Him. The circular banning *darshan* was one of His ways of intensifying the longing. In fact Baba is ever ready with open arms to meet anyone who has a daring heart. While concluding his personal opinion about the ways of the Master, Sule added, "If you honestly feel the urge to meet Baba, why don't you try now?" This reminds me of Baba's words. As far as I remember they were, "In trifles take no risk; in business take a few risks; in spirituality take every risk." Thus a young group of seven Baba lovers resolved to risk a visit to Baba in Ahmednagar and Madhusudan was one of them.

Soft Light Flooded Madhusudan's Soul

In the morning on August 21, all of them presented themselves at Adi's office in Khushru Quarters, now called Meher Nazar. The preparations for the New Life were being made at breakneck speed. Adi was overworked with the details that he had to see to. When he found this group in the office he was amazed and said, "Haven't you read the circular? Who advised you to come over here for Baba's *darshan*?" The group was nervous; no one expected a cold reception at Baba's office! Someone apologized to Adi for troubling him. But the way in which all behaved and the overflowing longing that was visible in the visitors' eyes made Adi say, "You see, Baba is very busy and He does not see any visitor. In the morning I drove Him to Meherabad; in the evening I shall take him to Meherazad. If you can wait till evening, and can risk waiting on the road, nearby the railway station, I will drive slowly and you may have a glimpse of Baba. This much I can do and nothing more." "Thank you, Adi Kaka," said one. "We really do not want to disturb Baba, but somehow we could not help coming over here," added another. The auspicious moment was decreed and the group left the place quite happily.

By late afternoon all began to stroll or sit under the shade of the trees, about the spot fixed by Adi. The eyes of all were set in the direction of Meherabad. They anxiously waited and waited but there was no sign of the blue Chevrolet carrying Baba. Time weighed heavily on their minds. It was past seven. The last bus for Poona was at eight and yet there was no car in view. Though unwillingly, they decided to leave for the bus stand in a few minutes. Madhusudan folded his hands in the direction of Meherabad as a salutation to Baba. Just then a car was sighted. It was Adi's car and in Baba's time — the moment of relief when self-centered efforts are surrendered to the Divine Will. Madhusudan felt that a tender beam of soft light flashed from the car and flooded his soul. As the car passed by rather slowly, he saw Baba smiling; beauty and majesty seemed blended in His expression. Baba's marvellous look reminded him at once of the dream he had had the previous night.

Baba Blessed Madhusudan

In the dream, Madhusudan had seen the huge and mighty, but most tender and noble figure of Lord Vishnu, the Sustainer (*Parvardigar*), gracefully smiling. As he moved on to approach the Lord, His form miraculously disappeared and in its place there shone a disc of bright light, rotating and rolling farther and farther away. At last it entered a very small temple of Lord Krishna — the Flute Player. As the halo touched the statue, it got merged in the idol of Krishna. Was it to signify that *Paramatma* — the Infinite God, through the symbolic aspect of Vishnu — the Sustainer — assumed the form of Krishna and later of Meher Baba? With the vivid recollection of this meaningful dream and with the vision of tender light touching the core of his heart, Madhusudan could not contain himself, he lay on the road as if dazed.

Adi's car moved some distance and stopped. The Poona group hastened, rather ran, to meet Baba. He called all near Him and blessed each of them. At Baba's instructions Vishnu, one of Baba's disciples, helped Madhusudan walk to the car. Baba smiled and placed His healing hand on Madhusudan's head. He gestured, "I know you love me. Continue to love me and remain happy. My *nazar* is on you." And the car sped off in the darkness of the night and within a minute it was out of sight. But the light of love, kindled in the hearts of His young lovers, was inextinguishable. The risk was richly rewarded!

MEETINGS DIRECTING THE NEW LIFE

Madhusudan's fondness for music was an excuse for Baba to draw him in the orbit of His love, in His own unique way. In the aforementioned dream, when Madhusudan found himself at the threshold of Lord Krishna's temple, there came out the words from the inner chamber, "Sing a song." And he sang one. Baba's divine touch not only inspired Madhusudan to sing but even to compose beautiful songs for Baba. His compositions in Hindi and Marathi were later very much appreciated by Baba. Many of these songs were sung in Baba's presence and in the public meetings too. Especially the *arti, Meher mana arti swikaro* (I offer my mind to Thee, O Meher, accept it as my *arti*), was sung in chorus before Baba by hundreds of His lovers. This *arti* carries with it a unique Baba perfume; many feel so and I whole-heartedly agree with them.

"I Am the Servant of the Universe"

In the last week of August, like the group from Poona, a batch of four from Uttar Pradesh had a chance to meet Baba. This audience was in connection with the *darshan* programs in the district of Hamirpur (U. P.). Through the circular Baba had banned correspondence and visits of His devotees to see Him. These few, however, were called to Meherabad to discuss the plan for a public *darshan!* Baba had definitely decided to enter the New Life, yet He wished to discuss the plan for meeting the masses. His only concern, it seems, was to fulfill spiritual needs, though sometimes His ways appeared rather contradictory. The Hamirpur group was headed by Shripat Sahai. Babu Ramprasad from Nauranga and Keshav Nigam accompanied him. Both of them were seeing Baba physically for the first time. The significance of this meeting was gradually revealed as years passed by; for this small group was instrumental in sowing the seed of Baba's work in the Hamirpur area — the garden of Baba's love.

This party had arrived at Meherabad in the evening of

August 29. The next morning, Baba, as usual, was at Meherabad by 7 o'clock. Soon they were summoned to His cabin. They were called for a five minute interview but Baba graciously spent half an hour with them. He spelt on His board, "People call me the Lord of the Universe but I am the Servant of the Universe. I am the Washerman come to clean the dirty clothing of humanity. You are all lucky to be here at the moment when I am about to enter my New Life." After some intimate chat Baba continued, "Now listen. Here are three instructions: do not touch money; do not touch a woman; observe fast for twenty four hours once a week. Think sanely and seriously over these points and communicate your decision to me before you leave the cabin. I will not be displeased if you express your inability to follow any one or all these instructions. But once you promise me to obey one or more orders, you must not break them. Be honest in your reply."

Then Baba discussed with them the subject of giving *darshan* in the district of Hamirpur. A draft of the leaflet regarding the programs was read out to Baba. He expressed His readiness to visit Hamirpur before October 16, if Sahai, Nigam and others would promise that the people coming for *darshan* would not fold their hands or bow down to Baba! Such an assurance they dared not give and so the mass *darshan* programs were cancelled. Was it for the postponement of the programs that Baba asked them to undertake such a long journey; two nights by train? This could have been done by sending a telegram. It was, perhaps, the deep and sincere longing of the lovers that compelled the Beloved to make an exception under some excuse and meet them personally. At the end of this interview, Keshav Nigam said that he would obey the first and the third order. The others also openly told Baba their decisions without any reservations. Baba was pleased with their sincerity. Enraptured, they left Baba's cabin. As they came out no one felt like speaking, for the highest joy often dwells in silence. After lunch they left for the railway station.

MEETINGS DIRECTING THE NEW LIFE

About his first meeting with Baba, Keshav Nigam wrote, "August 30, 1949 was not only the blessed moment of my present life but it also marked the culmination of all the blessed moments, of all my previous lives and the long vista of my evolutionary sojourn, for on that day I saw God Himself, on the earth, in the form of Avatar Meher Baba.... This first *darshan* of God-Baba initiated me into a new life and also bathed my heart in a new light. The flame of Baba's love was intensely kindled within me and before it, all the world and its mundane activities appeared absolutely petty and unreal."

Some Instructions

The date of the meeting called in connection with the New Life as mentioned in the registered letters was September 4, but later it was changed to August 31. I was one of those invited to it. By the afternoon of August 30, I reached Meherabad. As I got down from the *tonga* (horse-cab) and entered the hall, I saw Baba sitting with the *mandali*. He looked fresh and radiant but His eyes had an expression of deep thought. I gathered that He was discussing some serious matter. I folded my hands to Him. With a welcoming smile He gestured at me, "Sit down." Without disturbing anyone I took my seat at the end of the carpet. I noticed that Baba was holding a small hard rubber ball in His palm and was pressing it lightly. I wondered what the matter was. Later, I learned that it was due to Baba's love and compassion for Aloba, in teaching him the way to obey the Master.

When the discussion was over He made some casual inquiries about my journey and health. While leaving for Meherazad, He gave the following general instructions: "Tomorrow the meeting will commence at 8 a.m. Everyone must have a bath in the morning." Turning to Ghani He specially asked him not to forget this. Ghani was in the habit of bathing once a week on Friday. Jokingly he would say to us, "I wonder why you people have a bath every day! As I stay near Baba, I do not wish to wash off the holy dust of the *Avatar's darbar** that I daily collect on my body!" On August 31 we were not to fold our hands to Baba to offer *namaskars*. Baba instructed Padri that the stone flooring of the hall be washed by next morning. No one was to enter the hall after it was cleaned.

All of us were to get inside with Baba by 8 a.m. We were also told not to discuss among ourselves anything in connection with the New Life. The Baba people who had arrived for this meeting from the outstations included Dr. Daulat Singh, Kishan Singh, Minoo Kharas, Babadas, Dr. Deshmukh, Gadekar R. K., and Sadashiv Patel. After supper some of us gathered around Ghani and listened to the jovial and lively incidents from Baba's life which he narrated. We conversed on many topics of general interest except the forthcoming New Life.

In the Hall at Meherabad

Those who were staying in Ahmednagar and were called for the meeting arrived at Meherabad before sunrise. All of us eagerly awaited Baba's arrival. As He got down from the car He looked more than beautiful. No one was allowed to enter the hall before 8 o'clock so Baba sat on a bench on the verandah. We gathered around Him, particularly those who had come from the out-stations. Baba asked Gadekar and Babadas to come forward. Pointing at them, He made a joke, "Babadas has more *chelas* (disciples) than I have; and Gadekar more *gurus!*" Baba was thus referring to the fact that Babadas who had a long beard, wore long hair and used a *kafni* (long robe), was regarded by many villagers as a *sadhu* or a *guru*. They would revere him as a master. Gadekar was not particular about his dress though he was a high-ranking officer. As he had an innocent heart,

---

* The Royal Court.

he treated every *sadhu* as an advanced soul and would serve and revere him as a *guru*. In such a humorous mood Baba started inquiring about each and everyone called for the meeting.

Raosaheb Afseri had been the principal of the Hazrat Babajan School at Meherabad in 1927. Later he stayed with his family at Bombay. He was asked to attend the meeting. But it was noticed that he had not yet arrived. Baba conveyed, "If he comes after eight he will neither be allowed to enter the hall nor to attend the meeting." Just then the Bombay-Manmad railway train passed by Meherabad and we saw Afseri waving a handkerchief at those standing on the road. Baba ordered that a car be rushed to the station. The one going in the car was instructed to take Afseri right to the bathroom in Meherabad. This was to help him finish his bath in time to be ready by eight. The plan worked out well and a few minutes before eight o'clock we all, including Afseri, entered the hall, Baba leading. The stone flooring was covered with a green carpet. In the left wing was Baba's chair, and in the corner lay a small table. In the right wing some old photos of Baba with the *mandali* were displayed on the wall. An old clock was marking time, facing Baba's seat and it is still there.

Baba alone walked to the right wing and all of us stood in the left. He called Padri and asked him to walk across the hall seven times, in between the wings. He gestured, "The sight of a cat crossing the road is regarded as a sign of ill-luck by the Hindus and Padri's walking will ward off anything that is evil!" This was, perhaps, the last joke of the day, for once the meeting commenced the atmosphere remained exceptionally serious. Baba took His seat and motioned us to sit down. Before starting the work at the meeting, He asked Padri to close all the doors and the windows of the hall. Behram, Baba's brother, who arrived a few minutes late could not enter the hall and attend the meeting.

Choice of Joining the New Life

The momentous meeting commenced. All were extremely anxious to hear what Baba would explain about the New Life phase. He passed a cursory look over the gathering and conveyed, "From amongst the many I have specially called a few of you to attend this important meeting. Be very attentive. Think thoroughly over what you hear. Those who will soon get a circular should carefully go through it and arrive at an honest conclusion." The meeting began with the reading and recitation from the Holy Books. Kaikobad recited a part from *Zend Avesta*; Khaksaheb offered *namaz*. Baba was pleased with Khaksaheb's melodious and appealing voice. He gestured that if God were not to listen to such a heart rending prayer, He must be either deaf or dead. Donkin read the Crucifixion of Jesus from the New Testament. Kalemama concluded this program with the reading of some verses from the *Bhagavad Gita*, the Lord's Song.

The different Holy Books were placed on the table. We all, along with Baba, stood up, facing the Books and Baba's framed coloured picture on the wall which is still there. On behalf of Baba the following prayer of forgiveness was read aloud:

> I forgive each and every disciple, devotee and follower, all his weaknesses up-to-date, and any disobedience on his part up till now. And, on behalf of myself I forgive myself for any pain, injustice, or wrong that I may have done any of them.

There were also some members in the hall who were not to receive the circular about the New Life conditions. They were called the Arrangementwallas. After Baba's entering the New Life these were the persons entrusted with the work of taking care of the families and those people who had dedicated their lives to Baba and had been dependent on Him for years. To those whom He intended to give the choice of becoming His companions in the New Life, He addressed as follows:

> I want you all who receive this Circular to understand once and for all that I am 100% serious about this New Life. Although you have stood by me faithfully and lovingly all these past years, with perfect faith and sincerity in spite of receiving nothing from me, and although you all might be prepared to lay down your lives for me, yet there is the possibility that your and my habits of understanding and misunderstanding each other during the last so many years, might mislead you into *not* taking this *most seriously*.
>
> Therefore I want you all to go through this Circular word by word most carefully before you decide. It would be best if you accompany me and abide by all orders and conditions 100% thoroughly. But although your faith, love and service for me have been greater than mine would have been for my own Master, yet these conditions might prove your undoing. So unless you are ready to live the life of complete *satyanashi* [utter ruin] and absolute obedience it would be better to stay behind and obey instructions that will be given to you. But all this is by way of statement of facts and confessions. The decision is entirely to be made by you and you alone. May God give you the required strength. . . .

"You, and You Alone Are Responsible before God"

Ramjoo gave a short talk in Hindi especially for those who did not understand English well, explaining in a nutshell the clauses and terms comprising the New Life. Donkin then read out the original text in English. Everything mentioned therein was to be seriously thought over by those who wished to join Baba in His New Life by being physically near Him. Here follows the gist of some of the points from the circular.

Everyone who received a copy of the communication

was to inform Baba of his decision with a clèar "Yes" or "No"; not a word more. If anyone decided not to go with Baba, his spiritual connections with Him would not be broken off. Such a one was to receive a few orders from Baba and he was expected to observe them sincerely. If one failed to answer either in the affirmative or negative his connections with Baba would automatically get severed. Everyone was expected to ponder over the following seven points with due consideration. To quote from the circular:

(1) In this New Life of complete renunciation you will be utterly at the mercy of all kinds of good or bad treatment that may be meted out to you by others. Whatever happens, you, and you alone, will be held responsible before God.

(2) If, by accompanying Baba your dependants or your business or private affairs suffer in any way, you, and you alone, will be held responsible before God. . . .

(3) If, due to physical or mental exhaustion, exposure to extreme weather, lack of food. . . etc., etc., you fall ill or die, you, and you alone, will be held responsible before God.

(4) If Baba should give you any order that may result in your being sent to prison or in your being assaulted or even killed, you, and you alone, will be held responsible before God.

(5) If you should disobey Baba and He should send you away from Him you will not hold Baba responsible before God for your future, whatever that future may bring. . . .

(6) The decision that you give to Baba will be considered by Him as irrevocable, and He will not accept any change of decision from anyone. . . .

(7) If, as a result of your having been sent away by Baba, you should take any misguided step . . . you, and you alone, will be held responsible before God.

These clauses are enough to give an idea of the expected degree of preparedness from one who would want to join Baba in His New Life. In short, only those whose hearts dared to sing the song of perfect surrender to Baba's Will were eligible to follow Him. And such a response automatically implied complete faith in Baba's life of Compassion irrespective of its outward expression.

Baba Takes the Oath

In the circular, Baba had made it clear that by accompanying Him no one was to reap the slightest spiritual or material benefit. On the other hand, one had to be in readiness for every kind of disappointment and adversity. No special care for any ailment — physical or mental — was to be expected.

In spite of this, those who wished to go with Him were to affirm their resolve before God — the Infinite. Baba too was to take the Oath about His determination to lead the New Life. Some of the standing injunctions for the companions of the New Life were: not to touch a woman; not to touch money; not to discuss politics; not to tell lies; not to create circumstances that might invoke homage, etc. The circular also stated: "It must be clearly understood that although every condition and standing order listed in the communication is absolutely binding on all who decide to accompany Baba, Baba Himself is not only *not* bound by any order or condition but is also absolutely free for all time to give any order to anyone. And that such orders might change or even nullify any or all the standing orders and conditions...."

When Donkin finished the reading of the entire circular a deep silence prevailed in the hall. Everyone seemed to sense the immensity of the New Life phase. Baba and all of us stood up. On behalf of Baba the following Oath was solemnly read out:

Before God the Absolute whom those who have

realized know as their own Self and whom believers believe to be All-pervading, All-knowing, All-loving and All-merciful — before this Infinite Existence, Baba on behalf of himself and his followers, asks forgiveness for all mental, physical and moral weaknesses called sins, and for all lies and false dealings, and for all impure and selfish actions.

Before this Infinite God who ever was, ever is, and ever will be, Baba decides today on the New Life that he and those who accompany him will enter from October 16, 1949, and lead on till the end. This New Life will be based absolutely on all that has been dictated by Baba in the Circular of conditions; and Baba invokes God to make him stand by it as firmly and steadfastly as his companions in his New Life are required to be.

All the people, from the list approved by Baba, received a copy of the circular. All were asked to go through each clause carefully, word by word. No one was expected to approach Baba for any clarification whatsoever. Everyone was to convey his decision by writing just one word on the last page — "Yes" or "No" — and to add one's signature below it. This copy was to be personally handed over to Baba. When the distribution of the copies was over, the doors were opened and Baba ordered a break for tea and refreshment. It was perhaps meant to offer some time for each to go through all the pages thoroughly, to think well of the consequences and to arrive at a final decision.

The Blessed Day in My Life

The resident disciples who already knew about the nature of the New Life had perhaps arrived at their final decisions. They did not look very preoccupied but those from the out-stations seemed indecisive, or so it appeared to me. As I was having tea, Gadekar said to me, "You must have decided in the affirmative to go with

MEETINGS DIRECTING THE NEW LIFE

Baba." Before I could speak a word another of my friends seconded him and added, "You are right, Gadekar." I felt rather astonished and asked him the reason for his inference. He related that a few days ago he had visited Meherazad. There, during an incidental conversation, Baba mentioned that I, being unmarried, might prefer to accompany Him in His New Life. Baba's indirect hint that I might accompany Him removed any hesitation I had and I completely resolved to go with Him.

Here, I must also mention an earlier incident that contributed to my decision. In the morning I was standing with Sadashiv Patel near Mohammed — the resident *mast* of Meherabad. I was never interested in purposely meeting the *masts* or in asking them anything. I was just strolling with Patel. Coincidentally Mohammed, however, with his far off gaze turned towards me, stammered just a sentence, "God bless you." Patel told me that this uninvited utterance meant something auspicious. And indeed August 31, 1949 was one of the best and most blessed days of my life. These two incidents strengthened my original decision to accompany Baba, at any cost.

I must admit that I had no idea what day-to-day living with Baba was like in the Old Life, much less what it would be like in the New Life. But deep down in me I felt, "What else could be better than being in close company with Baba, the Beloved Master!" In a way this was extended selfishness. I was given the choice and I wanted to make the best of it. The only thought that clouded my conscience a bit was whether my accompanying Baba would prove burdensome to the other companions. I was ignorant of the tests and trials—physical and mental — mentioned in the circular. God willing, ignorance is not only bliss but sometimes makes it easier to decide such things! Anyway, I regarded this chance as the greatest opportunity in my life and with all sincerity I wrote, "Yes" at the end of the circular, signed it and returned it to Baba.

The Three Groups

After refreshment as we gathered in the hall, Baba made us sit in three groups. The first was of the Arrangementwallas — Sarosh, Meherjee, Nariman and Ramjoo. They were entrusted with the work of carrying out certain arrangements approved by Baba. The second group was of the "Nowallas". They were those who wrote "No" on the circular as they gave it back to Baba. Padri, Deshmukh, Gadekar and a few others were in this group. Baba was surprised to find Padri, one of His long-standing intimate disciples sitting among the Nowallas. Baba, however, conveyed, "Pendu, Padri, Adi and Vishnu are the four pillars of Meherabad. Three have decided to accompany me, in my New Life. In case anything untoward happens to them, at least one of the pillars is safe." Some Nowallas looked rather dejected at their inability to join Baba in His New Life. To console Gadekar who was almost in tears, Baba gestured, "May God always keep Gadekar in my heart." Pointing at Deshmukh He conveyed, "He will always be near and dear to me." He asked both of them not to worry over what they had decided.

Among the Yeswallas, those who decided to accompany Baba, Jal Kerawala's decision was a pleasant surprise. According to Baba's previous instructions, he was to be regarded as one of the Arrangementwallas. But inadvertently he received the circular and instantaneously determined to give up his high ranking government post and leave all his worldly ties. Baba appreciated his love and courage but as a special case, there and then, He absolved him of his resolve. He was asked to continue his services and to help the Arrangementwallas. Excluding Jal Kerawala there were 22 men in this third group: Gustadjee, Adi, Donkin, Nilu, Ghani, Pendu, Patel, Vishnu, Murli (Kale), Anna (Jakkal), Babadas, Daulat Singh, Kaka, Eruch, Baidul, Aloba, Minoo (Kharas), Pandoba (Deshmukh), Kishan Singh, Chhagan, Manek (Mehta) and Bal (Natu). Out of these twenty-two eventually 16 accompanied Baba in His New Life.

Referring to the Yeswallas who had come from the out-stations, Baba instructed, "Be thoroughly prepared to leave your home and everything connected with your worldly things once for all. If there are any difficulties, try to overcome them, but do not inform me or ask me anything about them. You are responsible for your decision and everything connected with it. Be at Meherabad by the morning of October 1. When you step into the premises of Meherabad, don't have any money with you. Be here in the dress that you generally wear. No extra clothes. You may, however, bring one *kambal* [coarse woollen blanket]. That's all." After lunch some of us, with the firm resolve to be at Meherabad as ordered by Baba, left for the railway station.

The New Life, it seemed, had already commenced.

4

Old Life Ends; New Life Begins

1949 — Part IV

Yeswallas Who Stayed Behind

OUT of the 22 Yeswallas* who decided to go with Baba, a few came in for special attention. Minoo Kharas from Karachi (Pakistan), was entrusted with an important job by Baba. He did it during the given time limit to Baba's satisfaction and Baba felt so pleased that of His own He released Minoo from joining the New Life physically, though he would remain in the Yeswalla category. Pandoba (Deshmukh) from Ahmednagar who had stayed in the *ashram* at Meherabad in 1926-27, approached Baba in the first week of September and wished to be included in the group of the Nowallas.** On second thought, Pandoba felt himself physically unfit to bear the strain of the New Life. Considering his age, Baba granted the request. He, at the same time, asked him to follow some special instructions.

For quite a long period Kishan Singh had been repeatedly imploring Baba to allow him to stay near Him permanently. He was ready, at a signal from Baba, to leave his job and family. In view of this situation, Adi wrote to him in June 1949 that he should not go to Meherabad with his bag and baggage, unless definite instructions from Baba to that effect were received. In the interview that followed, Baba asked him to attend the meeting on August 31. It was quite evident that Kishan Singh had decided to join Baba in His New

---

* Those who resolved to accompany Baba in His New Life.
** Those who preferred not to join Baba in His New Life.

OLD LIFE ENDS; NEW LIFE BEGINS

Life. But God willed otherwise!

After his return to Delhi he found that if the necessary papers were not signed by him before October 16 his family would face some legal difficulties in receiving his pension. He wrote a letter to the Controller of Accounts, asking him to speed up the process. He also forwarded a copy of it to Adi for his information. In this letter he mentioned an inquiry in connection with a false charge made against him. The investigation in progress, it seemed, would not be over by October 1949. When this letter was brought to Baba's notice, He directed Adi to send the following telegram to Kishan Singh:

In view of your letter, I forgive you and free you from your "Yes" promise and want you definitely to stay home as up to now and, rest assured, your spiritual connections with me will remain as before.

The contents of the above telegram were quite disappointing to Kishan Singh who ardenty longed to accompany Baba. He wrote to Adi about this who sent him an apt reply, a part of which follows: "I realize how very disappointed you have become at the sudden receipt of Baba's telegram cancelling your joining Him. In this respect I would like to tell you that you should not in any way be very much dejected and lose hope of your aspirations being fulfilled.... The chances of circumstances changing favourably can never be ruled out and accordingly as and when Baba wishes your aspirations will be fulfilled...." As predicted by Adi and wished by Kishan Singh, in the year 1953, Kishan Singh did have the unique opportunity of staying near Baba, with the resident disciples at Dehra Dun.

Manek Mehta was conducting an organization at Bombay called Meher Mandal. He was the head of the Mandal. Realizing his difficulty, Baba, of His own, advised him to wind up his personal activities connected with it and to dissociate himself completely from the organization, to join Baba in His New Life in 1950. Manek, however, failed to resign himself to Baba's wishes. Master proposes and devotee disposes!

Chhagan, one of the old-time disciples staying with Baba, happened to ask Him whether his personal decision to be with Baba in the New Life was appropriate. Asking Baba's advice about one's decision was against the spirit of the conditions outlined in the circular. Baba felt rather sad and ordered Chhagan not to join Him on October 16. Instead, He gave him three instructions which he had to follow. The first one was to sell the ornaments he possessed. The money received was to be used to feed Mohammed, the *mast* at Meherabad, as well as to provide for his other needs, if any. The second was to serve somewhere or to find some suitable vocation for his maintenance. He was not to leave Bhingar, a place about three kms. from Ahmednagar. The third order was to beg for his food, starting December 15, for one year.

As soon as Chhagan received the instructions he felt that he should not have changed his mind, but it was too late. The arrow had left the bow. Now the best he could do was to obey Baba, and he did so literally. The last instruction proved to be a real test. To beg for food at a place where one owns a house and a farm and where one is regarded as a man of some status is indeed an ordeal of a high order! Chhagan had to pass through this ego crushing process ungrudgingly. The date fixed in advance by Baba for the one year's begging happened to be the day following the death of his dear father. All his relatives — there were many — gathered at his house. The very next day, after his return from the cremation ground, in this atmosphere of intense bereavement, Chhagan had to pick up the begging bowl and satchel. As was customary among the Hindus, the funeral rites were carried out for fourteen days. During the last two days special feasts were arranged in honor of the dead but Chhagan could not participate. According to Baba's instructions he had started begging for food daily at five houses and ate whatever was received in *bhiksha,* irrespective of the bitter comments from the people. What a peculiar predicament! No wonder that when Baba learnt about this He was immensely pleased at Chhagan's obedience.

Leaving All to Follow the One

Now about myself. By the evening of August 31, I reached Kurduwadi. The next morning, the first thing I did was to see the headmaster of the high school; I tendered my resignation giving one month's notice. As I did not reveal why I was leaving my job so abruptly he was a bit surprised. Indirectly he blamed my "mystical attitude" which he thought had blossomed in me ever since I observed silence, a month earlier. He, however, asked me to reconsider the matter. To me this was unthinkable. The moment I had written "Yes" and signed my name at Meherabad I was dead to the world and yet strangely alive. I was in a carefree mood. I bore ill-feeling towards none; I did not feel specially attached to anyone. I was silently bidding farewell to whomsoever I met. Perhaps it was a fine speechless performance! I was not expected to reveal to others my intention to accompany Baba for good. Nevertheless, I was allowed to give some idea about my determination to one of the responsible members of my family. The married ones were to convey the resolve to their wives.

Being a bachelor I decided to disclose my decision to my dear younger brother, Prabhakar. After taking the necessary promise that he would not reveal the news to anyone before October 16, I narrated to him in a nutshell the account of the last meeting at Meherabad. He was astonished. Our dear mother had recently passed away; I was the eldest member in the family. In spite of this Prabhakar agreed to shoulder the responsibility of the joint family. He was indeed very co-operative in all matters.

We owned some land and a house in a village. A small

bank account and some shares of a sugar company were in my name. I had to finish the legal act of transferring all these to my brother's name. Whatever could be done was attended to and the rest of it was left to the Will of God. We were ready to forfeit the property if the legal procedure remained incomplete or needed my presence after October 1. In those days Baba had bestowed on me a most carefree attitude and I must admit that at present I do not possess it to that degree. In those days nothing seemed to bother me. I used to recall the following lines (I am not sure about the exact text) from the Song of the *Sanyasin**by Swami Vivekananda:

> They know no Truth, who dream such vacant dreams,
> As father, mother, children, wife and friend.
> The sexless Self....
> Is He who is but One,
> And know thou art That, *Sanyasin* bold.
> Say *Om Tat Sat Om*!

I was told by one of the old-timers that Baba in the early *ashram* days, at Meherabad, would sometimes refer to these lines to bring home the importance of renunciation and in the light of this I had resolved to "leave all" and to follow the One in all.

In the first week of September, I was under the impression that I had to present myself at Meherabad with just a coarse woollen blanket on my shoulder and nothing else. But in the second week I received a letter containing a long list of things — clothes and other articles of daily use — which I had to take with me. The first item was two cotton *kafnis* (long robes), one white, the other blue; the second was a brown woollen *kafni*. In India I had never seen anyone wearing either blue or woollen long robes. But Baba's instructions made such thoughts irrelevant. I went to the tailor and asked him

---

* One who has renounced the ways of the world to realize Truth (God).

OLD LIFE ENDS; NEW LIFE BEGINS

to take the necessary measurements. He gave me an inquiring look as if I had gone mad! In addition, when I told him to sew a woollen *kafni*, he seemed extremely surprised. I come from a middle-class family and he knew woollen clothing was a luxury for me. When I ordered these robes he tried to ask me some direct questions. I was deliberately evasive in my replies and changed the subject.

The headmaster, the tailor, and some other acquaintances probably regarded me as someone losing his mental balance! Once you come in the love orbit of Meher Baba, the God-Man, you may have to pass through this phase. And people are noticed remarking, "He is a good man, very rational and sane in his conversations except for anything belittling Meher Baba's orders and Divinity." Such words remind me of the meaningful lines of the Urdu couplets Ghani once recited. I hope the following translation will give some idea of the depth of meaning contained in the couplets:

Dear friend, following the Perfect Master, brings in its wake resurrection under the garb of desolation.
Don't judge the Master and His Divinity from the tests and trials that you are put in.
Never think that He does not know His mind. In spite of anything that He asks you to do, He is indeed the Wisest of the Wise....
O worldly wise, what do you know about His Game of Love!

The list included other things like toothpaste, a shaving set, shoes, etc. Even the size of the trunk was specified. I found that the trunk purchased by my brother was a bit too long; I had to buy another, of the required dimensions. I was eagerly waiting for the sun to set on September 30, to start by the night train for Ahmednagar. But, at the end of the list there was a note informing me to reach Meherabad on October 5. I thought, "From October 1, I shall be relieved from my teaching job. Then my neighbors and friends will know that I have left the school. Maybe some will visit me at home, inquiring about my future plans." And I was thoroughly prepared for this Baba joke!

A Jeremiad to *Saqi* (The Wine Seller)

I do not know much about the difficulties of those staying at Meherabad or Meherazad, except for those of Ghani. He was one of the Yeswallas but the necessity of providing his wife and children with a minimum income after his departure for the New Life continued to bother him. It was specially in relation to the property at Lonavla. Two decades earlier Ghani owned five houses at Lonavla, a place forty kms. from Poona. At that time he owed 16,000 rupees to a money lender who through legal maneouvres was successful in getting the court to order all those houses transferred to his name. In fact, the estimated value of the whole property was about 60,000 rupees. The decree of the court was a great blow to Ghani. The day this order was to come into effect, the moneylender and his wife were surprisingly murdered. The police department, in the investigation, tried to find out if Ghani, in any way, was involved in this heinous crime. Fortunately, in those days he was staying with Baba. The police for lack of evidence did not level any charges against him.

The whole affair, however, weighed so heavily on him that on his return to Lonavla, Ghani thought of committing suicide. One night in a desperate mood he went to a nearby lake and cursed all the Masters in the world including Baba for being so unjust and unkind to him. At the last moment, nevertheless, he dared not throw himself into the lake. The next morning, most unexpectedly, Baba visited Lonavla and asked Ghani why he had been calling on Him (Baba) so intensely the previous night! This revealed to Ghani, Baba's omniscience and thereupon he decided to resign himself to the *karmic* debts and dues, ordained by the Divine Will.

OLD LIFE ENDS; NEW LIFE BEGINS

He also promised Baba to stay near Him, whenever called. Ghani had appealed the decision of the court and in 1939 he got back 3/5ths of his property. Later, he dedicated this property to Baba.

In 1949, when the arrangements connected with the New Life phase were being discussed, Baba casually mentioned that He had it in mind to make some definite provision for Ghani's wife and children, especially while disposing of the property at Lonavla that was dedicated to Him. As the days passed by, Ghani noticed that his particular personal problem was neither attended to nor even referred to by Baba. So thoughts about the future of his family members continued to disturb him. He had anticipated Baba doing something to help in this matter. In September, he gave vent to his uneasy thoughts through a *ghazal* which was read out to Baba.

Baba appreciated the frankness of Ghani but at the same time asked Khak (named Abbas), one of His disciples, who too was a poet, to give an adequate reply to Ghani, as from Baba. I intend to quote a few excerpts from the English translation of these two Urdu *ghazals*. They give an idea of Baba's relationship with His close disciples, and also the way He stirred up the emotions of those near Him and how, in due course, He restored harmony. The title of Ghani's *ghazal* was "A Jeremiad to *Saqi*" He wrote:

> Tonight the members of the tavern are meeting in a session;
> Tonight the Master of the tavern also is gracing the occasion. . . .
> Tonight if permitted I wish to unburden my heart,
> Hereafter the Love and Lover and this Divine Night will only be a dream.
>
> I am notorious in the world as a free thinker; . . .
> Excuse me if the wailing tune is not sweet to the ear.
> O *Saqi!* Hear for once the groans of the faihful ones,
> This bemoaning is, nevertheless tinged with love.

O *Saqi!* Do you recall to mind the plethora of promises?
These — the uninvited gestures of kindness and favors,
Shattered our reasoning and vanquished our resistance.
We were caught just on the threshold of our lives.

O *Saqi!* Do you remember the postponement of your promises, to June and September?
We often recall such incidents for amusements.
You begin to evolve subterfuges and excuses.
There is no one to beat you at this game.

Often you have played the game of construction and destruction.
No sooner we felt settled, there was unsettlement.
The breeze of destruction, however, was never so strong as on this occasion;
It seems — the present game implied perfect destruction.

The school of Love for years underwent a routine course,
What seized you to change suddenly the curriculum so drastically?
Mere words can never remove the age-long ruts of temperament and nature,
When it is a problem even for advanced souls!

Saqi's Reply to the Jeremiad

At the next meeting, Khaksaheb as instructed by Baba was ready with the answer. It was in the form of couplets.

This *ghazal,* on behalf of Baba, was read out openly before Baba and His close disciples. Some of the lines are given below:

OLD LIFE ENDS; NEW LIFE BEGINS

Inmates of the tavern, do you know whose is the wailing note today?
The voice evidently is one of our ... beneficiaries.
How dare he complain about the tyranny of the *Saqi*?
Can he truly say that the Wine eternal has not benefited him at all?

Don't disgrace the name of free thinking!
A free thinker never caters for name and fame.
The *Saqi* has not forgotten His promises,
And His uncalled for gestures of kindness and favors.

It would be near the mark if I were to call you short-sighted.
Whatever I did was just the right thing in your case.
The so-called freedom of your dreams, like death,*
Would have dragged you down to the depths of ignominy and shame!

In the world, for one beautiful there is one better;
In intellect and learning, there are hundreds superior to you.
Just explain what particular qualification you possess,
That amongst others you become "select" in my eyes.

The process of purifying the heart is not a child's game.
The ordeal of surrender and resignation is long and tedious.
Your hasty temperament has blurred your vision,
In this Path, there is tardiness, but not niggardliness.

Listen to the *Saqi*, don't lose heart.
Success depends on the will to do and die.
Give up all considerations of profit and loss,
The All-merciful Master of the Tavern will no doubt,
Make you drink one day, the Wine of Immortal Life!

---

* Ghani's attempt to commit suicide at Lonavla.

Baba, the All-knowing and Compassionate One, guided Ghani inwardly to maintain his mental poise. In connection with this incident, Ghani wrote in the *Diary of the New Life,* "Over some misunderstanding in the matter of adjusting the disposal of Lonavla properties, an ugly situation developed, which Baba eventually tided over, thereby saving for Dr. Ghani the dire consequences of his rebellious mood over the question."* Ghani was a very outspoken person. Once he said to me, "I am here (with Baba) not only for *Khuda* (God) but also for *khurda* (money) — coins of different denomination." Perhaps he was joking. Whether he was or wasn't, his capacity to quote appropriate couplets from Urdu and Persian *ghazals* and poems, to Baba's satisfaction, was remarkable. Besides, his wit and humor were superb and Baba felt happy and relaxed in Ghani's company.

In this great game of material dispensation, Baba heard that a certain mill owner often spoke proudly of having helped Baba's cause, in cash and kind, a decade ago. So Baba sent two of His disciples, including Sarosh Irani to meet this person. He was given to understand that it was not he who obliged Baba with his services but in fact he was fortunate enough to be blessed by the *Avatar* by His accepting them and he ought to have felt grateful for this to Him. From the boastful remarks he had made earlier it was clear that he had failed to understand this fundamental principle. Hence, in that very same meeting, to his great astonishment, and in spite of his repeated refusals he was fully recompensed. Poor mill owner! It was too late for him to rectify his mistake.

As for the correspondence from the West, I learnt that Gabriel Pascal from the U.S.A. sent a cable inquiring when he should visit India to see Baba in connection with the film that Pascal wished to produce on Baba's life. Baba cabled back to him, "The New Life phase

---

* Ghani's unpublished *Diary of the New Life,* (October-November 1949) p. 2.

OLD LIFE ENDS; NEW LIFE BEGINS

that I have just decided upon will not make possible our meeting in December, 1949 for Avatar film. See me sometime, somewhere just for the meeting of love."

The Training Center at Belgaum

In the second week of September, Baba discussed with His companions the preliminary phases of the New Life. The first period of training, which would include physical labor, was to be at Belgaum. The second period comprising of *bhiksha* (begging) and wearing of *langoti* (loin cloth) was to be at Benares and during the subsequent march on foot, the third period, consisting of the gypsy life, was to be practised on the way to Hardwar. At the end of this meeting Baba conveyed, "In order to help and guide the Yeswallas... I desire to give training by being easy with them at first, as after the end of December, 1949 this New Life with me will be an absolute *satyanashi* [utter ruin]. From January, 1950 — May God help you all!" Thus Belgaum, about 375 kms. to the south of Poona, in the Karnatak State, was to be the first training center.

In the entire month of August, Baba did not disclose whether He wished to lead His New Life at a certain place or in a particular area. He would just gesture, "I can't say anything. We may go anywhere!" In September, He casually let out the secret that He intended to have a small piece of land near Hardwar. In the end, a small estate was purchased in the village of Manjri Mafi, four miles from the city of Dehra Dun, on the way to Hardwar. The work Baba wished to conduct from Manjri Mafi was mostly connected with the twin pilgrimage centers — Hardwar and Rishikesh. So, Baba generally referred to this estate as the Hardwar property. This was to be the headquarters for His New Life activities. The minimum essential arrangement for lodging was under construction and it required some time for its completion. Therefore, in the beginning, a short stay at Khuldabad, near Aurangabad was considered.

This was changed and it was decided to stay at Belgaum.

Nearby this city, at Thalakwadi, (a suburb), Vishnu, one of Baba's disciples, owned a piece of land. He volunteered to put it at Baba's disposal. There was already a small structure on this farm which could be used as a shelter for the four women disciples accompanying Baba. As for the Yeswallas, a small hut (20'x30'), with tiled roof and bamboo matting on the sides had to be erected. Vishnu took upon himself the responsibility of finishing this job by October 16. Belgaum was a good distance from Ahmednagar and there the possibility of the public approaching Baba or His companions with various inquiries was much less. To ensure that the curiosity aroused by His presence, and His *mandali*, would not lead to any complications, Baba asked Sarosh Irani, who was a person of considerable influence with the government officers, to inform the superintendent of police at Belgaum, about Baba's activities and his proposed stay for about a month and a half there.

A Game of "French" Tennis

According to Baba's orders, I was at Meherabad on October 5. Before getting down from the *tonga* I gave the driver nearly double the amount of the fare. He looked pleased and surprised to receive this large tip from a commoner like me. I too was very happy for according to Baba's instructions when entering the premises of Meherabad I had to be penniless and I now was. All the Yeswallas had come. In a way, this was simply the summation of all that He had been saying directly or indirectly during the past weeks. The new points which Baba mentioned were: "All Yeswallas are bound ... to the fulfilment of two responsibilities. (1) To bring my body after death to Meherabad Hill. (2) Also to bring Mehera's body after her death to Meherabad Hill and to bury the same beside my tomb." He also asked the Arrangementwallas to adhere sincerely to the responsibilities assigned to them.

OLD LIFE ENDS; NEW LIFE BEGINS

The next morning Khaksaheb read some *ghazals* to Baba. I still recall the following simile which Baba appreciated. It runs as follows: "O Beloved, if you were to ask me about the splendor of the scars of longing on my heart, I may dare say that it is brighter than the brilliance of the heavenly bodies; thank you!" After an hour or so Baba was busy in His cabin calling some of the disciples to assign them some work or to give them a few instructions. In the afternoon He played "French" tennis with us. In this game one has to hold the tennis racket right on the toes; the other players have a tennis ball. When the ball is thrown at the batsman he has to hit it. He can move the racket to any side but not change the position of his feet. If he is caught he is out; if the ball hits the batsman below his knees, he is out. Baba had His own way of forming new games! By a fluke I hit the ball well that day.

When the game was over, while returning to the hall, I felt a pat on my shoulder. That was Baba's. He gestured, "You played well today." I just kept quiet. He continued, "Do you play cricket too?" I replied, "I used to play when I was in the High School." "Not now?" Baba asked. "No," I answered. "Why?" Baba inquired. "When I was in college I had a severe lung hemorrhage which was subsequently diagnosed as tuberculosis. Since then I haven't played cricket," I added trying to clarify the situation. "Will you be able to walk 15 to 20 kms. a day in the New Life?" Baba asked pointedly. In a low voice I said, "I will try my best Baba."

Thereupon Baba instructed me, "Come to Meherazad on October 8, morning. There is a program of distributing food-grain and cloth to the poor and the other deserving people. Whatever duty shall be given to you, do it with your heart. Then I may tell you 'something!' " Baba looked so compassionately at me that Ghani who was standing near me could not help remarking later. "Bal, Baba seems to be very considerate in your case. You are lucky!" I neither understood what Baba meant by "something" nor what Ghani implied by calling me

103

"lucky". I must, however, admit that from the very beginning Baba has been most considerate and compassionate towards me, in all my life with Him. Perhaps every Baba lover feels so and I believe that everyone is perfectly right.

According to Baba's instructions, I went to Meherazad. The poor people from the nearby villages had gathered in the open space. I was asked to help Baba's *mandali* in separating the men and women into rows and then leading them by turn to the room where Baba washed the feet of each and handed over a bundle of *prasad* wrapped in cloth. For a short time I was allowed to stand near the room, watching Baba at His work. That was a wonderful experience. When all the people had dispersed, He called me near. Dr. Donkin and Dr. Nilu were standing near Him. He pointed at my frail body and asked the doctors if I could bear the hardships of the New Life. Nilu touched my collar-bone and ribs. The two doctors exchanged a few medical terms which I could not follow. They reported the matter to Baba and He asked me to be present at Adi's office in Ahmednagar the next day at 9 a.m. Savak Kotwal was to take me in his jeep from Meherabad to Nagar.

Baba Assigns My Duty

On October 9, I was at Adi's office. Baba had already arrived and Ramjoo was discussing some points with Him. Soon I was called inside. Without asking me anything. Baba conveyed through gestures. "I am pleased with you and your love for me." Then He asked Ramjoo to take out the mimeographed copy of the Circular of the New Life conditions that was signed by me on August 31. Baba told Ramjoo, as far as I remember, to write, "Bal will be with me in my New Life [to the very end]." Then he put his signature under it. Turning to me He conveyed, "Without any fault of yours, of my own Will, I free you from joining me physically in my New Life. Go back to your place. Continue the

OLD LIFE ENDS; NEW LIFE BEGINS

type of life that you were leading before. You have left your service, I know; so if you need some money, I will arrange for that." All this was so unexpected that I replied only to the last statement, "Baba, with your blessings I can manage without asking for financial help from anyone." Baba added incidentally, "There is one order for you. Don't touch a woman with an intention of lust." Really this was a great blessing bestowed on me. This order from Baba, I felt, proclaimed His inner and outer help in my attempt to refrain from any lustful action. Respectfully I lowered my head to convey my consent and said, "Yes, Baba."

Baba continued, "Last night I had a thought about Mauni; you know him. In the last interview I had asked him to see me after a period of six months. According to the conditions of the New Life, no one is expected to visit me after October 16. Therefore contact him and convey my message that he should whole-heartedly carry out the instructions* given to him. But now he must never, never try to see me even if he happens to know my whereabouts." I answered, "Baba, Mauni left Kurduwadi a month ago, to stay either at Hardwar or Rishikesh. I do not know his address. How can I find him?" Baba appeared displeased with this reply. On the board He spelt out that it was a duty given to me and that I had to do it. I felt ashamed and thought. "I shouldn't have answered the way I did." I silently stood up, feeling rather guilty, Baba gestured that I should wait a little while outside the room.

After some time He called me again. I found Him in a good mood, beaming and radiating joy. He gestured, "Don't worry about anything," and smiled. I took it as a promise of guidance for the rest of my life and felt greatly relieved. A loving farewell! I was given ten rupees and Baba instructed, "Take a *tonga* to Meherabad. Have your lunch and leave immediately for the railway station to catch the train." I humbly bowed

---

* *Glimpses*, Vol. II, Chapter 3.

down to Him. I had left my job and my family to stay permanently with Baba, but now after just four days I was being sent back, with no possibility of ever seeing Him again. For me it was an astounding situation. It gave me a glimpse of what life is like with the Master.

As I came out of Khushru Quarters I found a *tonga* waiting at the gate. I regarded it as a Baba-sent conveyance. As I reached Meherabad some were surprised to see me leaving so abruptly. I told them in a nutshell what had happened. Someone remarked, "Minoo and you are lucky!" I did not know then that Minoo was also excused from physically being with Baba in the New Life. Even now I do not know the reason for this. I had my lunch, I collected my articles and within an hour left for the station. I purchased a ticket for Kurduwadi — a place which five days ago I felt I would never visit again for the rest of my life. My brother and those at home as well as my colleagues were much surprised.

When I told the headmaster that I wished to resume my duties in the school, after the winter vacation, he had every right to criticize me. Can one ever convince others, logically, of one's life with the God-Man, unless one belongs to the same flock! My friends too probably took me as a crazy person but no one said anything openly. The New Life, in fact, was to begin on October 16, but for me the new life had already been inaugurated! Baba inwardly guided me to perform the duty he had assigned me, but to maintain the chronological sequence, I intend to narrate the details of it in the next chapter.

General Circular about the New Life

In September, Baba conveyed to his disciples and followers, through His secretary, Adi K. Irani, that He had completely stopped accepting anything from anyone in the form of a gift. On October 10, a special circular was issued for all the Baba people in the East and West disclosing the most unanticipated news about the New Life. It read as follows:

OLD LIFE ENDS; NEW LIFE BEGINS

Baba ends His Old Life of ... multifarious activities, and with a few companions begins His New Life of complete renunciation and absolute helplessness from October 16, 1949. Although Baba's and His companions' New Life will be known to everyone and their whereabouts will be no secret, no one should try to see Baba or His companions for any reason whatsoever, as Baba will not see any of them, nor allow His companions to do so. No one should try to communicate with Baba or His companions under any circumstances or for any reason whatsoever.

— By Order of Baba

Only Elinor (Elizabeth and Norina) from the U.S.A. were allowed to cable Baba in connection with the work that was entrusted to them during their interview with Him in the first week of August 1949.

All who learnt of this short but most unexpected circular were greatly astonished; its contents were entirely incomprehensible. To most of them the terms Old Life and New Life, were not only completely new but completely unintelligible as well. They only loved and knew about Baba's Divine Life. The One whom they loved so dearly was, all of a sudden, departing never to return again. No one could imagine why. The circular had forbidden them from even wishing their dear Master a heart-warming farewell. In addition they were not permitted to express their feelings through letters. They had to keep quiet. "Can the Compassionate One be so harsh? What sort of New Life is this?" some thought.

Even to this day, Baba's New Life phase is the most difficult to comprehend. The external details — the journeys and the diaries — are there. These, and more information gathered later from those who accompanied Baba, form the data for this narration of His New Life. But it is hardly an attempt to explain it. Who knows, perhaps some statements Baba made during this period may whisper the secret of this phase to some of His dear ones, even now. All I can say is that Baba as the *Avatar* — Infinite Consciousness — had to work and to express Himself through a finite human form, and this helped create both the enigma and beauty of Him and His New Life.

On October 12, Baba conveyed to the Yeswallas, "This continual one month's working day and night, personally seeing every detail of winding up the Old Life and arranging for the endless New Life . . . have made me literally dead exhausted, both mentally and physically. . . . Therefore, I order my companions beforehand that from October 16, to October 22, . . . I will be in a relaxed mood, tired and easy, towards my companions, in order to be free from physical and mental strain. . . . We leave Meherabad in early morning of October 16, and my companions should walk a furlong ahead of me and the four women companions. The men should laugh, talk and be cheerful without jeopardizing the conditions. . . ." Baba's program was to enter the first New Life journey by walking the distance, on the Ahmednagar-Poona Road, as far as Chas.

A day prior to the commencement of the New Life, Baba arrived at Meherabad fairly early. He gave final instructions to the Arrangementwallas—Sarosh, Ramjoo, Meherjee and Nariman. Padri and Sidhu were to stay at Lower Meherabad. Mansari and Jerbai were to reside at Upper Meherabad — the hill. Sidhu's duty was to serve and look after the *mast*, Mohammad. Baba inspected the travelling bags of those who were to accompany Him. He instructed the Yeswallas to retire as early as 7 p.m. and to wake up at 2 a.m. A bath was compulsory. After having tea, everyone was to get himself ready to bid adieu, for good, to Meherabad by 4 a.m., on October 16, 1949. After the inspection and instructions Baba agreed to sit for a group photo with those present. The atmosphere of the day was of mixed emotions. That most eagerly awaited day was almost there. It was indeed a serious affair, and yet it had a strange thrill of its own.

OLD LIFE ENDS; NEW LIFE BEGINS

The New Life Phase Begins

Accordingly, on October 16, in the early morning, Baba's New Life companions were taken in a bus from Meherabad to the railway crossing, near the Ahmednagar station. Baba, with the four women disciples, arrived from Meherazad. He permitted Sarosh, Adi Jr.,* and Savak Damania to wave good bye. Just while leaving, it began to rain and Sarosh suggested that up to the first halt, he be allowed to follow the Baba-party very slowly in his car. And in case it began to rain heavily the car would be at Baba's disposal. Baba agreed.

The New Life march began at the railway crossing. After walking a short distance, Baba bade every companion to stand behind Him. Then He Himself and the companions reverentially touched the ground with their fingers. While bowing down to the ground, Baba silently took an oath, the contents of which He never disclosed. After a minute, with upraised hands, Baba asked all to utter the following prayer, "O God, make this New Life for all of us a success and joy eternal." The journey on foot continued for a few furlongs. The wind blew harder and brought more rain. In place of raincoats the companions, like the Indian farmers, put gunny bags on their heads. Baba seemed happy with this whim of the weather and gestured, "A good sign!" The rains continued unabated; therefore, Baba and the companions were taken in cars to Supa, a distance of about twenty four kms. from Ahmednagar. The first halt at Chas, as previously planned, was skipped. At Supa, Sarosh and the others bade farewell to all and returned.

Baba and the women occupied the rest house at Supa. The men accommodated themselves in small rooms near a kitchen and a garage, in the same compound. Baba, squatting on the stone flooring, in the midst of His companions, explained the "three periods" preceding the New Life. The first was of relaxation; the second was

---

* Meher Baba's youngest brother.

of training in hard labor, begging, etc. The third which He termed as a "vacuum period" was to be of ten days, at the fag end of 1949. He concluded the chat by stating, "From January 1 onwards, characterizing the New Life, there will be 100% hopelessness and helplessness which even the gods will envy!"* Baba assured all of His help in attuning themselves to the New Life. The earnest response expected of each companion was a literal compliance with Baba's orders. He also conveyed, "All should try to be hundred per cent truthful and speak the truth and truth alone whatever be the circumstances and consequences."

A new way of living started from the very first day. At Supa, Baba ordered all to take a bath and for this everyone had to fetch water from a well a furlong away. To Ghani it was an ordeal. Seeing him panting heavily, while carrying the bucket of water, Baba lent Ghani — His childhood friend — a helping hand. As if to compensate for this life which the Yeswallas were not used to, Baba, with a cheering smile, distributed chocolates and dried fruits to all. This trait of teasing and pleasing the companions was reminiscent of life with Baba in Manzil-e-Meem (Dadar, Bombay) in 1922 when He used to mix freely with His disciples.

During the first halt on the second day, Baba, sitting with the companions in the unfurnished garage, explained, "We are all on equal footing, from now on, in the New Life.... Baba is to be looked upon and treated as a friend.... In one respect alone Baba will be a Master towards all — and that is in respect of demanding implicit obedience. In all other respects... perfect freedom of behaving towards Baba should be observed. Such a freedom of behaving should not smack of *beyadabi* [impudence]. Barring this, all are free to indulge in humor, joviality, jokes and laughter. Nothing will please me more."** Perhaps such a relationship holds

---

* Ghani's unpublished, *Diary of the New Life*, p. 7.
** Ibid., p. 12.

the seed of the New Life wherein one has to be simultaneously friend and slave of the God-Man; fully free to remain honest to oneself, yet bound outright to the Divine Will of the Beloved. One has to be in readiness to share the Supper and to shoulder the Cross too. Was that the secret of the New Life?

Exhausting Walk and Delightful Treat

In spite of the cloudy weather Baba decided to walk on foot, in one hike, a distance of 25 kms. from Supa to Ghodnadi. He gestured that whether it rained or not, the march was to be continued. Subsequently on October 18, as early as 4 a.m., the Baba-party set out for Ghodnadi. The men walked ahead and the women with Baba followed a little later. After a while Baba wished to communicate with some of the Yeswallas, so He clapped but in the open air His clapping could not be heard by the companions. Goher blew a whistle but as it was rarely used, the cork balls got stuck inside. Eventually the companions heard the call and stopped. Baba joined them and impressed upon them that it should not happen again. But in fact one of their orders had been not to look backwards. So naturally they could not guess how far they were ahead of Baba. If they had walked rather slowly to avoid getting too far ahead, there was a good chance that this would have displeased Baba. As someone later remarked, "Baba expects one to sit and stand at one and the same time!" True. To live with Baba is a constant challenge to I-consciousness.

After walking half way they came in sight of Narayangaon. Baba suggested that tea would refresh the companions. Kaka Baria, however, was the only Yeswalla permitted to carry some money and he had proceeded to Ghodnadi to make the lodging and boarding arrangements. The rest of the party were the penniless companions of the perennial *Fakir*, Baba. Eruch, however, remembered that according to the previous plan there was to be a halt under the shady trees at Narayangaon.

Besides, a person staying in that village had been paid in advance for milk, etc. That was good news. Baba asked Eruch and Donkin to hasten and find that person. They contacted the man and all had good refreshing tea. This incident could be regarded as the beginning of the coincidences that followed later in the New Life.

In the morning it was cool and the walk was pleasant. But soon it started getting warmer. By 10 a.m., the October heat, as it is experienced in India, is quite oppressive. Now the walk was tiring. Baba's toes developed sores and Donkin had to put adhesive tape on those spots. A small group of villagers, as they passed by the women disciples carrying umbrellas, perhaps sensed their plight and suggested that there was convenient bus service to Poona. The women smiled away the suggestion by saying, "It's all right. Thank you." As the party approached Ghodnadi, Ghani felt extremely exhausted. He had a slight heart attack. Baba made him sit under a tree and splashed some water on his head. A little rest helped him resume the journey. The rest house on the outskirts of the city, where the Baba-party intended to halt, was already engaged by some government officers. So the advance party had to make the lodging arrangements in a cinema house that had closed down and was vacant. The theater was in the heart of the city. The women, who had led a secluded life for years, felt shy as they walked through the crowded streets, avoiding the inquisitive glances of the strangers. It was now past midday. The lunch was ready. All relished the food after the strenuous walk and preferred to relax the rest of the day.

The next day was *Diwali*, the Festival of Lights. From the early morning, indeed throughout the night, firecrackers and sparklers were set off by children and grown-ups alike. The sound of exploding firecrackers was deafening. In spite of this disturbance, most of the companions enjoyed an undisturbed sleep as they had had a tiring walk the day before. After breakfast all felt energetic, though the stiffness of their limbs often re-

OLD LIFE ENDS; NEW LIFE BEGINS

minded them of the long journey. Here again Baba ordered all to bathe. Therefore, unroofed urinals were cleaned; these were turned into improvised bathrooms. In the afternoon *laddoos* (sweets) were served with tea; the previous day all had *jilebis* (sweets). These two treats were not intended to celebrate *Diwali*: these were meant to celebrate the two narrow escapes from serious injury — one to Nilu and the other to Baba.

On the first day while getting down from the luggage lorry, Nilu had inadvertently slipped and fell to the road on his haunches but did not hurt himself badly. On hearing this, Baba sanctioned the expense of ten rupees for sweets as the mishap had been averted. The next night, Baba was resting on a dinner table that served as an improvised bed. Generally the least sound would wake Baba but that night Baba fell into an unusually sound sleep. It was after midnight when someone knocked and shook the door violently. Baba woke up to get the door but as the dinner table was much higher than a regular bed, He missed His footing and fell heavily on one side. Fortunately He managed to support His body with His palms and was saved from any unfortunate consequences, except for a rude shaking.

Eruch tried to find out who had knocked, but in vain. It was not known who shook the door so furiously — a stranger or a spirit! Baba later disclosed that for the first time He felt immensely relieved of the burden of the Old Life, and as a natural consequence He had an exceptionally "sound sleep". When He conveyed the whole episode to the companions, Ghani suggested that this narrow escape too should be celebrated, befitting the person concerned! Baba responded good humoredly by alloting twenty-one rupees for *laddoos*. Thus, these two events provided timely *Diwali* treats for all, Baba discussed the transport arrangements from Ghodnadi to Belgaum a distance of about 440 kms. The companions were to travel in a special bus. Pendu and Kaka were asked to go with the luggage truck.

At Belgaum, the First Training Center

On October 20, at 2 a.m. the companions got into the State Transport bus bound for Belgaum. The Baba-party travelling via Poona, Kolhapur and Nipani reached Thalakwadi (Belgaum) by 4 p.m. the same day. It had rained enough so that the road leading to the hut on the farm on the outskirts of the city was muddy and slushy. The workmen were still at work and the flooring was quite damp. To cheer up the companions Baba mentioned that whatever was happening (whether offering comforts or discomforts) was in keeping with the New Life. The temporary structure for the women was a furlong from the men's quarters but it was on the same farm with a well nearby. For everyday use the men had to fetch water from this well. Life at Belgaum was indeed a phase of hard labor, as Baba called it. In the evening the companions had only wheat bread and curry for supper. No vegetables. At night it rained periodically. This made the floor of the hut even damper and in both rooms in the women's quarters there was ankle-deep water.

In one of the sittings Baba explained, "Up to now, the life, so to say, has been of pain and suffering.... In 1950, the life will be still more acutely painful, but this pain you will enjoy. This enjoyment of pain, will in itself constitute a challenge to God. I cannot say anything more...." On October 22, Baba dictated a general circular for His followers. It contained information about the three phases connected with the New Life and their duration up to the end of 1949.

Before inaugurating the physical labor phase at Belgaum, Baba distributed sweets to the companions. He then assigned different duties to one and all. Kaka was in charge of cooking; Baidul and Murli were to help him. Adi, Pendu and Nilu were to draw and supply water from the well. Vishnu was given the work of marketing but he was not allowed to engage a coolie to fetch articles from the city. Eruch was to attend to

OLD LIFE ENDS; NEW LIFE BEGINS

Baba for odd jobs and Ghani had to write the day-to-day diary of the New Life. Anna was to keep watch at night. The women including Mehera willingly shared the work of cooking, washing and sweeping which they had rarely done before. Mani was in charge of cooking. She was not as adept as Naja, Pendu's sister, in preparing dishes. One day at supper time it was found that the vegetable stew lacked flavor. Baba suggested that the patties stored in the cupboard be mashed in it. This gave it such a delicious taste that the women referred to it as "Bhagwan Stew" — a famous dish of Poona.

It occasionally rained at Belgaum and the rain water dripped from the tiled roof. Hence, floor cleaning was an additional but necessary task. Mehera and Mani used to sleep in one room. As the temporary structure was in a farm, one day Mani had a rat bite and it began to bleed; Goher had to give immediate first aid. Another day Goher suddenly got up from sleep. She felt that Mehru was calling her for help. In fact it was only an owl hooting at night. In spite of the hard labor and discomforts the men and women remained cheerful. This pleased Baba.

The second period of training, in begging, was to be carried out at Benares, in Uttar Pradesh. Sadashiv Patel and Babadas were to be sent in advance to find a secluded place where Baba and the party could stay for three weeks. They were also to find a person, a friend or an acquaintance, who would accept 500 rupees and in return feed the Baba-party for twenty days. There was no special condition about the quality of the food. Baba instructed them that the negotiations with the person concerned should be carried out so skillfully that the donor should in no way feel that he was obliging the party. They were also to be on the lookout for two cows and she-donkeys which they could purchase. This task seemed difficult but the companions had to try their best. Patel and Babadas left Belgaum for Benares on October 26.

There were a few occasions when the companions

came in for an admonition. Gustadjee's duty was to sweep the hut. Baba noticed that he was not particular enough in attending to his work. On another day, He found that Nilu was talking with Adi about the good old days of the Old Life. He even expressed a wish, "May those days return soon!" This remark displeased Baba. He made it clear to His companions that such thoughts were not expected of the Yeswallas. Through such directions Baba was trying to drive home the real nature of the New Life to all.

Daulat Singh Returned to Bangalore

By the first week of October, Daulat Singh, according to Baba's instructions, arrived at Meherabad. He was one of the Yeswallas. It was about this month that his youngest daughter was to get married. She had lovingly pleaded with her father saying, "Can't you postpone joining Baba in His New Life for a few days? As soon as my wedding is over you may gladly leave us all. This is my last request of you, dear father and I hope Baba too won't object to it." Daulat Singh tried to console her but had to refuse and arrived at Meherabad on October 5. Family ties are hard to untie; they are like the knots of silk thread, very tender yet very powerful. At Belgaum, one evening after helping Eruch wash the utensils, he sat alone at night outside their hut, silently sobbing over his helplessness to grant his dear daughter's simple request. Perhaps that was the day of her wedding. He thought that he was all by himself but Baba most unexpectedly arrived at the companion's quarters and approached Daulat Singh. He asked him to tell frankly why he was weeping and what troubled him so deeply. Daulat Singh had to say what he thought and felt. Baba quietly listened but said nothing at that time.

In view of this and some other incidents, Baba once again offered the choice to all the companions, to go back to the Old Life, if they so wished. At the request of the Yeswallas, Baba had a private interview with each.

OLD LIFE ENDS; NEW LIFE BEGINS

He cleared the doubts and difficulties of some in connection with the different phases connected with the New Life. Availing himself of this opportunity, Daulat Singh, who was very worried over his unsettled affairs at Bangalore, sought Baba's permission to return home for two months. He felt sure that within this period he could set matters right and would then be able to rejoin Baba with a free mind and heart.

A day later, in the presence of all the companions, Baba looked at Daulat Singh with compassion and conveyed, "Listen carefully, my friend, I have now decided for you to go back to your Old Life. I send you back without any fault on your part, and on your not having failed me in the least. . . . But as I am sending you of my own free will, your spiritual connection with me remains as before, if I am what you take me to be. The special orders for you are: (1) Till you die, no lustful action, even with your wife; (2) You will never lie, whatever the consequences; (3) One month, in every year you will wear the *kafni* that I will give you and during this month, you will live on begging. . . . If these three orders are obeyed by you one hundred per cent, you will be sharing my New Life one hundred per cent."* Daulat Singh, who in spite of having suffered several reversals in his life, loved Baba intensely and therefore felt very reluctant to return home permanently. He, nevertheless, dared not disobey Baba. It was a most touching sight to see him bidding farewell to the companions at Thalakwadi, with uncontrollable sobs and tears rolling down his cheeks.

The way Daulat Singh was drawn to Beloved Baba is rather exceptional. It was in a dream that he first beheld Beloved Meher Baba's face, aglow with matchless radiance and an inviting smile. But he neither knew Baba's name nor His whereabouts. "Is He the Awakener of this age? Is He Nanak** come again?" he thought of

---
* Ibid., pp. 34, 35.
** Nanak (1469-1538 A.D.), a Perfect Master, was the first Guru of the Sikhs and he is regarded as the founder of Sikhism.

the face he had seen. Ever since this significant dream his eyes always longed to see the face of that Enlightened One, in flesh and blood. This was what he genuinely wished but hardly dared hope for. This vision seemed very significant to him (it was a sign from the sphere of ever shining light, he knew) but not knowing what to do about it he became very restless. In those days he was living in Srinagar, the capital of Kashmir. He was practising there as a doctor and was well placed in life.

In the early 1940s one of Baba's devotees visited Kashmir to spread His name and message. He carried pictures of Meher Baba with him. Once he displayed a few of these in one of the small shops on the main road in Srinagar. By a stroke of luck, Daulat Singh happened to pass by and at once recognized the face as that of the One he had seen in his dream and for whom he was desperately searching and pining. He embraced that devotee with great fervor as tears of joy trickled down his cheeks. That day he first heard the Holy Name of this Age — Meher Baba. A wonderful lover had thus been drawn to the wonderful Beloved, in a wondrous way.

In the riots that sprang up in Kashmir after the partition of this great subcontinent in August 1947, Daulat Singh unfortunately lost a big part of his property and he had to move with his family to another part of India. Once he was a wealthy, well-to-do person and now it was not easy for him to manage his family affairs well. He was put in a miserable predicament. This, however, did not lessen his love for Baba even a bit. His circumstances had not changed much when he joined Baba in His New Life. It was in consideration of this plight that the All-knowing Master, Baba, relieved him from accompanying Him any further. Daulat Singh implicitly obeyed Baba's three standing orders. He generally referred to Beloved Baba as the *Huzoor* (the Lord). His last meeting, prior to his death, with his Lord Baba was very moving, when the lover and the Beloved were

OLD LIFE ENDS; NEW LIFE BEGINS

in each other's embrace. More about this event as we come to it in the course of the narration.

The Song of the New Life

Returning to the account of Baba's New Life phase at Belgaum, it was the period when Baba resumed His fondness for playing a *dholak* (a cylindrical drum with leather on both sides), to the accompaniment of a harmonium, which Adi played while also singing *ghazals*. During one such performance Baba asked Ghani to compose a *ghazal,* comprising the cardinal qualities expected of the companions. He spontaneously dictated the following chorus in Urdu:

Suno Meher Babaki khamosh bani, isime hai sab ashikonki kahani,
Hai jeena tumhe gar nai zindagani, karo tark dilse ye duniyae phani.

(Listen to the silent words of Meher Baba,
The life story of all lovers [of God] is based on the practice of these words.)

Baba then dictated some points to Ghani who later incorporated them in the *ghazal*. These were put into verse in nine quatrains. Baba again suggested a few points and asked him to include them at the end. He jokingly remarked that if Ghani failed to do this job well by next morning, his punishment would be a hundred *baithaks* (a kind of Indian exercise of rigorously sitting and standing). The couplets were set to a musical score. The tune was approved by Baba. This song was usually sung with the accompaniment of a harmonium and drum. Sometimes Baba played on a *dholak*, Adi on harmonium and Nilu on *tals* (small cymbals). Baba instructed that this song be sung as a morning prayer for some days during their stay at Belgaum. This *ghazal* is known as the Song of the New

Life. The next to last quatrain is as follows:

> Even if your heart is cut to bits, let there be a smile on your lips.
> Here I divulge to you a point worth noting.
> Hidden in your penniless hand, is treasure untold;
> Your beggarly life will be the envy of kings
> [of the world].

In November 1949 the complete song was published and sent to Baba people, along with its translation in English by Meher Publications, Ahmednagar.

Baba's New Life, Visible yet Veiled

Baba had regular sittings with His companions. Once noticing the discomforts of His friends, owing to the cold weather, He made provision for a *ghongdi* (very coarse woollen blanket) and an extra bedsheet for each member. During one of the meetings at Belgaum, Baba stated, "When I myself make inquiries about anyone's personal difficulties, then only should he tell me his difficulties honestly, frankly and truly without a tinge of spite or exaggeration.... In the New Life, to commence on January 1, 1950, I might at times, make you do things which I might also do. Sometimes, I will make you do things which I might not do. In either case, we shall all be sharing the New Life.... Extraordinary and abnormal things will be done by me and carried out by you too.... What exactly I mean by extraordinary and abnormal things, I cannot tell you now. Such happenings will go to make the New Life and the sufferings therein, enjoyable. I assure you, the New Life, in spite of its acute sufferings, will be *wet* inside and outside. ... The greatest help to me will be to do willingly and unhesitatingly anything, even to my person when I give the order."*

---

* Ibid., pp. 36, 37.

OLD LIFE ENDS; NEW LIFE BEGINS

During the stay at Thalakwadi, Baba once asked one of His companions to slap Him. He then asked all to stand in a line and He touched their feet with His hands. Such actions remind me of the instruction given by a Zen Master to his disciples, perhaps to initiate them into the impersonal aspect of the Divine. In connection with this deeper form of meditation, this Zen Master once instructed the aspirants, "Even if you happen to see the glorious form of the Enlightened One, discard it and go ahead." Was this a hint to merge oneself in the Vital Void, the Everything comprising the Nothing? The New Life activities of Meher Baba were quite visible and understandable but their spiritual significance lay veiled and mysterious!

External activities of the New Life were to be carried out at and near Hardwar. In view of this particular phase of work, a small estate was purchased in a village called Manjri Mafi, a few miles from Dehra Dun. The property was in the name of two of the companions. This small estate with two rooms, a veranda, kitchen, bathroom and a court yard was situated on the road leading to Hardwar. Baba remarked that in case He moved to some other place the house could be used by the companions.

When someone raised a question as to the legal position of the property when all of them would drop their bodies, Baba in a light vein of humor cited the title of a detective novel by Agatha Christie, "And Then There Were None." In relation to the name of the village, Manjri Mafi, which in the vernacular means "cats are forgiven," Baba joked, "Here at Belgaum we have rats to trouble us; in the village [where] we intend to stay, cats are forgiven. So let us hope that at Manjri Mafi we will be free at least from rat trouble." While conversing with the companions, no subject was too important or too trivial for Baba. And the companions felt that every action of Baba's carried with it the spark of His Divinity.

The training period at Belgaum was to end by the

middle of November and the begging phase at Benares was to be over before the end of December. About *bhiksha* (begging) Baba explained to the companions, "We have to beg for food only and not for anything else. Food includes everything cooked or raw, liquid or solid — anything and everything. We should not, during begging, ask for anything special.... Ghani should not say, 'Give me mutton' and Nilu should not ask for milk or *barfi*. You ought only to say, 'Please give *bhiksha*.' How to beg and what to beg, I will instruct you fully at Benares. If people offer clothing, accept it, but don't ask for it. You cannot accept money under any circumstances.... Animals offered voluntarily must be refused, but while thus refusing you can say that if a white horse is given, you would accept.... Food or clothing when given, should be brought and placed before me first.... This much we decide today."*

On an earlier occasion Baba conveyed, "From January 1, 1950, you all know we have no money. We either beg or earn for food. One point that is to be remembered by one and all is that no food should be preserved for the morrow, on shifting from one place to another. Every day will be a new day for us in this New Life.... If the picture I have in mind takes shape, the abnormal and extraordinary happenings for you all, from April, 1950 onwards will be an everyday affair. Although I said we stay at Hardwar for two or three months, it does not mean we stay there for all the time...."**

Some Suggestive and Profound Indications

In the month of November the companions found Baba in a communicative mood. So they tried to elicit some details about the nature of the impending New Life. This attempt did not prove very successful. Nevertheless, some statements made by Baba during this

---
* Ibid., pp. 42, 43, 46, 53.
** Ibid.

OLD LIFE ENDS; NEW LIFE BEGINS

period were suggestive, a few were rather obscure but profound. One day Baba conveyed, "In this New Life you must be prepared to witness and see Baba being humiliated in all sorts of ways by you, outsiders, *masts*, saints or *yogis*. You must, therefore, help [me] by not interfering unless I order you to do so."* He mentioned that the four principles underlying the conditions of the New Life were not to touch money, not to touch a woman, to carry out all orders of Baba most willingly and to remain cheerful under the most trying circumstances.

When asked if this type of New Life had been undertaken by anyone in the past and what need had He to lead it, Baba's laconic answer was, "This is whatever it is.... I cannot say anything more than this." For the latter part of the above question He clearly stated, "This much I know, I have got to go on, and on, with you or alone. By trying to dig out something from me with regard to this New Life, you will not gain anything further. On the contrary, you will get more and more puzzled if not dismayed.... I have been waiting these long years for this New Life, and if we live through it, it will mean life that has no end."* This clearly shows that Baba was reluctant to divulge the secret and subtleties of the New Life.

A local paper at Belgaum published news of Baba's stay at Thalakwadi. This became the talk of the town. In spite of Baba's instructions, some visited the companions' hut to know more about Baba and His work. It was difficult for the companions to satisfactorily answer the queries made by the visitors. They were told that Baba did not permit *darshan*. Yet some of them tried to approach Baba. As they came closer, Baba Himself bowed down and touched their feet. They were taken aback. They knew that Baba was observing silence and so did not ask Him any questions. Quietly they left the place. In anticipation of future incidents, the compa-

---

* Ibid., pp. 53, 59, 60.

nions requested that Baba give them a few pointers which would help them to explain, to some extent, the nature of the New Life to such visitors. Baba agreed and dictated the following statements:

> Hopelessness means renunciation of all hopes.
> Aimlessness means renunciation of all aims.
> Helplessness means renunciation of all help.
> No Master, no disciple means renunciation of spirituality.
> And the New Life I have in picture [mind], eventually means absolute renunciation.*

From this it seems clear, Baba was not very concerned how much these statements clarified the New Life.

Baba Leaves Belgaum for Benares

From November 1, Adi, in the company of the companions, started singing daily the New Life song in the morning. This indirectly meant coaching some of the Yeswallas to sing in a chorus, though very few of them had melodious voices. Baba continued to spend much of His time in the hut. Once He dictated a few extemporaneous couplets in Urdu about the life ahead of them. The gist of the lines is given below: The New Life will bring about a state wherein no one will depend on anyone for anything. (This could be the end, if there would be any, Baba later added). The life led in adherence to the oath taken (on August 31) will keep us together. There will also be a phase which can be termed as "enjoyment of suffering" wherein deep disappointment (a stone in the heart) and great delight (a wine glass at the lips) will go together. And I hope that Ghani will stay on with me as my companion (*sakha*).

On another occasion, the couplets Baba composed when freely translated conveyed: Whether morning or

---
* Ibid., p. 63.

evening, day or night, makes no difference for us. They are of equal importance and significance. We are not concerned with what others think about us. We are preoccupied with the agony (perhaps intense longing for a life of perfect renunciation). In the last couplet Baba's sense of humor, which was always present, exerted itself and with reference to the "beggarly life" He teased Ghani by saying that the only cash they had was the poverty in Ghani's pocket! Baba as a teenager used to compose poems in Gujarati, Hindi, Urdu and Persian under the *nom de plume* of Huma.* These early poems were mostly on spiritual subjects. Even after God-realization His love for composing poems continued, in later years they chiefly expressed His sense of humor, sometimes mixing words from different languages.

In the second week of November, Baba inquired of His friends (companions) about their day-to-day requirements, if any. He asked Eruch to note down all such items, viz. soap, thread, buttons, etc. The next day he was sent to the city to purchase the necessary articles. Marketing was usually entrusted to Vishnu but he had been sent to Poona on a special job. When Vishnu returned to Belgaum he was asked if he had brought any special news. Vishnu, in accordance with Baba's injunctions, could neither meet his old acquaintances nor read the newspapers. He, however, related that while moving through the city the newspaper boys were shouting the headlines. One of the bits of news he heard was that the persons connected with plotting Gandhiji's assassination were to be executed on November 15. It was also brought to Baba's notice that, that was the date of their projected arrival in Benares.

One of the companions mentioned that there was a group of people in Uttar Pradesh who were against the pro-Pakistan and pro-Mohammedan policy of Gandhiji. This state of affairs eventually brought about the

---

* Huma is a bird mentioned in the Scriptures. It is supposed that this bird in its life span never lands on earth.

tragic end of Gandhiji's life, on January 30, 1948. In view of this political situation it was anticipated that there might be an upsurge of communal unrest in the city of Benares and it might result in the enforcement of section 144 of the Indian Penal Code by the District Magistrate. Naturally this would ban any group activity as well as visitors from entering the city. One of the companions added that ignorance of the law would not be accepted as an excuse. So he suggested that the reading of newspapers by the companions would be helpful to them in keeping abreast of such situations.

He asked Baba to reconsider the prohibition on reading newspapers. He was indirectly voicing the wish of a few others who for years had been interested in reading the day-to-day news. A few of them for certain periods had regularly read the newspapers to Baba. Baba could easily guess the motivation behind this proposal. Instead of cancelling the previous order totally, He asked Donkin alone to read *The Times of India* every day. He was instructed to mark all the news relating to the promulgation of new laws, riots, curfews, floods, etc. These cuttings, Baba added, could be read by those who so wished! He also told Donkin to forget (!) the other news and to destroy the remaining pages. Baba did not consent to changing the date of the party's entry in Benares. By the way, it may be stated that the persons involved in the Gandhi case filed an appeal against the judgment and nothing untoward happened on November 15 in the cities of Uttar Pradesh.

On November 12, in the early hours of the morning, at 4.30 a.m., Baba and His companions left Belgaum as quietly as they had arrived. The first phase of physical labor at this center consisted of cleaning and washing, sweeping and dusting, cooking and fetching water from the well. Perhaps all this was more related to the dusting and cleansing of minds and hearts of their old habits and temperaments, or it was a warming up exercise of the New Life! For Baba's companions the end of the stay at Belgaum marked the beginning of a life which they could not anticipate. This was the beginning of a life untouched by hope, envy, fear or passion for possessions, as was sung in the Song of the New Life:

> We neither wail over lost hopes, nor complain about [broken] promises;
> We neither covet honor, nor shun disgrace;
> Backbiting we know not nor do we fear anyone;
> This is now the color [phase] of our New Life.

5

Benares to Moradabad

1949 — Part V

The Telegram Episode

MEHER BABA with His companions reached Benares via Poona, Bombay and Moghulsarai, on the morning of November 15. They were on their way to Hardwar, the place where the external activities of the New Life were to take shape. They had left Belgaum by train on November 12, and were at Poona the next day. Here, the party had to change trains for Bombay.

On the same day, after contacting Mauni at Hardwar in October, the duty assigned to me by Baba, I happened to visit Poona on some work. After getting out of the railway station I chanced to see Dr. Donkin, one of Baba's companions. In view of Baba's instructions I did not approach him. Not knowing Baba's program I did not dream, even remotely, that Baba was having a stroll at the end of the platform where I had gotten down. A strange coincidence of personal significance! Later the same day I learnt from Gadekar that he saw Baba and Nilu (Dr. Nilkanth) at the station. But because of the instructions in the circular he dared neither to contact any of the companions nor to linger there.

Personally I had no idea that Baba had been at Belgaum for three weeks and was on His way to Benares. I had seen Him last on October 9, when He freed me from physically joining the New Life. He permitted me to resume, if possible, my work at school. Returning home I found that the headmaster did not seem to favor rehiring me. As there were only a few days of school left before the long *Diwali* vacation, I resolved to meet my dear friend Mauni, the mendicant, in October and convey to him Baba's message. I regarded this work as a sacred, spiritual obligation which I must not delay.

As a child I had stayed in North India with my father. But during the last decade I had not even journeyed once through this part. Hardwar was over a thousand kms. from Kurduwadi, I had no acquaintance in those parts except Kishan Singh who was staying in Delhi. I did not know his address, so I sent a telegram to Adi, "On October 16, leaving Kurduwadi for Hardwar. Send Kishan Singh's Delhi address." To this I received a prompt reply but it was a bit puzzling. It read; "Whether Hardwar or Marwar* never, never try to see Baba stop Kishan Singh's address 55 Pandhara Road, New Delhi." I wondered about the first part of this communication. I thought, "Why should Adi reply so humorously?"

This problem was resolved on my return journey from Hardwar when I stayed for two days at Ahmednagar. There I met Dattu, a clerk in Adi's office. He knew about this telegraphic communication. I asked him about the unconnected contents. He related that my personal telegram to Adi was handed over to him in Baba's presence. In the course of attending to other matters Adi read my telegram to Baba. I had not mentioned therein that I was going to Hardwar to contact Mauni. Baba knew that very well but sometimes He could seemingly be most ignorant! He conveyed to Adi, "I have freed Bal from accompanying me physically in my New Life. I had asked him to continue his serivce; instead he is starting on October 16, on his own for Hardwar. Does he intend to join the New Life against my order?" So the first sentence of the telegram was dictated. "Whether Hardwar or Marwar never, never try to see Baba." When I heard this from Dattu I felt very sorry I had not sent a clear-cut telegram to Adi.

In fact, I had not the least intention of disobeying

---

* Marwar is a part of Rajasthan, one of the Indian states which I never intended to visit.

Baba. I did not know that the headquarters of Baba's New Life activities was to be near Hardwar. October 16 was chosen by me as the auspicious date because Baba was entering the New Life on that day. I wondered how, unintentionally, the situation had gotten distorted. "Have I displeased Baba? What a pity that I have been the cause of disturbing Baba's mood, maybe for a minute!" I thought. This had such a serious effect on me that for many days I felt rather uneasy, especially when alone. I would often implore Baba to forgive me and after some days Baba appeared in a dream and consoled me. With a benevolent smile He bade me forget the whole affair of the telegram and not to worry over it at all. With this dream the psychological tension entirely vanished. Thus, the telegram episode had a happy ending.

In Search of Mauni

Before narrating further the activities of Baba's New Life, I intend to give an account of what I did about the order that He personally gave me on October 9, 1949. As soon as I received Adi's aforementioned wire, I made the necessary preparations for that long journey to the foot of the Himalayas. I took sufficient money and clothing for a stay of over a month or more in those twin places of pilgrimage — Hardwar and Rishikesh. I had decided to search every *ashram* there to find my bearded friend Mauni and to deliver Baba's message to him. Only after discharging this duty did I wish to resume my teaching, not before.

So on October 16, by the early morning train, I left Kurduwadi for Bombay and reached New Delhi the next day, by evening. On that very long railway platform I did not see Kishan Singh to whom I had sent a telegram about my arrival by the Punjab Mail. I dared not take out my luggage and was planning to proceed to the main station, Delhi. Just as the train whistled I saw the tall figure of Kishan Singh, coming with long strides towards my compartment. "Baba be praised!" I muttered and jumped out of the carriage, pulling my bag and bedding behind me. Kishan Singh had received the telegram but the sender's name was changed from Bal Natu to Balnath. He did not know who was arriving by the train but thought it best to come to the station. For a day I stayed at Delhi. I asked Kishan Singh to keep the extra money that I had with me. It was a provision in case I lost my purse or baggage during my stay at Hardwar. Come what may, I had determined to find Mauni and deliver Baba's message.

The train for Hardwar was overcrowded. It was night and I managed to huddle on a bench but could rarely sleep. By early morning the train reached Hardwar. It was bitter cold which I was not used to at all. A *sanyasi* was sitting beside me. I asked him about the lodging facilities. By chance he happened to be in charge of a *dharmshala* (a free rest house), near the station. He led me to a big room where I found some pilgrims already resting. I doubted whether my belongings would be safe there, but trusting the honesty of my co-travellers, I planned to move freely through the town till lunch time.

During my round I noticed that some roads were thronged with persons wearing ochre clothes. In those days Hardwar seemed to me a town of *sadhus*. Moreover, I learnt that *ashrams*, small and big, stretched about the town, particularly by the banks of the Ganges. In this *sadhu*-crowded area I wondered how I would find the place where Mauni stayed. I recalled the instructions given to him by Baba: "Beg for food; don't cook food. Stay at one place." So I guessed that he must be staying near a center where free food was served. I inquired about such places and was told that in Rishikesh there were some big centers of this type. I had also heard from Mauni that during his last visit he stayed for some time at Rishikesh. It struck me that instead of Hardwar I should search for him in Rishikesh.

Baba Orders; Baba Guides

My *sanyasi* friend gave me an address and a personal note to one of his friends who had a spacious hut at Rishikesh. It was in a secluded section of the bank of the Ganges. Luckily the person, Parameshwaranand, was there when I reached the cottage. I handed the note from his friend to him and introduced myself. Unlike the crowd in the room at Hardwar, there was only one person here, the owner. A thought crept in, "Am I safe here? Is he really a good man?" The mind is very tricky; it doubts both ways.

It was about 3 p.m. and I left the place to visit Gita Bhavan, Swargashram, Laxman Zula and other places. But my main concern was to inquire about the chief centers where food was served to spiritual aspirants without charge. I learnt that the two main places were Kali Kamliwale or Punjabi Kshetra (center). The next day was *Diwali*, the Festival of Lights. At sunrise, facing the holy Ganges I offered my prayers, repeated some cantos from the *Bhagavad Gita* and prayed to God with all sincerity to guide me in discharging the duty entrusted to me by Baba. It was indeed a marvellous morning. The whole atmosphere seemed to be charged with a divine presence which filled my heart with confidence. I felt that I would return to my town only after completing the work assigned to me by Beloved Baba. That would be a real *Diwali*, I thought.

I had to walk a mile or more to reach Kali Kamliwale Kshetra. My plan was to visit one such place each day, right from its opening till it closed. By 8.30 a.m. I was there. After about an hour *sadhus* and *sanyasis* began to form a queue. Everyone had a cotton bag, like a satchel, and a plate or a mug. A few of them seemed absorbed in meditation even when standing in a row. The whole scene was reminiscent of the ancient Indian culture. And good heavens! There was Mauni standing at the far end of the line. I could not believe my eyes! His presence made me immensely happy. He too was much astonished and delighted to find me there. God had surprisingly and speedily answered my morning prayers!

Mauni told me that he was staying in a room in the Brahmanand *ashram*. It was on the way to the hut where I stayed. Upon reaching the *ashram* I told him Baba's message. He was asked to observe, with heart and soul, all the instructions given by Baba. The only change was that he was not to see Meher Baba after the stipulated period mentioned at Meherabad during his last interview with Baba. Mauni willingly agreed. I felt greatly relieved. Then I told him what little I knew about Baba's New Life phase.

I had anticipated spending a long time in that area looking for Mauni. Everything went so well it was as if it were pre-arranged; the only thing was that I did not know the arrangements in advance. Baba's orders imply perfect guidance, I learnt; Baba gives orders but He also gives one that guidance which allows the orders to be fulfilled. Mauni experienced the preciseness of this vital spiritual principle all the more during the concluding part of his *sadhana*. He later related to me an account of the last seven days of the period stipulated by Baba, when he had to observe a fast on water. He found that in the Brahmanand *ashram*, the place where he stayed, it would be difficult for him to draw water from the deep well. Hence, as Baba had given him the option, he wished to shift to a room near the bank of the Ganges.

He inquired if he could be lodged in a secluded hut for a week. But that was the period of the Kumbha Mela at Hardwar which is regarded as the biggest religious fair in India. This time, over half a million pilgrims were expected. Hundreds of *sadhus*, *nangas*, *bairagis*, and *sanyasis* of different sects had reserved certain areas for their followers. So accommodation in a special hut, meant for a single person, was not possible. But miraculously enough, Mauni got a very small hut, just for himself, and there was also a tiny pitcher to store water, the one thing he needed most.

On the last day of his fast Mauni felt very weak and feverish. He had no strength to go to the river and fetch water, even in that tiny pitcher. He lay alone in the hut, remembering Baba. Sometimes he felt extremely exhausted and depressed too. Just after midnight, when the period of seven days was over, Mauni, to his great wonder and delight, saw Beloved Baba's exquisitely fascinating face, compassionately looking at him from an undefinable distance. The vision was so comforting that he felt indescribable vibrations of bliss and peace within him. All his agonies vanished, and a new life was infused in him. The experience corroborated the fact that Baba had been with him all the time during the *sadhana*. Suddenly with great speed the face commenced drawing closer and closer till Mauni felt that its radiance touched and filled his heart. It was indeed Baba's glowing gesture to bless him.

By this time, he had also learnt about Baba's stay somewhere near Hardwar. But in obedience to His orders, he never tried to approach Him. Perhaps to get over the temptation of seeing Baba, and also for reasons of health he soon left Rishikesh for Benares.

Lila Sustains Reality

In October 1949, after delivering the message to Mauni, I felt relieved and enlivened. In that happy mood I decided to pass a few more days visiting the different areas sanctified by the presence of saints and *masts* contacted by Baba. I specially visited Swargashram, where in the summer of 1942, Baba had stayed with a group of Westerners in the bungalow of the Rani of Singhi. In the course of my stay I happened to meet a renowned *swami* who was a founder of an international society dedicated to spiritual ideals, including *yoga*. I stayed in his *ashram* attending different programs for two or three days. This short stay provided me with an opportunity in 1953 to revisit Rishikesh with Baba. About my personal meeting with the *swami*, on a moonlit night, sitting on a parapet in his *ashram* that stands by the bank of the Ganges, I intend to narrate later.

On my return to Kurduwadi, I met the headmaster again who seemed unwilling to take me on the staff. I wrote a short letter to him with a request to let me know his final decision. I could sense that he was somewhat prejudiced about my connection with Meher Baba. To be frank, I regarded my contact with Meher Baba as the most sacred and personal affair. At the same time, I was very particular that my relationship with Baba did not have any adverse effect on my work at school. It was true that I did not mix with or join my colleagues in visiting shows or going out for picnics, but the fact was that I had no liking for them. And perhaps, in the eyes of the headmaster this conduct was objectionable.

I did not personally approach the office bearers of the institution or the headmaster with the request to reconsider my case. But à day or two later, to my surprise, the school peon brought the news of my reappointment. I was asked to resume my duties the same day. What made the management change its mind so quickly I do not know. All I know is that Baba *knows* best, the when and the how, of every incident connected with the lives of those who come in the orbit of His love. My break in the service was also later condoned. It appears to me now that the headmaster's initial response to my request for reappointment was negative only so that I would feel inspired to fulfill Baba's order first and actually there was never any doubt about my eventual reappointment.

This detailed personal account may or may not be regarded as a digression. But as these incidents are directly connected with Baba's orders and the wonderful way in which they automatically got worked out, I succumbed to the temptation to include them. Before entering upon the New Life, Baba had given different types of orders to different people closely connected with Him. The above narration may give an idea of the way Baba helped all in carrying out His instructions. The orders of the God-Man and the subsequent happenings are not two separate parts; it is one inseparable phenomenon. Such events, though they come to pass in a most natural way, deepen one's faith in the companionship and the compassion of the God-Man — the *Lila* that sustains Reality — and thus simple things imply profound potentialities.

Had not Baba been in the New Life I would surely have met Him to recount my meeting with Mauni. The coincidence of my visit to Poona, when Baba was at the station, revealed to me a glimpse of His omniscience. For thus He indirectly "heard" without my telling Him the thoughts I fervently wished to convey to Him. With all its simplicity the life of the God-Man can be so mystical! His formless Presence and the enformed Personality are creatively multi-dimensional, wherein simplicity and surprise are superbly mingled.

In Nati Imli at Benares

Resuming the account of Baba's journey by train from Poona, the Baba-party reached Benares on November 15, 1949. Babadas was at the station to receive Baba. He and Sadashiv Patel had been sent earlier from Belgaum to find and rent a residence at Benares which fulfilled certain conditions laid down by Baba. Both of them had become very much disappointed in their search and were on the point of sending a telegram to Baba, conveying their inability to secure a place fulfilling the requirements.

At the eleventh hour, Dr. Nath agreed to the unusual terms for lodging and boarding the Baba-party. Thus Dr. Siddheshwar Nath became the chief host of the Baba-party. He was a well-known physician and opthalmologist. In addition to working as the honorary surgeon in the Civil Hospital, he had his own clinic on Kabir Road. He was an absolute gentleman who had spiritual leanings and held saintly personalities in high regard. He had neither met Baba nor heard of

Him before. Babadas and Patel did not reveal Baba's name but only talked to him about a party on the way to Hardwar. How Babadas and Patel, who could not speak English or Hindi well, succeeded in convincing a highly educated person like Dr. Nath to be their host is still inconceivable! Dr. B. S. Khare was an assistant to Dr. Nath. He was also working as a Professor at Benares Hindu University. Dr. Nath with the help of Dr. Khare agreed to entertain this incredible party of 16 men and 4 women who were total strangers to them.

The demands and the terms of the Baba-party aroused such deep interest in Dr. Nath that he went to the railway station in his car with his wife. When Baba got down on the platform, He cursorily looked around and then, pointing at a couple standing on the overhead bridge at a considerable distance away, asked Eruch to inquire about them. Eruch and the other companions arriving by the train neither knew nor cared where they were to stay at Benares or who was to be their host. The couple told Eruch that they were waiting for a party enroute to Hardwar which intended to stay for a few weeks at Benares. It was clear Dr. Nath was the host.

As Eruch conveyed this information to Baba, He was displeased with Babadas for asking the host to visit the station. He also sent Eruch back to meet Dr. Nath and inform him that as his visit to the station was a breach of the terms, the head of the party (Baba) wished to proceed to some other place, cancelling the halt at Benares. To this message Dr. Nath politely replied that on learning that there were four women in the party, he had wished to give them a lift in his car, to the place where they would be staying since it was rather far from the station. This explanation and Dr. Nath's attitude pleased Baba and He accepted his offer on condition that Dr. Nath accept only one rupee for the lift, and the rest of the expense be accepted by Dr. Nath as his gift (*bhiksha*) to the party.

Thus Baba's arrival at Benares marked the beginning of the phase of *bhiksha* (begging). Dr.

Nath was all the while standing at a distance wondering about the messages conveyed from the head of the party, but according to the terms he dared not ask the name or the whereabouts of the party. The women companions left the station in Dr. Nath's car, driven by the driver and the men companions left on foot, with their luggage carried on hand carts.

The residence was near Nichi Baugh (garden), a place near the Bharat Milap section, in the Cantonment area. The building was inside a big compound with an unkempt garden. It was in a secluded place but had water and electricity. The women stayed on the first floor. Two statues, standing as sentinels, on each side of the staircase, a remnant of former grandeur, greeted the visitors. Inside the main room there was a lot of furniture, mostly chairs. Baba, however, asked the women not to use any chairs. The next day all the furniture was neatly placed outside the room. The costly carpets were also removed. No comforts! In the adjacent building Baba allotted a place for each companion; Donkin was accommodated in a side room. The disciples had to carry and arrange all the things by themselves; for some, the work was very tiring especially after the tedious night journey. Nevertheless, a sumptuous breakfast arranged by the host refreshed them all.

According to the conditions, previously conveyed through Babadas and Patel, Baba sent Eruch to give six hundred rupees to Dr. Nath and to Dr. Khare towards the party's expenses of lodging and boarding for three weeks. They sensed that this was not an ordinary party and so hesitated to accept the money but they did not want to risk violating one of the conditions again and so they accepted it. The quality of the food was left to the choice of the host, though soon many a message was sent concerning the flavor and savor of the meals sent. It was really commendable and even astonishing that during Baba's entire stay at Benares, these two devoted families willingly carried out all of Baba's instructions. They were blessed souls indeed.

BENARES TO MORADABAD

Power Blended with Helplessness

The next day Vishnu brought the news that a package booked from Belgaum was missing. Because of this the clerk at the railway station was not willing to deliver the rest of the packages which had arrived. This caused great inconvenience and after their bath the companions had to put on their dirty clothes. Luckily a day later the undelivered luggage including the missing package was handed over to Vishnu and all felt relieved. Baba sent Adi and Eruch to Dr. Nath to give him seven hundred extra rupees. With this amount he was asked to purchase two good milch cows and two female donkeys for the Baba-party. Why? Even the companions did not know. Any additional amount required for the purchase of these animals was to be offered by Dr. Nath as *bhiksha* (which literally means anything donated in response to an appeal to one's generosity).

On that day, Baba discreetly sanctioned a small sum for each companion to buy shoes, gloves and other necessary things to protect themselves from the cold. No one was to bring back the unspent money. It could be given to beggars but they were not allowed to use it for tea or snacks. A few days were set aside to visit the famous *ghats* — the broad and long steps leading to the Ganges. The sight of burning corpses and of the city's sewage rushing into the river repelled the holy feelings of some of the companions. It is noticed that in the holy and spiritual places in India good and bad go hand in hand. Maybe it's a test, or call it a spiritual jest, but the fact cannot be denied.

One day out of fun, Baba instructed Ghani to greet Him each morning, on His arrival in the companions' room, like the Pathans, in the Pushtu language. The peculiar intonation of the words of greeting, ending in *hai, mai, tai,* made everyone smile and perhaps forget all inconveniences. Ghani was also asked by Baba to repeat in a sing-song way a few rhythmic lines in Urdu, as a way of wishing Him good night. The free rendering of these lines is as follows:

> How differently have passed the days of the Old Life!
> Somehow today has passed too!
> Tomorrow be damned! We are not in the least bothered by what happens next!

One day the owner of Nati Imli visited the estate and was talking with the watchman. He wanted to know if the visitors were in any way inconvenienced; he wanted to be of some help. But his visit displeased Baba and He sent a message to the landlord to leave the place immediately and the landlord unhesitatingly did so. Strange!

This brings to mind an incident which occurred when Baba was touring India contacting the *masts*. One night He was staying in a government rest house at Miraj (M.S.). It was summer and very sultry. However, according to His habit Baba asked the one on night watch to close all the doors and windows of the room. He did not even permit the fan to be turned on. Baba's suite was on the second floor. At midnight He complained that the sound of the ceiling fan from the ground floor was disturbing His sleep. "Could it be stopped?" He gestured. So Eruch went down the stairs and softly knocked on the door. The person seemed annoyed but reluctantly opened the door. Eruch gently pleaded that he and his elder brother, who was not keeping well, were lodging in the room just above the one he was in. He explained that the sound of the revolving fan kept his brother awake. At the end Eruch added, "It will be a favor if you will kindly turn off the fan." He also assured the man that if he wished, his cot and bedding would be gladly moved by Eruch and those accompanying him to the open veranda. Strangely enough the person consented to this.

In the morning this man asked if he could visit their room to express his good wishes. When this was conveyed to Baba, He gave His permission. As the man entered the room he at once recognized that he was in the august presence of Meher Baba. With deep reverence he bowed to Baba. He considered himself fortunate to have Baba's *darshan*. It then turned out that the visitor was none other than the Executive Engineer — the one in charge of all the rest houses in the district. Eruch wondered why the chief engineer had agreed so readily to his midnight suggestions. Maybe it was an excuse for Baba to bring this soul in His contact and indirectly offer him a chance to be of some help in His spiritual work. In Baba's New Life also, we come across some events where we find that even in the phase of "helplessness", the "power" of His presence was obviously expressed.

On the day in question, Baba sent His men to Dr. Nath to tell him that henceforth no one, including the owner, should step in Nati Imli as long as Baba stayed there. This was perfectly observed.

Baba's First *Bhiksha*

The second period of training comprising of *bhiksha* was to begin at Benares. On November 20, while sitting on the veranda which had an aura of stark austerity, Baba explained the subject of *bhiksha* to His companions. The main tenor of the New Life song was helplessness, and to live by begging was a part of it. They were instructed to go barefoot, wearing white *kafnis* and green turbans, with a begging bowl and a cotton satchel (bag) having separate compartments for food, grains and flour. They were to address the householder politely, "Mother/brother, with love please give *bhiksha*." Whatever food was offered had to be accepted, but no money was to be taken. If *bhiksha* were denied, the companions had to pass on to the next door without getting in the least perturbed. Baba often colored His instructions which presaged tests and trials with His sense of humor. Today, with a twinkle in His eyes, He concluded, "Do not beg at the sweetmeat shops or at the door of a eunuch!" Whatever was received was to be placed before Baba. He also set up a schedule for the begging: who was to go where, and when, etc. Nilu, a *Brahmin*, was to beg in the Muslim colony and Ghani, a Mohammedan, was to go begging in a *Brahmin* locality. On this day, before explaining the above details, Baba on His arrival dictated an Urdu couplet to Ghani which meant:

> Today our helplessness has bestowed upon us a rare fortune for which we had been longing for years.

A profound indication!

As the saying goes, example is better than precept; Baba Himself wished to inaugurate the phase of *bhiksha* on November 24,* at Dr. Nath's residence. At this time no one other than Dr. Nath's family was to be present in the house. Before leaving for *bhiksha* Baba called all the companions and touched their feet, every time lifting His hand to His forehead. Was it a prerequisite for the *Avatar* before going to beg? He asked Ghani to read a special prayer, a part of which is given below:

> Today the 24th November is a very significant day for me in the New Life. I ask the most merciful God to forgive me and my companions for any shortcomings and any conscious and unconscious mistakes done singly or wholly [collectively] or towards each other, or personally or impersonally, relating to the conditions or otherwise, as [and] also for any lusty [lustful] angry, greedy or Old Life thoughts or desires.
> ...I ask God to forgive us all, not merely by way of ceremony, but as a whole-hearted pardon.**

---

* Coincidentally this happened to be the last Thursday in November which is celebrated as Thanksgiving Day in the U.S.A.
** *Circular NL 2*, issued on 23-1-1950.

BENARES TO MORADABAD

About this incident one of the companions wrote:

> While this prayer was being read, the atmosphere, one could feel, had undergone a change. Baba Himself became very serene... and the glow on His face was that of one on the judgement seat, overflowing with love, kindness, compassion and mercy. He seemed to be the judge, the crime and culprit rolled into one.... All through He listened to the prayer in rapt attention and then, making a gesture of forgiveness, brought the invocation to an end.

As planned, Baba walked barefoot to Dr. Nath's house, about a km. from Nati Imli. He carried a brass pot in His right hand and an ochre satchel hung on His shoulder. Eruch accompanied Baba. Dr. Nath and his family had the unique fortune of offering the first *bhiksha* to Baba. When this was over he requested Baba to allow Dr. Khare, his colleague who was helping him with all the arrangements, and his family members, the privilege of offering *bhiksha*. Dr. Khare was staying a few kms. away in the university area. So, for the sake of convenience Baba was invited to Dr. Nath's place for a second time on November 25.

It was on this day that Dr. Nath, not having told anyone of his intention, took the snap-shot in which we find Adi accompanying Baba. Perhaps this was the first picture taken since Baba entered the New Life. It was from this photo that Dr. Nath ascertained that the head of the party was no other than Meher Baba. While the Khare family was offering *bhiksha*, a piece of it fell on the ground. Baba very naturally bent down, picked it up and put it in His begging bowl.* Baba had become a perfect beggar! Or maybe He could not part with anything which was offered with such love. Fortunate were these two families who

---

* The bowl and satchel are preserved in Meherabad Museum.

had the honor of being the hosts of the Divine Beggar, Baba, the Ancient One.

On November 26, the program of begging by the companions started. They had to go out in pairs approved by Baba. They wore green turbans and were in white *kafnis*. When Nilu and Kaka visited a Mohammedan locality some remarked, "You are quite robust; you look like wrestlers from Punjab! Why don't you work for your living?" And they were right, for Kaka and Nilu were blessed with good physiques but this proved to be a handicap for getting *bhiksha*. Various were the experiences of this begging phase — some pleasant and a few unpleasant. In one of the villages they were asked to wait a while so that they could be served with fresh baked bread.

Some Events at Benares

The breakfast time at Benares was 5 o'clock in the morning. It was winter and quite cold. All the companions had to get up for breakfast which usually was just a cup of tea and a *chapati*, otherwise some would have preferred to continue sleeping under their coarse warm blankets. There seemed to be no reason to rise so early; Baba had given no other instructions about bath, meditation or any other work. Could not the breakfast time be changed? But no one could defy Baba's order; that would have been against the conditions of the New Life. Ghani, as Baba's childhood chum, enjoyed a special latitude in Baba's company for making jokes. With an oblique reference to the early morning breakfast time he casually remarked that the New Life meant doing routine things at odd times! And some companions had a hearty laugh over this. The next day Baba asked if Ghani were joking or serious about his remark. Baba felt relieved when Ghani and the companions assured Him that it was just a joke and nothing more. Baba, however, asked the companions to pinch His ear for He had doubted Ghani's intention! The New Life phase veiled Baba's Divinity under the guise of a few common, human weaknesses!

After some months (April, 1950), a great religious fair (*mela*) which is known as the Kumbha Mela was to be held at Hardwar. Baba asked Vishnu to find out the main dates for the Mela. On another occasion, He asked Baidul and Babadas to collect information about the *masts* and saints who were expected to visit Hardwar. Hearing this, someone asked whether Baba's activity of contacting *masts* had not ended with the termination of the Old Life. Upon this Baba explained, "The *mast*-activity of the Old Life had exclusive importance for me; but hereafter this work will have importance for all. Henceforth, the work with the *masts, sants* and *sadhus* will be absolutely different from what it had been in the past. I might make you serve them; or I shall myself serve them in your presence which was never the case before. I might even humiliate myself in your presence or in the presence of others, in a manner that would be shocking to you all. So I need *masts, sadhus* and *sants* for a different kind of work altogether."* Such statements from Baba did not clarify the nature of His work with the *masts*. And to ask Baba to give any more explanation, particularly in and of the New Life, was to make the subject more enigmatic. So no one tried to ask any more questions.

According to the original plan Baba was to spend three weeks at Benares. But after some days He expressed a wish to camp for ten days at Sarnath, a place closely connected with the life of Lord Buddha. It is about 9 kms. to the north of Benares. The Baba-party was to start to Sarnath on foot. The luggage was to be carried in two bullock carts. In an informal discussion it came out that the two carts would not be sufficient to carry the luggage of the companions. Adi suggested that they get a camel cart. Baidul, when in the prime of his youth, had stayed in Iran and knew how to look after a camel.

---

* Ghani's unpublished, *Diary of the New Life*, (October-November 1949), p. 89.

Dr. Donkin, before joining Baba in India, had gained some knowledge about handling a camel during his visit to the Sahara Desert in Africa. This was enough for Baba to find favor with the idea of purchasing a camel cart.

Baba sent one of the companions to Dr. Nath to inquire if he could purchase the required camel cart. The noble doctor was in a mood to carry out any instruction from Baba. He readily agreed to get the desired vehicle for the Baba-party but was unwilling to accept any money for it. Had he not been so willing, Kaka Baria, the Treasurer of the party, would have been required to subtract this amount from the sum earmarked for the fodder of the animals and that would not have been easy. Some days passed and Baba sent two of His companions to get information about the purchase of the animals and the camel cart. In addition, Dr. Nath was asked to find and rent two bungalows at Sarnath for the Baba-party, as Baba intended to stay there for ten days. With the help of his brother, an influential person, Dr. Nath succeeded in getting the required accommodation within a few days. In the New Life there were occasions when Baba's instructions appeared entirely impractical and practically impossible but they invariably worked out very well.

The companions were not allowed to speak among themselves either about political or spiritual subjects. They were neither to read the dailies or the weeklies, nor were they permitted to talk about anything related to the Old Life. For some it was not easy to transcend their old habits and interests. They felt bored. Knowing this, in one of the sittings Baba stated, "Though the sufferings of this stage are dry and uninteresting, the suffering of the New Life [to commence] in real earnest after 1st of January [1950] though 100% more severe will be wet and enjoyable. The New Life will be wet through and through."* It seems He wanted them to

---

* *Circular NL* 2, issued on 23-1-1950.

live happily from moment to moment and the secret of doing this lay in their willingness to do anything or nothing when it was at Baba's bidding.

Once the topic of journeying on foot from Sarnath to Hardwar was discussed. The provisions had been made for a period ending in December. It was brought to Baba's attention that taking into account the absolute minimum requirements of the party and the accompanying animals, the money in hand was insufficient. Various ways of meeting the deficit were thought of. At the end Baba suggested that some belongings of the companions, especially trunks and clothing, be given to Dr. Nath and to Dr. Khare. They were free to retain or sell these things and in return they were to give the extra money the party needed. In short, in return for their loving offer to provide a camel and a camel cart to the Baba-party and their willingness to contribute the amount needed to meet the deficit, these two doctors were to receive the used clothes and trunks of the companions! From November 25, the host knew for certain that the head of the party was the eminent spiritual personality, Meher Baba, who was regarded by many as the Perfect Master. He did not divulge this recognition of his to Baba's companions but he felt himself most fortunate to be of some service to Meher Baba.

After hearing Baba's message, Dr. Nath with perfect courtesy said, "We will very happily give the sum of money you need. Is it necessary that in return we must accept the clothes? We can gladly get the clothes washed and return them to you, too." At this Eruch pointed out that the head of the party did not want that. In a graceful way the doctor continued, "In that case, I hope, the clothing you mentioned includes the clothes of the 'head' also." Eruch could not give any direct answer. He returned to Nati Imli and told Baba of Dr. Nath's reply. Baba appreciated Dr. Nath's demeanor and consented to add one of His scarfs to the bundle of clothes. In due course, the clothes and the trunks were handed over to the host. At the close of this gesture of giving away the clothing, Baba, with a charming chuckle, conveyed to the companions, "While leaving Meherabad on October 16, we were comparatively speaking 'light weight'; at Benares, with the disposal of the trunks and 'Old Life' clothing, we have become 'feather weight' and after January 1, 1950, who knows (I don't promise) we might become 'air weight.' "*

Prayer in the Cellar at Sarnath

On December 1, the Baba-party shifted to Sarnath. The women and Baba were lodged in one bungalow and the men companions in another. One morning Baba asked Mani to write the names of the known *Avatars* on a piece of paper. She wrote: Zoroaster, Rama, Krishna, Buddha, Jesus, Mohammad and Meher Baba. Baba kept this paper in one of His coat pockets and later led the women companions to one of the underground passages around Sarnath. It turned out to be the place where He later sat in *langoti* (loin cloth) with His companions. This noteworthy event happened during their visit to a subterranean cellar associated with the life of Buddha — the Enlightened One. It is believed that Gautama after attaining *Bodhi* (Enlightenment) preached his first sermon to his five disciples at this place. One morning, after reaching this particular spot, Baba asked His men to wear only a *langoti*. They were asked to sit and repeat mentally for fifteen minutes the following prayer, a copy of which was given to each companion. It read thus:

> God, give me strength to follow the conditions hundred per cent. God, help me to speak the truth and not to tell a lie under any circumstances. God, help me to control anger, and to keep away from lusty [lustful] and greedy desires. God, help me to be just, fair, honest and kind towards my companions

---
* Ibid.

and towards those who come into contact with me.*

When the silent repetition of the prayer was over, Baba asked the men to don their clothes and to get in a line. Baba looked very radiant and stood at one end of the passage. He greeted everyone with a warm handshake. Then He asked each companion to come and hand Him the prayer note. With a beaming smile He asked Ghani to then repeat loudly, seven times in Hindi, *"Ho-gaya"* (meaning accomplished or completed). And in a very delightful mood Baba Himself participated in each of Ghani's repetitions by raising His right hand. Was the reading of this prayer a revival of Lord Buddha's teaching, particularly the first sermon, in a different way? Baba instructed those who were present to mark the loin cloth they were wearing; it was not to be worn again, unless Baba specially told them to.

God's Gift to the Gardener

While returning, Baba took His companions to the bungalow where He was staying, specifically to point out the old gardener working there. Baba had once remarked that the game of Love is not for the weakling. This gardener outwardly looked like a skeleton but possessed a robust heart, bubbling with unadulterated love for God. He was a real hero. He would invariably get up before 4 o'clock in the morning, sit on his low rickety bed that was open to the skies and would melodiously repeat, "Rama, Rama, Sita-Rama," for hours, irrespective of the changing seasons. Baba conveyed to the companions, "This old man is thoroughly content with what little he has. He is one-pointed in his devotion. Though he does not wear the ochre robes, he is a real *sadhu*."

Once, according to Baba's instructions, Goher

---
* Ibid.

approached the gardener and asked him if he wanted anything. His prompt reply was, "God be praised. I do not want anything. *Thakurji** (the Lord) provides me with anything I need." Hearing this Baba felt pleased and sent Goher again to inquire if he really needed anything. When persistently pressed he replied, "A box of matches!" What a demand! On another occasion Baba called this gardener to Him and presented him with a good blanket which he delightfully and most reverentially accepted without any hesitation saying, "I am blessed. This is *Bhagwan's* [God's] gift." Did he recognize Baba as *Bhagwan*? That is unclear. But surely the God-Man had spotted His lover and the Divine Gardener seemed pleased with the blossoming of this "flower" in His garden of Love.

The premises of the bungalow where the companions stayed at Sarnath presented a strange sight. During the stay at Belgaum, Baba had sent specific instructions to Padri, staying at Meherabad, to deliver a coach (later known as the New Life caravan), along with the bullocks to the Baba-party at Benares. Dr. Nath, in fulfillment of Baba's instructions, had purchased and handed over to the companions a camel cart with a camel, two milch cows (one had a newly born calf) and two female donkeys. In addition to these animals, there was one white horse. According to the conditions of the New Life money was not to be accepted from anyone; if someone offered any animal it was to be politely rejected. But, while refusing, the companions were permitted to say, "The only animal we can accept is a white horse." In response to this, Dr. Khare had presented the Baba-party with a spotless white horse as *bhiksha*. All these animals were tethered to pegs in the compound.

Baba Bows to Buddha

In one of the informal sittings a point was raised

---

* Devotees of Lord Krishna address Him as Thakurji.

whether any new person could join Baba in His New Life and stay with Him. One of the companions remarked that such an admission would mar the charm of the New Life. Baba conveyed, "The importance of the New Life is not from us but from those who keep it alive. If we were to fail in the conditions we would disgrace the New Life, and if an outsider were to obey the conditions 100% he would uphold the honor of the New Life."* Perhaps it was in this sense that Baba once stated, "The New Life will live by itself eternally...." At the end of the above meeting it was agreed that Baba could permit anyone to join Him as one of the companions. Baba, before October 16, had indirectly promised Kaikobad Dastur that He would accept him as one of the Yeswallas. Later in the light of this discussion Baba sent the necessary instructions to Kaikobad who was asked to join the Baba-party directly at Dehra Dun. Kaikobad was the only one who was not originally a Yeswalla to join Baba in His New Life. As for the women, Naja (Pendu's sister) was the only one to join the women companions, also at Dehra Dun.

In another meeting when the topic of the journey on foot from Sarnath to Hardwar was discussed, it was suggested that the extra luggage should be sent in advance by railway to Hardwar. This seemed practical and convenient too. The question of railway freight was brought up. This required extra money as no provision had been made for such an expenditure. So Baba asked most of His companions to surrender their wristwatches to raise the money. Donkin, Pendu and Adi, who had to attend to duties which brought them into contact with the outside world, were allowed to retain their watches.

One day at Sarnath, which is studded with shrines and temples, Baba visited a place that enshrines the figure of Buddha. The walls were beautifully painted, representing different incidents from the life of Siddhartha

---

* *Circular NL* 2, issued on 23-1-1950.

Gautama. In the center was a splendid statue of Lord Buddha. Baba asked those accompanying Him to pay their respects to that graceful piece of sculpture and He Himself bowed most reverentially, to set an example as to how one should honor the God-Man, who in fact is omnipresent. To some an idol, a portrait or a painting of the God-Man is the silent symbol of His omnipresence. In its right perspective, I personally think it is like a telescope through which the wonders of the Formless One are revealed. It is a window to the ever inviting Eternal.

On Foot to Shivapur

On December 12, Baba with His companions, some driving the carts, some driving the animals, commenced the journey on foot from Sarnath to Jaunpur which was about 60 kms. away. This was predominantly a phase of gypsy life. Generally the march began by sunrise. Baba with Eruch walked ahead and the women followed them. A little later the companions, wearing white robes and green turbans, followed. At first Baba had suggested that the women companions wear blue *kafnis* and gray turbans during the march on foot. But later He cancelled this instruction and asked them to wear light blue *saris* only once, on the opening day of the march. The chiming of the camel bells was very melodious. Gustadjee and Ghani were in charge of the donkeys, a hard job indeed. Nilu and Aloba had to look after the cows.

After going a little distance Baba wanted to attend nature's call. There were no latrines by the road and so Eruch led Him to a suitable place, a little distance away and returned to the highway. This march on foot with such an unusual group of animals and with people belonging to different religions had aroused deep suspicions in the minds of the police officers. One of them accosted Eruch and began to ask different questions about the party's itinerary and intentions. Eruch, who skillfully managed to give satisfactory answers, stated that the group consisted of people who shared the intention of going to Hardwar for the Kumbha Mela (fair). From distorted reports the officer had received previously, he had suspected that they belonged to some political party or were engaged in some anti-government activity. His last question was, "And where is that man who was walking with you?" Eruch told him the truth and before Baba returned the officer went away, feeling that he had done his duty well. He did not know what a precious opportunity he had missed by just a few minutes! One can be quite close to Baba and yet miss His *darshan* while someone else may be far away and yet the circumstances will be so arranged that he soon finds himself at the threshold of the God-Man. Astounding are the ways of the *Avatar!*

The first halt was at Shivapur. Baba and the women were waiting at the outskirts of the town for the men companions. The women described the scene of their arrival as follows:

> They arrived later than was expected, but we shall never forget the scene. It was like a beautiful pageant being enacted before us. All the companions were dressed in their white robes and dark green turbans. First came Dr. Donkin with an Arab-like headdress leading the white horse which looked tall and beautiful, walking proudly, without a saddle. Then followed the bullock-carts and the stately camel drawing a cart. The camel had a large sized bell round its neck which gave a melodious sound as it walked. Some of the companions were driving the carts while the others were accompanying them on foot. Lastly came the caravan drawn by two bullocks. Gustadjee was in charge of the two donkeys who were stubborn and would not walk. They were tied to the caravan and were being dragged. One of the bullocks drawing the caravan was Raja, the English bull which Baba had fed milk from a feeding bottle when it was a calf

in Meherabad.*

All the companions had arrived except Nilu. He was very fond of milk but this fondness had gotten him in trouble. At Sarnath Baba told Nilu that as he was fond of milk, he would have to look after the milch cow! It had a young calf too. After a journey of about a km. the calf could not keep pace with the mother cow. It began to stagger and fall to the ground. So, poor Nilu had to carry it on his shoulders for some distance. He fell behind; the party had already walked into town when, at the octroi** outpost, Nilu was to pay the tax. The clerk thought Nilu had come to sell the cow. According to the New Life conditions he was not permitted to carry a single coin with him. Fatigued and annoyed as he was, it was hard for him to convince the clerk that he was a pilgrim on his way to Hardwar. God be blessed, in the end he somehow managed to prevail upon the official to let him by. Later, the same day, hearing the plight of the companions in charge of the animals, Baba agreed to sell some of them and also to send some by railway to Hardwar.

Parade of Animals

It took four days for the party to reach Jaunpur. Those were the days which gave them the first taste of the gypsy life. The companions, in spite of the cold weather, had to spend the nights in the open, under the trees, beg for food and remain content with whatever was received in *bhiksha*. (It is rather difficult to express in English the exact meaning of the word *bhiksha* when used in different contexts. In general, it can be anything which one receives as one begs for something, especially food.) The party spent one night each camped at Shiva-

---

* *The Glow.* Vol. VIII, No. 1, February 1973, p. 5.
** In India a small tax is levied by the city municipality on things brought for sale, from the outside area.

pur, Babatpur and Rehata. The march would generally commence before sunrise and continue till mid-day. Dried wood, if conveniently possible, would be collected on the way. At each stop, Pendu's work would be to look after the fodder of the animals and to take them to water. Kaka Baria would be in charge of cooking. The companions and even Baba begged for food in the villages. Generally the villagers were more hospitable in offering *bhiksha* than the city people.

There was a small two-flapped tent for Baba, the two ends of which could be tied to the caravan which provided shelter for the women companions at night. Anna would keep watch at night; in the *mandali* he was known as Anna 104. He did not understand English but in the 1920s when he was running a high fever some Baba people visited him. As everyone entered the room he would greet each with the word 104! When Baba visited him Anna loudly cried out, "Baba, 104!" And since then he was known as Anna 104, the nickname Baba gave him. Mehera, Mani and others knew that it was getting colder and colder. So they sewed some blankets together and made a warm sleeping bag for Baba. This was to protect Baba's physical body — the fairest flower of creation — the most delicate and the most powerful form! During the night the women would rest in the coach (caravan).

About this journey the women companions wrote:

> Early in the morning, often before 4 o'clock, we would be awakened by Baba's knock on the door. Goher would roll up her bedding and she and Meheru would jump out of the caravan clutching their warm clothes, hurrying, so Baba would not be kept waiting. Baba would enter the caravan, ask how we had slept and tell us how cold it was outside, that we should take care and put on our warm clothes. While we washed and prepared hot water for Baba's washing and shaving, we were drawn to the warmth of the open fire, like a pin to a magnet. The caravan was

well insulated and warm compared to the air outside.

Breakfast — a hot cup of tea, was most welcome and with it Baba would give us a *chapati* or two — anything that we had received in *"bhiksha"* the day before. Milk for the tea was provided by the cow. Patil [Patel] would milk her and Kaka made the tea. Mehera would pour the tea for Baba and we would have breakfast. After tea we would wash up and hurry with our packing as best as we could with our fingers numb with cold. Baba would go over to the men *mandali* to see how they were faring. They had to tend to the animals and then to themselves and pack the carts. In the carts were packed the *mandali's* belongings, their beddings and household utensils, hurricane lanterns, fodder and grain for the animals and parched rice and lentils that provided for our meals.*

At every halt there would be a crowd of visitors — men and women with eyes filled with inquisitiveness. This made the women companions feel rather uncomfortable as they had spent most of their lives in secluded places. The villagers marvelled at the parade of animals and the strange group wearing long robes and turbans. Some thought that they were a group of refugees from Pakistan, for this was the period following the partition. Some inquired if the companions belonged to a circus troupe! A few were curious about the inclusion of the donkeys with the other animals. Nowhere in India had they seen or heard of any spiritually minded group leading donkeys to a place of pilgrimage! It was extremely difficult for anyone to satisfy their curiosity.

Years later, Kaka Baria, one of the companions, commented that through the animals taken with them in the New Life, Baba gave a fresh impetus to the work done for the animal kingdom in His past Advents. The white horse, according to Kaka, represented the work

---

* Ibid., p. 6.

accomplished by Zoroaster and the cows that by Krishna. The donkeys were the medium for recharging the spiritual push given by Jesus and the camel that by Prophet Mohammad. Kaka, as Baba's dearest disciple and personal attendant, might have asked Baba about the significance of this "parade of animals" in the New Life or this might be entirely his own interpretation, I am not sure. Had Kaka told this to the villagers, some might have laughed at him and perhaps this explanation would have intrigued them all the more. Leaving such queries apart, as soon as the villagers knew that this group was on its way to Hardwar, the famous place of pilgrimage in India, their minds and hearts would be filled with deep respect and devotion. They would ask if they could be of any help to them.

The Vacuum Period

Suitable accommodations at Jaunpur could not be settled in advance by Babadas and Adi. So a place called Kai-Bagh about a km. from the city was hired. Even in the New Life, Baba's habit of building and dismantling, planning and replanning continued. The activities of the God-Man are not meant for immediate tangible results but they are symbolic expressions of the inner work in which the *Avatar* is engaged. At this place Baba instructed some companions to sell the camel, the camel cart and the cows. The coach, the bullock carts and the two donkeys were to be sent by rail to Hardwar. The white horse was to be retained. At Jaunpur, Baba disclosed to the companions that before leaving for the New Life He had asked Meherjee Karkaria to set aside one thousand rupees for each of the Yeswallas. This amount was to be given to any companion who, without any fault of his, was sent back to the Old Life by Baba.

But in the same meeting, a little later, He asked each one whether he would willingly forego this provision made by Him. And He smiled the God-Man's smile. Whether the *Avatar* gives something or takes away anything from any of His dear ones, it is equally graceful! All readily agreed to remain penniless, whether physically with Baba or away from Him. This pleased Baba very much and He asked all to go wash their hands and faces and return to Him. Then He poured some water on the palms of each companion. In India, this simple, visible action stands for complete acceptance of a deal between two people.

The next proposed halt was to be at Moradabad, a place over 150 kms. to the east of Delhi. Baba instructed Adi to contact Harjeevan Lal, one of Baba's dear ones at Delhi. He was directed to help Adi find a suitable place at Moradabad for the Baba-party. The next day, Baba, His beautiful and graceful bearing radiating a carefree feeling, conveyed, "We have left the Old Life and there is no going back to it now. The Old Life is practically dead. I have heard it said that when a person is dead, the spirit has [a] connection with it for three or four days, and before the spirit gets established in the new sphere, there intervenes a wee bit of a time which may be said to be a sort of a vacuum between the old and new life. Similarly speaking, our Old Life is dead since October 16, 1949. From that date up to December 21, our New Life has had a kind of connection with the Old Life."

Then turning His beaming face towards all the companions He continued, "I have, therefore, decided that the vacuum period should be from December 22, to December 31 (both [days] inclusive). During these ten days there will be observed a complete suspension of the ordeals of the training period."* He also made it clear that within those ten days the companions would neither wear *kafnis* nor beg. It would be a period of complete relaxation, and they could even have good food during it. This unexpected declaration filled the hearts of the listeners with a rare delight. Was Baba demonstrating to the companions that in the New Life,

---

* *Circular NL* 2, issued on 23-1-1950.

if they accepted every happening of any day as it came to pass, without any grumblings, there would be occasions that would fill their hearts with delight and courage, helping them to follow Baba till the very end?

The journey to and the stay at Jaunpur provided the experience of begging and gypsy life alike. Baba would be sitting in His two-flapped tent, with a hurricane lantern, right from the early morning, keeping all the companions engaged in the work assigned to them. All had to get up as early as 4 o'clock and Baba would see that each companion was "out of bed". An hour later, after a hot mugful of tea, all would take their "posts" for the "quick march".

The Stay at Moradabad

Adi, with the help of Harjeevan Lal, an advocate and Keki Desai, was trying to find a place at Moradabad for Baba and His companions. At the last minute he was successful in securing a building called Ram Leela Grounds. As planned earlier, Baba boarded the Dehra Dun Express at Jaunpur bound for Moradabad which He reached in the early morning of December 22, 1949. The women accompanying Baba narrated the arrival and stay at Moradabad as follows:

> We arrived at Moradabad station in the middle of the night. The *tonga* ride in the dark to our destination seemed endless. It was 2 in the morning and bitterly cold and Mani was not feeling well at all. When we reached the place it was pitch dark. There was no chair or bed or bedding on which to make Mani comfortable. She sat huddled on the floor and we started shutting the doors of the house to keep out the cold. There seemed numerous doors to that one room — 12 in all — and the floor was not yet dry, it had been recently washed, and puddles of water had formed here and there. At last some luggage arrived and we hurriedly opened a bedding roll for Mani.

Next morning while we were unpacking a *Brahmin* came along and scolded us for occupying the place. He was taken to the men *mandali* and things explained to him that permission for our stay had been granted. This was a *Dharmshala* for the Hindus where pilgrims stayed during a fair that took place here. The *Brahmin* thought we were squatters. Baba did not stay in the room. His tent was pitched on the broad veranda. Along both sides, close to the house, were paths which led to the city. Almost all day there were passers-by. There was very little privacy. One afternoon when we were on the veranda Baba wanted to rest. He said He was not to be disturbed. While He was resting in the tent, a *sadhu* — a monk — in ochre clothes and bald pate stood before the door, demanding *bhiksha*. He said he wanted flour. There was no such thing in the house as we did not do any cooking. Goher told him to forgive her for refusing it and go to the men *mandali*. He looked at her curiously and said that flour should be where the women were. Goher tried to get him away as fast as she could so that Baba would not be disturbed by his loud talking. Baba later said that he was a genuine seeker.

The camel and the cart had been sold at Jaunpur as it was not practical. The cow and the calf were sold at Moradabad as the calf gave much trouble. Dr. Nilu had been responsible for the cow and he often had to carry the calf on his shoulders so that the mother would follow. The white horse had to be hitched to a *tonga*, but it refused to budge. An expert *tongawala* (coachman) was called to break him in. After a tussle the horse was hitched to the *tonga*. Another *tonga* and filly were also bought and another bullock cart to replace the camel cart. Baidul drove the *tonga* drawn by the white horse with Kaka behind with provisions for our meal. They would go ahead so that the meal could be prepared and kept ready when our party arrived. But it was not easy to get the temperamental horse to start. If there was weight in the *tonga* it would not budge. Otherwise he would start with jerks and Kaka would have to run after the carriage, putting the packages in the *tonga* and jumping in himself. This, more than anything, was responsible for the heart attack he had at Najibabad. Adi drove the other *tonga* with Dr. Ghani, his companion. They had the job of collecting *bhiksha* on the way.*

Baba — The Emperor and the *Fakir*

At Jaunpur, all the companions had willingly consented to forego the one thousand rupees that had been allocated to each in case they, without any fault, were sent back to the Old Life by Baba. Now Baba was free to utilize this amount. Once Baba had money He rarely spared any part of it for long. He was a real *Fakir* who owned nothing! To clarify this status of being the Emperor and the Beggar at one and the same time, I wish to quote a few lines from one of the Life Circulars:

> Baba, the Divine Beloved, carries within Him the most precious treasure of Infinite Love which permits no room for worldly wealth. As such, He has always been and is the Perennial *Fakir*.**

The residence at Moradabad was far from the city. So out of the above-mentioned amount, to facilitate transportation, two *tongas* were purchased. This being the vacuum period, the companions were not to beg for food. Hence, a part of this sum was used to pay the boarding charges and other expenses of the party. A certain part of this amount was earmarked for building small huts or for buying portable tents for each companion, after reaching the headquarters, near Hardwar. The remaining money was to be utilized for meeting

---

* *The Glow*, Vol. VIII, No. 1, February 1973, pp. 8, 9.
** *Life Circular* No. 30, 1-9-1950.

the ferry fares, pilgrim taxes, fodder for the animals and such other most essential expenditures. Baba stayed at Moradabad till December 31, 1949 and by the time He left the city they had practically no money left.

In the earlier years, Baba sometimes would put His hands in the pockets of His coat, which contained some letters from His lovers, and would jokingly gesture, "The pockets are big; they can admit a few more letters," and with a smile He would add, "But they have holes [!] and as such they cannot hold any coins [money]." Throughout His life Baba was indeed the Perfect *Fakir*.

Without affecting the begging conditions laid down by Baba, Harjeevan Lal, Kishan Singh and Kain wished to offer, purely in the form of *bhiksha*, some eatables and warm clothes for the companions. Baba kindly accepted the proposal. He allowed them to send these articles before January 1, 1950. They were not to deliver these things in person but to send the same with a person approved by Baba. Harjeevan Lal sent mufflers and sweaters, socks and monkey-caps, woollen jackets and blankets. As it was December, a fairly cold season in U.P., the warm clothing was not only useful, but one might say essential. Without these woollen clothes the companions would have suffered tremendously from the severe cold. In two separate trunks, he also sent many nourishing things — jam, dry fruits, ghee, etc. This timely offer was very much appreciated by all. He also asked Baba's permission to send some pyjamas and sugar before the beginning of the next year. The companions felt that to live with Baba was to live with the Emperor and the *Fakir* in one. A note was sent to Harjeevan expressing Baba's happiness for this unconditional and unselfish offering, but at the same time, he was warned that henceforth he should have no communication or contact with Baba during His New Life. To Baba's people any message from Him was the harbinger of blessedness; it meant the Master regarded them as His own.

BENARES TO MORADABAD

Mystical Lining of the New Life

The stay at Moradabad was a period of relaxation. The food was brought in *tongas* from the hotels but it was only vegetarian. One day Ghani remarked that he did not feel satisfied with this "grassitarian" stuff. "In this vacuum period why can't we enjoy the non-vegetarian dishes?" he concluded. Hearing this Baba turned His gaze towards him and conveyed, "Today I permit you to visit any good hotel you like. You can satisfy your palate to your heart's content, with as many dishes of any non-vegetarian food as you want." Ghani felt greatly delighted.

On the other hand, among the companions, Nilu had been a strict vegetarian for the whole of his life. He disliked the non-vegetarian dishes. But dogmatic dislikes bind as much as explicit likes. Perhaps for this reason Baba asked Nilu to accompany Ghani and taste a bit of anything and everything he ate. This was a real test for Nilu. But with the spirit of obedience embedded in his love for Baba, he underwent this ordeal fairly cheerfully.

On that day, perhaps it was Christmas, Ghani enjoyed a mixed grill at a grand hotel. The next day Baba asked Ghani if he really felt happy. He inquired of him about the dishes and delicacies he had had. Ghani said, "I had mutton chops, chicken chops, fish and...." At this Baba smiled and gestured, "Fine." Then He continued, "I am happy you obeyed me. Today here is another order from me for you. Put on your *kafni* and visit the same hotel to beg for food!" Ghani sportively and willingly agreed to this. As he approached the hotel. the manager, as well as the servants who had received tips at Ghani's hands, were greatly surprised to find the respectable customer of yesterday today calling out, "Brother, give *bhiksha.*" How could one expect them to understand the sense of humor of the Perfect Companion and one's companionship with Him? Anyway Ghani played his part well and this pleased Baba. He also permitted

Baidul and Aloba to have a non-vegetarian feast. But as they had not grumbled about the vegetarian diet, they were not sent out for *bhiksha*.

The New Life had throughout a mystical lining. For some companions it provided a few intense inner emotional experiences, while for others it provided a deeper understanding of life. With Baba this phase was never a freak, superficial religious insanity; it was rather a profound expression of universal Divinity, sowing the seeds of the New Humanity. It was a demonstration where kingly and beggarly life were beautifully blended. But to inherit a little of the treasure of the New Life, special preparedness is expected of a person. Francis Brabazon, one of Baba's close disciples, once read the following lines to Baba. These point out the qualifications needed to be a companion to the Eternal Beloved and they also give a taste of what life with Him is like:

> The qualifications for the path of love are these:
> A gale of destruction to oneself, to others a soft dawn-breeze.
>
> When a man can suffer heart's tempests while his forehead smiles
> He is fit for sea travel, deserts and mountain defiles.
>
> When he becomes both the fabled lion and lamb at play
> He will meet that master who can set his feet on the way.*

---

* Francis Brabazon, *In Dust I Sing*, p. 69.

6

Termination of the "Gypsy Life"

1950 — Part I

On New Year's Day in the Morning

WITH a smile beaming on His face like dawn at the horizon, Meher Baba gestured, "Happy New Life" as He offered a piece of cake to each one of His companions. It was the first morning of the year 1950. The "vacuum period" or relaxation was over and Baba had decided to continue the journey on foot. The baggage consisting of bed rolls and odd things was loaded in the carts and by afternoon all the companions, in white long robes and green turbans, left for a place a few miles from Moradabad. It was a bright day with warm sunshine but by evening the sky was laden with black clouds. At night it began to rain. The showers, however, stopped as abruptly as they had set in. Yet, during that short span it rained so much that Baba's bedding in the tent got wet. The plight of the companions who had no proper shelter over their heads can well be imagined. Next morning the march was resumed and all camped at Haryana. The next two halts were at Amroha and Ratangarh. This was a gypsy life with its alternate joys and discomforts.

On this journey there would be an advance party going ahead in a *tonga* to arrange a place where the whole paraphernalia of animals and vehicles could be accommodated. Baidul, who drove one of the *tongas*, in an attempt to overtake another one, damaged one of the wheels of his vehicle. He somehow managed to get the *tonga* to the halting place. On Baba's arrival the mishap was brought to His notice. He, however, did not approve of being detained at that place. He ordered an early morning start for the next day. Hence, the repairing of the wheel which could not be done there became a pressing problem. It was learnt that there was a wheelwright in a nearby village. The damaged wheel was disjoined and taken in another *tonga* to the wheelwright. Baidul, Adi, Donkin and Pendu left for the village where the wheel could be repaired.

By sundown they reached the wheelwright's house. He was reluctant to work at night but after a little persuasion he agreed. Some wooden spokes of the wheel had to be replaced, and then the iron plate round the wheel had to be refixed. From the demeanor of the visitors the wheelwright knew that they were not conventional customers. He requested them to take their seats on a *charpai* as the work would take a long time. It was getting darker and colder too. Out of courtesy the wheelwright asked them if he could offer them tea. In India any time can be tea time! The man was very surprised at the nature of their acceptance, for they were willing to have it only if it were offered as *bhiksha*. And yet these four fair skinned robust men were prepared to pay reasonably well for the repair charges. Strange! The wheelwright explained that he was not joking; the companions answered that they too had been serious in their reply to him. All this was beyond the wheelwright's comprehension. He just said, "Sir, whatever it be, please accept tea at my house!"

When it was served all felt happy to have a hot drink in the cold weather. But at the first sip they had a surprise. As was customary in that part of India, salt in addition to sugar had been added, and this was not to the companions' taste. When the work was done, the wheel, along with the iron plate, was placed on a circular formation of cow dung cakes that were set aflame. The plate with its rubber tire was then hammered and fixed to the wheel. Because it was so dark a friend of the wheelwright was requested to guide them to the main road leading to the camp of the companions. By the time they reached the halting place it was after midnight. A fire was kept burning to ward off the cold. Donkin and the others attached the repaired wheel to the damaged *tonga*. Donkin was so exhausted by the work that without unrolling his bedding he just rested his head on it and passed the night by the fireside. As had been decided the party started before daybreak. In the New Life everyone tried to carry out Baba's wishes cheerfully. That was their only pleasure.

Baba Uses a Proxy

During these wanderings, Baba would lead the way, Eruch accompanying Him. Keeping a little distance behind, Mehera, Mani, Mehru and Goher would follow; about a furlong behind were the men companions. The women generally carried a flask of fresh water for Baba. Finding that Baba did not ask for water, and since it was winter when one wouldn't ordinarily develop much of a thirst, one day they did not fill the flask. On that very morning Baba felt thirsty! The women were very sorry but they were helpless. Just then Baba noticed a man fetching water from a well in a field that was by the road. Eruch, on Baba's indication, was quick to get water from him for Baba. Before quenching His thirst Baba called Eruch and placed His forehead on Eruch's feet. He was then instructed to repeat the same gesture before conveying the words of thanks to the farmer. Eruch did as he was told and it was tantamount to Baba bowing down to that person. He used Eruch as His proxy. Baba had on some occasions used this method of extending His help to needy persons through the medium of His disciples and close lovers.

This brings to mind an incident in the early 1940s. Baba had sent Eruch on special work to Poona. Previously someone had offered Baba a packet containing money. Baba did not wish to accept it. The man was pained and he begged Baba to accept the packet. Baba then asked Eruch to pick up the packet. He told him to give that sum to a needy family. He also instructed Eruch to keep the money with him whenever he went out visiting some town to fulfill the work Baba had entrusted him with. Eruch looked a bit puzzled but Baba assured him that He would inwardly guide him to whom the amount should be given. After some months Eruch went to Poona. It was summer. He felt thirsty and visited a sugar-cane juice stand. There were a lot of customers. A few of them, sitting beside Eruch, were loudly debating on the present day condition of human virtue. One stated, "Honesty has become a sin and dishonesty a merit." The topic arrested Eruch's attention. In support of this "modern" policy one among the group related a true story wherein an honest, pious person had to suffer much for his righteousness. The owner of the shop also participated in this discussion.

When these people left, Eruch approached the proprietor and requested him to tell him the name and address of that person. At first he hesitated. When Eruch convinced him that his elder brother (Baba) intended to help such people, he related the whole story and gave him the man's address. It seemed this man, now middle aged, lived in Bhor, a place about 40 kms. from Poona. Formerly he had held a good post in the Municipal Office. His uprightness and impartiality had thwarted the corrupt schemes of some Municipal members. Being in power, these individuals brought false charges against this employee and he was demoted to an ordinary octroi clerk. Because of his family he dared not leave the job as it was not easy to get another. Eruch knew Baba's instructions concerning such families and also the conditions under which some monetary help could be offered to them.

That same afternoon he left for Bhor. On reaching the town he found the residence of that oppressed person. He was not at home. His wife and two daughters, finding young Eruch wearing khaki pants and a shirt, with a hat in hand, took him to be a police officer. Were they to face a police inquiry? The women were afraid.

TERMINATION OF THE "GYPSY LIFE"

The girls became evasive and hesitated to divulge any real information about their father. Eruch with great skill explained the philanthropic work of his elder brother who lovingly helped respectable families in distress. Slowly and hesitatingly they revealed that the head of the family was at work and would not return till late evening. The wife explained that if the help was in the form of a loan they would not be able to pay even the interest, let alone the principal.

Eruch clarified that the money would be given as an unconditional act of grace — help from the Brother to a brother. "He will give and forget; you receive it and forget; that's all," concluded Eruch. To them this seemed unbelievable. Eruch during the conversation personally discovered the authenticity of the information he had casually overheard. He told the woman that he would return the next day with the money and requested her to ask her husband to remain at home. With this instruction he left for Poona to attend to other Baba work.

Karmic Debts and Dues

The following day Eruch met the head of the family at home. Surprise and suspense were writ on his face. Without wasting any time Eruch conveyed the purpose of his visit and asked for a jar of water. He asked the man to stand and washed his feet while the other family members looked on wide-eyed at both. After drying the feet with a towel he placed his forehead on the man's feet and handed over to him a sum of five hundred rupees saying, "Please accept this, on behalf of my elder brother, as *prasad* from God and oblige us." He did not disclose that the gift was from Meher Baba — God in human form. As the person counted the currency notes he was overjoyed and tears rolled down his cheeks. It was a most unexpected gift for him, amounting nearly to his year's salary.

To him this was indeed divine intervention for he

confided to Eruch that had he not received the message yesterday, his family members would not have seen him alive today! For in a mood of desperation, made especially bitter because of his helplessness in raising money for the marriage of his dear daughter, he had resolved to end his life. He saw no ray of hope, and had prayed to God most sincerely as his last resort. The clerk in a mood of great relief ended the conversation by saying, "After hearing about your loving request that I stay at home, I decided to postpone committing suicide to see what you would do. Now I firmly believe that God is not only compassionate but He never lets down those who sincerely pray to Him. May God bless your compassionate brother!"

The whole incident made Eruch quite happy for the money had reached a most needy person as Baba had wished. But he also wondered over the way everything had worked out, as if it had all been prearranged. He left the place without disclosing Meher Baba's identity. What would have happened had the person known that the help was from Baba? Would he have become one of His ardent lovers? Baba knows best. The *Avatar's* game of concealing and revealing His name depends upon the spiritual necessities of the situation. History proves that even the idea of God in human form is not palatable to some good-natured souls; they lack the closer connection essential for that personal touch and subsequent acceptance.

Baba, in a letter addressed to one of His disciples in England, Will Backett, had referred remotely to this subject. He wrote: "To some it is a greater help to know me through my disciples. Not all can understand the human side of God. It is more difficult for some to follow and obey God in the human form, due to preconceived ideas of God."* The God-Man knows perfectly how and when to bestow the conviction of accepting Him, on His terms, and the spontaneous love for

---

* *Meher Baba Journal* (November 1940), p. 34.

TERMINATION OF THE "GYPSY LIFE"

His Form that symbolizes His everlasting Formlessness.

The above incident brings out one more aspect of Baba's inner working. As I already mentioned, while accepting the money (which Eruch subsequently disposed of), Baba had remarked that He would spend the amount in His own way and time. The donor did not know the donee; the recipient did not know the contributor. The God-Man thus becomes the medium for the repaying and recovery of *karmic* debts and dues, whether in cash or kind. Baba's casual concern in the monetary affairs of His people was solely spiritual; it was to free them from intricate monetary ties. The *Avatar* as Infinite Consciousness works out innumerable problems on various levels. But these responses of unconditional compassion give rise to apparent contradictions and make the God-Man's life appear enigmatic. And this is all the more true with Baba's New Life. Has not Baba said, "Don't try to understand me. My depth is unfathomable. Just love me and you will know what you need to understand."

Baba's Slightest Displeasure Grieved the Companions

The march on foot continued from Haryana to Amroha, on to Ratangarh. During this walk, sometimes, soon after dawn, the companions would notice smoke rising above the huts. It was a sure sign that the women folk were busy preparing food. On some such occasions Baba would send Eruch to those distant huts for *bhiksha*, to rejoin Him again on the main road. Eruch's experiences of begging were pleasant and amusing too. He observed that those living in mansions were not large hearted, but the village folk readily offered something from what little they had. An owner of a sugar-cane crusher, for example, presented him with a *chatty* (a big earthen bowl), full of sugar-cane juice as *bhiksha*. Eruch had difficulty carrying it on his shoulders to Baba, who shared its contents with all. One person felt such affection for Eruch that he requested him not to beg and in return, though it seems unbelievable, he was ready to have Eruch as his son-in-law!

Aloba also had a heart-warming experience. At Benares, Baba had asked him to visit a slum of supposedly low caste people for *bhiksha*. In white *kafni* and green turban, Aloba, who has a fair Iranian skin, appeared very impressive. When this young "beggar" stood before a low roofed cottage and said aloud, "Mother, please give *bhiksha*," a woman in a faded *sari* appeared at the door. It had never occurred to her that such a distinguished looking beggar would be at her door! With a look of astonishment she said, "Do you mean what you say?" Aloba answered that he did. He requested her to give him any cooked food that she could willingly part with. Upon this the woman felt so happy that she carried Aloba's bowl into the hut and filled it to the brim with whatever she had. When Aloba returned to Nati Imli (Benares) where the party had camped, Baba mixed this *bhiksha* with the rest of the food and distributed it to all the companions. Baba always regarded *bhiksha* as something very special. At Ratangarh, Baba Himself went out begging with His bowl and satchel. God knows who were the hosts of honor of this Perfect Beggar!

It was January, a season of severe cold in northern India, but the companions had to pass some nights with no proper shelter. Some slept under the open skies, some under the trees or whatever other accommodation was possible. At Ratangarh, to ward off the cold, Nilu and Aloba slept near a temple, a bit away from the camp. One night Anna 104, who was the night watchman near Baba's tent, blew a whistle. According to Baba's standing instruction, when this emergency call was sounded, all had to gather near the tent. By the time the companions got there it was discovered that the alarm signal had been given by mistake; Anna had been frightened by what turned out to be nothing more than a shadow. In no time all returned to their "beds" perhaps cursing Anna for disturbing their sleep for nothing.

TERMINATION OF THE "GYPSY LIFE"

Next morning while joking about this funny incident Baba casually asked whether all had assembled at the call. Nilu and Aloba admitted that owing to their sound sleep they had failed to attend. Hearing this Baba seemed displeased and admonished them both severely. He conveyed, "If you can't be alert enough to follow my standing orders, why should you accompany me? You are good for nothing!" At times Baba would scold the *mandali* very harshly, over seemingly insignificant things. Though Aloba's violation of the order was unintentional, he, being sentimental by nature, took Baba's words to heart. He became emotionally disturbed, for the thought of displeasing Baba was unbearable to him. He did not express this openly to the others but he secretly thought of ending his life rather than be a burden to Baba. However much he tried, he could not ward off the black clouds of dejection.

In the middle of the night, he went to a nearby well and was on the point of committing suicide. At the last moment Baba's saving grace enlightened his heart. He started revising his decision. He thought, "Will the ending of my life lighten Baba's burden or worsen it? Perhaps there will be a police inquiry and what not. And all this will be a great nuisance to Baba in leading the New Life." He thus realized that his very attempt to be of some help to Baba would actually create obstacles in Baba's New Life. Aloba was at his wit's end. Finally he relinquished the idea of committing suicide and instead he slapped himself hard fifty times on each cheek. In a sullen mood he returned to his bed but he could not sleep at all. He did not tell his companions about his self-mortification, but his face did disclose a slight swelling over the cheeks. Next morning while sitting with the companions Baba again stressed the dire necessity of being alert to His standing orders, and He looked at Nilu and Aloba. It was one of Baba's practices that having delivered the reprimand there would follow a few words of cheer, a gentle pat or even a comforting hug.

On this occasion He embraced Nilu and Aloba and pardoned them for their unintentional failure. Then He asked the question, "Who didn't sleep last night?" Aloba raised his hand. Baba, the All-knowing One, did not ask him the reason but just conveyed, "Try to have a good sleep tonight." Aloba tried his best but he had to spend most of the time watching the stars. He feared that the next morning, Baba might again ask him about his sleep and He did. Aloba had to again reply that he hadn't slept. Without any further inquiry Baba ordered him to sleep well that night. Aloba had not yet recovered from the shock of disobeying Baba and he was worried about successfully carrying out this latest order. So he bound a scarf tightly over his eyes and kept it on from night till early morning. True, he did not succeed in having a sound sleep, but he did doze off occasionally. He had done his best and that was what Baba expected of him. Baba did not inquire again about his sleep. Baba's soothing embrace and His promise of forgiveness gradually comforted Aloba's heart and after a fortnight he succeeded in sleeping normally.

Sentimental disturbances need a considerable time to heal. For those who stayed with Baba, whether in the Old Life or in the New Life, it was agonizing to bear His slightest displeasure. They regarded each of Baba's actions as a selfless expression of Divinity — of Divine Wisdom in action. So they felt that to displease Baba meant offending God. Hence, whenever Baba got annoyed with any of the closer ones, it became very painful for that person and Aloba was no exception.

Here, I am reminded of an event that Aloba once told me. In the early days it was very difficult for Aloba to control the expression of his love for Baba. In the 1930s he once went to see Baba at Bombay, at Kaka Baria's house. Quite a crowd had gathered to have Baba's *darshan*. The moment Aloba saw Baba he tried to prostrate before Him but he suddenly fell like a log of wood with a big thud at Baba's feet and became oblivious of his surroundings. Baba's gentle touch helped him to regain his senses. As he got up beads of tears were trickling down his cheeks.

During this program, with a winsome smile, Baba offered him a big rose garland that He had on. After reaching home, Aloba dried all the flowers and leaves and turned these into powder. He consumed it by taking a pinch of it for about a year. Perhaps this *prasad* had strengthened Aloba in later years to bear the radiance of Baba's presence. To some this may sound strange but any spontaneous response of love, awakened by the grace of the God-Man is most sublime and holy. In the later years if Baba asked Aloba to do anything, he would be so quick and enthusiastic in complying to His wishes that Baba once jokingly gestured, "I have to be cautious in giving instructions to Aloba; he gives me a fright!"

Incredible Becomes Credible

After three day's stay at Ratangarh, the party marched on to Natore, Akbarabad and Hussainabad. From the last stop Baba sent Adi, Ghani and Babadas a day in advance by rail to Najibabad to make the necessary arrangements for lodging and boarding the companions. He asked them to try and conform with the following conditions:

1. To find a place where the men and women companions, with their carts, coach and animals, can stay for a period of three days. If possible, to arrange a hot bath for the whole party.

2. To make arrangements for the meals, lunch and supper and also morning and afternoon tea for the companions, to be provided in *bhiksha*!

3. To find someone who would voluntarily pay for the railway fare of the companions from Najibabad to Dehra Dun.

All these conditions appeared obviously incredible. One often wonders if such a life of "planned uncertainties" and incredible actualities has ever been lived by any Master! To some extent Baba's New Life seemed to have a Zen flavour about it. In this life those who accompanied Baba had to have implicit allegiance to His orders. So Adi with Babadas and Ghani left for Najibabad. Baba gave them enough money for their railway fare and transportation in town. But they were not permitted to spend a single pie from that amount for food or soft drinks. They were to carry food with them from Hussainabad. In case the stock of food was exhausted and they felt hungry they were to beg for it. During the journey by rail, the trio felt so hungry that by the time they reached Najibabad, they had finished all the food they had brought with them. They had not previously visited this place. They had no idea where to go or whom to contact and yet the work entrusted to them had to be completed soon for Baba was to arrive the next morning.

Adi approached the manager of a *dharmshala* who did not readily agree to allot them a room. The three cots practically filled their room and left very little space in between to move about in. Ghani was a heart patient and on that day, all of a sudden, he felt very weak and had to rest in bed, while Babadas, who had developed sciatic pain, expressed his inability to accompany Adi. So Adi hired a *tonga* and asked the driver to take him to prominent citizens of the town; he visited some but no one expressed any readiness to accede to any of the three conditions as laid down by Baba. Moreover, they were expected to fulfill these terms without inquiring much about the party's whereabouts!

After some time the *tongawala* politely asked Adi about the nature of his work. After learning Adi's intentions he remarked, "Why didn't you tell me about it in the beginning? That would have made this job easier." So saying, he took Adi to a cloth merchant named Makhanlal, a very generous person. Adi explained to him the three requirements of the Baba-party. Makhanlal frankly replied, "Don't depend on me for any residential arrangements. As for the meals and the tea I shall willingly do what you want me to. Be assured that I can manage it not only for three days but even for three weeks!" Adi was quite surprised with this answer and felt greatly relieved. A big problem was solved. He thanked Makhanlal and told him that he would tell him their place of residence after the party's arrival.

Now the *tongawala* became a guide. He led Adi to another merchant, a wholesale dealer in catechu (one of the substances used in the preparation of *pan*). It seemed that Adi's luck had changed. The businessman readily agreed to pay the railway fare of the companions going from Najibabad to Dehra Dun. He did not press Adi for the whereabouts of the party. The casual information that the group was on its way to the Kumbha Mela proved sufficient for his consent. He called his *munim*, accountant and cashier, and introduced him to Adi. He also directed him to go to the station and to purchase, when requested to, the railway tickets under Adi's direction. For this second surprise of the day, Adi heartily thanked that large-hearted person.

The problem of lodging was still unsolved. While going towards the station Adi noticed an unkempt garden. The gate was closed but not locked. There was a spacious platform inside which Adi thought could be used for spreading the bed rolls of the companions. Standing by the gate, he was just wondering who could be the owner of that place, when coincidentally a man accosted him and asked him about his interest in the garden. Adi told him that his party was on its way to Hardwar and the companions were expected to arrive at Najibabad the next morning and he was looking for a place where they could stay for three days. On hearing this the stranger replied, "If you think that the open space in the garden would serve your purpose you can occupy it during your stay. The garden belongs to me. Just open the gate and go in."

In a very cheerful mood Adi returned to the room in the *dharmshala* but felt sad to find Ghani and Babadas still unwell, resting in bed. They welcomed Adi's arrival and were glad to share the news. But they were feeling weak and especially hungry. Baba's instruction was not to spend money on food or soft drinks. They had no food left with which to appease their hunger. The only solution was to get some in *bhiksha*. But after his hard, active round through the city, Adi had no energy left for going out and begging.

The *tongawala* was still waiting to be paid. As Adi went out to pay him, he thought of a plan and asked the man, "How much money should I give you?" The man answered, "Ten rupees, sir." Adi replied, "You have really been of great help to me. I will be happy to pay you twenty rupees for your services." The person did not expect such a big sum. In that mood of surprise the *tongawala* said, "It is too much, sir. I am very thankful to you. What more can I do for you?" At this Adi gave him another surprise by saying, "If you really mean what you say, you may offer food to the three of us, as *bhiksha*." The man looked confused and said, "Sahib, what are you saying? I can arrange or pay for your meals at any hotel. Why do you talk of *bhiksha*? Are you joking?" Adi explained that he had meant exactly what he had said. In the end, though with much hesitation, the *tongawala* brought enough food for three people. Before receiving it Adi instructed him to say aloud that it was offered in *bhiksha*! The poor man, with an astounded look, somehow managed to mutter some words, saluted Adi with respect and left the companions to themselves!

The room in the *dharmshala* was rather stuffy. Yet the trio soon went to sleep. By midnight Ghani got up in his bed and began to grumble and groan, whispering to Adi about some trouble in his chest. He began to twist and contort his fingers. He was having a second heart attack, though a mild one. Ghani began to shiver with fright and pain. Adi, as he gaped at the strange scene, tried to be brave but he could not shake off his nagging fears. It was hard to find any medical aid in the dead of night. As a last resort he asked Ghani to remember Baba whole-heartedly; Baba — the only hope of their lives. Miraculously enough the pain lessened and he slowly resumed his sleep and began to snore. By sunrise he felt quite refreshed. Babadas's energy seemed also to have been restored. And according to Baba's instructions, the trio was ready at the entrance of the town to receive Him.

Najibabad to Dehra Dun

By late morning the party arrived. The first question Baba asked Adi was about the lodging facilities. Adi answered that he had arranged open air accommodations on a platform in an unkempt garden. This was not heartening news and Baba admonished Adi for not trying harder to secure a better place. Adi silently submitted to Baba's reprimand but in the course of their talk told Him about the food and the railway fare arrangements he had made. This pleased Baba. Baba's sneering and cheering were equally significant. They were meant to free His dear ones from the binding snares of "I did it." A Sanskrit line states, "Even the anger of the God-Man is verily a blessing." The party with its coach and carts was led to the garden. The animals were tethered and Pendu began his work of looking after the needs of these dumb creatures.

Adi went to the town to inform Makhanlal that lunch was needed. From the uncommon conditions, this merchant intuitively felt that the party he was going to entertain must be an extraordinary group. Within a few hours he brought a nice lunch to the garden. He was taken to Adi's "elder brother". In His flowing hair, Baba looked incredibly beautiful; His presence commanded respect. When Makhanlal saw Baba, he could not help but touch Baba's feet by way of offering his homage. Adi gathered that Baba disliked this devotional gesture of

Makhanlal. So in soft Gujarati Adi told Baba that he had not disclosed His identity to the visitor. A pleasing look reappeared on Baba's face and He gladly accepted the food. Upon request, He permitted Makhanlal's family to visit the garden the next day. For practical reasons, he was told that morning and afternoon tea were to be ordered from the railway station.

From the beginning, at Sarnath, villagers seemed to express special concern and curiosity about the two female donkeys named Sakhu and Thaku. Carrying them to Hardwar while on pilgrimage to the Kumbha Mela struck them as rather unusual. The donkeys too were not very co-operative in marching with the other animals. In the beginning poor Gustadjee, who was observing silence, had great difficulty in driving and dragging them on to the camp. Later Mani and Mehru by loading them with odd things somehow managed to get them moving ahead.

At Najibabad, Baba wished to sell them. Sadashiv (Patel) was asked to take them to the market. On the first day the customers offered a very low price and so they were brought back. The next day Baba fixed a price and instructed Sadashiv to settle the bargain with a person who would of himself propose to have both for that particular amount, not more, not less. On that day no one offered the "fixed price" and Sadashiv returned again unsuccessful. On the third day a customer approached Sadashiv and on his own offered exactly the price confirmed by Baba, and off went Sakhu and Thaku with their new master. Maybe Baba wished that this particular person should own them and so the deal was delayed by two days. A mysterious New Life dealing!

During this stay at Najibabad, when Adi was standing near the gate, a stranger approached him and began to inquire about the party's intentions. Adi tried to be evasive but the man persisted in asking rather pertinent questions. When Adi looked annoyed the person said, "Do you know that the garden where you are staying belongs to me? And you are trespassers." This was

TERMINATION OF THE "GYPSY LIFE"

startling news. Adi went inside and talked to Baba about the situation. He also told Baba how two days earlier another stranger whom he had coincidentally met there had gladly permitted the party to stay in the garden. Of course this had been done orally and nothing had been given in writing. Hearing this, without the least perturbation, Baba gestured that under such circumstances it was better that they leave the garden and move somewhere else.

Adi met the person and apologized for the intrusion. He also informed him of their intention to vacate that place then and there. With this answer the person calmed down so much that in turn he asked Adi to forgive him for being discourteous. He also told him that he would be pleased if the party continued their stay in the garden till they all left for Hardwar. Further he explained that he had lodged a case in the court for the legal possession of that garden and that the respondent might have deliberately misguided Adi. With this cordial conversation the forthcoming inconvenience was warded off and the whole matter ended well. Sharp thorns sometimes bring us closer to the flowers!

Owing to the physical strain of the New Life, Kaka Baria had a severe heart attack at Najibabad. Two days earlier Ghani too had had grievous chest trouble. In the gypsy life, comforts and discomforts changed hands in quick succession. The sickness of the companions made Baba confirm His former intention of travelling from Najibabad to Dehra Dun by railway. Some companions were to drive the carts and the coach (caravan) by the main road so as to reach the headquarters, at Manjri Mafi, within a week. With this decision, Baba asked Adi to inform in advance the wholesale dealer in catechu to arrange for the railway tickets. The date of departure was January 12. They were to board the Dun Express passing through Najibabad by early morning.

According to the agreement, the merchant had consented to hand over the tickets and not money to Adi. He had allotted this work to his *munim*. Accordingly he was instructed to be present at the station by 3 a.m. and he was. When the train arrived it was so crowded that it seemed impossible, especially for the women, to get into any of the third class compartments. Also they had a lot of luggage with them. Baba hurriedly sent Adi to contact the *munim* again and to ask him to pay the difference for transferring some third class tickets to first class. The *munim* on his own, without the prior consent of his master, agreed to this extra payment. The express train's halt at Najibabad was very short. It was not possible to contact the ticket inspector and get the due receipt for the change in class. So, informing the railway authorities and approximately calculating the money, the *munim* gave the necessary sum to Adi. The women somehow got into the first class compartment and most of the luggage was dumped in there.

The companions managed to get into other third class carriages. At the next halt, Baba learnt that instead of regular railway tickets Adi had accepted money to be remitted to the ticket checker. Accepting money was not allowed in the New Life. So Baba instructed Adi that after getting down at Dehra Dun his first duty would be to refund the balance, no matter how meager the amount, by money order to the person concerned. Baba was particular in matters, small or big alike, and Adi literally followed Baba's instructions.

To narrate every event of this gypsy phase is neither possible not practical. Nevertheless, the happenings at Najibabad mentioned above offer a glimpse of the inconceivable nature of the New Life led by Baba.

7

New Plans in the New Life

1950 — Part II

Kumar's First Meeting with Baba

PRIOR to the commencement of the New Life in 1949, Baba had called one of His lovers, Keki Desai, from Delhi to Meherabad. He was given the duty of purchasing a small piece of property near Dehra Dun in the name of Baba's companions. This was to be the headquarters for Baba's New Life activity. Keki was asked to build a small tenement on the plot and to dig a well nearby. The work did not go as scheduled and could not be completed prior to Baba's arrival. So Desai with the help of Harjeevan Lal, an advocate from Delhi, made a tentative arrangement for the party to stay in Mrs. Pratt's bungalow on its arrival in Dehra Dun. The women left for that place but Baba was requested to wait a while in the waiting room on the railway station for lunch.

The plot purchased for the headquarters was in a village called Manjri Mafi, now called Meher Mafi, a place a few kilometers from Dehra Dun. In the adjacent plot lived Shatrughna Kumar Ghildial, an agriculturist. Baba called him Kumar. Kaikobad Dastur, one of Baba's *mandali*, was sent in advance to Dehra Dun, in October 1949, to stay on the property at Manjri Mafi. Out of convenience Kumar was asked to arrange for Kaikobad's meals. Kumar also supervised the construction work on the site. Keki Nalawala, one of Baba's dear ones at Dehra Dun, was entrusted with the work of feeding the party on its arrival. He asked Kumar to see to this and Kumar willingly agreed to send food on Baba's arrival. The Baba-party reached Dehra Dun by 10 a.m. on January 12, 1950. It was time for food to be served to Baba. Kumar had come to the station to receive the Baba-party and Eruch asked him about the food. Kumar knew that Meher Baba whom he was meeting for the first time was very particular that one be punctual. So he left for his residence on his motor-bike and soon returned to the railway station with good hot food.

In the waiting room Eruch started serving food to Baba while Kumar was standing by His side. Baba casually asked him, "Why late?" Kumar told Him that it was due to a slight misunderstanding on the part of his dear wife, Subhadra. She thought that the guests would visit their residence for the meal. With the intention of serving them steaming hot food, especially rice, she was waiting for the guests to arrive. This was the cause of the delay.

Looking at Kumar, Baba held the morsel of rice in His fingers and expressed His happiness over its preparation. Baba was a good judge in appreciating different dishes and delicacies, their flavor, taste, everything. Very casually, He asked Kumar, "Did you feel perturbed over the delay? I hope you did not get angry with your wife." At this first meeting Kumar was deeply drawn to Baba but he did not expect Him to ask such a personal question. He, however, replied with an open mind, "Yes, Baba, I did feel annoyed that the food was not ready in time." With a suggestive smile Baba added, "Right. One should be particular about time. Did you admonish your wife for this? I hope you didn't hit her!" Kumar might have thought that this was rather meddling too much in his personal affairs but he could not help saying, "In that mood of impatience I did strike her, though very slightly." Hearing this, Baba pushed aside the plate of rice and with a grave look conveyed, "How can I eat food associated with ill feelings?"

The situation became tense. It was true that Kumar

had lost his temper over a petty affair but it was because of the inconvenience caused to his honorable guests. He conceded that he had treated his wife roughly but he didn't see why Baba should express such anxiety over someone else's personal affair. Yet Kumar did not express any annoyance but simply apologized for ill treating his wife. This was perhaps the first time in Kumar's life when he unhesitatingly expressed his regrets over a personal affair before someone he was meeting for the first time! In the course of time it was revealed to him that this "someone" was the Ancient One and the most intimate One to whom the life of each one was an open book. The above incident clearly shows that Baba expected men to treat women with respect and courtesy. In fact, "Respect Life" is one of Baba's teachings.

This verbal acknowledgement from Kumar did not seem to satisfy Baba. He told him that only if Kumar promised not to repeat any ungallant behavior towards his wife, Subhadra, would He (Baba) partake of the lunch that was served on the table. He even stretched out His hand inviting Kumar to promise Him. Things were moving so speedily that the rebellious spirit of Kumar had no chance to think about either complying or protesting against Baba's gesture. Kumar placed his hand in Baba's as a token of affirmation. Baba looked pleased and started eating the food. A little later He took a morsel from His plate and offering it to Kumar He indicated that Kumar should eat it. To the politically minded Kumar such an act of intimacy was totally new but he did not refuse it. In this meeting, by offering *prasad* to Kumar, Baba sowed the seed of a close relationship with him that was to blossom in the years to come. During different phases of Baba's work in the New Life a few families which would not have met Baba in the ordinary course of events coincidentally came into His contact and became His ardent devotees. The New Life brought Kumar's family into Baba's love orbit. Baba, the Eternal Fisherman, even now continues to adopt marvellous means for "netting" His lovers.

A Challenge to Mr. God!

The significance of Kumar's promise to Baba can rightly be understood only when correlated with an event that occurred some years earlier and another incident that took place years later. This backward and forward sweep in narration shall reveal, to some extent, the profundity of Baba's actions. Kumar as a youth belonged to a revolutionary party. Those were the days when India was ruled by the Britishers. Kumar, as a staunch patriot, wished to free his motherland, India, by any means whatsoever, including violence.

During the Second World War, India was still a British territory. Some Indians, especially those belonging to the revolutionary parties, concentrated on overthrowing the British regime and were jailed. Kumar was one of them. In the beginning Kumar was at the Devali (Rajasthan) Detention Camp, and later he was taken to the Bareilly Camp in Uttar Pradesh. The main political party, the Indian National Congress, co-operated with the British and so when the war was over, although independence was not granted, many political prisoners were released as a good will gesture. However, terrorists, who were regarded as a special threat, continued to be detained and Kumar was one of them. During his imprisonment Kumar noticed that some of his friends would regularly offer prayers to God. He would sarcastically laugh at those who prayed. He had no faith in prayer for he was a staunch atheist, not even an agnostic.

One evening he thought, "Should I experiment with prayers? With a clear conscience, why should I not test God's existence?" He wanted to be very concrete and practical in his experimentation. One evening he addressed the Impersonal Presence as follows: "O Mr. God, they say you are omnipresent and omnipotent. If you are really that, hear what I have to say. You can call it what you may, a request or a challenge. You know I am in jail for no fault of mine except my love for the motherland, India. I am a married person and my dear wife and family members have to suffer for nothing. If you are compassionate or at least reasonable, I sincerely agree to abide by the following terms: if you effect my release from the prison by tomorrow early morning, I shall accept your omnipresence. In that case I assure you I will dedicate the rest of my life in your service. This is my promise to you. And Mr. God, if I am freed any time after tomorrow morning, I shall treat this as chance or anything but your doing. In that case I shall not be bound to you or to anyone to keep this promise."

Kumar knew that the jail office opened daily at 10 a.m. and that the time to discharge any political prisoner could not be earlier than that. However, whatever Kumar said to himself or thought that evening was not done as a joke. In some remote corner of his being, he felt that something extraordinary might happen! "Nothing is impossible," he thought, "if the One I prayed to turns out to be the Omnipresent One, the Omnipotent One! After all, this is a sincere experiment and I must remain open and also take some risk." In that peculiar frame of mind Kumar even started collecting his belongings, in case Mr. God sympathetically considered his case! With a mixed feeling of belief and disbelief he was unable to get any sleep.

In the early hours, much before dawn, a jail officer visited Kumar's cell and handed him a note saying that he must be ready to leave the prison premises shortly. He was immediately taken to the office where the Superintendent was present. It was a surprise to Kumar to find him there at such an unusual hour! The Superintendent rifled through some papers and told Kumar that he would be immediately released from the Bareilly jail and that he would have to wait outside the gates to collect his railway warrant, etc. No more explanations were given. With this unexpected event Kumar felt greatly astonished. "What a humorist God must be!" he thought. It was still dark and Kumar waited on the road to receive his allowances and railway warrant. This release from prison before sunrise brought a change in Kumar's outlook towards life itself. The atheist became an agnostic. Yet he had no idea that instead of indirectly experiencing the Impersonal Presence of God, he was to meet God in human form, face to face and that in fact He had the greatest sense of humor.

Some years later Kumar came in close contact with Baba and had the unique fortune to stay with Him as one of the *mandali*. He would regale Baba by narrating interesting stories. In 1954 during Baba's stay at Satara, Kumar would accompany Baba in the mornings for a stroll. His duty was to carry an umbrella to hold over Baba when needed. One day, during a morning walk, all of a sudden Baba turned to Kumar and gestured, "Do you recall the promise that you gave me?" Kumar could not understand what Baba meant. In 1953 during Baba's Fiery Free Life, Kumar had been with Baba for a number of programs, in different parts of India. He had witnessed thousands of people clamoring for the *Avatar's darshan*. He had also been present when Baba had given instructions to some of His lovers. Kumar did not realize that Baba was referring to the particular promise he had given Him in the waiting room at Dehra Dun. So he said, "What promise, Baba?" Baba further gestured that He was referring to Kumar's promise to treat Subhadra (his wife) with respect. Kumar recollected the event and assured Baba that he was implicitly following Baba's instruction. Baba looked pleased and conveyed, "You have kept your promise. Good." And with a smile He added, "I also kept my promise!"

Through this statement Baba was indirectly indicating God's eternal promise to respond to prayers. For want of a definite context Kumar could not gather what Baba meant. At this point Baba gave him a meaningful look and all of a sudden Kumar remembered the challenge and the promise he had given to God when he was in prison at Bareilly. The incident which had remained dormant in his subconscious for about a decade vividly flashed before his mind, in complete detail. Emotion brightened Kumar's face and his eyes glistened as he related to Baba, for the first time, the whole story. At the end Baba smilingly gestured, "I am Mr. God! I am God in human form." What a mysterious and time penetrating corroboration! Later, whenever Kumar wrote letters to Baba, he would address Him as, "Dearest *Khuda* [God]." Baba's casual act of taking a promise from Kumar at Dehra Dun had such a profound context. Every act of the *Avatar* is immensely meaningful. Indeed, unfathomable is His *Lila*!

In Mrs. Pratt's Bungalow

Mehera, Mani, Goher and Mehru left the railway station at Dehra Dun in a car that took them to a fine bungalow owned by an English lady, Mrs. Pratt. This villa, in contrast to the unkempt premises at Najibabad, had a lovely garden with fine rows of rose bushes and many other flowering plants blossoming in the sun. There was a lovely lawn and a small orchard too. A fine view of the snowcapped Mussoorie hills offered a delightful sight. From whatever angle you looked it was a vision of sheer beauty. Inside, the bungalow was well furnished. It had a good kitchen with an electric stove. Hot water could be had at any time. They hadn't had a good bath for weeks, so this pleased them all the more. But in fact they were more concerned about Baba. They thought that now Baba's clothes could be washed. Lukewarm water could be made available to Him at any time. He will have a good rest here. They deeply felt that Baba's delicate body needed at least a few minimal comforts, especially after the strenuous gypsy life. They, however, did not know that their stay in the bungalow was to be for just a few days.

In one part of the bungalow stayed an English couple,

Mr. and Mrs. Angelo. Mr. Angelo had retired from the military service as an officer. But at that time he was depressed for he had lost his two sons in the Second World War. He was also suffering from some serious eye trouble and was gradually losing his sight. In addition, he didn't have enough money to return to England. Baba sent one of His companions to meet this couple. In the friendly talk that followed Mr. Angelo revealed his plight. Baba, hearing of this, later managed to offer him some financial help, through Dr. Donkin, to proceed to England. Maybe because of the Angelos' past connections Baba agreed to that very short stay in Mrs. Pratt's bungalow. It has been noticed that Baba's movements, with all their unexpected changes, have a sublime spiritual motivation.

"Baba *Jāne*" — Baba Alone Knows

Another incident during this stay which I find more astonishing is connected with Todi Singh and his first meeting with Baba. He was a cream contractor from Aligarh, a place over 100 kms. to the east of Delhi. In the second week of January, 1950, he had an unusual dream. In that fortuitous dream he saw Baba in His long white *sadra,* effulgence radiating from His beautiful body. Baba's flowing hair added spiritual splendor to His personality. Todi Singh was in rapture and felt blessed. He reverentially touched Baba's feet. In the dream, Baba lifted him up and He spoke, "At present I am at Dehra Dun. Come there. Serve me. Feed me." He had not heard of Meher Baba before. But the dream was so powerful that he felt convinced that the personality whom he had seen in the dream was his Master and he intuitively addressed the Master as "Baba." The dream awakened him from his slumber of worldliness. With eyes streaming with tears, he decided there and then to visit Dehra Dun to meet the Radiant One. It was a divine call.

Without knowing the name of his Master or His

address, he left for Dehra Dun. He carried with him a good many things, packets of butter, fruits, sweets, etc., to offer in "Baba's" service. He was confident he would definitely meet Him somewhere in that extensive city. A heart filled with love knows no doubts. Through some coincidences Todi Singh eventually reached the house of Keki Nalawala, 36 Lytton Road, Dehra Dun. He remembered that he had seen this particular house in his dream.

Overwhelmed with feeling he knocked at the door. Keki Nalawala came out to find a stranger requesting him to accept a cart load of things he had brought. Keki asked him his name and where he was from. He also asked him why and for whom he had brought these things. The only two words that Todi Singh repeatedly uttered, in answer to any and all questions, were, "Baba *Jāne*" meaning Baba alone knows. Baba's arrival in Dehra Dun had not been disclosed to Baba people except for a few very close ones connected with the activities of the New Life. Keki was forbidden to give anyone Baba's address. He wondered how Todi Singh, from a distant city, Aligarh, managed to visit his house just at the time when Baba was visiting Dehra Dun. With Baba's permission, however, Todi Singh was taken to Mrs. Pratt's bungalow.

As soon as Todi Singh saw Baba he became oblivious of the companions and everything else except Baba. He muttered to himself in Hindi, *"Wohi to hai, wohi to hai"* (He is the same One, He is the same One) whom he had seen in the dream. Instantaneous recognition, surprise and delight flashed across his face. Overpowered with blissful feelings he could not say anything but shed tears of joy. Anyone can imagine with what fervor he must have prostrated at Baba's feet! All those who witnessed this scene were greatly touched by Todi Singh's devotion. After he offered all the things he had brought, Baba made Todi Singh sit near Him and patted his back. In spite of the New Life phase, Baba did not object to Todi Singh's expression of love and reverence. It seemed Baba knew about Todi Singh's dream.

Referring to the packets of butter he had brought, Baba commenced teasing him, "You have brought the cans but who will cook the eatables in clarified butter [ghee]?" Todi Singh gladly and promptly replied, "I shall regard myself as most fortunate if you allow me to do that. I shall go and bring my wife and family here to render such service." Surprisingly enough, Baba unhesitatingly agreed to this proposal; it was an authentication of the instruction in the dream, "Serve me, feed me."

Todi Singh went back to Aligarh and within a few days returned to Dehra Dun with his wife, daughters and a son. By this time Baba had left Mrs. Pratt's bungalow. The whole party had moved to Mahant's *Kothi* (house) in Manjri Mafi. From January 16, through January 21, Todi Singh fed Baba and His companions with tasty vegetables and other nutritious food. He looked exceedingly happy while serving Baba. He would be seen shedding tears of joy for this unique opportunity to serve the Lord of love. He was so absorbed in Baba's love that he evinced little interest in obtaining any information about Baba's earlier life. To him Baba was God in human form and hence he never thought of getting any personal information about Baba's earlier life. He was blissfully content in meditating on Baba's form and mentally repeating His name. He would not talk much with the companions and if someone asked him anything about his family or business he would repeat his pet phrase, "Baba *Jāne*"

After a short stay, Baba instructed him to go back to Aligarh and this made him extremely sad. On the day of his departure he bowed down to everything and anything that Baba had touched. He was trying to suppress and swallow the grief of parting from the Divine Beloved. He strived to restrain his sobs but big bead-like tears often lingered at the edge of his eyes and subsequently flowed down his cheeks. Todi Singh's first stay with Baba turned him into a semi-*mast* and his eyes looked intoxicated with Baba's love. He intensely longed to be with Baba for a second time, and in response to his love, Baba called him again to Manjri Mafi in the summer of 1950. But this was just for a few hours in connection with a business Baba intended to start at Delhi.

Todi Singh had very devotedly served Baba and His companions with good food. This incident brings to mind the time when a person staying at Bhivandi (Maharashtra) lovingly arranged a light refreshment for Baba and His people. This event is also connected with a dream and a march on foot. In 1923 Baba was staying in Manzil-e-Meem at Dadar, Bombay. During this period, with some of His disciples and devotees, Baba left Bombay on foot for Sakori where Upasni Maharaj — one of His five Perfect Masters — was residing. Sakori was over 400 kms. from Bombay. After walking a distance of about 80 kms. the party reached Bhivandi.

Here, unexpectedly, the Baba-party was received by a government servant. He told Baba that he had been anxiously waiting to meet Him and asked Baba to kindly condescend to have some refreshment which he had arranged at the government rest house. Why? In the course of conversation he revealed that in the early hours of that morning — which are regarded as very auspicious — he had had a dream in which he saw a party of mendicants, headed by a saintly personality with flowing hair and a bright silvery halo. The leader was wearing a long white cloak. When he awoke, the memory of the dream was so vivid and convincing that he began to await his spiritual guest. And then he met Baba. Baba accepted this breakfast served with love. Whether in the Old Life or the New Life, Baba's work of drawing His dear ones to Him through love continued, and this heart orientation still goes on even more marvellously though Baba has dropped the cloak He had donned for some years.

The incidents connected with Major Angelo and Todi Singh have made Baba's short stay in Mrs. Pratt's bungalow much remembered by the companions.

Revising Some Conditions

Baba had cancelled the journey on foot from Najibabad to Hardwar and with some companions He left the city by train for Dehra Dun. It did not seem practical to ship the animals and the carts by rail. So it was decided that these should be led to the headquarters (Dehra Dun) on foot. Pendu was in charge of this work. The cavalcade of vehicles was led by Donkin; he held the reins of the *tonga* while Pendu was the "guard" driving the caravan. In between were the vehicles of Baidul, Sadashiv and Aloba. After journeying some miles, at one of the crossroads, some local people suggested a shorter route to Dehra Dun. With the intention of reaching the destination earlier, the companions forgot Baba's hint to journey by the highway. This detour ended up causing them great inconvenience and they ended up regretting their decision.

When the animals were crossing a rivulet, the caravan, owing to the heavy load it carried, stuck in a marsh patch. In spite of great efforts the bullocks could not get it out. At last, with the help of some villagers, they removed the muddy soil that lay near the wheels and instead spread some dried twigs and branches there. This plan worked well and the caravan was pulled out. The road ahead wound through a forest area infested with wild animals. To make up for lost time the party continued to drive. It was getting darker and darker, and the way led through a jungle. Fortunately they came across a rest house built for the forest officers. Circumstances forced them to break the journey. They lit a camp fire to keep the wild animals away. They tethered the bullocks and horses round the fire. At night it began to drizzle. So, with the permission of the caretaker, Donkin, Pendu and the others passed the night on the veranda of the rest house. At daybreak they resumed their journey. Because their short-cut had prolonged their trip, they didn't have enough food. So for the last two to three days, before reaching Manjri Mafi, the party had only one meal a day. Baba was residing in the Mahant's house as the erection of the huts on the plot purchased had not been completed.

After reaching Dehra Dun, Baba thought of revising some of the conditions to be followed by His companions in the New Life. They had passed through the phases of training, begging and gypsy life. These phases had offered Baba's companions some objective lessons which had helped them to understand their own weaknesses and merits. Everyone had enough experiences of the comforts and discomforts, the thrill and the fatigue of the New Life phase. This life had many surprises, some aggravating, some soothing. They had to pass through them all with considerable unconcern. Sometimes it was natural for them to feel depressed and dejected but they had to laugh it off soon — the sooner the better.

Baba, however, never lost his celebrated wit. His breezy humor would reach the hearts of the companions, whispering to them a message of cheer — to take things easy. But as the deeper levels of emotions were occasionally stirred up in the New Life, sometimes it was not easy for the companions to keep really cheerful. Baba's benign smile, however, helped them in such situations. During Baba's stay in Mrs. Pratt's bungalow, He had several open and intimate conversations with the companions, and by the time He left this house He had practically dictated the final draft of the revised conditions for the New Life. He seemed to be waiting only for the arrival of Pendu's party to disclose the three plans.

The Three Plans

On January 15, in a meeting with the companions, Baba communicated the following: "You all should honestly and whole-heartedly consider these three plans in their entirety. They are of my own making, and my own free will and accord, and you must accept one of them as being my wish and order. By accepting one of these plans collectively or individually, you will still remain one hundred per cent my companions in the New Life. These three plans make me free to live the New Life in my own way and yet keep you all one hundred per cent in the New Life. . . . These three plans are based on the labor phase. The other three phases of begging, gypsy and *langoti* life will be personally carried out by me alone or with the companions staying with me. . . . In these three plans, the two points of 'responsibility before God' and 'no spiritual benefit' stand good for ever." *

The first plan was divided into three independent units, A, B, and C: "A" was to be worked out collectively; "B" was to take effect either collectively or individually; "C" was to be undergone personally by any companion. The second plan allowed anyone to open any business he wanted or to take any job. The third plan called for total adherence to all the conditions agreed to in the meeting at Meherabad on August 31, 1949.

Here is the gist of some clauses included in these three plans. Plan I-A (Collective): All the companions would co-operate and help one another in adjusting things each doing his best to keep the plan going. The earnings of the companions from their jobs, farming or business, would belong collectively to all the members. Baba would have nothing to do with money or accounts. In their spare time the companions could come together for casual conversation with Baba or entertain Him with music and songs. This Plan I-A, in a sense, offered full freedom to Baba for His work and also enough latitude for the companions. If, instead of all, only a few agreed to act according to the clauses mentioned above, such a small group was classified by Baba under I-B. Baba proposed to keep the carts, *tongas* and animals

---

* *Circular NL* 3, issued on 10-2-1950.

at the disposal of this batch.

In Plan I-C (individual) Baba permitted the companions to lead the New Life at their place of residence. Some of the terms in connection with this option were the same as in I-A. Such a one was allowed to earn money by taking a job or opening a business. After keeping the money necessary to support himself he was to send the balance for those who would decide to stay with Baba. He had, however, to give up hope of ever being in Baba's *sahavas* again. Those in this plan were also prohibited from having any correspondence with Baba of their own.

Plan II was similar to Plan I-C (Individual) in many respects. The companion who chose this plan could go to any place other than the one he had been residing in, in the Old Life. Of course he had to follow a few conditions laid down by Baba. In one of the clauses of Plan II the following was stated: "No duties will be allotted to you by me [Baba]... and you can lead an absolutely independent life...." Because of this "independence" offered by Baba no one dared to join Plan II. Who would ever want to free himself from the privilege of being guided by the God-Man? Plan III was for those who were thoroughly prepared to accept the original conditions circulated during the first meeting about the New Life in Meherabad hall.

The necessary copies of these three plans as suggested by Baba were mimeographed. On January 21, He called another meeting of the companions and everyone received a copy of these plans. They were to study seriously all the conditions before deciding to join any plan. They were to meet again after two or three days when everyone had to convey his decision to Baba. It turned out that Plan I-A was dropped since it required unanimous approval. Donkin came forward to work out I-B. Kaka and Gustadjee joined him and Donkin shouldered responsibility for them. Adi, Ghani, Babadas and Anna 104 wished to abide by I-C. No one thought of joining Plan II.

The remaining eight companions, Nilu, Pendu, Baidul, Eruch, Murli, Vishnu, Sadashiv (Patel) and Aloba decided to accept Plan III *in toto*. All the companions had to affirm their decision by taking an oath before God — the Impersonal and the All-knowing. Each one had to follow most sincerely and honestly all the clauses mentioned in the plan of his choice. Some of the standing instructions mentioned in all the plans were: not to touch any woman with lustful intention; not to discuss politics; not to criticize anyone; not to tell lies; not to create situations (directly or indirectly) that would invite homage and above all to remain cheerful, thus maintaining the "Don't worry and expect nothing" attitude. It seems that anyone who wishes to be Baba's companion in His eternal New Life has to lead it voluntarily and cheerfully, but the aforementioned injunctions have to be observed as well. Baba expected the companions to remain intrinsically detached from any activity, though in the thick of it. Baba's New Life phase was a symbolic demonstration of a life of unreservedly committing oneself to the Divine Will.

To be in the company of the God-Man and to serve Him to His selfless satisfaction was not an easy-going affair. Those who stayed close to Baba had to pass, time and again, through "fires". Sometimes the mind would rebel and the heart would be in low spirits, but the God-Man, being infinitely skillful, played with each of His companions a thrilling game to its farthest limits. To illustrate how in the lives of Baba's dear ones — whether in the Old Life or the New Life — the emotional crises were initiated and resolved, I quote below a letter from Baba sent in the early 1930s to Quentin Todd, one of His lovers from England. Baba dictated:

> I have all your loving letters and know how you long to be of service to me. You have been and will be still more, dear boy. Why should you feel yourself "unworthy" and that I am pulling on [putting up] with you and so on? For I love you *as you are*. You

have a nice, frank, receptive heart that can and does love, in spite of the constant reverses, as you say, from the head. And that is all I want.

When one completely depends on me and leaves things to me as you have, I see that the reverses from the head gradually give way. I will order everything for the best, as you desire. The way you feel, your own weaknesses open your way and lead you to rise above them. They all have to come out once and the sooner the better. It is because of this that you feel as you do, but you, dear Todd, needn't at all worry. For it is all for the better. Things are being stirred up and they are all brought out to prepare you for the greater future that is to be yours. Love me more, and that will take care of other things, consuming all in its flame, till nothing but pure Love Divine remains. That is all I want you to do, more and more.

The merits or the weaknesses of His followers and lovers did not matter much to Baba. He was and is concerned with their total and willing surrender to Him. He is ready to accept anyone *as he is*. In the New Life Baba often stirred up the companions' emotions and then helped them to face their weaknesses. The plans and the many changes in the external aspect of the New Life were made by Baba to keep the spirit of the New Life intact while at the same time accommodating the natural weaknesses and proclivities of His companions. After all, He is the Compassionate Companion!

8

Stay at Motichur

1950 — Part III

New Life Phase; A Spiritual Emergency

ON January 25, Adi, Ghani, Babadas and Anna 104, having accepted Plan I-C, left Dehra Dun for their respective places. As they embraced each other farewell, tears sparkled in the eyes of the companions. According to the New Life conditions, they were not to meet each other again in the future. Donkin, as per Plan I-B, was to be a medical practitioner at Dehra Dun. He had willingly agreed to shoulder the responsibility of providing for Kaka, who was still unwell, and also for Gustadjee who was too old to get any job. For the group of eight who were in Plan III, Baba appointed Vishnu as their manager for the household affairs. Obedience to Baba's orders continued to be of paramount importance. It should, however, be noted that obeying Baba, the God-Man, was qualitatively different from obeying anyone else, however great.

The New Life phase appears to some as a period of spiritual emergency. Accompanying Baba in this phase was not compulsory, but from those who decided to be His companions, He expected implicit obedience and unfailing loyalty. Whether through planned journeys or aimless wanderings, reasonable doings or reasonless dealings, Baba's work of awakening the hearts, continued on different planes of consciousness to reveal in time to come the Divinity latent in each. Baba's life was Divinity in action. So the fortunate ones who were given the option of participating in His work had to obey the God-Man whole-heartedly.

STAY AT MOTICHUR

In one of the meetings Baba had clearly stated, "You may believe that I am the *Avatar*, God, Devil or anything or anyone you please, but you must understand that although I may live among you as if I were your brother or friend, I will in fact be your Master whom you must obey absolutely." At the end of the meeting Baba pointed out that from March 1, He expected complete obedience from those who had accepted Plan III. Was the Compassionate One becoming the Merciless One? After studying the methods that Baba used in His relationship with the companions, one would in fairness agree that He had beautifully blended the ways of Marpa and Milarepa, the Tibetan Masters, in an incredible integrity. Baba's orders and statements were not irrational but super-rational, beyond the grasp of the human mind.

In the midst of these serious discussions, an amusing incident occurred which provided a little fun. Anna 104 of Plan I-C while leaving Dehra Dun unwittingly carried Gustadjee's baggage instead of his own. That bag contained Gustadjee's warm clothing and other necessary things. Dear old Gustadjee who was observing silence tried to express his inconvenience and displeasure through gestures to all, including Baba. This aroused sympathy for Gustadjee who was going to suffer the discomforts of the severe cold. Gustadjee through his lively gestures and irrepressible facial expressions had so many times entertained Baba with humorous and funny stories, but this time he himself had to play the tragedian. This event, however, ended happily for after some days Gustadjee's belongings were collected and sent back to Dehra Dun.

When Has God to Worry?

In the next meeting, Donkin was asked by Baba to visit Bombay to purchase some medical appliances and surgical instruments for his dispensary at Dehra Dun. While returning he was instructed to bring a typewriter for Mani and some sewing material and aids. Baba had previously hinted that the women accompanying Him might be asked to take jobs or earn money by doing odd work like stitching clothes. In those days Mani and Mehru were not keeping well; it was tiresome for them to attend to the work in the kitchen. So Baba asked Donkin to meet Naja at Nariman's place in Bombay and, if she was willing, to invite her for a stay at Manjri Mafi. This was not an order from Baba, but it was a choice given to her. The only condition she had to observe strictly was that she was not to refer to any incident or person from the good Old Life. In Mahant's house people were not allowed to meet Baba, but He was easily available to the family members of Nalawala and Kumar (Ghildial). They were lucky people indeed to be in Baba's physical presence when His dearest disciples and devotees were not allowed to have even a glimpse of Him.

Kumar had newly come into Baba's contact, but Kaikobad (Keki) and Freiny Nalawala had met Baba a few years before. In April 1941, when Baba was staying in Dalanwala on New Road, Keki had Baba's auspicious and heart warming *darshan*. Later in 1946 he helped Papa Jessawala find a quiet bungalow near Dehra Dun for Baba's special spiritual work. It was located about five kms. away from the city, in a village called Niranjanpur. Baba stayed here with a group of His disciples for about eight months. Baba wished to remain undisturbed, so His stay at Niranjanpur remained a closely guarded secret. In *The Wayfarers,* an account of Baba's work with the God-intoxicated souls, Niranjanpur was only referred to as a "place of seclusion".

Yet, on some mornings, Baba allowed Keki to see Him. As a way of accepting the whole-hearted services that he had rendered, Baba consented one day to have a simple meal of rice, *dal* and *chutney* at his home in Dehra Dun. Baba instructed that the lunch should be prepared by his wife Freiny in complete silence. It was an indirect opportunity given to her for remembering

Him whole-heartedly. This indirectly helped her clean and purify her mind and heart to receive the radiance of Baba's love. This was her first unforgettable meeting with Baba. It was during this visit that their son Naosherwan,* a two month old baby had the unique fortune to rest in Baba's lap. A blessed family!

This breeze of compassion continued to blow towards this lucky group even in the New Life. In 1950 Baba paid another visit to their house. He lovingly inquired about each. Freiny told Baba that Keki unnecessarily worried himself sick about certain things in life. Baba flashed a carefree smile and in simple words gave some profound advice: "If you worry about yourself, God does not worry about you. And why should He? If you stop worrying, God has to begin to worry for you. Remember Him whole-heartedly; leave your worrying to Him and be free to remain cheerful." Had not Baba been in the New Life, He would have replaced the word God with Baba. For, a year later, in a similar situation, He authoritatively conveyed, "Whenever my lovers one-pointedly call on me, I dare not ignore them."

All residing in Mahant's house were kept busy with some work. Baba gave different duties and instructions to different companions. He told Pendu and Vishnu to sell the vehicles and animals. The money received in this transaction was to be handed over to Donkin to work out Plan I-B. The white horse was not to be sold. It was received in *bhiksha* from Khare. So the horse was given to Donkin. He was free to keep it or give it away to anyone. The four bullocks worth 2,500 rupees were donated by the women companions to an institution called *Nanhi Duniya,* Children's World.** Baba told the Principal that the work done by creating opportunities

---

* Naosherwan Anzar, the editor of *Glow International*.
** Mani, Baba's sister, once said, "What can I say about children? If Baba hadn't loved children so much, He wouldn't have loved us so much! Wherever Baba was and where there were any children, they somehow always came to Him. I remember in 1952 on the plane to the U.S. — of course, nobody knew who Baba was — the

in which good qualities in the hearts of innocent children blossom and flower, was and is always noble and commendable in "the eyes of God." Baba encouraged him to carry on with this meritorious work in a spirit of selfless service, leaving the results to the All-knowing Will of God. Nalawala and Eruch Mistry (Elcha) were directed to find a suitable flat in the city for Donkin to use as his dispensary. Eruch (Jessawala) was often sent to see Kumar to find out how the construction of the hut, the extension of the old building and the newly dug well, on the Hardwar property, were coming along.

Baba's Game of Love

By February 10, Donkin returned from Bombay to Dehra Dun with Naja, Baba's cousin and "master cook". Naja knew Baba's likes and dislikes about food better than anyone else. Her services became indispensable, especially after the two accidents. The day she arrived at Manjri Mafi, Baba entrusted her with the work of preparing *rava* for His forthcoming birthday. According to the Zoroastrian calendar it fell on February 12. On this day it was very chilly in the morning. When Baba was sitting with the companions, He, as usual, asked them about their sleep and the weather. To this Nilu replied that he could not sleep and added, "It's cold, cold, cold."* This evoked Baba's sporadic mood to compose a short stanza. He dictated:

We are neither young or old,
Our everything is sold,
Neither we have silver or gold
There is New Life all told.

---

children would walk down the aisle and constantly stop where Baba was sitting and caress His coat or look up at him. And their mothers would be after them, 'Don't disturb that gentleman!' Then Baba would smile, the mothers would relax and forget to scold.... I think they wanted to come and caress Baba too!" (Laughter.) *The Awakener.* Vol. XIII, Nos, 1 & 2, p. 77.

STAY AT MOTICHUR

To this Donkin added,
  From March, it will unfold.
And Baba concluded,
  For those who are real bold,
  Conditions hundred per cent to hold.*

Was it Baba's birthday message to the companions to be buoyant and bold, in spite of the grim and cold "weather"— the discomforts of the New Life?**

Some families were invited to participate in the informal celebration of Baba's birthday. Baba distributed *rava* and *prasad* to the visitors. In addition He also gave good *bhajias* to all, followed by tea. Those who attended this program still remember with great delight and reverence this pleasant occasion, when they received delicious *prasad* at Baba's hands. To commemorate this festive occasion they continue to share *rava* with their friends and Baba people on their Beloved's birthday.

The next day Donkin left Manjri Mafi for Dehra Dun in connection with the dispensary work. Sadashiv Patel left for Poona. He was to help Arrangementwallas, Nariman and Meherjee, in some legal matters. Manek Mehta of Bombay had been given the option of joining Baba's New Life as one of His companions from January 1951. In spite of this concession he had not let Baba know his decision. So by the end of January, Baba sent a letter to him through Adi, but once more no reply was received. A reminder was then sent which too remained unanswered. Eventually it turned out that Manek who had composed devotional songs on Baba's Divinity, had been deluded by *maya's* trick and lost the chance to be with Baba in the New Life. Such incidents

---
* *Circular NL* 4. issued on 7-3-1950.
** To a follower who was dejected, Baba once conveyed, "If you don't want to be old before your time be cheerful in deed and word and in appearance — most of all in appearance. It is a divine art to look cheerful, it helps others."

reveal how, in spite of having had Baba's close *darshan* and intimate contact, it was possible, in the case of some, not to realize how precious these opportunities were! Baba had said, "I am most slippery." On the other hand we also come across some Baba people who had only casually heard of Him or had caught a glimpse of Him but were impatient to leave all and to follow Him with unfailing fidelity, and Baba had to order them to wait. No one is to be blamed. Baba, the Infinite One, alone knows the "moves" He plays through us all in His Game of Love.

"Big Mistake" Remains a Secret

From the second half of February the companions had tea and *chapatis* for breakfast at 5 a.m. Soon after Baba would visit them. The weather during the month was unpredictable and so were Baba's moods. It all depended on the spiritual work He was engaged in. Sometimes, Baba would be in a pensive mood or get upset over ordinary matters. There were occasions when He would ask a few of the companions to pinch His ears for losing His temper. Though it happened rarely, there arose a few situations where under some pretext He would ask someone to slap Him. This order had to be obeyed immediately. What an incredible companionship!

It was not a life meant for the weak-kneed. Once Baba had quoted a couplet of Hafiz wherein the poet stated that the aspiration for God-realization is in itself an indication of stark madness! One could however say that to stay with the God-Man during His different phases of work such madness was essential. Only those who, with His grace, surrendered their intellect to Him and became devotedly pliable, could stay with Him. Spiritual blossoming depends upon the showering of the Master's compassion from beginning to end. For most of the time Baba was very considerate about His Companions' faults and was forgiving. After an early supper, He would generally spend half an hour with them in light talk. To find Baba in a really cheerful mood was an occasion of great delight to all. During such moments He would look exquisitely graceful, His face beaming with an extraordinary glow about it.

A few days earlier Baba had sent one of the companions to visit Hardwar and bring back water in two jars from the holy Ganges. In the third week of February, He instructed Baidul to empty these jars in the current of the Ganges at Rishikesh, to refill them and to bring them back to Manjri Mafi. Was Baba symbolically sanctifying the flow of the Ganges from Rishikesh to Hardwar, for the thousands of *sadhus* and pilgrims who were expected to visit these places of pilgrimage, to have a dip in the river, during the Kumbha Mela? On Baidul's arrival, Baba used water from one of the jars for His bath. Water in the second jar was to be utilized on March 1, the day of the new phase in Baba's New Life.

Nalawala and Elcha Mistry were successful in securing a place at Dehra Dun for Donkin's dispensary and the necessary papers for leasing it were executed. Baba agreed to visit the dispensary on its opening day. Murli, one of the companions, was asked to give homeopathic treatment to the patients coming from the nearby villages. One day, while returning on foot from Mahant's house, an old woman approached Baba. Her son was ill in bed. He had vomited many times and was also suffering from acute dysentery. On Baba's instruction Nilu gave free medical treatment to him. There was a rapid recovery and within a few days the young man visited Baba's residence and profusely thanked Nilu. Even in the New Life, Baba's loving concern for the sick and the poor and the afflicted, whom He incidentally met, continued.

Baba had given a special interview to Norina and Elizabeth in the first week of August, 1949. At that time He had promised Elizabeth that He would visit the West. In connection with this matter, He directed Donkin to write a letter to Elizabeth inquiring about the possibility of His visiting the States in the near future. The conditions of this visit were previously explained to her. Adi, who had accepted Plan I-C and had returned to Ahmednagar, sent one thousand rupees to be used for the requirements of the companions. While strictly adhering to the conditions of the plan he had saved this amount from the insurance business he had entered on his return from Dehra Dun. This pleased Baba and He sent an encouraging telegram to Adi.

In view of the thousands of *sadhus, sanyasis, nangas* and *bairagis* who were expected to visit Hardwar in large numbers for the Kumbha Mela, Baba decided to shift His headquarters temporarily to Motichur. It was a village about five kms. from Hardwar. From this place it seemed convenient for Him to visit the premises of the Kumbha congregation. On March 1, Baba asked for a small pair of scissors and cut a lock of hair from the head of each companion. Then He had a bath with water from the Ganges brought by Baidul. He gave no explanation about this particular "hair cut and bath" and no one asked Him about it. On March 3, Baba was to leave for Motichur with Pendu, Eruch, Baidul, Gustadjee, Murli and Aloba. Vishnu and Nilu were to stay at Manjri Mafi to look after the women companions and also to take care of Kaka who was still unwell.

In the morning, Baba asked the companions under Plan III to wash their feet; He then placed His forehead on the feet of each. He apologized to them in case He had hurt their feelings. Simultaneously He pardoned them all for the mistakes committed by them, if any. At the end He conveyed the following: "During the period between October 16, 1949 and March 1, 1950 I have committed consciously and deliberately one big mistake and I want the companions to kick me so that God forgives me." Then He gestured to the companions to obey His order. You can imagine the plight of those who had to kick hard the Beloved of their own hearts, for whom they were ready to lay down their very lives most willingly. Baba never disclosed, even in the later years, what this "big mistake" was for which He underwent that submissive act of chastisement.

The Origin of the Kumbha Mela

As was planned, Baba, with a few companions, left for Motichur by the noon train. The rest set out in a bullock cart with the necessary luggage piled in it. Baba liked the house at Motichur. According to Baba's instructions, in one of the rooms a hut was erected with a thatched roof. Outside the room a small tent was also pitched. Baba was to be in seclusion in this hut. In the evening He distributed *chapatis* and cooked vegetables to the companions. This was their simple supper. Baba wanted Jal S., His younger brother, to stay with Him at Motichur. So some days back a letter had been mailed to Jal. However, Jal expressed His inability to join the Baba-party, owing to his illness. The life at Motichur was austere and the diet frugal. In the morning, the companions had tea with a little milk, while in the afternoon it was without milk. The companions and Baba had only one plain meal a day. Baba Himself swept His room, washed His clothes and cleaned the pots He used. Was Baba indirectly contacting, through these austerities, the spiritually minded people who were also leading disciplined lives and were due to arrive for the Kumbha Mela? On March 7, Baba walked to Bhimagoda. Eruch, Baidul and the other companions were asked to collect information about the different camps of the *sadhus* and the *mahatmas* and their expected arrival dates at Hardwar.

There is an interesting mythological (*Pauranic*) background to this fair. It is believed that when the ocean was churned by the *devas* (gods) and *asuras* (demons), fourteen mysterious things came out of it. Next to the last but one was a jar of deadly poison which Shiva drank. Then there came out the *Kumbha* of *Amrit* (pitcher of Nectar) that had a quality of bestowing immortality. The *asuras* wanted to possess this pitcher while the *devas* wanted to carry it to the heavens. During this dispute and subsequent pursuit the bearer of this pitcher, while rushing to heaven unwittingly spilled a few drops of nectar in the river beds at four places — Nasik, Ujjain, Allahabad and Hardwar. Therefore the Kumbha Festival is held at these four places. The exact dates of the fair are connected with certain astronomical positions. Anyway, March 1950 served as a good opportunity for Baba to bless thousands of pilgrims and hundreds of *sadhus* and *mahatmas* with His divine physical presence.

Baba wished to begin His work at Hardwar on March 15. Prior to this, He planned to visit Rishikesh and accordingly He paid visits to the Kailas and Mangal Ashrams. He also contacted many aspirants residing in different cottages, huts and caves. He either touched their feet with His hands or, in some cases, placed His forehead on them. In the Old Life, the disciples accompanying Baba were not allowed to witness Him touching or bowing down either to the *masts* or spiritually advanced souls. From the New Life onwards there was no ban on watching Baba pay His respects to the *masts* or to the poor.

Unburdening an Old Life Burden

After a week's stay at Motichur, Baba returned to Manjri Mafi for two days. He was pleased to find Kaka in good health. Coincidentally, Donkin too, had come from Dehra Dun and met Baba. In the course of the conversation, he brought to Baba's notice the contents of a letter he had received from Ghani (Ganoba). Baba did not approve much of Ghani's way of indirectly calling Baba's attention to his problems concerning the Lonavla property. It seems, however, that Baba had a soft corner in His heart for His childhood chum, Ghani. The next day He sent a letter to the Arrangementwallas explaining the circumstances which had made Him consider Ghani's case rather differently. In the circular to be issued He Himself begged His Old Life disciples and devotees to help Him discharge the debt, which He treated as an Old Life burden. This debt, which in fact was one only because Baba had so declared it, was thus fully repaid.

In Meher Baba's life receiving and disbursing money was a significant activity. He had turned down grand offers and sometimes asked for small sums. His acceptance and refusal of money was qualitatively different from that of an ordinary man. He neither desired to possess money nor was opposed to it. He used it for the spiritual upliftment of the *masts* and to fulfill the material needs of the poor. Baba's love for His lovers was so great that sometimes, overlooking their weaknesses, He went out of the way to help them monetarily by begging money from His other loved ones.

As far as I recall, Meher Baba had once stated that that person is really rich who knows how to spend his wealth well — irrespective of its extent. One who hoards money with selfish ends (however small or large the amount may be) is really poor. Through the above mentioned circular, it was as if Baba had offered His dear ones a chance to be "really rich". Ghani was given the sum fixed by Baba and not a rupee more was accepted by the Arrangementwallas for this specific purpose. Call this method what you may, a benediction or bait, but this too was one of Baba's ways of winning His dear ones for their spiritual benefit. In one of the Discourses* Meher Baba has explained why the Master tolerates the failings of the disciples with unfailing patience and subsequently how these lapses are used to awaken them to higher aspects of living.

What Sort of *Bhagwan* Is He?

Baba was at Motichur. One day while having His

---

* Meher Baba, *Discourses*, Vol. II. The Ways of the Masters.

meal, He remarked that the rice was not cooked well. A little later He expressed regret about this grumbling and asked one of the companions to pinch His ears. Having become man, Baba was demonstrating how easily men lose their temper over trifles. Having His ear pinched was Baba's way of reminding His companions to become aware of their ordinary actions. Otherwise, why would Baba have complained about the rice, for in the past He had immensely enjoyed eating hard, stale pieces of bread given Him by the *masts*!

Baba's visits to different *ashrams* in Hardwar and Rishikesh continued. This particular area is typically oriental, evocative of the ancient spiritual traditions. Under the skies of these twin places, aspirants for centuries have longed and nourished noble, selfless feelings while their minds pondered deeply over the significance of life and the timeless Reality. Unfortunately, at present, that glorious past is being exploited by hypocrites. Some seem to don ochre colored robes for everything but God and it is difficult to differentiate between real and false *gurus*. During His wanderings, the All-knowing Master, Baba, as He moved through these people, knew the spiritual worth of each. In 1950, Baba contacted over ten thousand *sadhus* and *sanyasis* during the Kumbha Mela. The spiritual significance of these contacts was not revealed to those who were with Him. The outward expression of these contacts was so common that those who accompanied Him had no idea of the "give and take" which transpired on the inner levels of consciousness. The following incident that took place earlier in this area reveals the depth of Baba's contacts with *sadhus, yogis, masts* and saints.

In 1946, Baba was staying at Niranjanpur, a suburb of Dehra Dun. Krishna* from Kerala, was staying with Him as a night watchman. One night, while quietly

---

* Krishna (not Krishnajee), a boy brought to Baba by His brother Jal at Bangalore, in 1939. Later, he served Baba as a night-watchman but was sent back home before Baba started for the New Life in 1949.

sitting by the door, he was badly bitten by mosquitoes. He very lightly slapped his legs to get rid of them, but that little sound disturbed Baba's sleep, and He called Krishna near Him. He began to admonish him for disturbing His sleep. Krishna wanted to complain about the mosquito bites, but Baba ignored his words and dismissed him with an instruction to be more careful in his duty. Krishna felt annoyed with the way Baba had treated him. As he returned to his seat, Satan seemed to possess him. In that mood of irritation he began to think, "Baba is quite comfortable in the mosquito net but can He not realize my inconvenience? He says He is God in human form, but has no pity for those who serve Him. What sort of *Bhagwan* [God] is He?" He was restless throughout the night.

The night watchman was usually allowed to rest and sleep till late in the morning after his night duty. But that night Baba unexpectedly instructed Krishna to accompany Him during His visit to Hardwar, early next morning. Krishna had to forego his rest and sleep for he was also ordered to arrange for transportation to Hardwar. On reaching Hardwar, Baba disclosed that He had it in mind to contact only a *mast* type *yogi* who for years had been in the habit of standing on one of his legs. For most of this time he had been observing silence. He had some followers who revered him greatly. Yet when Baba arrived none of them were present. No sooner did Baba approach him than the *mast* became ecstatic, folded his hands and with tears of joy streaming down his cheeks, broke his silence saying, "You are *Bhagwan*, God in human form. O God! I was waiting for you for years and at last you have come. How blessed am I!" Krishna, as he heard these sentences, felt that this visit was in answer to the disbelief he had entertained the previous night. Baba did not stay any longer with the *mast* but quickly returned to Dehra Dun.

That night, though feeling drowsy, Krishna tried his best to be diligent in his duty, thinking that he would have a long rest the next day. But just when he was leaving Baba's room after his night watch was over, Baba ordered him again to visit Hardwar in the morning and to meet that *yogi* like *mast* for a second time. He was to go alone. Krishna was on the verge of putting forth the excuse that he was too exhausted, but the words of the *yogi* ringing in his ears restrained him from saying anything.

When Krishna reached Hardwar he noticed that a crowd had gathered around the *yogi*. They had assembled there for his last *darshan* as he had breathed his last. The bliss of meeting the *Avatar* can be so shattering that sometimes, even an advanced soul cannot contain it. Krishna noticed that this *mast's* (*yogi's*) face looked blissfully calm, radiating peace all around. His last words to his devotees were, "I met *Bhagwan*, face to face and He blessed me. My life's desire is fulfilled." Disclosing this secret in a very cheerful mood he dropped his body. It dawned on Krishna that as he had doubted Baba's Godhood, He, in His love for those who serve Him, had provided direct evidence of His All-knowing nature through this episode. Krishna realized how blessed he was for the opportunity to wait on Baba as a night watchman! The mosquito bites now seemed insignificant. He thought to himself, "What an incredible *Bhagwan* is Baba!" Such incidents, whether in the Old or the New Life, occasionally revealed the significance of Baba's contacts with the *masts* and other spiritually advanced souls.*

"I Give Love; I Receive Love"

Returning to the narration of Baba's New Life activity, in March 1950, He often paid visits to the different *ashrams* in Hardwar and Kankhal. In the early morning

---

* *The Wayfarers*, by William Donkin, gives a detailed account of Baba's contacts with the *masts*. In his book, on page 242, he has stated that Baba visited Hardwar at different times with different people and that it was difficult to mention all the contacts made. The incident mentioned above is one not included in *The Wayfarers*.

with four companions, Gustadjee, Baidul, Pendu and Eruch, Baba would leave Motichur on foot and return by late afternoon. Throughout the day, He would walk from place to place, in the hot sun, contacting seekers and *sadhus,* mostly in ochre clothes. In that area anyone wearing such clothes was referred to by the people as a *mahatma.* Pendu was the "scorekeeper". After a fortnight, Pendu's record showed that Baba had contacted over a thousand persons from the different sects of *sadhus,* including those from Nirmali and Udasi. The strain of this work especially affected Baba's eyes, but He would not agree to discontinue these strenuous visits. When the number of people contacted reached 1,300. Baba went to Manjri Mafi for a two-day stay. It was March 21, *Jamshedi Naoroz,* New Year's Day for the Zoroastrians. On His arrival all greeted Baba with "*Naoroz Mubarak.*" Baba's vital presence filled the hearts of all with great delight. Baba, however, looked tired and His personal doctor, Nilu, noticed the ill effects of the physical strain in Baba's eyes. Baba permitted him to prescribe treatment for His eyes, but He also decided to go back to Motichur the next day.

Some people interested in spirituality heard about Baba's stay at Motichur. They visited His residence for *darshan.* But He rarely gave an audience. On one rare occasion, when the visitors expressed their wish to have His blessing. He conveyed to them, "In New Life, I give love and I am happy to receive love. No disciple-Master relationship." This remark expresses that the New Life meant giving and receiving love and love alone on a friendly footing. Baba had become a companion to all and His New Life will ever sing the note of companionship, a free and fearless relationship of man with God.

Baba continued His visits to Hardwar where the *sadhus* and *sanyasis* from different parts of India had assembled for the Kumbha Mela. In those days it seemed that any person with a long beard and hair, or clean shaven, or in an ochre robe was worthy of receiving Baba's attention. As He walked through the crowded streets He would cast them a special glance. It would be so penetrating but so quick that the person concerned would hardly realize how significant and potent it was. Sometimes Baba would touch the feet of these people with His finger tips. On such occasions, He would look gracefully divine and yet perfectly human. The person contacted would be struck with Baba's elegance and deep concern about him. But perhaps being blinded by Baba's unseen radiance, he could hardly discern the worth of this sanctifying touch. Once the contact was made, Baba would not wait a moment more. In this way Baba continued to bless many spiritual aspirants. To illustrate this particular method of paying homage, which Baba adopted during those days, He once held one end of a walking stick in His hand, with the other end in Baidul's. The next moment He gestured to His companions that He was ready to bow down to anyone Baidul would lead Him to. This method of contacting *sadhus* and the like continued throughout Baba's visits to Hardwar and Rishikesh. Baba could thus use any of the *mandali* as an instrument for His spiritual work.

The Eclipse of the Moon

March 27 was one of the important dates in the Kumbha Mela. On this day *sadhus, bairagis* and others, belonging to various sects, were expected to march in procession towards the banks of the Ganges to bathe during the specified hours mentioned in the Indian almanac. So thousands of people, fired with excitement, swarmed near the bathing *ghats* to witness the ceremony of the day. Because of the crowds, Baba preferred to stay at Motichur. He spent the time washing His own clothes and cleaning the pots, etc. The next day He visited some camps to contact *mahatmas* and *matajis* (literally mothers, woman aspirants). At a place known as Nirmal Akhada, a *mahant* (chief of the sect) was giving a discourse to a large audience, explaining the spiritual bounties derived from the *darshan* and *sahavas* of saints and Masters. The people had no idea that the One worthy of *darshan* and *sahavas* was intently listening to this talk for about half an hour. It was rare for Baba ever to spend such a long time listening to a spiritual discourse.

While bowing down to the hundreds of *sadhus*, Baba had to bend His back and neck again and again. This strained the muscles and nerves of His tender frame. Perhaps the serious suffering He endured during the 1960s owing to neck trouble had its origin in this wearying work. Though repeatedly requested by the companions, Baba refused to use any conveyance to reach any *ashram*. In addition, He also observed a fast on certain days. While returning to Motichur, He often looked very fatigued and walked with heavy steps. The eye trouble did not subside and His health was not good; He, however, seemed totally engrossed and devoted to this "*darshan*-taking" phase.

April 2 was another important day connected with the fair. It was the full moon day which concurred with the lunar eclipse. Hindus regard this coincidence as having great spiritual potential which can be utilized beneficially by devoting this particular period to the worship of God or the God-Man. Especially those who are after occult powers and are known as *tantriks* repeat certain disciplines and *mantras* as they stand in the river to revitalize their psychic powers. In the early days, Baba had been asked whether there was a grain of truth in such a belief and He explained, "It is a scientifically acknowledged fact that the stellar regions, planets and stars do exert an influence on the life and activity of this planet earth. And since this earth of ours has the highest evolved organic life, the human happens to be the nearest to the spiritual planes; the phenomenon of eclipse does indirectly affect the world spiritually. The *rishis* of old knew too well the astronomical basis and the spiritual influence of such heavenly occurrences. Looking at the average mentality of the masses of their times, the *rishis* could do no better than issue cut and dried instructions as to prayers and penance and austerities... rather than give a rational and spiritual elucidation.... There is, however, no denying the fact that a few prayers... undergone with keen concentration, concurrently with the eclipse of the sun or the moon do result in... spiritual benefit to the individual concerned."*

By the way, I would especially like to add here that on some occasions I had the opportunity to stay with Baba during eclipses. He, however, did not give any special instructions to those who stayed with Him. There was not even a mention of the eclipse during the day. I gathered that any moment spent in the whole-hearted remembrance of the Timeless One (Baba) is spiritually more beneficial than offering prayers or doing penances on astronomically auspicious times. On April 2, Baba did not visit Hardwar. Yet, He seemed to participate indirectly in the mass bathing of that day; He had a bath with Ganges water brought to His residence by Baidul. At night the *sadhus* and the like were expected to continue their prayers and other ceremonies on the bank of the Ganges, during the period of eclipse. At the appearance of the full moon, as per tradition, all were to bathe for a second time before returning to their camps. The next morning, April 3, Baba left Motichur as early as 3 a.m. for the Kumbha grounds to meet these holy men. This was the most active and strenuous day for Baba. Without rest or respite He moved between Hardwar, Kankhal and Neeldhara for about ten hours. Through His loving presence and sanctifying touch, Baba quietly poured His radiance upon the "ochre-race" — *sadhus* and *sanyasis*, and silently inspired and strengthened them to lead a life of honesty and selfless dedication in their search for God. At the end of the day's work He felt extremely tired but preferred, as usual, to walk back to Motichur on foot.

---

* *Meher Baba Journal*, February, 1939, p. 76.

STAY AT MOTICHUR

Raja, The English Bull

During each visit to Hardwar, Baba had to walk about 20 kms. and had to spend six to eight hours in the sweltering sun, meeting and bowing down to the mendicants and *mahatmas* residing at different places. In spite of the great physical exertion, Baba would not agree to use any conveyance. Very rarely He consented to hire a *tonga* to reach Motichur. In fact there was an ox cart at His disposal which had transported the party's odd things — utensils, etc. — from Manjri Mafi to Motichur. It was drawn by a single ox called Raja, brought from Ahmednagar along with the caravan. As a calf Raja had been presented to Baba by Sarosh. Baba had a special fondness for him and he was occasionally fed by Baba. Raja was an English bull and looked very noble. It was brought to Baba's notice that Raja needed some work and the cart could easily take Baba to Hardwar. Baba agreed that Raja should have some exercise and He told Murli to yoke Raja daily and visit Hardwar to purchase good fodder for him. He, however did not comply with the request of the companions to make use of the ox cart for Himself.

Murli commenced his daily cart drive. One day when he was returning to Motichur someone driving a car honked from behind. Raja, licking his nostrils with his rough tongue, was leisurely swaying his neck from left to right but did not move aside. The road was rather narrow; the car could not pass, so the driver repeatedly honked his horn and got annoyed with Murli who was holding Raja's reins. Finally the car overtook the cart and its driver, a British officer, stopped the car, got down and grumbled at Murli for his indifference to the traffic rules. Upon this Murli humbly apologized to him and softly added, "But sir, that was not my fault; I tried my best but the bull did not respond to my language. Perhaps it will understand you better; he is an English bull!" Raja's expression of unconcern and Murli's sense of humor made that grim Englishman not only smile but also laugh merrily. He spent a few minutes more, asked some questions about Raja and had a good chat with Murli. In the evening when Baba heard the story about Raja it provided Him with a few moments of joy and relaxation after His exhausting work during the day.

At the end of the conversation, Baba suddenly announced that Raja should be unconditionally donated to any good institution. This habit of immediately declaring some plan or order about a person or object which had come up quite incidentally in the conversation was typical of Baba. In the light of Baba's instruction, Pendu, while returning from Motichur to Manjri Mafi,* contacted Sister Miraben (Miss Madeline Slade), a close associate of Gandhiji, who was maintaining *Pashu Lok*, an animal farm, near Dehra Dun. She personally wanted to have Raja but the rules of the institution prevented her from accepting him. So, in the end, Raja was donated to *Goshala* — House of cows and calves.

This incidental mention of Miraben's name brings to mind a controversial statement linked with her name in Rom Landau's book entitled *God Is My Adventure* published in 1935. With reference to Gandhiji's meeting with Baba on the steamer *Rajputana* in September 1931, the author writes:

> I was travelling to America in the same boat as Miss Madeline Slade, Gandhi's English disciple and companion. I asked Miraben (as Miss Slade was called) about Baba's conversation with Gandhi. "I know all the details about the connection between the two men," she said. "It was always Shri Meher Baba who went to see Gandhi, never otherwise. Shri Meher Baba sent round a word, asking whether Gandhi would receive him. Gandhi of course, consented. They had

---

* Although the decision to give Raja away had been made at Motichur, this was not actually accomplished until after the group returned to Manjri Mafi.

STAY AT MOTICHUR

a talk, and after that Shri Meher Baba visited Gandhi again in London."

This information is totally distorted. On the contrary it was Gandhiji who, after receiving a telegram from Jamshed Mehta, the Mayor of Karachi, desired to see Baba.

Baba's secretary, F. H. Dadachanji (Chanji) who was well-acquainted with Gandhiji, brought the above statement to Gandhiji's notice. Later, Gandhiji himself wrote a letter to Chanji as follows:

Sevagram,
Via Wardha (M.P.)
20-9-41.

Dear Dadachanji,

With reference to the alleged interview with Miraben reported by Rom Landau, you may announce to the curious that it was not Meher Baba who sought me out on the Rajputana but I had sought him out in his cabin and it was I who used to go frequently to his cabin. And ... you were Baba's interpreter of the alphabetical plate which he held to converse with the world. You know the spiritual nature of our conversation. I had further invited Baba to meet me in London during the time I was there....

Yours Sincerely,
M. K. Gandhi*

I also know a few similar incidents when ill intentioned and superficially interested persons have tried to malign Baba and His cause, but these will be dealt with later. All such reactions, I noted, have their root in contempt prior to honest investigation.

---

* The photostat of the original letter is with Meher Baba's disciples.

Omniscience Without Knowledge

These regular visits to Hardwar bring to mind another incident depicting Baba's role as a seeker. In the Mela grounds He bowed down and touched the feet of *sadhus*, whether pseudo or real, sitting or standing by the roadside. He also visited the *ashrams* located on the banks of the Ganges. During one such visit as He reverentially bowed to the head of an *ashram,* Baba was offered some *prasad*. He, however, turned away swiftly as He always did after each contact, unwittingly not accepting the *prasad*. At the end of the day's program, before returning to Motichur, Baba conveyed to His companions, "I feel I should have accepted the *prasad*, then and there, that was offered by the *Mahant*." Eruch replied, "What you think is right, Baba. I personally feel that in the spirit of the New Life it should have been accepted." Upon this, Baba asked Eruch if he could find that particular *ashram* and meet the person again. Eruch assured Baba that he could and accordingly he met the *Mahant* again. Eruch apologized on behalf of his elder brother — Baba — for not accepting the *prasad*. The *Mahant* was pleased to re-offer it. This was later distributed by Baba in a devotional mood to His companions. Whatever role Baba assumed He played it to perfection. This reminds me of Baba's words, "*Sadguru* acts, *Avatar* becomes."

It is believed by some Indians that, though very rare, witnessing the mating of crows is a sign that foretells the death of a person, very dear to the observer. Once, while Baba was on His daily march to Hardwar with the four companions, one of them witnessed such a mating. Knowing this, Baba, like an ordinary superstitious person, seemed very concerned over this matter. He asked the companions what should be done to avert the death of a close one. Fortunately, every superstitious peril has its own amusing antidote! As Baba seemed very grave it was agreed that the death (!) of someone should be announced in order to avert real physical death. Baba suggested that as He was the dearest person to them all, His name should be used in a telegram to a person connected with the New Life activities. Eruch suggested that Baba's name would be too much of a shock to that person. And in case that person immediately communicated this news to Adi at Ahmednagar, who generally circulated news about Baba to His disciples and devotees, it would cause serious complications. In the end it was agreed that Pendu's name should be used and that a little later another wire would be sent cancelling the news of Pendu's death. Could anyone imagine that the Deathless One could express such concern about someone dropping his body?

Accordingly, a telegram was sent from Hardwar to a Baba lover in Delhi. But strangely enough, the first telegram was received after the second. And instead of any confusion, it gave the family members a good laugh. This revealed to them the absurdity behind such a superstition. Do we not know that devoid of any hypocrisy, birds live a natural and simple life? They are not lustful like men who are often overpowered by lust. But what an irony that man, who is the crown of creation, claims that the birds' playfulness and innocent passion predicts an evil happening! Having lust is entirely different from being lustful. Through this whole affair it seems that Baba has very skillfully disclosed the foolishness embedded in any superstition. In the New Life, Baba had become an ordinary seeker, but it cannot be denied that all the happenings during this phase had their origins in His divine wisdom. Baba's New Life expressed His omniscience without knowledge and omnipotence without power.

Baba Returns to the Headquarters

Baba and the companions visited Hardwar each day from Motichur. Aloba stayed at home but he was not keeping well. So Baba allowed Kumar to send a young boy from the hills to guard the house and also to cook the evening meal. This lad, named Satpal, was simple and sincere in his work. He once expressed his concern about the poor quality of the meals that all of them had. He suggested that at least a teaspoonful of ghee should be served with the food. Baba approved the suggestion. The next day the companions were allowed to purchase a tin of ghee and they carried it to the headquarters. The first evening, Satpal served each one a spoonful of ghee and all felt happy about the added flavor and nourishment. During the meal Baba smiled and casually warned the boy to take care of the tin.

The next evening, to the surprise of all, no ghee was served. Baba inquired and the boy sorrowfully told Him that there was no ghee left in the tin. The details which he gave later were amusing. A stray dog, lured by the fascinating smell of ghee, stealthily entered the room and carried away the tin. In his attempt to open the lid he knocked the tin over and, in the hot sun, the ghee soon flowed out to be licked up by the dogs. When Satpal noticed the tin was missing, he first searched for it in the house. Finally, he found it dirty and almost empty outside. Hearing this Baba had a meaningful smile. He did not get angry at all with Satpal. It seemed that in the New Life discomforts could not be avoided. The New Life Song of the companions reads:

We are merrily singing, the song of helplessness;
We are inviting all calamities and difficulties.

On another occasion, Satpal felt that after their strenuous wanderings on foot the Baba-party needed at least a tasty meal. However, he dared not suggest anything extra be served and certainly not ghee. He knew that they were not having enough milk in their tea, not to mention fruit or any other nutriment. But there was no question of changing the menu, much less preparing a feast. Even so, Satpal once devised a way to serve them a better meal. On that day the companions relished the *dal* and praised Satpal for its preparation.

However, after a few hours, all of them began to feel uneasy in their stomachs and developed diarrhea. They sensed that something must have been wrong with the food. They called Satpal and asked him what he had done. He explained that to make the *dal* rich in nutrition, he had soaked it in sweet oil before he cooked it. The good intention of the cook made the *dal* very tasty but it also acted as a light purgative. From then on Satpal never thought of preparing any other dish than the usual food.

Throughout this stay, Aloba was particularly not feeling well. It was hard for him to digest any food. He fasted for some days but this made him weaker and once he fainted near the bathroom. The entire stay at Motichur was very tough and rigid. Various were the "tastes" and tests in the New Life; Baba sharing them with one and all as the Real Companion. While Baba was thoroughly engrossed in His work with the *sadhus* and the like, a few security officers were busy gathering information about Baba's activities from the companions residing at Manjri Mafi. The officers felt curious about the nature of Baba's work. They wanted to ascertain whether it had any anti-social or communistic bias to it. Baba had instructed His people to abide by the laws of the government, so they willingly furnished the authorities with the necessary information about Baba's external activities. They were soon convinced that Baba's work posed no threat either to the government or to its policies.

Dr. Donkin who had accepted Plan I-B was at Dehra Dun practising medicine. He was allowed by Baba to communicate the New Life activities to Elizabeth Patterson, residing at Myrtle Beach in South Carolina in the States. In March 1950, he wrote her as follows:

> As far as Baba's New Life goes, not one of us (New Life companions) can make head or tail of it. Even the "3rd plan" people now with Baba do not expect to be there long and Baba has openly told them that

He does not want them with Him. It is all a mystery, a mystery and again a mystery, and very difficult both for those who are with Baba and those away from Him.

I went into Plan B, (taking a temporary job), since that is what I felt Baba wanted me to do; but whether it is a frightful waste of money I really don't know. Also I don't know, as you can realize, how long Baba will let me keep at it (practising medicine in Dehra Dun), whether for a month, a year or a life-time.... As far as Baba Himself goes, He is as adorable as ever...."*

This excerpt from the letter is enough to express the unpredictability of the New Life.

On April 4, Baba left for Belwala to continue the work of bowing to the mendicants and sages. At the end of this visit, Pendu, the scorekeeper, declared that the grand total of the holy men so far contacted had reached ten thousand. Baba seemed pleased to hear this. Before coming to Motichur, He had it in mind to contact personally a large number of those who had come for the Kumbha Mela. Reaching the residence He conveyed to the companions that the purpose of His stay at Motichur was accomplished and expressed His intention of returning to Manjri Mafi the next day. Gustadjee, Eruch, Baidul and Aloba were to follow two days later. Pendu and Murli were to drive the one ox-cart drawn by Raja carrying the belongings and other sundry things of the Baba-party. One of the companions accompanied Baba to Manjri Mafi and returned. Thus a very wearying yet greatly significant stay at Motichur was over.

---

* *The Awakener*, Vol. VII, No. 1, (1960). p. 19.

9

Leaving Manjri Mafi

1950 — Part IV

Participation in Baba's Suffering

ON April 5, Baba returned to Manjri Mafi at noon. Those staying at the headquarters rejoiced at Baba's arrival. He visited the men's quarters in the afternoon. All were happy to hear that Baba's work at the Kumbha Mela was accomplished to His satisfaction. They felt especially delighted at this achievement because they knew how hard He had had to exert Himself in contacting the spiritual wayfarers in spite of His frail health. Dr. Nilkanth (Nilu) wrote, "Baba looked tired and overworked. He appeared to drag His feet. While making inquiries, He was frequently coughing. Though He was not in good health, His face was lustrous and His eyes were brilliant. His face looked so beautiful and charming that our eyes refused to look anywhere."*

Some hours later it saddened them to find Baba fatigued and worn out. The next day when He arrived He looked more radiant and agile. But in fact He had had no sleep due to a fever and cough. He discussed with Kumar the practicality of staying at Manjri Mafi during the impending rainy (monsoon) season. With the first showers, puddles of water were forming in the surrounding area. This informal discussion was a prelude to Baba's decision to soon leave that place for good. Baba's indifferent health worried the companions. Baba's personal doctor, Goher, consulted Donkin and Nilu about possible treatment and precautions they

---

* *Circular NL* 8, issued on 23-5-1950.

should take. The doctors always did their best for Baba, but the results depended mostly on Baba's inner spiritual work. The internal crucifixion will not necessarily be mitigated by the administration of an external prescription.

The companions too, one way or the other, seemed to participate in Baba's sufferings. They were allowed only one meal a day consisting of *chapatis* and *dal*. The only variation permitted was to have some vegetables instead of *dal*. In the evening, milkless tea was served. The weather and living accommodations did not suit them, and they were not used to such a life. Yet, the morale of the companions was high and they cheerfully tried to obey each of Baba's instructions. Nevertheless, their physical bodies had to bear various afflictions and ailments. After all, they were made of clay! The following paragraph from Nilu's diary is sufficient to give an accurate picture. On April 9 he writes:

> The New Life is now nearly six months old and during this period, the companions had undergone such trials and tribulations and certain ordeals that their general health was not only much affected, but it had given each of them a certain infirmity — Pendu with pleurisy and pain in the chest; Eruch with lumbago and sprained foot which was becoming chronic; Murli with broken wrist-joint, still weakened by the labor; Vishnu crippled down with a rheumatic knee joint; Nilu with sciatica and left knee joint trouble due to water-carrying duty; Ali Akbar (Aloba) weakened and fatigued by fever, water-carrying and other hard labor; Kaka with his chest trouble; Baidul with all sorts of body ailments, and Gustadjee with his old age and increasing weakness.
>
> Individual suffering and ill-health may not mean much, but the collective result of the whole party's illness is not very cheerful and bright.... This weariness is due to natural and unnatural circumstances; due to normal and abnormal circumstances. In spite

of all this, one could easily observe the genuine attempt the companions were making to maintain a cheerful face with jokes and humor amongst themselves. It is true that the companions have their innocent and harmless faults and weaknesses, and why? Because they are simple human beings, and beyond that they do not claim anything.*

The above mentioned facts bring out how hard it was to stay with Baba in His New Life phase. In the Old Life, Baba would express great concern over the slightest sickness of any of His dear ones, and now, for the most part, He seemed unconcerned about it. As for one's relationship with the Beloved Master one of the Urdu poets has aptly stated, "O Beloved, in our first meeting, how lovingly you spoke to me and stole my heart! But now, O Thief of thieves, you are withdrawing yourself, not even casting a sideways glance at me!" In spiritual life, a short spring can usher in a long drawn out autumn. What a strange inversion! And this phase entails an incredible internal tug-of-war, sustained only by the grace of the Master's companionship.

The Beginning of the New Plan

April 11, 1950 was one of the important days for the companions. From Baba's casual remarks they had gathered that there was going to be a major change in the course of the New Life. From the beginning of the meeting held on that day, the atmosphere was serious and fraught with doubtful expectations. Baba looked very solemn. He was curt in admonishing the companions for the slightest mistakes they had committed. When Baba was conveying anything the eyes of His companions were fixed on His face and gestures. If He gave a severe look to anyone, by way of a rebuke, the heart of the recipient seemed to jump into his throat!

---

* *Circular NL* 8.

To live with Baba implied one's readiness not only to enjoy the soothing glow of His radiance but also to bear its blazing glare.

Every activity of the New Life was strictly conducted, according to Baba's orders. At times, in spite of the utmost care, the companions had to yield to Baba's severe criticism. In Baba's New Life it seemed that a little violation of His instructions on the part of His closer ones resulted in a hindrance — like the anticlockwise movement of a cog — in the subtle operation of His work, on the inner planes. Baba's reprimand or anger was a compensating as well as a comforting factor, for it was meant to relieve the companions from any harm that might come to them through disobedience. So it can well be termed another aspect of His compassion.

In this meeting, to avoid future lapses on the part of those who were with Baba, He decided to free them from the three phases — begging, gypsy and *langoti* life. He wished them to lead only the labor phase. He reserved the first three phases for Himself. With gentle piercing eyes and a serene unworldly expression on His face, Baba conveyed from the board the following: "I feel that everyone of you in Plan III is trying his best to carry out the conditions one hundred per cent... [but] to carry out Plan III seems impossible under circumstances due to the gulf that exists between you and me in the matter of understanding while executing the conditions.... I, therefore, decide today... that from 1st May 1950, none of you remain in Plan III. I shall remain alone to carry out the three phases of New Life of Plan III, and I order you all companions of Plans III and I-B, to join a new plan which will enable you to earn your livelihood and yet make you stay in one group near me.... My help in the form of guidance ... I shall give as far as possible to make this new plan a success."*

---

* *Circular NL* 8.

LEAVING MANJRI MAFI

All willingly agreed to execute this plan, and Baba's beautiful face looked more pleased and tranquil. Dr. Donkin suggested that if Dr. Nilu were allowed to work with him as a colleague and Pendu and Murli were permitted to assist him, then he would open a clinic that would easily maintain the whole party. Baba liked this idea, but it was kept pending for lack of funds. In this meeting, He told all that it did not seem practical for Him to continue His stay at Manjri Mafi and that He intended to shift to Delhi. For further discussion He wished to hold another meeting on April 15.

Blessed Hours at Kumbha Mela

While recounting the events that took place during the stay at Motichur, Baba told the companions who had stayed at Manjri Mafi about the large crowd of *sadhus* of different sects. They had assembled at Hardwar from various parts of India. They represented a fantastic cross-section of the different sects of the Hindu traditions. They had camped on both banks of the Ganges, eagerly awaiting the most eventful day of the Kumbha Mela; it fell on April 13. All of them were supposed to bathe in the holy river during a specified time. The various groups exhibited widely divergent ways of living. Some wore costly costumes, while some put on threadbare robes and a few had no clothes on at all. Some, with large and heavy bodies smeared with ash and matted hair reaching their knees, proudly paraded through the streets, while others, with shaven heads and lanky frames, meekly moved on the roads without any glamor or show about them. Indeed it was a heterogeneous multitude assembled with the motive of quickening their journey to heaven! Baba proposed and decided to take all the men and women companions to Hardwar for this particular occasion of *Purna* Kumbha.

Accordingly on April 12, Baba left Manjri Mafi for Hardwar in a station wagon, with Eruch and the women companions. Those remaining left the headquarters the next day by the morning train, walking five miles to reach the station. At Hardwar, Baba stayed in a mansion situated on the bank of the river. On the second day, He sent Eruch to Neeldhara, a particular spot, with special instructions to fetch water from the Ganges. A day later, on April 13, Baba took a bath with that water and when all the companions arrived He summoned them to Him. He asked Donkin to read out a prayer which was similar to the one read at Benares before He stepped out for the first *bhiksha*. After the prayer, He touched the feet of every companion with His hands. A most serene atmosphere always prevailed on such occasions. Baba seemed to pray like others, but it was never like others' prayers; it was matchless.

As if to get over this solemn mood, Baba led all to the terrace which offered a panoramic view. They saw crowds of gay pilgrims on both banks of the Ganges, and the distant blue mountains. After midday the great procession of the Kumbha Mela was in sight. It was led by *nangas* followed by different *mahants*. The dust raised by thousands of feet marching prevented a clear view. Nearly a million people had assembled there from distant parts of India. Man wants to travel externally, while God wants him to journey internally — within himself. What a paradox!

The auspicious hours of the Kumbha bathing were in the afternoon. During this time, Baba sometimes strolled on the balcony. It has been observed that occasionally when Baba found it hard to bear the burden of His inner work, He would walk briskly up and down the room. On the terrace of that house Baba sometimes stood and looked at the pilgrims and *sadhus* through a pair of binoculars, as the banks of the river were not very close to the house. Was He contacting certain persons through these frequent appearances? This seems quite possible because one of Baba's dear ones, Keshav Nigam, later recounted his wonderful experience of that day. He had had Beloved Baba's first *darshan* at Meherabad in August 1949.

LEAVING MANJRI MAFI

That first glimpse of Baba set his heart aflame to see Him again, but this had become impossible as Baba had entered the New Life and did not allow any of His disciples or devotees to see Him. Keshav came to know about Baba's stay at Dehra Dun from Babadas who, on his own, had selected Plan I-C. Now Keshav could not restrain himself from visiting Hardwar where he expected Baba during the Kumbha fair, and luckily he had Baba's *darshan* too. His heart swelled with delight and his eyes were filled with adoration as he gazed at the brilliance on Baba's radiant face. About this incident Keshav wrote:

> I made a pilgrimage to Hardwar during that Kumbha. For me Kumbha bathing meant nothing but a chance to take Baba's *darshan*. At that time Babadas was with us. With his help I was able to reach... the bank of the Ganges' canal... on the opposite bank stood the building in whose upper storey Baba was staying alone with His New Life companions. Sometimes Baba would come out of the room, stand on the balcony and look at the thousands of pilgrims through binoculars. Sometimes, He would stroll all over the balcony. This gave a good opportunity to... His lovers to see Him during the entire Kumbha day and take His coveted *darshan* to their heart's content. The Kumbha hours began at about 3 p.m. and ended at 7 p.m. For me, the Ganges was where my Beloved Baba was. As such, on that very spot of the Ganges' canal I took my dips in His Name, and with each dip I again got what I longed for — the *darshan* of Baba.... It was dark enough at 7 p.m. and yet even in the darkness I could clearly see the bright form of Baba on the balcony after every dip. My Kumbha pilgrimage was fully rewarded and my Kumbha bathing was one hundred per cent fulfilled! I felt extremely happy and blessed!

When the special hours of the procession and bathing

in the Ganges were over Baba left Hardwar by train for Dehra Dun.

Passing Away of Vishnu's Mother

After the party's return to Manjri Mafi the next day, Baba asked some of the companions how they would respond to the news of the passing away of their dear ones. They assured Baba that they would receive this information calmly and with composure. At the end, Baba asked Vishnu how he would feel if his dear mother, staying at Meherabad, were to drop her body. Vishnu conveyed that the news would not disturb him. At this moment Baba disclosed that a telegram had been received by Dr. Donkin from Ahmednagar. It said that Kakubai, Vishnu's dear mother, had passed away. Vishnu did not express any outward sign of emotional turmoil. He did not shed any tears, instead he attended to all his duties including marketing. Later on Baba praised Vishnu's attitude of tolerance and embraced him in appreciation of his even temper and his "brave" heart.

Kakubai was an old contact. In 1920 Baba was staying in Kasba Peth at Poona. He had started gathering the *mandali* round Him and Vishnu was one of them. He frequently visited Sadashiv Patel's house where Baba resided. Baba indirectly asked Sadashiv about this young boy. Once, on His own, Baba visited Vishnu's residence. His mother Kakubai was at home and Baba had a good chat with her. As the number of such visits increased, the relationship became more informal and intimate. Sometimes Baba would ask Kakubai to prepare a certain hot dish called *pithla*,* and he enjoyed having it for lunch with *bhakri*,** or rice.

Once, when Baba visited the house, He learnt that Vishnu had paid a visit to the theater. Hearing this, in

---

* Prepared from gram flour.
** Millet bread.

the presence of Kakubai, Baba gave him a sound slap that turned his cheek red. Vishnu with lowered head said nothing. The next moment Baba said, "If you want to visit the theater, you may do so at any time, but only with my prior consent. And every time you decide to go do not fail to collect the necessary money from me!" And He heartily smiled! Maybe such slaps and pamperings paved and quickened the way for the *mandali* to surrender to Baba unconditionally. Soon Vishnu left his education and permanently joined Baba, and later Kakubai stayed as one of Baba's women *mandali*. Vishnu was her only son. She was deeply grieved when she learnt about her son's decision to accompany Baba in His New Life. A mother's love for her son is very deep rooted indeed. Vishnu loved his mother immensely, but in one's life with the Master everything has to be forsaken cheerfully and voluntarily at His beck and call.

The meeting that was adjourned on April 11 was resumed on April 15. Baba visited the men's quarters before 7 a.m. The points mentioned in the earlier meeting were discussed again from different angles. In addition, Baba informed the companions that He was expecting a cable from Elizabeth Patterson about His forthcoming visit to the United States and that it would be either in 1950 or 1951.* At the end of this meeting, He asked Eruch to proceed to Delhi the next day and to inquire about suitable accommodations for the Baba-party in the capital of India. In connection with the new plan of starting a business, Eruch was to speak to Keki Desai and Harjeevan Lal. The work of the meeting was to be continued after Eruch's return from Delhi.

Baba was not keeping well. The slightest effort would tire Him. Nilu's diary states: "Some companions had become so weak that to send them out to beg for food was out of the question. The remaining companions

---

* In fact, this visit to the West was delayed till April, 1952.

were somehow managing to pull on with the duties entrusted to them." In addition, the weather was windy, cold and wet. Vishnu suffered from a high fever and, owing to a severe cough, he could not sleep at night. So Nilu had to do the marketing. It was as if the body and mind of each companion were being tested.

"Loving" the God-Man Is "Living" with Him

About this time, Rustom S. Hansotia, Gustadjee's nephew, came to visit Baba with the intention of joining Him as one of His New Life companions. He was working for the railways. After studying the New Life circulars, he decided to follow Baba and stay with Him. He informed his father who tried to dissuade him from his intention. Rustom had already resigned his post and soon left his town in search of Baba's place of residence. After visiting Hardwar and Motichur, he finally reached Manjri Mafi. He met Pendu who explained to him that in the New Life, Baba did not permit interviews. Rustom said that he was ready to obey Baba implicitly, but with one exception. He feared that Baba would say to him, "Go back home." And he expressed his inability to carry out this particular instruction because he had determined to stay with Baba under any conditions.

Pendu informed Baba of Rustom's arrival. Baba pointed out that as there was going to be a change in the external aspect of the New Life with the introduction of a new plan, the visitor should be told to go back and await the final decision at his home town. It would be conveyed to him by Baba through a letter after He had a special meeting with His companions. In a depressed mood Rustom asked Pendu for Baba's *darshan*. "This is not possible," Pendu explained. At the last moment Baba, however, allowed the visitor to have a glimpse of Him from the other side of the road, and it was quite a long distance. Rustom looked at Baba with insatiable eyes, while sweet tears of joy and agony partly blurred his vision. He left Manjri Mafi with a heavy heart.

Baba did not visit the men's quarters for over five hours because of Rustom's presence. Was it so difficult for Baba just to walk over there from the main house? Maybe a visit planned on one's own is not the approach that qualifies a person for his meeting with the God-Man. It has to be the other way. The meeting can bear fruit only at His choice. Rustom's visit to Manjri Mafi reminds me of a similar incident, over a thousand years earlier.

A seeker who felt deeply drawn by the teaching of Prophet Mohammed approached him and expressed a keen desire to stay near him permanently. This person was from Yemen. The following lines in Persian expressed the Prophet's reply to the seeker:

Garbaomani daryamani pishamani
Garbimani pishamani daryamani

When freely translated in English these lines mean:

O seeker! If you really have me (i.e., if you have love for me) in spite of your staying away from me at Yemen, in fact you will be residing quite close to me. And O dear! In spite of your living with me in my close vicinity, if you fail to love and obey me, it is tantamount to your staying away from me — even further away than Yemen.

With this laconic reply, Mohammad asked the person to return to his homeland. He, nevertheless, assured him that carrying out his instructions would make him feel strongly the Prophet's presence.

It is good to long for the physical presence and company of the God-Man. But it is not good to seek this against His wish. He expects us to love and obey Him, and to live in accordance with His teachings. There are some instances when Baba had asked His lovers who wished to stay near Him permanently to return home and to lead a normal life. In Rustom's case, within a fortnight after the above mentioned meeting, he was informed that he should not come to Hardwar, but he was free to lead his life according to the conditions of the New Life. He was not allowed either to correspond with Baba or see Him in person. Unfathomable are the ways of Baba in dealing with His lovers.

Two Aspects of Companionship

During the next meeting with the companions, Baba reiterated the points connected with the implementation of the new plan. Different suggestions as to how to faithfully carry out this plan were put forth by the companions. This honest expression of opinions, however, provided quite a few heated discussions. Baba silently listened to this unreserved and frank exchange of concepts and sentiments. In the end, with an air of benignity and brotherly love, He asked them to wait for a few days for His final decision. He instructed Eruch to visit Delhi to make further specific inquiries in connection with the forthcoming business in ghee.

About the daily schedule at Manjri Mafi, the women companions later reported: "Despite the cold and rain, Baba rose at the early hour of 4 o'clock. After Todi Singh and his family left, Mani, Mehru and Mehera did the cooking and *chapatis*. At 8 o'clock Baba would come and ask if food was ready, and we would say, give us half an hour to have it ready. At 12 noon we had afternoon tea, and the evening meal would be over by 5 o'clock, and by 6 o'clock the dishes washed. In the evening Baba would sit with us and ask us to say something amusing or relate a story we could remember. We could not read books or newspapers, and not even the wrapping papers provided for packing."* Mani later

---

* *The Glow*, February 1973, p. 11.

recalled that the articles they required would reach them wrapped in newspapers mostly in languages they could not read or understand. With Baba's *mandali* the time for tea and food varied widely during the different phases of His work. In the early '60s at Guru Prasad, Poona, I remember afternoon tea was immediately followed by a cold drink, *sharbat*. We would pass in a line and Baba would fill our glasses with delicious *sharbat*, mostly pineapple. At Manjri Mafi, after an early supper, Baba would usually retire very early.

After the pre-monsoon showers the weather became cold, wet and windy. Goher and Mani fell ill. Water from the well on the premises of the headquarters had such a stink that it could not be used for drinking or cooking purposes. Water was fetched by the companions from a distance of about half a mile. Nilu, one of the inmates, commented on the life led during this period as follows: "Lack of proper food, clothing, sufficient quantity of good water... added to semi-privation, starvation, physical and mental tension and exhaustion, with continuous chilly weather during the six months of the New Life, had run down Baba's and the companions' health."* In spite of this all had to attend to the duties assigned to them by Baba. Once Vishnu had a high fever, 103°, but the day his temperature became normal, he had to be carried on a pushbike to Dehra Dun on some important business.

Why had Baba, who, at Belgaum at the beginning of the New Life, lovingly carried a basket of vegetables on His head from the women's quarters to serve His dear companions, become so callous? Whatever Baba's intention was behind this rigid discipline and apparently cold attitude, it was clear that the companions had to suffer much physically and mentally too. Baba also suffered with them, and His suffering was not just personal. For the companions, the New Life was a journeying through a series of painful yet fruitful

---

* *Circular NL* 8, issued on 25-5-1950.

"rebirths;" each time a different aspect of their being would be confronted and revealed. Once you come into the love-orbit of the God-Man whatever happens either compensates for, or complements, the innate needs of the spirit — the involving consciousness. The God-Man as Man suffers immensely to fulfil His mission which is to help humanity attain its rightful inheritance of Godhood. The *Avatar's* life represents the struggle of humanity with its attendant joys and sorrows, and the New Life phase stands out as a typical aspect of Baba's work.

In spite of such circumstances the companions would sometimes find Baba in a gay, jovial mood. On such occasions He looked very lively and even had a twinkle of mischief in His eyes. He would then be seen beaming with delightful radiance. This change would warm the hearts of the companions, replenishing them with zeal and confidence. One day Baba agreed to attend a sugarcane juice party. That was a very happy time for all. On some mornings, He used to play badminton with Nilu and Kumar. Once He suggested that they play cricket and that was great fun. There was no regular playground and the fielders had to run after the ball bouncing and gliding through the trenches when it was hit for a boundary.

On the last day of April 1950, one of Baba's favorite Indian games, *gilli-danda,* was played. In the early '20s, He often used to play different Indian outdoor games. Sometimes He would explain the spiritual significance attributable to these games. *Gillidanda* needs a wooden rod (*danda*) about two feet in length, and another small piece (*gilli*) about six inches long with two pointed ends. In playing this game the shorter stick is skillfully tapped at one end so that it is lifted high up in the air, and before it falls to the ground it is hit hard for a second time by the same stick.

Baba explained the spiritual background as follows: "... when a Perfect Master selects a disciple as worthy of God-realization, he invariably strikes at the lower part of his nature, his self-egoism. This corresponds to the striking of the smaller piece of wood by the rod in hand, to enable the former to lift itself in the air. The egoism or the lower self of the disciple once shattered, the second step consists in driving him onwards towards the Goal of Self-realization. This second ordeal is explanatory of the second stroke which sends the piece hanging in the air to a distance proportionate to the force of the impact conveyed."* The Old Life association of the companions with Baba can be likened to the first, light touch, while keeping companionship with Baba in the New Life resembled the second, hard hit.

From a different angle, Francis Brabazon, in one of his *ghazals,* expressed this relationship thus:

How simple was this matter of love in the beginning—
Glad night, sweet sleep and awaking to the magpies' singing.

The sun rose each morning as a peal of bells from the sky,
Calling our spirits to another day's glad journey.

None of us thought that that journey would lead to this bitter
Helplessness, with the stoutest an eyeless palm-joined sitter.**

And in another *ghazal,* he presented another aspect of one's relationship with the Beloved as follows:

May our enemies never know our hardships. Yet, we rejoice,
For we were free men who became your slaves out of free choice.***

---
* *Meher Baba Journal,* September 1940, p. 682.
** Francis Brabazon, *In Dust I Sing,* p. 18.
*** Ibid, p. 40.

And Baba had thrice warned and asked the companions to exercise their free will fully before each one decided to join Him in His New Life.

The New Plan

On Eruch's return from Delhi the decisive meetings were held. A brief summary of the decisions taken is given below:

All the members of the new plan were to abide by the conditions that Baba set in January 1950 under Plan I-B. The following eleven members were to take part in this project: Kaka, Gustadjee, Pendu, Baidul, Eruch, Nilu, Vishnu, Murli, Donkin, Ali Akbar (Aloba) and Sadashiv (Patel). At Delhi, Keki Desai's residence was to be the headquarters and the head office of this new business. Todi Singh of Aligarh was the chief promoter and organizer. In his capacity as a businessman, Todi Singh assured the companions of a steady, good supply of cream through his old contacts in Nainital and Kathgodam. Todi Singh's connections with Baba and Baba's love for Todi Singh seemed to have resulted in choosing this ghee business. Maybe, through this occupation, Baba wished to shower more of His blessings on Todi Singh by offering him opportunities to share some work in the New Life.

All the "partners" in this business were expected to earn their livelihood through honest transactions. They were to work as one team. At the start, Baba agreed to provide some money for their initial capital. This amount was to be raised by selling the very property occupied by the Baba-party. Of the four phases of the New Life as mentioned earlier, Baba declared that He would lead the first three phases on behalf of the whole group, whereas the companions were to carry out the fourth, i.e., the labor phase for themselves and also for Baba. Gustadjee and Kaikobad were totally exempt from any type of work. Dr. Donkin, who was getting himself established as a leading physician in Dehra Dun, was asked to close his profession and to dispose of the things he had in his clinic.

As the property* where Baba stayed was to be sold, He planned to occupy the place where Donkin had his clinic. It seems that Baba's trait of building and dismantling things and plans continued rather intensely throughout the New Life. He was to stay at Donkin's place till a suitable house could be leased in Delhi. Kain and Harjeevan Lal of Delhi were asked to help the companions if conveniently possible.

After Ghani's departure, Baba had ordered Nilu to maintain a diary of daily events. In one of the meetings this order was cancelled. With the discontinuation of this diary it turned out that some important dates and events of the New Life went unrecorded.

The time fixed by Baba for a special *bhiksha* was the morning of May 1. The same day at 5 p.m., the companions were to be freed from undergoing the first three phases and were to be admitted to the new plan which consisted of hard physical labor. From the many sittings and meetings of the New Life it can be noted that Baba did not deal with the so-called philosophical subjects or metaphysical themes. However, while giving instructions, whether ordinary or extraordinary and when making casual remarks, whether meaningful or apparently meaningless, He did what was perfectly human and natural.

Bhiksha Ends for the Companions

According to Baba's instructions, on May 1, all the companions got up at 4 a.m. It was pleasantly cold and

---

* This property was sold for a few thousand rupees, though the expenses incurred on the well alone were over 2,000 rupees. Baba's first condition was to get money in cash and only a short time period was allotted for the sale. He hinted to those who had come in closer contact with Him during the New Life to purchase the estate, but they failed to raise enough money. In the end it was purchased by a photographer in Dehra Dun.

the early breeze was delightfully refreshing. When the morning duties were over, all the members of Plan III wore white *kafnis* and green turbans. On Baba's arrival, Nilu and Kaka helped Him to put on the green turban. He looked incredibly beautiful and profoundly serene. Baba's solemn mood superimposed a gravity on the quietness of the morning. No one dared to break the profundity of the prevailing silence.

After sunrise, Baba, accompanied by the band of companions, left on foot for the dry, sandy bed of the Rispana. On the bank of the river, Nalawala's and Kumar's families were to offer *bhiksha* to the Baba-party. Freiny, the wife of Kaikobad Nalawala, decided to prepare a dish of rice called *pulao*, to be offered in *bhiksha*. The time fixed for this program was 7 a.m. She woke up early to begin work in the kitchen. At about 6 a.m., Freiny found that in spite of her utmost care the *pulao* was not perfectly cooked. They did not want to be late and Keki Nalawala knew that Baba expected them to be present by the river bank a little before the appointed time. So it was hard for them to allot more time for cooking. This put them in a dilemma. What should they do? Should they carry the rice as it was for Baba, or should they delay the appointment? Kaikobad insisted on obeying Baba's order and they hurried towards the bank of the Rispana jogging along in a *tonga*. Their hearts were filled with mixed feelings of worry and delight.

At the appointed time, they saw a group of mendicants in white robes, with Baba in the lead. Soon the party reached the specified spot. Baba, with sparkling eyes, sweetly smiled at those present and their hearts rose up as on a wave of delight. They felt blessed to offer *bhiksha* to the God-Man and it was indeed a rare privilege. Baba's loving and gentle glances carried the message of love from His heart to each one, and they forgot their worry about the raw *pulao*. At a signal from Baba they brought out the food and Baba very lovingly accepted the *bhiksha*; the companions also followed suit. All quickly returned to Manjri Mafi. While going back, Baba asked all the companions to observe complete silence; it made this *bhiksha* all the more memorable. On reaching their quarters, Baba conveyed to the companions that it had been their last turn to go for *bhiksha*. They would not be required henceforth to beg for food. Baba would, however, carry out this phase as and when necessary. With His own hands Baba served *pulao* to all. He also declared that according to the decision in the last meeting, after 5 p.m. on May 1, the companions of Plan III and Plan I-B would come under the new plan.

Freiny after reaching her house realized that in the overwhelming presence of Baba she had totally forgotten to mention that the *pulao* was undercooked. After a few days when they had another opportunity to visit Baba's place, they humbly apologized to the companions for offering the half-cooked rice on May 1. No one could understand exactly what they meant for each of the companions had immensely enjoyed that day's food. A few even remarked that it was exceptionally delicious. The secret of "raw" turning into "ripe" remains concealed to this day.

Kathgodam Stay — A Retrospective View

In the second week of May, the companions left Dehra Dun for Delhi to conduct the ghee business. The property at Manjri Mafi was already sold. With the first installment of money received through this deal, the wheels of the new occupation were set in motion. Baba with the women and Baidul and Vishnu shifted to the house on 29 Lytton Road used by Dr. Donkin for his clinic. During this short stay, Baba in a light mood once visited a circus show. While watching the pranks of the clowns, He felt so delighted and laughed so much that His cheeks glistened pinkish and He covered them with His palms, as was His habit. On another day He paid a visit to the Botanical Garden and had a good stroll in it with an amusing look, perhaps wondering over His creation! Sometimes He seemed to be seriously engaged in His work. As for the companions, after reaching Delhi they commenced their hard labor phase. They were accommodated at Keki Desai's place, 4 Hussain Building, Nicholson Road, Delhi-6. On each alternate-day, Todi Singh would visit the Nainital and Kathgodam regions to dispatch the cans of cream.

With this casual reference to Kathgodam, I am reminded of some past interesting events which occurred during Baba's stay in this little town. It was July 1942, one of the years of Baba's special work with the *masts* and intensive seclusion. A secluded hut about two miles from the town, overlooking the slopes of the hills, was tentatively rented. The four disciples accompanying Baba were Gustadjee, Baidul, Kaka (Baria) and Adi. Baba had asked the four men to keep a two-hourly night watch by turn. On the first night, through a small window, Gustadjee saw a ball of light moving over the foot-path of the hills. He was astonished. The next day he expressed through gestures — as he had been observing silence since 1927 — the marvel of the night. Adi remarked that it was all Gustadjee's fanciful imagination. Baba too did not take any cognizance of it. The next night Baidul saw the same wonder and related it to the others. Adi began to have second thoughts about his skepticism. On the third night Adi himself observed a small globe of light gliding along the path and wondered what it could be!

He later told this to Baba and asked Him what sort of phenomenon it was. Baba, who had shown indifference on the first two days, now revealed that the trailing lightball was a yogi visiting a cave situated in that area. Baba also brought to Adi's notice that it was not a thing worth paying any more special attention to. So many wonders are strewn on the spiritual path! Baba has repeatedly stressed that love for God is what matters most; and the rest of the things, if necessary in one's journeying, incidentally accrue. And this love is to be

LEAVING MANJRI MAFI

kept constantly and secretly alive in one's normal life.

The second incident of Kathgodam is also worth mentioning. In the mornings Baba used to move freely on the slopes of the nearby hills. On July 14 the *mandali* woke up at 3 a.m. and left the hut at 5. Baba walked briskly, His white *sadra* flowing about Him. After plodding for two hours the Baba-party reached a plateau. Here, Baba began to walk fast in different directions. His combed hair, that was hanging on His shoulders, gracefully flowed back and forth with His quick pacing. As He walked with elegant and authoritative dignity, He stopped a while at some places on the plateau deeply absorbed in His work. Returning to a flat surface, Baba selected a spot where He intended to settle all alone by Himself, unobserved by anyone. He asked the four disciples to take their posts in four different directions at a distance of about 150 meters away from Him. They were not to look at Him unless He clapped. Earlier He had also informed them that He might even break His silence! What a thrilling occasion! Suddenly some unnameable emotion stirred the hearts of the four disciples. Would they hear the Original Sound, and what would be its spiritual impact on world consciousness?

What Baba did under the blue sky no one knows! But when He stood up and clapped He looked exceptionally glowing with spiritual splendor. The disciples gazed at Baba's luster and beauty, radiating from His face. No wonder that their hearts soared high as on a gale of gaiety. Baba too was very happy and He instructed Adi and the others to collect some earth from the spot where He sat, and it is still preserved. It was on the above mentioned slopes that the cattle continued to graze and it was from these herds that Todi Singh collected the cream for the New Life business in ghee. Perhaps too remote a context! But it is a Baba context, in Baba time!

Dishonesty, Baba Never Permitted

Returning to the narration of the new project in Delhi the work was really well planned. There were different groups attending to different matters. Some had to go to the railway station to bring the cans of cream, some had to empty them in the churner barrel. After adding ice, some had to rotate the barrel with the handle provided with it. All this was hard work. The process of rotating, separated the cream into butter and toned milk. One group would heat the butter on a big Indian-style *"hibachi"* (brazier)-like charcoal stove to the boiling point. To know the exact temperature when butter is clarified, giving out a delicious odor, requires experience and skill. Todi Singh was an adept in this art. A few were entrusted with the work of filling the containers of different sizes with ghee. They were also to paste the labels Nav Jeevan (New Life) Ghee on them. Finally the containers were soldered.

Sometimes owing to adulteration of the cream purchased or a fault in their method of boiling they would not get good butter. In that case, to compensate for this loss, the stuff had to be turned into sweet cheese in the form of *pedhas*. Once, in an attempt to sell these, one of the companions shouted on the roads of Delhi like an ordinary hawker, *"pedhas*, good *pedhas*, for sale" to attract the attention of customers. A funny experience! Even getting a good market for ghee was a problem. The bare cost of production turned out to be higher than the standard rates of ghee in the Delhi market. The thought of making a profit was out of the question. It was discovered that even the best ghee was, to some extent, mixed with some inferior stuff by other producers.

During Baba's visit to Delhi this state of affairs was brought to His attention. He did not feel surprised. But the lack of sales had resulted in a piling up of stock. What next? Should they continue with the business or close it? To compete with the stuff in the market Dr.

Donkin asked if they could follow the course of other businessmen. Baba's instantaneous and emphatic reply was, "No, No, No." Baba never permitted dishonesty in any form. He simply mentioned that He would let them know about the business later.

Yoga Implied Spirit of Dedication

May is generally the hottest time of the year in Delhi. The companions sweated profusely as they worked near the charcoal stoves. Most of the time they would wear underwear and T-shirts only, but that too was not comfortable. The peculiar smell of butter milk, cream and ghee all mixed together was nauseating.

The entire ghee affair can be termed as a *"paseena"* phase (perspiring phase) of the New Life. This sort of hard labor phase had its parallel in the summer of 1924. At that time Baba was staying at Meherabad. He kept the *mandali* extremely busy with the work of dismantling and rebuilding a few rooms at lower Meherabad. All had to put in eight hours of intense physical labor every day, in the hot sun. The food they had was millet bread and vegetable curry. They had no weekend off. Using shovels and pickaxes they had to fill iron pans with mud, mortar and stones which they had to carry to different places. Baba would often visit and supervise the work.

Once when He was inspecting the site, a clean-dressed, spiritually inclined person who was also practising some *yogic* exercises approached Baba. He knew that Baba was regarded as a Perfect Master. The person, however, had been conditioned by conventional ideas of spirituality and its usual disciplines. He was amazed to find Baba's *mandali* working like coolies (hired labor). In his conversation with Baba on spiritual subjects, He could not refrain himself from asking the following question of Baba. He said "I have studied *Dnyan Yoga, Bhakti Yoga, Karma Yoga* and *Raja Yoga* and other *yogas* too. But I would like to know what *yoga* you teach to your followers!" Baba, with His inimitable sense of humor simply said, "*Ghamela Yoga!*" This made the visitor look all the more confused. *Ghamela* literally means a broad iron pan, and it was the most commonly used tool that the *mandali* worked with. It is not known whether the person correctly understood Baba's words or not. But it was obvious that Baba never underestimated physical labor in relation to the spiritual disciplines that are commonly known.

There was also a time when Baba and the *mandali* used to grind flour on a big grinding stone, a *chakki*. And this period was called *chakki yoga*. It means that anything that one honestly and sincerely feels like doing, or everything that is carried out under the Master's instruction can be termed as *yoga*, for that particular person. Such a course of life will ultimately lead him to Real *Yoga* — union with Beloved God.

Spirituality does not necessarily consist in practising *asanas* or meditating for a specified time. It is a way of total living. It is not the outward form but the inner attitude of dedication that really counts. The hardships of the ghee business in Delhi might have reminded the companions of the *ghamela* days, 25 years earlier, at Meherabad. The *paseena* phase in a way was the silver jubilee celebration of the *ghamela yoga!*

The Secrets of Spiritual Life

During Baba's second visit to Delhi, the ghee problem was again brought to His attention. Another point for consideration was that even after making their best efforts a suitable apartment for Baba's stay in Delhi had not been secured. These two subjects were discussed from various angles in Baba's presence. At the close of the meeting, Baba quite unexpectedly suggested that in the prevailing circumstances, He would prefer to return southwards, to His favorite area between Poona-Satara-Mahabaleshwar. It meant that the business in Delhi had to be closed. So, according to Baba's instructions, the companions began winding it up. They feared that it had not been a profitable venture; that was true. By May 24, 1950 they washed their hands completely of the business by selling all the things connected with the affair, lock, stock and barrel. The money recovered from the sum invested was to be spent by the Baba-party for travelling towards the south and on other daily requirements, till the companions started earning money through odd jobs. No one had the slightest idea about the future nature of the New Life; no one worried about it.

The women companions residing at Dehra Dun were also completely ignorant about the life that lay ahead; but they were blissfully happy about it. Baba had instructed them to work and earn. Donkin had brought the hand sewing machine from Bombay, and the women spent their spare time sewing clothes. Some would cut different designs from colored designed cloth and this applique could be embroidered or sewn onto a dress to make it more attractive. Mani revived her art of making puppets. She remembers that she made a charming figure of Krishna with a lovely bluish complexion and a cruel looking butcher having a black moustache with an open knife in his hand. What a contrast! Through this business and other sundry indoor occupations, the women earned about three hundred rupees.

On May 25, under Baba's order, Eruch wrote to Jal Kerawala, one of the Arrangementwallas, about the forthcoming shift from the north to the south. Baba expressed His intention to stay in a moderately big town that had a mountain and a river nearby. The climate should be temperate, not hot in summer and not too cold in winter. It seems that Baba's inner work had some connection with the outer geographical environment. On certain occasions Baba would insist on a specific site or a venue before making a move to that place. In that letter to Jal, Baba expressed His special preference for the region near Satara-Mahabaleshwar. In spite of its heavy rainfall, He seemed to have a special affinity for Mahabaleshwar. The next best place was Satara. On May 27, Baba sent Eruch to help Jal secure the required residence. Eruch was successful in hiring two bungalows in the camp area in Satara, which was sparsely populated and had a quiet atmosphere. Soon, with the women and a few men companions, Baba left Dehra Dun on June 14, 1950 for the south, a journey over a thousand kilometers. The servant companions at Delhi boarded the train for Satara two days later. And by the middle of June the temporary headquarters of the New Life at Manjri Mafi were left for good.

Baba's activities in the north from November 1949 to June 1950 were characterized by great extremities and tribulations and a challenge to the old ways of living. Baba Himself suffered much physically. He did not reveal the reason behind this. Perhaps some secrets are not to be spoken of, and even if words dare to convey these, they are not much understood. Rather, such an attempt makes things more confused. Baba preferred not to explain certain things for He expected His lovers to have the daring to live by faith and love, not reason. Baba was passing through an unparalleled phase of "helplessness" which was concealed from the sight of the companions. An occasional glimpse, however, would reveal the grandeur and enormity of the New Life. This sustained the morale of the companions in staying with Baba.

This was also the time when the companions physically endured much beyond their normal limits, and as such they had to face inner crises. Why did the companions choose to suffer and be with Baba? Because they had complete freedom to leave Him. A so-called free man shackled with rationality shall call this madness, but the liberated spirit of a lover shall regard this as a benediction. To learn the secrets of living a spiritual life, one has to know the art of dying to the past continually — an avenue leading towards the Eternal New Life.

10

Headquarters at Satara

1950 — Part V

An Incredible Eye Infection

BY the middle of June 1950, Baba left Dehra Dun and reached Satara. The nature of His work as well as its locus was now shifted from the foot of the Himalayas in the north, to the base of the Sahyadri range in the middle of India, Maharashtra. Two houses were rented in the camp area which was some distance from the crowded part of Satara city. Mutha's Villa where Baba stayed in 1947 was made available to Him for His residence and work. The companions occupied another place, Bhurke's bungalow. It was about four furlongs away from Baba's residence but quite close to the government rest house where Baba used to halt for a day or two during His earlier *mast* tours. The *mandali* knew the locality of Satara well. Baba often visited the men's quarters and sometimes He called them to Mutha's place.

This villa was a two-storey building. Mehera, Mani, Goher and Mehru stayed on the ground floor. Soon Kitty and Rano joined them. The second floor was reserved for Baba and for His meeting with the men companions. It was here that a local *qawwal* was engaged to sing the New Life song in Baba's presence, for the benefit of the companions. The song was sung almost daily in the same fashion and to the tune approved by Baba. This singing was accompanied by two musicians from among the companions, one playing on a harmonium and the other on a tabla.* The words and tune of

---

* A kind of drum.

the song ringing in the ears of the companions, helped keep aglow in their hearts the ideal of the New Life which was to harbor no regrets for the past and to have no plans for the future. All of them were expected to be like hollow reeds ready to play, voluntarily and happily, the music of each moment.

On June 7, the monsoons began in earnest. Small puddles of brown water were seen around the houses and bungalows. The climate, however, was neither chilly nor humid but moderate. The grass sprang up in the enclosures and along the streets. The roses blooming in the morning sun with a few raindrops on them looked very lovely. Owing to the change in the climate and the surroundings Baba felt relaxed, but He did not completely regain His normal health.

The fasts and physical strain He had gone through at Motichur and Manjri Mafi in Uttar Pradesh had greatly affected Baba's digestive system. Besides, His eyes were also giving him a lot of trouble. Most of the time Baba would have the feeling that He had sand or grit in His eyes. Occasionally the irritation would become so extreme that in the end while staying at Manjri Mafi, Goher, Baba's personal physician, decided to call a well known eye surgeon from Dehra Dun. His son was also an eye specialist. Both of them examined Baba's eyes very thoroughly, perhaps not knowing what a fortune it was to stare deeply into Baba's eyes. After a short talk with Goher the eye surgeon prescribed treatment.

Here I would like to mention that when specialists would call on Baba, His body would not show all the symptoms recounted by Goher. On such occasions Baba would appear quite well and instead of Him being the patient Baba would tend to treat the doctors as His spiritual patients. He would ask them questions about their physical and mental worries and would assure them of His inner help. In some cases He even suggested certain diets for them. And when the physicians had left, Baba would again start complaining to Goher about His ailments and indispositions! The same thing happened with the visit of this eye specialist.

Within a few weeks of Baba's arrival at Satara He began to complain that the gritty sensation in His eyes had started troubling Him again and that it was very painful. In fact, Baba's sufferings from various physical disorders and injuries form a unique medical case. It seems, however, that these disorders and injuries were closely related to His spiritual work on the inner planes of consciousness and were not a direct result of physical causes. There are a number of incidents which suggest such side effects of Baba's working and the sandy sensation in the eyes was one of these occurrences.

At Satara one day, Eruch was marketing in the city area and he happened to notice a sign of an eye specialist. He thought that until Goher was able to call some specialist from Poona or Bombay, perhaps this doctor would be able to provide Baba with at least some modicum of relief. With Baba's permission he arranged the eye specialist's visit to Mutha's Villa. This doctor had no idea whom he was to treat.

The doctor took Baba for Eruch Jessawalla's elder brother or perhaps as someone just visiting Satara for a change of climate. He arrived at the appointed time with the necessary medical appliances and set to work. He pried open Baba's eyes and noticed small granules beneath the eyelids. With a delicate pair of tweezers, he plucked many little globules as easily as one would pick grapes off of a bunch. That the famous eye surgeon from Dehra Dun had not detected the formation of these granules seems odd! Yet stranger is the fact that this eye specialist did not recognize his patient, whom he so closely examined, even during Baba's subsequent stays and *darshan* programs at Satara in the following years. Otherwise he would have realized his unique fortune. Baba was perfect in concealing and revealing His Divinity. Anyway, it is a fact that the extraordinary pain in Baba's eyes was completely cured with the casual visit of this eye specialist and He did not suffer from the eye trouble again. Isn't that incredible!

Kitty and Rano Called to Satara

Prior to the commencement of the New Life, Baba told Kitty and Rano that, owing to the prevailing political situation in India, He had decided not to have any western woman with Him in His New Life of wandering on foot and begging for food. So in October 1949, following Baba's instructions, both of them went to Bombay and stayed at Meherjee's place. They willingly agreed to abide by Baba's decision. Yet they kept a few necessary things packed in a small suitcase so they could leave Bombay and join Baba immediately if called. It seems that Baba often fulfills the sincere wishes of His dear ones, but not necessarily when they are looking forward to them. After some months in Bombay they received a letter from a place in the north, probably Dehra Dun. It was sent with Baba's instruction that there was no possibility of their being called to stay with Him and they were asked to get jobs. They had never, during their previous stay in India, sought paid work. But as Baba's wish was a command and a call of love to them, they earnestly tried to follow His orders.

They started contacting different people and institutions, such as the Y.M.C.A. as well as the different consulates. But it was difficult to obtain the sort of work they wanted, a job that would not violate the conditions laid down by Baba. One day Meherjee's wife, Homai, suggested Kitty see the Principal of St. Mary High School which Meherjee's daughter, Perviz, attended. Kitty had studied and taught piano in England and she sought an opening in that department of the school in Bombay.

The Principal, Miss Groom, was a very religious and loving person. At their first meeting Miss Groom formed a very good opinion of Kitty and agreed to appoint her as a teacher. Kitty decided to teach English instead of piano. During the course of their conversation Kitty mentioned Rano, and that she was also seeking a job. The Principal casually mentioned that she would try to get her on the staff. So Rano met Miss Groom and again the result was favorable; she was asked to teach drawing and painting part-time. Miss Groom was much impressed with Rano's paintings. Knowing that Rano was a novice as a teacher the Principal agreed to give her a small batch of students and permitted her to draft her own curriculum. At the beginning Rano introduced perspective to the pupils and they seemed to get on well with her. While Rano was working part-time, Kitty became a full-time English teacher. She was so conscientious that she worked overtime so that her students could acquire a thorough knowledge of English. She gave them extra lessons and this meant that she and Rano would at times work late into the night, correcting the exercises and preparing the lessons. A wonderful new life!

The pay they received in the high school had to be handed over to Homai. They had to ask Homai for whatever they required for sundry expenses, including bus fare. They were not allowed to eat out. Going to the movies was out of the question. Days turned into weeks, and weeks into months, but these two dear ones of Baba who, leaving their homes and countries, staying with Baba continuously since 1937, now spent their days in Bombay, a city they never dreamt of residing in. That was a totally unexpected participation in Baba's New Life. Above all, the thought of seeing Baba had to be put out of their minds. In a way this instruction helped them to keep Him in their minds and hearts all the more. In one's life with Baba, the Eternal One, one has to accept with cheerfulness not only the days of delightful sunshine, but also the so-called rainy days. And when He is pleased with the spirit of your resignation He spreads a feast. And soon this happened in their case. Quite unexpectedly they received a letter that brought the best of news. Baba had asked them to come for a month's stay with Him at Satara.

The explicit condition mentioned in the letter was

that they could come to Satara on condition that they could have their jobs back. Both of them had begun their duties at school with the special help of the Principal, Miss Groom. Resigning would have been easy for them. But as Baba wished, they had to ask for a long leave right in the middle of the term. When they had been hired they had made it clear that they should be treated as temporary teachers. Yet now they were asking for the special concession of being allowed to rejoin after a month's absence. Their visit to Baba depended on this particular favor from the Principal.

So with great hesitation and a lot of trepidation they approached Miss Groom who, to their surprise, readily sanctioned their leave without asking for any details or reasons. When they asked her whether they would be allowed to resume their duties Miss Groom replied, "Of course, yes." The whole affair was a sort of Baba surprise. Packing things and getting ready did not take much time and in the second week of July, perhaps on the 8th, Kitty and Rano reached Satara to be with Baba and the women companions. Both immensely enjoyed their stay since it was a unique privilege to be with Baba in the New Life.

Ganoba and Aloba

During the early period of Baba's stay at Satara, He once asked Aloba, one of His servant companions, to go to Bombay and get settled in business or seek a job. According to the New Life conditions, he could not dare question Baba's decision. He immediately left Satara and secured a job as a cashier in an Iranian restaurant in Bombay. Baba's reason for sending Aloba was revealed to some extent within a few weeks. The husband of Aloba's niece soon arrived in India from Iran. Had he not found Aloba in Bombay he would have created a scene among his fellow men, the Iranian Muslims. In the course of his search he would have tried to contact Baba and being a fanatic he might have eventually created such a scene that it would have disturbed Baba's New Life. Such a nuisance had occurred in the case of the Muslim boys from Iran studying at Meherabad in the Meher Ashram in 1928. Every action of the *Avatar* has a profound significance whether hidden or explicit, and as years pass by sometimes a few glimpses of this are revealed.

After some months Aloba managed to secure his own tea shop and he made good money. Some months later when it was in full swing, Baba ordered Aloba to close the business and join Him in the tours throughout India, during the phase of His Fiery Free Life in November 1952. Since then he has continued to stay with Baba as one of the resident *mandali*. Aloba's real name is Ali Akbar Shahapurzaman. He is an Iranian Muslim.

Baba's New Life commenced in October 1949, i.e., two years after the political partition of the Indian subcontinent into India and Pakistan. This division was decided not so much by geographical consideration as by religious bias. The Mohammedans especially claimed a separate state — Pakistan — where the majority of the people were Muslims. For a few months the religious fanaticism resulted in looting and killing innocent people in the name of religion, and the Hindus and the Muslims who resided on the boundaries separating the newly formed states suffered immensely. Even after a lapse of two years the bitter ill feelings between the Hindus and the Muslims had not entirely subsided. The march on foot of the Baba-party was through Uttar Pradesh where the majority of people were Hindus. Among Baba's companions were two Muslims. So to avoid any trouble caused by the inquisitiveness of the public, Baba nicknamed Dr. Abdul Ghani Munsiff and Ali Akbar as Ganoba and Aloba respectively; these sounded like Hindu names and made them a little more inconspicuous. Dr. Ghani passed away in 1951; Ali Akbar even after the New Life is known among the *mandali* and Baba people as Aloba.

Most Unexpected Meeting

Once while Baba was sitting with the companions in Bhurke's bungalow, He happened to notice someone wearing a *kafni* sitting on a culvert by the roadside. He asked the companions who they thought the person could be! As the man was sitting with his back towards them they could not say anything. Baba sent Eruch to get information about the stranger. As Eruch approached him, to his great surprise, he found that the person was none other than Dr. Daulat Singh. Both felt greatly astonished at this unforeseen meeting and fell in each other's arms, in a loving embrace. Daulat Singh asked Eruch if Baba were in Satara. Eruch replied that He was. He, however, asked Daulat Singh not to follow him and said, "Wait where you are till I come back." When Baba heard that the stranger was Daulat Singh, He asked Eruch to call him into the bungalow and to tell him that Baba Himself would offer him *bhiksha*. Listening to this, apparently unaware of it himself, tears started rolling down Daulat Singh's cheeks. Eruch reminded him that he should be very cautious about shedding tears in Baba's presence for that very act was the cause of his leaving Baba's company at Belgaum in October 1949.

Hurriedly collecting his satchel and bowl, he followed Eruch to see Baba, the Lord of love. As he approached the door he was extremely thrilled to find himself in Baba's overpowering presence. With a gracious gesture, Baba asked him to extend his bowl. He filled the bowl to the brim with food and his heart with love. With the love that shone in Baba's eyes, Daulat Singh began to weep all the more. The tears seemed to rush into his eyes from nowhere. It was a unique event in the sense that this was the only occasion in Baba's New Life when, instead of asking for *bhiksha*, He offered it. Baba allowed him to come inside the room. He asked him to narrate the whole story from the day he had left the New Life companions. A glorious glance again darted from Baba's eyes and Daulat Singh burst into fresh tears. In a hoarse voice he muttered something which was inaudible. Baba gestured, "Why are you weeping, Daulat Singh?" He replied, "Excuse me, Baba. Please believe me. I am not crying for anything; I am feeling overjoyed."

After a little pause he controlled himself, and began his narration. All that had happened to him since he left Baba came flooding back to him in vivid detail. He told Baba how happy his family members were to welcome him home on his arrival from Belgaum. But this happiness did not last long. As soon as they learned of Baba's orders that he had to observe, they were displeased. They could not bear the thought of Daulat Singh, who was the honorable head of a respectable family, begging. Daulat Singh, on the other hand, maintained that he would not mind begging in the city where they all stayed, even in the locality where he resided. His relatives tried to dissuade him. In the beginning they requested him, pleaded with him and later even threatened him, but Daulat Singh had resolved to carry out Baba's instructions to the very end.

When they failed in their efforts to convince him, the family approached the elders of the Sikh community and urged them to ask him to change his mind. The elders also failed totally in their efforts. Daulat Singh, who was very reasonable and sensible about the various subjects they talked about, refused point blank to modify the slightest part of Baba's orders. The leaders thought that such behavior would be a slur on the Sikh community and they regarded his decision in following Baba as sacrilegious. Thus Daulat Singh's life became a target of the intellectuals of his community and his friends questioned him, "Why put on a wanderer's robe and beg when God has given you a home and enough to eat? What have you gained by following Meher Baba?" They did not know the difference between following the code of religion and the commands of the God-Man. Even the thought of having any material or spiritual gain was alien to the conditions of the New Life. The entire episode infuriated the community and the family members found themselves in an awkward situation. After trying his utmost to stay at home for some months, Daulat Singh felt compelled to leave the house, locality, and even the city to carry out Baba's orders, whom he regarded as the Supreme Lord.

Though physically away from Baba, Daulat Singh indirectly seemed to participate in the different phases of the New Life practised by the companions, such as walking barefoot, resting under the open sky at night if no shelter were available and begging for food. Only the fire of his all-consuming love for his Beloved Master sustained his life of physical and mental suffering. His way of living reminds me of the following lines of Francis Brabazon, the great poet:

To those who are not ready he fulfills their desire;
To those who obey him he gives a consuming fire.

By ruin we have evolved to manhood from star dust;
From ruin God will raise us to Godhood — if we trust.*

Daulat Singh told Baba that from Bangalore he started towards Poona by the highway with no special intention except to obey His orders. He casually thought of staying for a day or two at Satara, not knowing why. His sitting on the culvert to rest was a divinely ordained coincidence which brought him that most welcome meeting with Baba, his Compassionate Companion of the New Life.

All present listened to this narration with great admiration. Baba's face glowed with a rare radiance. He conveyed, "I am pleased with you, Daulat Singh. Now I order you to discontinue this wandering on foot,

---
* Francis Brabazon, *In Dust I Sing*, p. 33.

wearing of a *kafni* and begging. Return home and lead the normal life of a practising physician as you had been previously doing. Go." Daulat Singh's eyes were fixed on Baba's radiant face. He caught Baba's eyes and felt that a shaft of luminosity had touched his heart and in a wonderment of delight he rose to leave the place. The buoyancy felt in the company of the Beloved Master made his eyes glisten all the more. The New Life had sighs of pain but it also offered at times tears of delight.

Daulat Singh was in Bhurke's bungalow for perhaps half an hour but he lost all sense of time in Baba's presence. At parting Baba conveyed, "Do not linger at Satara, go straight back to Bangalore where your family stays." Very lovingly Baba also added, "I am really pleased with your love for me, Daulat Singh. As you have come most unexpectedly to my door, one day you shall find me also visiting your home. This is my promise to you." Before leaving, Daulat Singh embraced Baba with great fervor and it appeared that he was encircling the whole world in his arms. I wish to mention here that Baba did keep His word by visiting Daulat Singh's residence after some years. At that time Daulat Singh, overwhelmed with Baba's presence, forgot to offer Him any refreshment or even tea! He was lost in Baba's wonderful presence and this was such a strong experience for him that soon after this meeting he dropped his body, perhaps to be united with the Divine Beloved, never to part again. His faith in Baba's *Avatarhood* and his spirit of resignation in the face of extraordinary circumstances and great suffering were exemplary and Baba's love for Daulat Singh also seemed unparalleled.

25th July, an Eventful Day

In the second week of July, Baba began His work with the mad and the poor. These persons were accommodated in the compound of the companions' bungalow. On July 21, in a meeting with the companions, Baba decided to send Donkin within a few months to the West for specific work. Baba's special message to His lovers in the States concluded: "My coming to the West in July 1951 is definite, and Elizabeth and Norina have undertaken to arrange this."* Baba was in the New Life and no one was allowed to correspond with Him. So this general assurance consoled those yearning hearts expecting the Ancient One to visit their "modern" land.

July 25, 1950 can be regarded as one of the important and eventful days of the New Life. The servant companions got up at 4 a.m. Before Baba's arrival, Pendu and Eruch thoroughly cleaned the stone flooring in the hall with water. Here, Baba was to hold an important meeting. All were instructed to have a bath by early morning. At 6.45 a.m. Baba arrived from His residence. He went directly to His seat and told all to get into the hall. He also asked one of them to close the windows and the doors of that big room as was done at the time of the first meeting about the New Life at Meherabad. At such meetings, Baba looked extremely solemn though His face continued to radiate a divine glow. Baba asked everyone to be very attentive about everything that would transpire during the day.

At the commencement of this meeting Donkin read Baba's following message which was later circulated to all His people:

> On this most eventful day of my New Life, I send salutations to all my Old Life men and women disciples and devotees ... and to all my New Life companions. I ask the Most Merciful God to forgive us all our shortcomings, failures and weaknesses, to help the Old Life disciples and devotees to keep firm

---

* Again, there was a change in this plan and Baba visited the U.S.A. in April, 1952.

in their faith and their love and their understanding of God and His Divine Manifestations, to give courage to the Arrangementwallas to fulfill their responsibilities 100%, and to give strength to the New Life companions to abide by Truth and the following of the New Life conditions honestly and faithfully.*

After offering salutations to His dear ones and asking God's forgiveness, Baba asked the men to go out of the room. When He was alone, He reaffirmed the oath of the New Life. Then each one was directed to enter the hall and to approach Baba. As each came to Baba, He pressed His forehead on their feet. Later Baba asked Nilu and Vishnu to recite a Sanskrit hymn in praise of the *Avatars*. The first and last verses are rendered into English as follows:

O Lord! I bow down to you. You are the Ruler, the Primeval, the Male, the Cause of creation, preservation and destruction of the universe. You are the animating Principle, assuming Form in answer to the call of Your Lovers....
In my heart I always meditate on You, O Supreme Brahman. You are birthless, deathless and You pervade the whole universe....

Now followed the Zoroastrian, Mohammedan and Christian prayers previously dictated by Baba. A part of the Christian prayer read by Donkin on behalf of Baba is given below:

In the name of the Father and the Son and the Holy Ghost, O Lord! Hear my prayers and let my cry come unto Thee.... I beseech Thee because Thou art Mercy Itself. I offer Thee all my thoughts, words and

---

* *Circular NL* 12, issued on 25-7-1950.

actions, my sufferings and my joys because Thou art the only Beloved.... I, therefore, beseech Thee my God! My Lord of Lords! the Highest of the High! The Ancient One!, to have mercy on me according to Thy Unbounded Mercy and let my cry come unto Thee. O My Beloved! Suffer me not to be separated from Thee for ever and ever. Amen!

After these prayers Baba directed Nilu and Donkin, the two doctors, to read the English translation of the *Bhagavad Gita*. The reading of the *Gita* continued for over an hour. Such a long reading was rather unusual for Baba. He also looked very solemn. Maybe Baba wished to counterbalance His statements about the extreme helplessness of the New Life with the most authoritative declarations He had made, in one of His earlier Advents as Krishna. Krishna, in the part of the Gita that was read (Discourse IX), has stated:

I am the Father and the Mother of the Creation. I am He who award to each the fruit of his action. I am the Receiver and the Giver.... I am equally in all and I am for all. Anyone who loves me comes to me.

At the end of the *Gita*, Krishna proclaimed:

Think of me, worship me, love me. I promise you that I love you dearly. Leave all the various ways of attaining liberation. Surrender to me whole-heartedly; do not fear, do not brood. I assure you [with my divine authority] that I will set you free from all sins — bindings created by *karma*.

I am specially prompted to quote the above lines because when Baba was journeying with the *mandali* in northern India, one of the visitors who had come for His *darshan* said, "Baba, what is your opinion about the *Bhagavad Gita?*" Baba's simple but laconic reply was, "I experience the *Gita,*" meaning the God-Man-State of the Ancient One.

The first part of the day's program continued inside the house and it ended with the recitation of the New Life song. Baba then stepped out of the bungalow to feed a *mast*. Later He served food to all the companions. After a short break, at 2 p.m., Baba commenced His work with the *masts,* the poor and the mad. The companions helped Baba shave and bathe these people. Each one of them was given new clothes, a shirt, a pair of pants and white pyjama. The poor, in addition, received a bed mat of cotton fibers and two coarse blankets. Baba was extremely busy throughout the day. He also fasted, abstaining from taking any solid food, as He used to on such occasions in the past.

Next morning when Baba visited the companions, He expressed His wish to go out begging at the house of the caretaker of the government rest house at Satara. It was a place where He had halted during previous tours. He broke His fast by partaking of the food received as *bhiksha* that day. The great Giver willingly becomes the Beggar if His work demands that He play that role.

While Baba was engaged in His external activities, as mentioned earlier, and especially in the New Life period, those who were with Him had to put in hard work without expecting good food or enough rest. The companions, however, had to remain cheerful, always. This did not mean that Baba was inhuman. He had His own reasons for setting such regulations. In one of the letters Donkin wrote, "Moods due to illness, want of sleep, etc., was one thing and this Baba understood and it was not deemed a fault, but if arising out of anger and irritation because of putting up with hardships, etc., then it would be deemed as a fault not to be tolerated. And Baba warned them all that He had complete freedom to send any away or to keep them with Him."* However, it was noticed that "throughout the New Life Baba was very strict and Baba was also very forgiving, and not without His jovial moods and eternal humour."**

Following Baba in His New Life was a thrilling ordeal and a profound challenge!

An Invitation from the Master

Before shifting from Satara to Mahabaleshwar, Baba, through Adi, issued a general circular to His Old Life disciples and devotees. This gave them news about Baba's activities and a tentative work program. The circular also disclosed the most unexpected but pleasing news about the possibility of meeting Baba in person, during a meeting that was to be held at Mahabaleshwar on October 16, 1950. To quote from the circular:

> Baba has resolved ... to free his present life-long servant companions on 16th Oct. 1950 in order to give them another chance to revise their decision whether to continue the New Life with Baba or become again disciples of Old Life of Baba.... After taking a very careful and complete retrospective view of their personal weaknesses and some pleasant but too many other painful experiences of the New Life with Baba, if they still choose to continue to stay with Baba ... then Baba will take some of them with Him for three months from 1st Nov. 1950 to January end 1951 to help Him in His work amongst *masts* and poor ... as well as for His three phases of begging, *langoti* and gypsy life.
> ... on the 16th Oct. 1950, He has decided to step into the Old Life for a short period of four hours and as soon as the period is over, He will immediately step into the New Life again.... Only all the com-

---
* *The Awakener*, Vol. VII, No. 1 (1960), p. 20.
** Ibid.

panions of the New Life will be given another choice to stay with Baba in His New Life.

...Those, other than servants of Baba... who desire to live that life are free to do so in spirit independently.*

This circular also conveyed the following information:

Baba invites all Old Life men disciples... and all Arrangementwallas to Mahabaleshwar to attend the program between 7 and 11 a.m. sharp on 16th Oct. 1950....

Those, who will accept the invitation, must make their own arrangements regarding boarding, lodging and conveyances.

...[They] are warned that they should not under any circumstances talk to Baba and his companions about their Old Life affairs.**

A few more points that Baba wished His people to note were compiled in a supplement to this circular. It was brought to Baba's notice that the amount on hand for the forthcoming *mast* work and work with the poor was not sufficient. In consideration of the importance of the work ahead of Him, Baba agreed to offer an opportunity to His people to donate money during the meeting; after its termination He did not wish to accept money from any of His people. A portion from the text of the supplement was as follows:

...Baba can accept and add to the *mast* account only during those four hours when He will step into the Old Life on 16th Oct. 1950.

Anyone who genuinely desires to give Him money during that period should do so from Rs. 50 (minimum) to Rs. 500 (maximum).

---

* *Circular NL* 17, issued on 11-9-1950.
** Ibid.

Adi K. Irani circulated the details of the October meeting to the Baba people staying in different parts of India. It was a pleasant surprise and everyone looked forward to the unique opportunity of meeting their Beloved Master. Baba groups, scattered over the country at Delhi, Dehra Dun, Hamirpur, Nagpur, Bombay, Poona, etc., started contacting Adi to say they were coming. Among these the Poona group seemed to be the youngest. In those days the young Baba lovers from Poona were referred to as Ghani's group. Ghani was one of Baba's New Life companions. At Dehra Dun, in one of the meetings, Baba had offered three plans to His companions. Ghani accepted Plan I-C and accordingly he returned to Poona in January 1950. He was most responsible for the formation of this young Baba band.

These youngsters generally gathered at Laxmi Narayan B. Thade's place. It was in the building where he worked as superintendent of a government hostel. Ghani stayed quite close to this hostel and often visited Thade. Fascinated by the Baba stories related by Ghani, a few of the boarders who were in their teens like Rangole, Bade, Pratap Ahir and some friends like Madhusudan as well as Thade's maternal uncles, (Narayan and Krishna), frequently gathered there to hear more about Baba. On every Thursday there was a meeting. After *bhajans, arti* and *prasad,* most of the youngsters would sit around Ghani and listen to his talk, interspersed with Baba stories. This would often continue late into the night. The boys would ask all sorts of questions and Ghani, with his superb sense of humor and without the least irritation, would explain to them the different facets of the *Avatar's* working and His words of divine wisdom in a pleasant and appealing manner. Sometimes Madhusudan would compose songs on the topics discussed with Ghani. In later years most of these songs were sung before Baba and were much appreciated by Him.

Once in 1950 these young boys, along with Ghani, visited the Theosophical Lodge where a famous theosophist was to deliver a lecture on some spiritual subject. At the end of his talk he invited questions. One of the youngsters asked, "What is *Nirvana?*" Perhaps the speaker did not expect this question especially from a teenager and he fumbled while answering it. One of the office bearers of the Theosophical Lodge felt awkward at this situation. Standing by the dais he sarcastically commented on the question about *Nirvana* by saying, "It is ludicrous that those who are not in the elementary grade expect an answer to a university question!" Ghani could not bear this satirical statement. He stood up and requested the chairman to allow him to have his say. He first explained the seven planes of consciousness. Coming to the subject of *Nirvana*, he explained that it was the state of *Fana* (annihilation of the individual mind) in which consciousness of absolute vacuum prevails. For the sake of intellectual understanding of the term *Nirvana,* he added that this state can be likened to the experience that one may have on immediately entering a pitch dark room after a long walk in the bright sun. Or it is like a feeling that dawns on someone as soon as he comes out of a totally dark cave into the dazzling light of the midday sun. You are in it but do not know it. *Nirvana* does not mean total extinction but it is the dying down of the last vestige of separateness. At the end he did not hesitate to declare to the audience that they had no idea of the quality of intense inquiry of those young "back benchers".

During the meetings at the center, Ghani encouraged all sorts of questions, even if they revealed the boys' ignorance. He, however, definitely asked them to be sincere and honest in understanding Baba's statements. He would also bring home to them the limits of human understanding. He said to them, "At present you are like coals that have just caught fire giving out smoke and sparks. That's natural. Baba willing, if and when you are completely ablaze, the smoke [the questions why and how] will cease of itself." In later years, with a growing conviction in Baba's divinity, the group slowly lost interest in dry, intellectual discussions, and began spending more time in singing the glory of the God-Man.

A Persian couplet states:

Akal go astanse door nahin.
Eske takdeerme huzoor nahin.

Although the intellect is not far from the threshold of God, it is not blessed with the fortune of having a glimpse of the Lord.

At Poona there were also a few other disciples of Baba like Khaksaheb, Gadekar, Sule and Baily Irani. They would also frequently visit Thade's place and would relate Baba stories which were helpful in clearing up the youngsters' questions. The boys gathered from them that love for Baba surpasses all spiritual disciplines. Baily narrated a funny episode of the early years. Once Baba visited Baily when he was on the point of taking poison after being disappointed in a love affair with a girl. Baba's timely visit dissuaded him from committing suicide. Baba had a free and intimate talk with him which greatly consoled Baily. Later, Baba pointed at a chair and asked Baily to sit in it. Baba stood at a little distance from Baily and most unexpectedly commenced revolving on the spot, faster and faster. This surprised Baily. But as he continued to watch Baba, he felt that the person spinning like a top wasn't Baba, but the girl he loved. Baba stopped after a while, made no comment, but immediately left the place. Baily, however, learnt that to love Baba was to love all. The God-Man is the Eternal Beloved of everyone.

Ghani also recounted different incidents from the lives of the *mandali*, revealing their intimate relationship with Baba. He also depicted how each one was different from the rest except in his rock-like faith in and love for Baba. These anecdotes were not recorded in any of the diaries as they were of a more personal nature. So Ghani would humorously refer to each of these stories as "inner boxing". He also told them many inspiring events from the lives of the Perfect Masters and saints who had *Vedantic* as well as *Sufic* backgrounds. To emphasize the fact that Baba was the Expected One, Ghani once read out to them the following words of Baba:

> From the viewpoint of Divine gnosis, the Muslims progress from Oneness (*Wahadat*) to Manyness (*Kasrat*) and the Hindus from Manyness to Oneness i.e. the Hindus and Muslims represent the extreme and opposite points of a diameter of a circle with God as the Centre. Zoroastrianism is mid-way between the two extremes and hence the choice at this juncture of a Zoroastrian Form in me as the vehicle of spirituality derived from Hindu and Muslim sources.*

Here I would like to mention that in this Advent, the *Avatar* of the Age chose the English language to explain spiritual truths. This indicates that Meher Baba is also for the Westerners, among whom a good many are Christians. As for Buddhists, I am reminded of a particular incident which I heard lately. One of the *mandali* once reminisced that while visiting one of the caves at Ellora which enshrines a statue of Lord Buddha, Baba gracefully pulled out the alphabet board that He was holding under His arm and, as others were watching Him in silence, He spelt only three words, "I am Buddha." And all felt that the entire cave was resounding Baba's statement. Baba did not convey anything more but left for the next cave. All these statements eventually signify that Meher Baba is equally for all.

The informal "talks" with Ghani gradually helped the Poona group to accept Baba whole-heartedly, on

---

* *Meher Baba Journal*, December 1940, p. 107.

His terms, as God in human form. When this young band got the news of the meeting at Mahabaleshwar, all felt extremely happy. They jumped at the opportunity of being in Baba's *sahavas* on October 16. Thus, this particular circular from Adi became the harbinger of glad tidings to many Baba lovers who were eagerly awaiting the chance to see Him.

At the beginning of October 1950, Baba left Mutha's Villa in Satara for Aga Khan's spacious bungalow in Mahabaleshwar where the memorable meeting of the lovers with the Beloved was to take place.

11

Sermon on the Mount at Mahabaleshwar

1950 — Part VI

"Coming Down" to the Old Life

A FEW hundred Baba lovers, men only, arrived at Mahabaleshwar, a hill station in Maharashtra, from different parts of the country on October 15, 1950. They were expected to be present at Florence Hall* by 6.45 a.m. the next day. Some of the hotels in the town were crowded with the Baba people and these began to bustle with activity in the early hours of the 16th as everyone hurried through his morning chores. By 6 a.m. with clean clothes, happy faces and expectant hearts, the Baba lovers walked along the quiet roads leading to Beloved Baba's residence. He was already present in the open yard, in front of the men's quarters by the time they reached there.

Baba was in the New Life yet all witnessed about Him the same Divine glow of the Old Life. He was standing on the veranda and small groups of visitors were waiting at a distance for His call. After a while, according to Baba's instructions, every congregant was allowed, one by one, to approach Him. Each one, irrespective of their previous years of contact with Baba, was introduced to Him by Adi. It seemed Baba had severed His connections with His lovers during the New Life phase! Or was it a blessed excuse to allow them to have an embrace? After a brief introduction, Baba embraced each one with much love and its sanctifying

---

* Formerly it was the estate of the Aga Khan, but now it is owned by the Poona Catholic Education Association Ltd.

warmth touched and kindled the hearts of all.

At the close of this "reception", Baba directed all to get inside an enclosure which was formerly used as a stud farm for race horses, by Aga Khan. In one of the wings of this meeting house, there was an ordinary wooden chair which Baba occupied. Near Him sat the New Life companions. Dr. Ghani was asked to sit on His right. The visitors occupied their seats silently. Baba looked at the assembly of His lovers and asked them to be comfortable and at ease. Before commencing the work of the meeting, Baba directed Vishnu, one of the *mandali,* to close the big, broad gate of the stable. As Vishnu reached the gate he noticed, at a distance, good old Gustadjee, one of the companions, still walking towards the gate. Perhaps he had gone out to urinate. Respecting his age, Vishnu waited for him to come in. But during this short interval another two or three people also slipped in. After Gustadjee's entry the gate was shut and both left together to join the assembly.

During this small interval of Vishnu's "exit and entry", the congregants were sitting in front of Baba and an air of delightful feeling prevailed. All had their attention focused on Baba. Some were looking intently at Him as He sat there, His mystical dignity and profound Divinity encompassing His fair features, especially His gestures. His casual glances pierced the hearts of His dear ones. It is hard to state what actually transpired during the informal, personal inquiries made by Baba, but it was clear that the inner revelations experienced by the Baba people were enormous. Some with tears silently streaming from their eyes communed quietly with the Divine Beloved. Baba, with His loving and overpowering presence, seemed to have touched the depths of their hearts. These were the preliminaries of that momentous meeting.

But at this point, the uninvited people who had sneaked in, directly approached Baba and not knowing His injunction, bowed down to Him with due reverence.

SERMON ON THE MOUNT AT MAHABALESHWAR

Baba reciprocated this action by pressing His forehead against the feet of each. Astonished, the people repeated the act of paying respect by prostrating themselves before Him. This made Baba all the more displeased. According to the conditions of the New Life, He returned their homage the way they offered it. All those who were witnessing this were taken aback by surprise. Just then some people explained to the visitors Baba's special instructions and brought home to them that it would be not only right but beneficial for them to remain quiet and act as Baba would ask them to do. They were convinced and obeyed Baba's order to leave the enclosure at once.

Baba now called Vishnu closer and asked why he had been late. He told Baba that he had to wait for good old Gustadjee to get in. But in this act of solicitude he had failed to obey Baba literally and instantly. This lapse on Vishnu's part had allowed the uninvited people to enter without his knowledge. Baba had been upset by their presence. Whenever Baba called any meeting, big or small, He was particular that only those who were invited attend it. And this gathering was no exception.

Baba, in the presence of all, severely admonished Vishnu for not being prompt in obeying His order. "Even if you had seen 'God' approaching the gate, you are not supposed to wait for Him to enter!" gestured Baba sternly. Even if He had slapped Vishnu, the displeasure on Baba's face could not have been more obvious. He was in an exceptional *jalali* (fiery) mood. Vishnu, however, stood there quietly, in total surrender to Baba's rebuke. This unexpected happening changed entirely the atmosphere of gaiety at the meeting. Vishnu admitted his fault, and to the assembly his behaviour was an example of the life led with Baba in His New Life. In all the different aspects of this life, obedience — complete surrender to the wish of the Companion — was the first and foremost requisite expected of each one accompanying Him.

This episode did not end with Baba chastising Vishnu; He openly asked some of His lovers whether it was right for Him to lose His temper. And without waiting for any reply, He motioned to one of His devotees to slap Him. This particular person felt so nervous that he hardly hit Baba's cheek. Baba was not pleased with this tender touch. He continued, "Is that the way you slap when you punish someone?" He then asked one of His dear ones from Karachi (Pakistan) to do the job properly. He at once rose up and gave such a harsh sounding slap to Baba that the visitors were astounded to see Baba's face turn red. Baba, however, looked very pleased and this enhanced the radiance about Him. The meeting had not yet begun in earnest. Some who were sitting at the back did not realize what had come to pass in quick succession. Various were the reactions in the minds and hearts of those who closely watched this unforeseen event. It may be assumed that this whole affair was a symbolic prelude to Baba's intention of "coming down" to the Old Life, from the profundity of the New Life, to conduct this meeting.

Every act of the Perfect Master (*Sadguru*), whether of honoring or humiliating his dear ones, whether of blessing or beating them, equally carries with it the secret significance of untying some of the deeper knots of the *sanskaras* of his devotees. Each of his gestures or actions, even when in his *jalali* mood, has its origin not in any personal hostility but in his impersonal Divinity. With reference to such *jalali* actions of Baba's Perfect Masters, I am reminded of a remark once made by Shri Upasni Maharaj. One day a newly-married girl visited Maharaj to offer her respects. He blessed her and permitted her to return home. The girl, however, continued to linger around him. So Maharaj asked her if she had anything special to convey to him. The bride in green *sari* and blouse, the conventional color preferred at wedding, shyly replied. "My mother-in-law has strictly warned me not to leave this place unless I had a beating at your hands. This," she added, "I am told is the best of blessings!" Maharaj smiled and said, "Yes, she is perfectly right. But you can neither demand nor put up a request for it. It is not so cheap. It happens; such intimacy is a rare fortune!" Then, with a few words of advice, he sent her home. In the life of Meher Baba, we notice that only the most intimate men *mandali* received this precious *jalali prasad* at Baba's hands; sometimes He severely reprimanded them, and Vishnu was surely one of His most beloved disciples.

The Simple, Significant Sermon

Baba declared that He had stepped down to the Old Life for this special meeting. In addition, He explained that His companions also had entered the Old Life. At the commencement of the meeting, Baba asked forgiveness of God for not being able to live the New Life as He wanted to. He pardoned His companions for all their weaknesses and lapses committed in the New Life and in return He asked them to forgive Him if He had done anything which had hurt their feelings. Forgiveness, the Forgiver and those who were forgiven had all become One; it was a Divine unifying performance. There was a fascinating grandeur of humility and of Divinity in Baba's bearing. As He looked at those sitting before Him, the light of love seemed to flow from Him, and with His vibrant presence, He appeared to open fresh reservoirs of feeling within the hearts of His lovers. All felt very delighted and relaxed.

Baba then asked Donkin to read aloud the Sermon. It was received with great solemnity and eagerness. The simple words of the Sermon, potent with profound significance, stole into the hearts of the audience. The first sentence, "Essentially we are all One" brought to the listeners the truth that Baba as the God-Man stepped down to the level of a common man to reveal that the two — God and Man — are One. The text of the sermon is given below. Meher Baba stated:

Being just now in "Old Life" for these few hours, I will tell you what I feel to be the established Divine facts:

Essentially we are all One. The feeling of our being otherwise is due to ignorance. Soul desires consciousness to know itself, but in its progress towards this Goal which it cannot realize independently of creation, it must undergo the experience which it gathers as the individualized ego and which is all imagination. Thus it is faced at the outset with ignorance instead of Knowledge.

Dual forms and illusionary creations are the outcome of ignorance: birth and death, happiness and misery, virtue and sin, good and bad — all are equally the manifestation of this same ignorance. You were never born and will never die; you never suffered and will never suffer; you ever were and ever will be, as separateness exists only in imagination.

Soul undergoes experience through innumerable forms such as being king and beggar, rich and poor, tall and short, strong and weak, beautiful and ugly, of killing and being killed. All these experiences must transpire as long as the soul, though it is one in reality and undivided, imagines separateness in itself. When soul is bereft of the impressions of these illusionary experiences it becomes naked as in its origin, to become now fully conscious of its unity with the Oversoul which is One, Indivisible, Real and Infinite.

The soul becomes free of the binding of impressions through various paths. And Love is the most important of these paths leading to the realization of God. Through this love, the Soul becomes entirely absorbed in God, ultimately forgetting itself completely. It is then that all of a sudden Knowledge comes as swiftly as the lightning bolt which burns to ashes all that it falls upon.

This Knowledge uproots illusions, doubts and worries, and apparent sufferings are instantaneously replaced by everlasting peace and eternal bliss which

SERMON ON THE MOUNT AT MAHABALESHWAR

is the Goal of all existence. Soul now free from its illusions, realizes its Original Unity of Being.

Let us not hope, because this Knowledge is beyond hoping and wanting. Let us not reason, because this Knowledge cannot be comprehended or thought of. Let us not doubt, because this Knowledge is the certainty of certainties. Let us not live the life of the senses, because the lusty [lustful], greedy, false and impure mind cannot reach this Knowledge. Let us love God as the Soul of our souls, and in the height of this Love lies this Knowledge.

The divinely Perfect Ones can bestow this Knowledge on any one they like and whenever they like. May we all gain this Knowledge soon.

The Hindi translation of the above Sermon was read by Dr. C. D. Deshmukh. Baba then asked everyone to get a mimeographed copy of The Sermon. "May we all gain this Knowledge soon," was a sort of assurance from Baba that He would help His dear ones to be worthy of His gift of Grace that bestows divine Knowledge. The copy of The Sermon that I received from Baba forms part of my personal, precious Baba treasure. A casual look at this old paper brings back to my mind the whole scene in that "stable", with its incidents glowingly alive. When the distribution of the copies of The Sermon was over, Baba saluted all the Old Life disciples and devotees. This was a lesson of how one should feel obliged at the opportunity of presenting Divine facts to others.

Pukar's First Meeting with Baba

The gathering was then informed that those who wished to offer money for Baba's work with the poor and the God-intoxicated ones could now make their contributions. It was a rare opportunity given to His lovers. This was not compulsory. No one knew what others donated. While this was happening, the audience saw a stout young man silently stand and take off all his clothes except for his underpants, a *langoti*. He was Parameshwari Dayal Nigam (Pukar) of Hamirpur. Before narrating what followed I intend to present some information as background to show what led to this spontaneous though unusual response.

In his childhood Parameshwari Dayal (Pukar) was immensely devoted to Rama. The *Ramayana* was the book he revered and loved most. He could recite line after line from it with great devotion for Rama, the God-Man. After finishing his schooling, he gradually got involved in politics especially because India was then under the British rule and he vowed to free his motherland, India. The interest in leading a spiritual life which he had in mind as a boy, slowly receded and he became a staunch revolutionary, one of the top leaders of an underground organization.

When he first heard of Baba he thought that Baba might be a British spy, trying to divert the attention of other Indians from the struggle for freedom. He also suspected that Baba might belong to that group of false masters who cheat the gullible. Besides, his mind vehemently rebelled against the claim Baba made of being the *Avatar* of the Age. He even decided to expose Meher Baba as a fraud. He openly expressed his views against His Divinity. But in spite of his efforts he found that a few of his close friends and relatives in Hamirpur began to worship Baba as God in human form and loved Him deeply. All this made him visit Hardwar and later Dehra Dun to see Baba in person; each time he missed Baba however. When he reached Dehra Dun, Baba had just left for Satara.

In the early 1940s Pukar wrote a few letters to Baba, challenging His authority. He criticized Baba's way of changing the dates of His programs so often and at the same time expecting implicit obedience from His followers. In one of his letters, he rather impertinently asked Baba why hundreds of people in Bengal (one of the Indian states) should die of starvation due to a severe famine when He claimed to be the *Avatar*. He also wondered when this could happen right under His "nose" in India, how He could possibly relieve humanity at large of its suffering! In those years, Baba was very busy contacting the *masts* and only important letters were attended to. Pukar did not receive any reply to this letter. Owing to his immature understanding of the spiritual work done by the Perfect Masters, he felt that Baba dared not reply to him. This made Pukar denounce Baba all the more. In spite of this severe criticism, his own relatives continued to love Baba, and he became more and more perplexed.

In this state of hostile bewilderment, he learnt about the meeting at Mahabaleshwar. Luckily, he received an invitation and decided to avail himself of this opportunity to solve or appease the conflict that had been raging within him for years. From the day he left for the meeting he experienced a few coincidences which made him feel strongly that Baba was drawing him to Him. There were also incidents that confused him, but after awhile he would realize that he had simply misconstrued the facts. It could not, however, be denied that the entire journey from Hamirpur to Mahabaleshwar was a significant and even glorious event in his life. On the way to Mahabaleshwar he participated in a gathering of Baba people at Poona. The *bhajan* program appealed to him so much that tears of unknown joy often rolled down his cheeks. He also heard with interest some *lilas* from Baba's life and was much impressed. In general, all this made him decide that if Baba was really the One He claimed to be, he would surrender his entire life to Him and would not go back home.

At Mahabaleshwar, on the morning of October 16, Pukar watched Baba very lovingly embrace each of the visitors. He was greatly moved. Baba seemed to have established a perfect rapport with everyone He met. As Pukar approached Baba he nearly broke down. Through the tears that flowed from his eyes, many of the doubts he had harbored about Baba's Divinity were washed away. In the stable, the meeting place in Florence Hall, he sat facing Baba and experienced an incredible awakening of the heart.

People with love and respect started giving money for Baba's special work. As this was optional, Pukar had not previously thought of donating any sum. But on the spot he felt so overpowered that he wanted to give whatever he possessed. He took off all his garments except his underpants — *langoti* — and made a bundle of them. Before doing this, he had hurriedly scribbled a note that he placed in the pocket of his shirt, along with the money he possessed. The short note read that he wished to surrender his money, body and mind at the feet of Meher Baba, the Perfect Master, all in the service of the poor. In tune with the spirit of this note, Pukar, as one of the integral components of the bundle, stood on it. Then he prostrated before Baba with uncontrollable sobs. As he stood in that gathering, nearly naked, a few thought that he was deranged, some even thought that he might be a *mast*!

It was all Baba's game. He gestured to Pukar to bring the bundle of clothes to Him. Someone helped him to go near Baba. Baba looked intently at the clothes, kissed the bundle and returned it to Pukar. Baba instructed him, "Put your clothes back on. When this meeting is over go back to Hamirpur. Continue the work that you have been doing. But remember one thing, that formerly you were doing it for yourself, now think that you will be doing it for Baba." In a way this was a response to the resolution he had made at Poona. In a casual way Baba also conveyed, "It is the inner attitude that counts and not its outer expression." These words of advice helped Pukar in the forthcoming years to understand that Baba's work of spiritual awakening is totally and qualitatively different from the propaganda and activities conducted by the philanthropic societies or political parties the world over.

This understanding was instrumental in his withdrawing from political and social fields and offering his services in Baba's cause. At the October meeting he had only a glimpse of Baba's Divinity. The firm conviction of His *Avatarhood* occurred a few years later. At the time of this first meeting, Parameshwari Dayal was the editor of a Hindi weekly called *PUKAR*, dealing mostly with the political and social issues of the time. Later this weekly was turned into a monthly called *MEHER PUKAR*, totally devoted to Avatar Meher Baba and His message of Love and Truth. And as Parameshwari Dayal came in closer contact with Baba, instead of calling him by his long name, Baba nicknamed him "Pukar", which is how he is known to this day.

When all who voluntarily wished to contribute had done so, it was declared that the money collected would be used only for the work mentioned in the earlier circular, during Baba's tour beginning on October 21, 1950.

Pankhraj Gets Married

The previous night all the Baba people staying in different hotels were advised that if anyone had had any difficulty in obeying Baba's orders which had been given to him in the Old Life, he should bring that point to Baba's notice. Such people were to write their problems on separate notes which were to be handed over to Baba the next day. After a short break the morning session continued. Baba inquired whether all had come back. Then He allotted time to attend to these problems. As Baba learnt the contents of each note, He spontaneously offered concessions or suggested adequate changes in the previous instructions. All these little alterations ex pressed Baba's deep spiritual insight, tempered with His sense of humor. This was most evident in the case of Pankhraj, who was earlier asked by Baba to get married in His physical presence. Before coming to this topic, I wish to relate a short account of Pankhraj's previous contact with Baba which reveals Baba's omniscience in drawing His dear ones to Him.

In 1940 Pankhraj was studying in a college at Nagpur. During summer vacation, he chanced to read some spiritual literature which impressed him so much that he decided to discontinue his education, much to the displeasure of his father. Instead of having a degree to lead a so-called rich and respectable life, he resolved to be a simple aspirant and seeker of Truth. He commenced leading a life of strict spiritual discipline. He took vegetarian food without salt, slept on a rough bed, maintained a day-to-day diary in which he wrote about his own weaknesses and made confessions. He formed a small group and prepared a code of conduct. He became a *sadhak* (an aspirant). This was not only a sudden but also a complete change from the life he had led in college. During his college days Pankhraj was a good sport and keen participant in college activities. He did not then have any interest in spirituality. In fact he used to criticize the lives of the saints. However, years earlier as a child there had been a time when for days and months he used to repeat the name of God, Rama, continuously for hours. Perhaps the seeds of spirituality had thus been sown in his childhood.

In July 1940, he attended a talk by Dr. C. D. Deshmukh on "The Need for the Awakener". The Awakener's (Baba's) message of love touched his heart. As he read and heard more and more about Baba, he felt that Baba was the personification of love and the embodiment of beauty. The more he became one pointed in his allegiance to Baba, the more he severed his connections with his former group of semi-ascetics.

In 1941 he got a temporary job in his father's office filling in for a clerk who had a 20 day earned leave. The day he received his first pay envelope, he decided to spend the money on a visit to Meherabad to see Baba. Dr. Deshmukh told him that Baba's whereabouts were not known. He suggested to him that he get an appointment. But in his fervor to see the Beloved, Pankhraj was not ready to wait any longer. He boarded a train at Nagpur and got down at the Ahmednagar railway station. He had not been to this place before; however, in one of the books on Meher Baba he had seen a picture of the Meher Retreat on the hill and remembered that it was by the railway track.

With this meager information he started walking along the railway lines until he reached the top of the hill. There he saw Pendu supervising some construction work. From him he learnt that Baba was not at Meherabad and he felt very sad. Pendu, who was the manager at Meherabad, nevertheless permitted him to stay in the *ashram,* down the hill. It was here that after so many months he drank tea and slept on a mattress. He gradually realized that Baba expected His devotees to lead a normal life of love and service, in His wholehearted remembrance, without imposing unnecessary restrictions. If you get a plain meal don't grumble, if you have a feast don't indulge. Parading of spirituality vitiates the core of spiritual life.

Coincidentally the next morning, Baba arrived at Meherabad and was busy calling different members of the *mandali*. They were meeting Him after a year's absence, resulting from His extended *mast*-tours and seclusion. As they were called to receive specific instructions, Pankhraj, through Vishnu, conveyed his request for *darshan* to Baba. But it being a phase of seclusion and special spiritual work, Baba refused to see him.

Pankhraj had come to Meherabad with the intention and mental preparation of staying permanently near Baba, but he found that he was not allowed to have even a glimpse of the One at whose feet he wanted to surrender his entire life. This was quite shocking. Instead, Baba sent a message that if Pankhraj could afford to, he might pay a visit to Kedgaon for the *darshan* of Shri Sadguru Narayan Maharaj, one of Baba's Masters. This was quite an unusual instruction. But it carried hidden significance. Pankhraj loved Baba but he was very skeptical about His Masters, especially Upasni Maharaj and Narayan Maharaj because of the perverted information published in a few Marathi journals. He had neither the urge nor the money to spend on this visit to Kedgaon. This message, though not acted upon, nevertheless helped Pankhraj to shed his misgivings about Baba's Masters. To be able to accept Baba as BABA on his terms, needs not only inner guidance but also His grace.

The denial of *darshan* greatly upset Pankhraj. In obedience to Baba's instructions he left the *ashram,* but remained sitting under a tree by the roadside asking each of the *mandali* going up the hill to place his "case" before Baba for reconsideration. He could not refrain from sobbing and weeping bitterly. After his going through a period of agony and restlessness for a fairly long time, Vishnu came with heart-warming news from Baba. Pankhraj was summoned by the Beloved, and in raptures he followed Vishnu up the hill. He was asked to stop at a distance of about 50 feet from Baba who was then standing on a cement platform under a tree. He wore a silk coat and looked very radiant. In the period of "special working", Baba would not allow anyone other than the resident *mandali* to come closer to His person. Pankhraj saw Baba; and His divine splendor stirred his soul to its depth. His joy knew no bounds. He stood gazing at Baba. Nothing was asked or conveyed orally but his heart communed with the Beloved's. After a few minutes, Baba gestured, "Isn't it enough? Now leave."

On the way down the hill, Vishnu asked Pankhraj some personal information about him and his family members and especially inquired as to why he wished to stay near Baba. According to Baba's instruction, Vishnu said to him, "If Baba gives you sufficient wealth to provide for all the amenities of life, will you be happy?" "I have not come here for this," was Pankhraj's reply. When this was conveyed to Baba, He was pleased and He called Pankhraj again for a second *darshan.* At this time Pankhraj was told that he would be called after a year or so and that Baba might then give him certain instructions which he should whole-heartedly follow. He was also instructed to return directly to Nagpur. However, before he left Meherabad another message communicated to him was that Baba's *nazar* (protective blessings) would be on him. With Baba's initial refusal to see him, Pankhraj found himself in the valley of dejection, but Baba's subsequent intimate concern and loving messages lifted him up to the skies. Baba, at times, used and is still using this "pushing away and drawing closer" technique to awaken the hearts of His dear ones to His love.

With a very warm heart Pankhraj left Ahmednagar. He had a passing thought to get down at Chitali, to see Upasni Maharaj at Sakori. But Baba's instruction to go straight home made him drop the idea. When he got down at Bhusaval, he saw the connecting train for Nagpur standing on the next platform. Instead of directly getting into it, his mind lured him into walking round the city before catching the next train. What a vain thought! It was the trick of the Devil tempting him to swerve from the spirit of obedience to the Master. Poor Pankhraj succumbed to it and after roaming about in the city he returned to the station but boarded the wrong train. Only after great inconvenience did he reach Nagpur but at least the lesson he learned stayed with him for the rest of his life: never to alter with selfish motive any of Baba's instructions. After Baba's *darshan* at Meherabad, he witnessed a considerable change taking place within him. The rigidity of *sadhana* was replaced by liveliness. He realized that Baba's guiding hand had been silently at work during the so-called good and bad times of his earlier life. They had all been designed to lead him to Meherabad for the *darshan* of the Eternal Beloved and the opening of a new chapter in his life.

In the summer of 1942 Pankhraj was specially called to Dehra Dun. Baba directed him to follow a few specific instructions and this gave him a strong feeling of being accepted by Baba. The years passed by and he came into closer contact with Baba. He wished to remain a bachelor but circumstances took such a turn that he had to ask Baba whether he should get married or not. Baba permitted him to remain engaged to a girl, another Baba lover. The marriage, however, was to take place in Baba's august presence. Time rolled on and Baba entered the New Life. In this phase, no one from the Old Life was allowed to see or correspond with Baba. So Pankhraj refrained from getting married. In the meeting at Mahabaleshwar, Baba permitted His dear ones to put forth their difficulties, if any, with the previous instructions given by Him.

In the course of the notes that were read out to Baba, Pankhraj's case was also brought to His notice. Only men were invited to this meeting so Pankhraj's fiancee, though a Baba lover, had not come. With a smile Baba asked dear old Gustadjee to stand up. He was to play the role of Pankhraj's "bride". Amidst laughter, Baba asked Pankhraj and Gustadjee to come closer to Him and to shake hands as husband and wife. They did so and Baba blessed the couple! He then instructed Pankhraj to go home and get married in any way he liked. Pankhraj wished to perform the wedding without any pomp or traditional ceremonies. So he visited the Registrar's office with Tara Raje, the bride, and in Meher Baba's loving remembrance, Rama Pankhraj and Tara signed the register. It was a human attestation to the Divine Registration! To this day, in their united love for Baba, the Real Beloved, Rama and Tara are leading a happy married life.

Baba thus attended, very lovingly, to one and all the questions brought before Him by His disciples and devotees. Rama Pankhraj's case is enough, I think, to give an idea of the magnitude of the other problems presented as well as of the love and loyalty with which Baba lovers obeyed and still obey Baba's instructions. When this item of dealing with the difficulties was over Baba looked relieved and switched to the next subject.

SERMON ON THE MOUNT AT MAHABALESHWAR

Perfect Divinity and Perfect Humility

In that enclosure behind Baba's seat there was a piece of cardboard displayed on the wall. In the centre of it was pasted one of Baba's pictures. On its right side was written in bold letters, OLD LIFE — Perfect Divinity, Divine Man, and on its left, NEW LIFE — Perfect Humility, Ordinary Man. To clarify the symbolic meaning behind these phrases, Baba had already prepared an explanation which was now read out. It revealed how these two aspects of Divinity in action get expressed through the life of the God-Man, to fulfill His spiritual work of awakening. Baba asked Donkin to read this special message which also included some other important points connected with His New Life. With reference to the phrases, Old Life and New Life, written on the board, Baba had stated in the message:

> If I am the One my Old Life disciples take me to be, I would wish them to endeavour whole-heartedly to stick to their faith and love, to carry out my Old Life instructions without any feeling of enforced bondage on their part, and to live a life worthy of real Love; and, irrespective of what I am, the Most Compassionate God, will surely reward them spiritually, even if they do not seek reward....
>
> My Old Life places me on the altar of Absolute Godhood and Divine Perfection. My New Life makes me take the stand of a humble Servant of God and His people. In my New Life I am the Seeker, the Lover and the Friend. Both these aspects — Perfect Divinity and Perfect Humility — have been by God's Will and both are everlastingly linked with God's Eternal Life. Anyone may believe me to be whatever he likes, but none may ask for blessings, miracles, or any reward of any kind. My New Life is Eternal.

In the earlier part of this message, Baba had offered the Yeswallas another chance to reconsider their decision of continuing to accompany Him in His New Life. He asked all of them to think seriously about their own weaknesses and to take an impartial survey of their past experiences before arriving at their final conclusion. About the forthcoming life Baba clarified:

> If in spite of all this, they [Yeswallas] decide to join me as servants in the New Life, they must know that they will have to try and obey me 100 per cent, and must do whole-heartedly whatever I want them to do. The servants' obedience to my orders must be spontaneous and devoid of any feeling of slavery or compulsion. They must carry out my wishes with a cheerful willingness, without in any way feeling it an encroachment on their freedom.

He also added that the conditions accepted in the first meeting of the New Life at Meherabad on August 31, 1949 remained unchanged.

The gist of this message, rendered in Hindi, was conveyed to the visitors by Dr. C. D. Deshmukh. Baba again distributed copies of the message in English to all and declared a recess for half an hour. Perhaps it was intended to offer time to the Yeswallas to think over this latest proposition from Baba. This short period also provided the opportunity for each of the congregants to receive *laddoo* (a sweet) as *prasad* from Baba. Everyone also had a cup of refreshing tea.

When all gathered in the enclosure for the third time, Baba expressed His satisfaction over the duties performed, despite great odds, by the Arrangementwallas. Before the beginning of this session, He left the chair and went inside a room to take the Oath of the New Life. When He returned, He was wearing a white *kafni* and an ochre colored satchel was hanging down His shoulder. In the New Life, He had used this satchel while begging for food. As He took His seat He declared that He had entered the New Life and asked every Yeswalla to announce his decision. Adi,

SERMON ON THE MOUNT AT MAHABALESHWAR

Daulat Singh, Anna Jakkal, Ali Akbar (Aloba). Minoo Kharas, Babadas, Pandoba, Kishan Singh, Bal Natu and Dr. Ghani decided to adopt the Old Life. Pendu, Vishnu, Eruch, Nilu, Donkin, Kaka Baria, Baidul, Gustadjee, Murli and Kaikobad (Dastur) resolved to be Baba's servants in His New Life.

Baba offered a prayer to God to give Him strength to live the New Life fully and completely as He wanted to. The Hindu, Muslim, Christian and Zoroastrian prayers were recited by different companions, the way they were offered at Satara on July 25, 1950. These prayers considerably changed the tempo of the meeting. Then followed the *qawwali* program. The *qawwal* who used to sing in Mutha's Villa at Satara was called to Mahabaleshwar. To the accompaniment of a harmonium and a *dholak* (drum) he sang the Song of the New Life. At the end of this singing, Baba slowly and gracefully got up and went out to bathe a *mast* known as Bapji. As Baba emptied mug after mug of water over Bapji's bare body the *mast* obviously enjoyed the bath. Baba also looked alive with the delight of some inner work done to His satisfaction. Bathing a *mast* in the presence of all was an unusual event. Maybe it represented cleansing some *sanskaras* of the visitors, through the medium of Bapji. Only a guess!

The meeting was over. As some visitors began to leave the premises a few tears rolled down their cheeks. With voices thick with emotion they took their leave of the companions. Some looked very buoyant while some were deeply absorbed in and impressed by the happenings at the meeting. Yet, everyone definitely felt, "What a wonderful day!" and with the fullness of this feeling they left Mahabaleshwar.

*Nawab** Selling *Bidis* and Matchboxes

On October 21, Baba and the companions offered the following prayer: "Grant us your guidance, Oh God

---

* A Mohammedan title for a nobleman.

Most High, and stir up our hearts with your love, Oh Christ the Everlasting Truth, that we may live the New Life with a faithfulness that will endure to the end." The same day, as was planned earlier, Baba decided to commence the tour of India for His *mast* work and His work with the poor. In the Old Life, He had personally contacted thousands of poor people in various villages and had given them, as *prasad*, cloth, money and food grains worth tens of thousands of rupees. It was not charity but a typical external activity to accomplish certain results on the inner planes of consciousness. How? Baba did not explain.

Collecting and contacting poor in India was not very difficult, but during the forthcoming tour Baba wished to offer large sums of money not to such individuals but to the heads of very poor families who were once rich and well-to-do. He did not reveal any reason for such a preference. It was a new phase of His work with the poor. The *mandali* never questioned Baba about His intention. They firmly believed that Baba's every action was completely selfless and that the Divine Will continuously manifested through Him. They knew that if they whole-heartedly carried out Baba's instructions, however difficult they might be, Baba's inner guidance would lead them to the appropriate persons and places. On this tour Pendu, Eruch, Gustadjee and Baidul accompanied Baba. Thirty-three families of the type mentioned above were contacted by Baba in different states of India, viz. Bihar, Orissa, West Bengal, Tamilnadu and Andhra. Only two such accounts are given here but this narration will give some idea not only of the type of families contacted but also the ways in which Baba delivered this financial assistance.

Baba was in Hyderabad (Andhra) when the *mandali* heard of a very wealthy Muslim *Nawab* who had literally become a pauper. In the earlier years when he used to travel by train he had his own special coach. He was wealthy enough to maintain elephants at his palatial residence. But the tables of fortune turned or, rather, crashed to such a degree that it was now hard for him to earn his daily bread. Friends and relatives who had thrived on his money totally deserted him. What a world! The *mandali* thought that the *Nawab* would be the kind of person that Baba would like to contact. So they made many inquiries about his whereabouts. At last they learnt that recently he had been staying on the open veranda of a *sarai* which afforded free lodging to the poor. There he had a small wooden crate in which he placed *bidis* and matchboxes for sale. This was his only source of income by which he had to feed himself and his wife.

When Baba and the *mandali* went there, they found that the man was ill and his wife had gone out to get some medicine, perhaps from a free dispensary. Eruch told the man about Baba's intention to help him financially and explained the routine He followed before offering this help. The man agreed to all these conditions. So he was asked to move to the edge of the veranda. He dangled his legs over the low parapet. Baba swiftly but very lovingly washed and dried his feet with a towel. Then Baba bent down and placed His forehead on the feet of that *Nawab*. But as He was lifting His head the old man suddenly collapsed and became unconscious. Luckily, one of the *mandali* caught the man and prevented him from falling to the floor. Perhaps his heart could not contain the joy of receiving financial help so unexpectedly! Maybe Baba's tender touch overwhelmed him. Whatever the reason, this complicated the situation.

A group of women who had been curiously watching the whole scene from a distance drew closer and out of sympathy for the old man they raised a hue and cry. Thinking him to be dead a few even beat their breasts. They openly accused the party of killing an innocent person for nothing. The *mandali* felt embarrassed but Baba looked calm and unperturbed. He asked His men to inquire if there were any responsible persons around who were related to the *Nawab* to whom the envelope containing the money could be given. In an indignant tone one among the crowd replied, "The old man's wife is his only relative and she has gone out to get medicine for him. Oh God! But of what avail is it now!"

While the women were engaged in making some accusatory remarks about the party, Baba Himself joined the *mandali* in lifting the *Nawab* and making him rest on a bed which had an unclean, tattered bedsheet. They also sprinkled water over his face and continued to fan him so that he might regain consciousness. As it was getting very stuffy inside the room, the *mandali* asked the crowd to disperse but no one would listen. However, after a while, the man gradually opened his eyes and the *mandali* heaved a sigh of relief. The *Nawab* was alive! Just at this moment the *Nawab's* wife arrived and she was greatly surprised to find people crowded inside the room, including a few persons whom she did not know, and her husband looking very wearied lying on a bed. With a bewildered look she said to the *mandali*, "Strangers, why are you harassing a sick person?" Eyes lit with gratitude, the *Nawab* softly muttered, "They are not strangers but God-sent angels!" His words calmed down the old lady and also alleviated the prevailing confusion and hubbub.

Eruch took this opportunity to speak with the *Nawab's* wife. He disclosed to her the purpose of their visit. He also introduced her to Baba as his elder brother who lovingly offered her the envelope containing the money. Eruch addressed her as follows, "This is offered as a gift from God and you will oblige us by accepting it." Baba also instructed her to use this amount towards their welfare. By this time the atmosphere in the room had completely changed and most of the people started praising and glorifying God. Baba, who would not wait a moment more when His work was done, left the place with the *mandali*, almost unnoticed. The *Nawab* never knew whether the money received by him was a God-sent help or the God-Man's *prasad*. No one from the *mandali* ever met this couple again! Perhaps such incidents in Baba's life are meant to set examples of how

SERMON ON THE MOUNT AT MAHABALESHWAR

to render help selflessly and anonymously.

Sincere Prayer Is Never Ignored

During this tour Baba visited Madras and was moving through the city to contact *masts*. At midday He consented to have coconut water, a very refreshing and cool drink of the south. Baba had a special liking for fresh coconut milk. He was standing under the shade of a tree and Eruch went to the other side of the road to get the coconut dressed. In the meantime Baba overheard some people talking at the *pan* shop about a person who had once been rich but whom the wheel of fate had reduced to a pitiable state. On Baba's instruction, Eruch approached the *panwalla* and told him of his big brother's intention to help some respectable poor families. The *panwalla* narrated the whole story, including the name of that unfortunate person and also that of the contractor who had swindled him and usurped his newly built home at Gudur in Tamilnadu.

Hearing the report, Baba decided to leave for Gudur immediately by the first available train. It was a journey of 2-3 hours. At Gudur, Baba, Pendu, Baidul and Gustadjee waited at the railway station. Eruch left to find the house where the person whom Baba intended to contact lived. He knew the name of the contractor who had finagled his way into getting possession of this man's new building. With this clue he first found that particular building and knocked on the door. A person with diamond rings on his fingers opened the door and politely said, "What can I do for you, sir?" Eruch told him the name of the person Baba wished to contact and added, "I hear that he is in dire need of help. My brother wants to help him. Can you tell me his address?" At this, the mood of the contractor changed. He even looked a bit annoyed and said, "Sorry, I do not know." But at this point a boy who was not even in his teens came out from inside and said, "Sir, I will show you the house of this person." This boy was either the son of the contractor or someone living in this family. The man got angry with the boy but Eruch skillfully interrupted, "Why do you not allow him to come with me, sir? I shall be thankful to you for this."

The boy willingly led the way while Eruch followed him. They crossed some lanes and by-lanes and Eruch was all the time observing their route, trying to remember the shops they passed since he would later have to take Baba there. By a narrow lane there was a row of adjoining houses. It was late in the evening. From a distance the boy said, "You see that house. I mean that door which has no small clay lamps with lighted wicks in front of it.* That is the house of the man you wish to meet." So saying the boy quickly left Eruch and hastened home. It was *Diwali* day but that particular house had no lamps lit before its doors. Standing at the door, Eruch saw in the semi-darkness a young girl, with her back to the door, standing before a life-size statue of Lord Krishna; she was absorbed in prayer. Ten minutes passed and her prayers continued. Finally, not wishing to keep Baba waiting too long at the station, Eruch lightly knocked on the door. The girl turned her gaze and invited Eruch inside. She must have been a well-educated girl for she spoke in fluent English.

Within a few minutes Eruch received corroboration of the information they had gathered at Madras. As he stepped into the room, he saw the girl's father, who was very ill, lying on the floor. He was an invalid. In another corner of the room was her sick mother. What a miserable situation! Except for the statue of Krishna, there was no other furniture in this room. Obviously circumstances had forced them to sell what they had. Eruch explained to the girl that his brother, out of His compassion for all, wished to render some financial help to her father, and that He had especially come to Gudur

---

* On *Diwali* days it is the custom for Hindus to have near the outer doors and windows, small clay lamps filled with oil lit by wicks. In the early hours of the morning and in the late evening these are kept burning for hours. Hence Diwali is known as the festival of lights.

from Bombay. He asked her to stay home till he returned there with his brother who was waiting at the railway station.

Eruch met Baba who was very eager to hear his report. Within a few minutes Baba, accompanied by Pendu and Eruch, left by a *tonga* to visit this particular family. It was unusual that the *tongas* in this city were drawn by bullocks instead of horses. Eruch, with his excellent memory, directed the *tonga* to the correct lane. The young girl was at home and a single little oil lamp was dimly burning inside the room. Eruch explained that before giving financial help his brother had to observe certain formalities. Her father who was running a high fever was made to sit on his bed. He was asked to put his feet in a basin. Baba washed his feet with lukewarm water and dried them with a soft towel. All these things, including water, were carried by the *mandali* whenever Baba used to go for such work. At the close of the contact, when Baba handed over the packet of currency notes worth five hundred rupees to the person, Eruch repeated in a soft voice, "My brother says that this money, given by loving hearts for deserving and needy persons is now offered to you. You should not take it as charity or feel yourself under any obligation whatsoever. Please consider it as a gift of love." These words brought tears to the eyes of the old man.

Baba left the house as soon as the work was over. Eruch thanked the girl. She looked so amazed that she could not express her feelings in words. As the Baba-party was leaving the house, Eruch saw her standing again before the statue of Lord Krishna saying, "How compassionate you are, O Lord! How quickly you respond to our prayers!" Little did she know that in her case the Lord of the Age Himself had blessed the whole family. Owing to their dire poverty, on that *Diwali* day the family had not been able to decorate their house with small clay lamps for "light". But Baba's presence must have lit the hearts of the trio, a real celebration of *Diwali*, the Festival of Lights. The God-Man bestows His blessings with such consummate skill that the recipient is not aware of the treasure conferred on him.

The work of helping poor families led the Baba-party to Bihar where the people were severely affected by the flooding of the Kosi River. Baba visited the interior parts of the state. After reaching Jhanjharpur and Madhupur in the district of Darbhanga, Baba walked through the ravaged villages to contact the poor afflicted villagers. He gave five rupees to each of the persons, male or female, He contacted. Baba's trip symbolized His silent participation in the sufferings of the people. Eleven well-off families who were severely affected by the floods also received substantial financial help at Baba's hands.

A Funny Scene on the Railway Platform

Side by side with the work of helping the poor, Baba continued His contacts with the *masts*. Baidul was in-charge of finding these God-intoxicated ones and in taking Baba to where they resided or roamed about. During this tour nearly a hundred *masts* had the blessed fortune to meet the God-Man face to face. In Bihar, Baba contacted such souls at Patna and Chhapra, in Andhra at Hyderabad and Secunderabad and in Tamilnadu at Madras. Though the places visited for the *mast* contacts are known, the names of the *masts* and their special traits have not been recorded. It seems that after the New Life phase no one asked Baidul about their names and the interesting incidents connected with this tour. However, as an exception, in a letter sent to the West, one of the events was reported. This happened during Baba's journey by train from the Nepal border to Calcutta. Baba had visited Janakpur in Nepal, a place of many temples and *ashrams,* where He blessed twenty spiritually advanced souls, though not *masts*. Then the party proceeded to Calcutta.

The following incident occurred at Colgon, a small railway station. Here there was a *mast* who was regarded by some people as mad. He passed most of his time in the station premises; he also roamed about the adjacent streets. Baba seemed pleased to contact this person. Later, the *mast* sent word that Baba and His party should spend the night with him, as his guests. Baba, as a rule, tried to accommodate the wishes of any *mast*. In this case, He sent a message to the *mast* through the *mandali* to cancel the invitation and to permit the party to proceed by the next train. The *mast* did not readily agree.

After some time he came to the railway platform and extended the same invitation. The passengers crowded around the Baba-party engaged in conversation with that so-called madman. In the beginning they felt amused but soon, for some unknown reason, the crowd felt so agitated with the whole affair that Eruch and Baidul were pulled about and a group of the people dragged the *mast* out of the station. Baba was silently watching and enjoying this comic situation. Just then the train arrived and the people rushed towards the compartments to get good seats. During this confusion and uproar the *mast* probably gestured at Baba to leave Colgon, and that is why the Baba-party also boarded the same train. What a funny contact!

As for the other *mast* contacts in the eastern states of India, it can be stated that the general method of meeting with them did not differ much from that followed in the Old Life, except that the companions were allowed to be with Baba while He paid homage or served these God-intoxicated souls. Whatever the city or town, Baidul would collect information about the *masts*. He would personally pay visits to them. If he felt that the person was a genuine one, Baba would consent to contact him. Most of the *masts* had life stories which, although true, if recorded would read like fiction. With a profound awareness of inner realities these lovers of God led a life of external and inner renunciation, unmindful of any discomforts. With them the abhorrence of luxuries was neither forced nor imposed. Their stay near urinals for years or their roaming practically naked in severe cold formed part of their natural living, in communion with their Beloved God.

In spite of the abuses they uttered they had real love in their hearts. In their mumblings ecstasy would rise as a song. When they would stare at Baba's face their eyes would shine brighter. After Baba's contacts their hearts would either be filled with peace and bliss or would be set aflame with His love. This also depended upon the nature of the work Baba had with them. During the present tour of different states, Baba offered many *masts* the things they seemed to like most as *prasad*. It was a tangible expression of His spiritual help to them. Baba's work with the *masts* can be regarded in many ways as the matchless *Avataric* activity of this Age.

Illustrative *Mast* Contacts at Bombay

Baba concluded this tour by visiting Kolhapur, Miraj and finally Bombay in Maharashtra State. At Bombay, He stayed at Nariman's house, Ashiana, on Warden Road in the Breach Candy area. This flat was kept entirely at Baba's disposal for twelve days, from November 25 to December 6, 1950. Besides those in the Baba-party, only the Arrangementwallas were permitted to stay at Ashiana and Ramjoo Abdulla was one of them. Ramjoo accompanied Baba during the *mast* contacts in Bombay and has written a graphic account of it. This narration will also help the readers get a picture of the other contacts made in different states during this whirlwind tour. Ramjoo writes:

> Baba started contacting the *masts* from the morning of 27th and completed the work on 29th of November. Baba maintained a uniform method of approach to all those whom He contacted. That approach was essentially one of great humility and submission. First of all, Baba used to be very careful and avoided causing the least disturbance or annoyance to the one approached. One of the *phirta masts* i.e., those who keep on roaming from place to place

without sticking to any particular place or locality, was found lying on a footpath near Mahim. The moment the *mast* was spotted, the car was stopped; and we all followed Baba quietly near the spot, where this semi-naked *mast* was lying huddled up, on the bare ground. In spite of the blazing afternoon sun, he was found fast asleep without any shelter over him. After watching him for few minutes, Baba decided not to disturb him at all and said, "We shall take another chance, some other time"; and with that we moved on.

Although Baba would not seek actual permission in order to pay His respects, He would not make an advance, unless He was satisfied that it was not likely to be resisted. But, once the contact was established, Baba would not leave the place without obtaining the express permission of the other party by word of mouth, nod of head, or any other gesture of assent. Once at Bandra, a *mast*, who puts up in a very simple but neat little hut over a hill, overlooking the sea, granted Baba's prayer for the asking; but he added, "*kabhi, kabhi aaya karo,*" i.e., "Visit once in a while." Baba at once stopped; He had the prayer repeated with the statement that He would like to go now and waited until He got the clear and unconditional assent of that *mast*.

Unless and until Baba could touch His forehead upon the feet of the *mast* and get an assent to His request from him, a contact was not supposed to be complete. It was while He placed His forehead on their feet that I [Ramjoo] generally used to repeat the prayer, "*Aap dua karayn kay inka ruhani kaam ho jai,*" meaning thereby, "You will kindly pray that His [Baba's] spiritual work is carried out." The response used to be received in various ways and words. The *Salik* (discerning) type, would say, "*Insha-Allah ho jaiga*" i.e., "God-willing, that will be completed." Some would merely nod their heads. Some boldly asserted, "*Ho jaiga*" i.e., "That shall be done." One queer type, at first did a lot of fencing by asking how he could dare interfere with the Will of God and the work of the Masters. But when assured that all that was needed from him was his own blessings, he suddenly went into an ecstasy and began to give sharp raps on the back of Baba, four or five times, saying that the work shall be carried out. . . .

The *masts* were found in all sorts of places, settings and circumstances, throughout the nooks and corners of Bombay. Nothing stopped Baba from carrying out His self-appointed pilgrimage with the briskness and thoroughness of an electioneering campaign. I [Ramjoo] will, for the present, stop with describing the case of one, who so to say, paid back Baba in His own coin! I would call him the Patiwala Baba — a short, robust, full-bearded Arab or Pathan type of a Muslim. We had to go to him twice, once in the morning and the second time late at night. He would let people collect round him. So, the second time, Baba decided to approach him with only myself by His side. In the sweetest and most persuasive tones that I could adopt, I began to plead with him that we did not mean to disturb him, and pointing to Baba, I [Ramjoo] said that He only wished to pay His respects. At last the "lion" roared. With a gesture towards Baba he said something to this effect, "He may be God, may be Mohammed; but why not leave me alone?" Baba quietly touched the old man's feet from a distance and beat an immediate retreat, asking me to leave him alone. "He is a fine fellow" repeated Baba more than once.*

During Baba's stay in Bombay He contacted nearly 20 God-intoxicated souls. He felt satisfied with this work and wished to relax for a few more days at Ashiana.

---

* Ramjoo Abdulla, *Meher Baba and The God-Determined Step*, p. 17.

SERMON ON THE MOUNT AT MAHABALESHWAR

Bhiksha and *Langoti* Phases Concluded

In the Mahabaleshwar meetings, Baba had informed the gathering that in the forthcoming tour He would be concluding the two phases of *bhiksha* and *langoti*, i.e., begging for food and wearing a loin cloth. These phases symbolically represented the helplessness of the New Life. During His stay in Calcutta one day He specially visited Dakshineshwar where the Perfect Master Ramakrishna Paramhansa stayed most of his life. It was morning and Baba with the companions moved briskly through the premises and all the temples. He inquired about the dining hall used by the disciples of the Master. The *swami* in charge of the *ashram* told Eruch that as they were not using the hall it was locked. On Baba's instruction, Eruch told the *swami* that his brother would like to retire a while in that particular place and asked him for the key. The *swami* without making any further inquiries readily offered it. Baba sat quietly in seclusion in that hall for about half an hour, wearing only a *langoti*. It was indeed fitting that Baba selected Dakshineshwar for this type of work, where *Sadguru* Ramakrishna, who was renunciation personified, had kindled the flame of *sanyasa* in the hearts of his close disciples. Thus ended Baba's New Life phase of wearing a *langoti*.

After the short seclusion at Dakshineshwar, Baba put on a *kafni*, took the "begging bowl" and hung the ochre colored satchel on His shoulder. He started "begging" at the stalls that lined both sides of the lane leading to the temple. No one gave Baba anything. Perhaps no one dared to offer that exceptionally radiant beggar the sundry things they possessed. Also it was a strange sight to them, for those who followed Baba had decent clothes, pants and coats. And, in addition, Pendu had a bag full of coins of low denominations, from which he gave a handful to each beggar or mendicant that Baba, with a glance or gesture, directed him to.

Where the line of stalls terminated, Baba turned to

the right and commenced begging at each of the adjoining houses on the side street. Eruch generally used to say at each house, "Mother, please, with love, give *bhiksha*." In the first few houses no one paid attention to this call of love. As the Baba-party neared a house with a latticed veranda and issued the call, the women of the house came out. They seemed greatly impressed by the Beggar standing at their door. Spontaneously they said, "Please do not move on till you accept *bhiksha* here." In a short time they filled Baba's bowl with freshly cooked vegetables and offered Him a good quantity of cooked rice. Baba looked exceedingly pleased. It was the last house where the Lord of this Age begged for food. How fortunate must be that family though the members never knew the great worth of their simple offering!

After leaving that locality, Baba stopped at a quiet place under a tree. He distributed the *bhiksha* to His companions and He Himself joined them for lunch. The food tasted very delicious. Thus ended the *bhiksha* phase of the New Life.* Baba then took off the *kafni* and put on the *sadra*, trousers and coat which He generally wore during such trips. While staying in Bombay, Baba also concluded the work of offering financial help to needy families by giving one thousand rupees to four families connected with Him in the Old Life who were in great need of help.

Having completed the different phases of work, Baba wished to relax and rest for some days. Of course, this only meant a change of "work". He consented to visit the Brabourne Stadium to witness the cricket matches between the Indian eleven and the Commonwealth team. Baba and the *mandali* sat in the North Wing of the public stand. He appreciated the enthusiasm and the witty remarks made by the spectators about the good drives and strokes of the batsmen and the easy catches

---

* Even after this, however, Baba went out begging once at Khuldabad in November, 1951.

which the fielders missed. On December 5, when He called the companions and the Arrangementwallas to His room, for no outward reason, He looked very tired and ill. He told the *mandali* that He would not visit the stadium on that day. By lunch time, when He gestured to turn on the radio, perhaps to hear the score of the match, the first news they all heard was of the passing away of Shri Aurobindo Ghosh, at Pondicherry in the early morning, at 1.30 a.m. In the Old Life, Baba would refer to Shri Aurobindo as one of the great saints of India. He asked Nariman and Meherjee to confirm this news from other reliable sources. Later, He decided to remain indoors for the whole day and was in a pensive mood. Why? He alone knew.

On December 6, Baba left Bombay and reached Mahabaleshwar. As He was very particular about the proper expenditure of money received from His lovers, He asked one of the companions to write down and check the details of their expenses during the tour. The balance was sent to one of the Arrangementwallas with the necessary instructions. The entire information was circulated to all Baba people. Sometimes Baba used to appear very lavish and sometimes very frugal. It all depended on the spiritual need of the time; money by itself had very little value. During the above trip, Baba was very economical about the requirements of the Baba-party though He gave thousands of rupees to help poor families. This itinerary like the other *mast* tours of the Old Life was full of hardships, little food eaten at untimely hours and only a few hours sleep for those who accompanied Baba. Baba's demanding but compassionate companionship, His challenging yet, at the same time, reassuring demeanor made this trip very trying but also fascinating.

Singing Program on Mehera's Birthday

During Baba's stay at Satara a little pony was purchased from the gypsies. Baba named it Begam (Lady).

At Mahabaleshwar when Baba, with the women *mandali*, would go out for a walk in the mornings in the bracing and cool climate, Begam would follow like a pet dog. In Florence Hall she would climb the veranda and go straight to Baba in the drawing room where He would feed her with carrots. Sometimes Begam would come earlier and expectantly wait for Baba. Baba's love for animals was one of the most loving facets of His life.

This year Mehera's birthday coincided with Christmas and Baba agreed to have on that day a singing program by the Poona *bhajan* party. This group was composed of young Baba lovers. R. K. Gadekar, one of Baba's old, close disciples, residing at Poona was asked to inform the youngsters about the program. The Thade brothers, Madhusudan, Pratap and a few others were given this news which greatly delighted their hearts. Gadekar was also instructed to send a passport size photograph of each member of the group. Baba intended to select one of these boys to stay with Him for a few more days after the program.

Dr. Ghani who stayed at Poona continued to feed the group with enlightening and inspiring Baba stories (*lilas*). He brought home to them how fortunate they were to be invited by Baba during His New Life. He strongly desired to accompany them but in the letter Baba had instructed that only the Poona *bhajan* party should visit Him. So he composed a *ghazal* and asked or rather requested the boys to sing it before Baba. On December 21, Khaksaheb, another of Baba's old *mandali* visited Thade's place. He had developed an intense urge to see Baba. But owing to Baba's injunction he dared not visit Mahabaleshwar. He too composed a very touching *ghazal* and asked the boys to include it in their singing program. Coincidentally, two days after this visit, Khaksaheb passed away and that particular *ghazal* turned out to be his last message to his Beloved Master. Gadekar was one of Baba's old disciples, yet he decided to join the young group of lovers because he used to join them in singing. A good excuse!

SERMON ON THE MOUNT AT MAHABALESHWAR

On December 24, in a very delighted mood, the party reached Mahabaleshwar. Vishnu looked after the lodging arrangements of the visitors. The same evening Baba happily agreed to have a program. When the group arrived Baba's eyes sparkled and with a sweet smile He conveyed, "I am happy you all have come. Tomorrow you have to visit Florence Hall again in the morning. Sing freely and whole-heartedly. But remember that you have not to refer to anything concerning the Old Life." Pointing at Pratap (Ahir) who was hardly in his teens, Baba asked if he could stay with Him for a few more days. Pratap's immediate reply was, "Yes Baba, Yes." A lucky chap! Then Baba signalled to commence the program. Baba was pleased with Pratap's singing and He asked him to sit near His chair. When the group sang Khak's *ghazal*, Gadekar, who was blessed with a childlike nature, looked very restless and wanted to tell Baba about the passing away of Khaksaheb. But because of Baba's earlier instruction concerning the Old Life, he tried to check himself. Baba noticed this and knowingly gestured at him, "Don't worry, I know." This calmed Gadekar down but a look of wonder shone on his face.

After a few songs, Ghani's *ghazal* was sung. Baba liked this composition through which Ghani, in his humorous style, had expressed his feeling of being "pushed aside" by Baba. The refrain of the *ghazal* was:

What a sunny day it was!
What a dreadful night it is now!
(I hope) God's hand is on the Wheel of (my) fate!

Ghani was Baba's schoolmate and close disciple too. He used to have free access to Baba. But in the New Life phase, after his return from Dehra Dun, Baba did not permit Ghani to visit Him except at the October meeting at Mahabaleshwar. Even then he had had no personal interview with Baba which saddened him. In the above *ghazal* Ghani poured out all his pent up feelings, spiced with humor. Ghani's *ghazal* did touch Baba though at the time He did not comment on it. A month later He sent Ghani an invitation through a short poem composed by Him. It is said that if anything ever touches the Universal Heart it is love, and also a real sense of humor. And Ghani was a great humorist.

Here I am reminded of another humorous refrain composed by Ghani in 1940 when Baba was at Bangalore. At that time, Meher Baba was busy with the formation of a Universal Spiritual Center and His work with the *masts*. He had assigned various duties to the *mandali* staying near Him. No one was expected to interfere with the work of others. Baba casually remarked that the one who could efficiently and economically manage his department would please Him the most. For some days Baidul was in charge of the mess. With the thought of winning Baba's favor by being extra economical, Baidul purchased a lot of pumpkins. They are very cheap and last for a long time. So every day the *mandali* would have a vegetable dish of pumpkin for lunch, and supper too. This continued for a week and a few developed an aversion to the food.

The *mandali* freely talked with Baba but they dared not complain about any instruction He had once given, unless He asked someone about it. Naturally everyone hesitated to bring this "pumpkin problem" to Baba's notice. Ghani could not bear this any longer. He had a brain wave. He knew that sometimes Baba asked a few of them to sing. He composed a *ghazal* and trained one of the inmates to sing it. The refrain of it was:

Our dear Baidul has cooked a *kola* [pumpkin] today,
And lo! He cooks it every day!

The song not only gave Baba a hearty laugh but it also conveyed to Him the *mandali's* grievance. He looked into the whole matter and instructed Baidul not only not to cook the pumpkin again but ordered him to bury the whole stock on hand that same day!

SERMON ON THE MOUNT AT MAHABALESHWAR

The next day, on December 25, the Poona *bhajan* party reached Baba's residence by 7 a.m. The group was led to a spacious hall where the program was to take place. Soon Baba arrived. He had put on a silk coat over a long white *sadra*. To the young Baba lovers He appeared very resplendent and in a relaxed mood. His expression belied the sufferings He had endured during the earlier tour. It had often been noticed that in spite of excruciating physical pain and spiritual suffering, Baba looked very radiant while meeting visitors.

The boys tuned the musical instruments and the hall resounded with the vibrations of sweet music. *Bhajans* glorifying the love of God, the Beloved, were sung. Baba looked very pleased. He gestured, "I like you all." And He sweetly smiled and added, "You have sung some Krishna songs; do you know any Radha song?" Baba might have proposed this because of Mehera's birthday. The boys remembered one such *bhajan* but they had not practiced it before. However, as they began to sing it, Baba liked it so much that after the refrain He took a *dholak* on His lap and Himself played on it. Padri who was present photographed Baba playing the *dholak*. During this two day program, Padri's camera clicked many times to register Baba's unique gestures. The singing continued for about two hours. Then the moment of departure arrived. A deep silence fell over the group. In that overpowering silence Baba communicated His message of love to each. The *bhajan* party left Mahabaleshwar the same day, their hearts singing merrily the name of the Lord of Love.

Rano and Kitty were also at Mahabaleshwar as the school where they worked in Bombay remained closed for Christmas. About that Christmas morning Kitty writes:

> Baba returned to Mahabaleshwar from the tour before Christmas. How well I remember that Christmas! We went into the jungles that surrounded our

villa, and dug up a small evergreen tree to place on the living room table. Mehera and Mani, with Mehroo assisting, made all its paper decorations. Mani insisted I make an angel for the top of the tree. The tree looked beautiful and I can still see that sweet, gentle smile on Baba's face as he stood by it on Christmas morning. Rano and Naja made their contribution — a table decoration. It was a wonderful cottage made out of cookies, icing and sugar. A face peered from one of its windows. It was lit up from inside by some quite simple contrivance, for we could not buy materials. Up the lane to the little house trotted, I believe on the snow, a deer. There in the middle of the jungle, Baba had this wonderful surprise — A Christmas tree and a wintry Christmas cottage! It is these small things which bring that not-so-frequent smile on Baba's face when suffering is acute.*

And the New Life phase for the year 1950 was thus concluded.

---

* Kitty Davy, Recollections Part II, *The Awakener*, Vol. VII. No. 1 (1960), p. 30.

12

Hundred Days' Seclusion

1951 — Part I

Service to the God-Man Never Goes Unrewarded

DURING the New Life, Baba's daily routine was full of activities which entailed hardships and suffering. It was a part of the arduous spiritual game He was engaged in. In early December, after His return from Bombay, He commenced planning another tour of contacting *masts*. The lease in connection with Florence Hall where the Baba-party stayed in Mahabaleshwar was to end at the end of May. Every year by the second week of June it starts to rain generally in Maharashtra and the monsoons bring torrential showers specifically to Mahabaleshwar. Sometimes the sun is not visible for days. So Baba wished to move to some place with a more moderate climate and He preferred Hyderabad. He instructed Adi to bring his blue Chevrolet to Mahabaleshwar and to drive Him to Hyderabad so He could select the two bungalows (houses) to be rented in June. While He was there, He also wished to contact some of the God-intoxicated souls. Adi promptly arrived and in the third week of January 1951, Baba, with a few companions, left for Hyderabad.

On the way the party halted at Sholapur where Baba contacted three *masts*. Ghuliappa was a typical *yogi* of the fifth plane. He referred to himself as if he were a woman! He resided in a clean apartment and had remarkable eyes. Mulla Baba was contacted a short distance from an Indian gymnasium where he was sitting in a filthy environment, oblivious of his surroundings. He had long dirty nails and a wild temper too. Despite his disposition, he was greatly revered by the local populace. They feared him, respected him and loved him as well. The party resumed their journey and reached Hyderabad on January 16. The guest house at Osmansagar was reserved for the Baba-party for three days. Before beginning the hunt for the *masts*, the *mandali* inquired of real estate agents about vacant bungalows. Baba had already specified the requirements for the houses to be rented and Adi appeared most concerned about checking every detail with the agents.

Adi had a good reason for being concerned. A few years back, in 1945, Baba had entrusted to Adi the work of leasing a house at Hyderabad. Adi did this job diligently and reserved a newly built villa for Baba on the Jubilee Hills. This Villa had a good swimming pool and a lovely lawn. After the arrival of Baba and the women *mandali* it was noticed that though the electric fittings for the fans and lights were perfect, the house lacked a direct connection with the power station. Since this was during World War II, regulations prohibited the establishment of any new connection and thus the house was without electricity. Even kerosene was not easily available. Those staying in the house did not grumble over the inconvenience. Baba, however, would often blame Adi for not being careful enough in observing the instructions given. Sometimes, He threatened Adi to the extent of His leaving the house and even the city where He had come for special spiritual work. Adi felt very sad over the whole affair.

It was only after thorough inquiry that he found that Dharam Karan, one of the Rajahs in the Hyderabad state, was the only person empowered to grant an extra connection under exceptional circumstances. He tried to meet this person but to get an official interview with this Rajah who rolled in riches, and in princely vagaries too, Adi had to wait patiently for over three hours. The Rajah, on his arrival, seemed most disinterested in meeting his visitor. Adi pleaded his case well, specially by stating that his elder brother (Baba) had come from

HUNDRED DAYS' SECLUSION

Bombay and that the party should be treated as the guests of the great city — Hyderabad. Had Adi disclosed Baba's identity, things would have moved very smoothly but that was not permissible. The Rajah somehow was convinced of the genuine need for "lights" and put his long and most illegible signature sanctioning the application. The head of the power house reluctantly extended the connecting wires to the bungalow where Baba and the women *mandali* were residing; and there was light!

This Rajah was in fact interested in paying his respects to the saints. One of his secretaries who was a Parsee had previously heard of Meher Baba and, anticipating his master's interest, he visited the house where the men *mandali* stayed. Adi met him and explained that since Baba was in seclusion, it was not possible for Dharam Karan to have Baba's *darshan*. Perhaps Adi had a grudge against this Rajah who had not behaved cordially towards him. Just then Baba who had recently arrived at the *mandali's* quarters, sent someone to the living room to inquire as to who had come and what he wanted. Hearing the report, Adi was called in and, to his surprise, Baba at once acquiesced to the Rajah's request for *darshan*. On some later occasions, Dharam Karan came to see Baba with his whole family. He became friendly with Adi. It seems that even if someone unconsciously renders any help in the cause of the God-Man, it shall be rewarded tenfold. Whether you love, serve, or hate the God-Man, nothing shall go in vain. Once the connection with the *Avatar* is established it will draw His blessings and compassion. And there are a good many instances to justify this supposition.

During the present stay — January 1951 — the owners of the two vacant bungalows were contacted and without any difficulty the due legalities were completed within a day. This made it easier for the companions to move freely with Baba for the *mast* contacts in Hyderabad. Baba's special intention, during the short visit, was to renew past contacts with the God-intoxicated ones. He resumed this work with a brilliant start and within a day and a half, He had met about thirty-one *masts*. It was rare for Baba to be able to meet so many *masts* in such a short period. It was as if these contacts had been prearranged by Baba, for no sooner would He arrive at a certain place than the *mast* would be spotted as if he were waiting for Baba. While returning to Mahabaleshwar, Baba halted at Gulbarga and Humanabad. There was also a short detour to visit Itka. Here Baba had to walk a pretty long distance to contact a spiritually advanced soul named Swami. This love-intoxicated person was found in a very jolly mood and readily accepted the sweets given by Baba, a favourable indication that the *mast* would be willing to shoulder spiritual responsibilities. Hence this diversion made Baba quite happy. From Gulbarga the Baba-party journeyed straight to Mahabaleshwar.

Ghani Invited for a Short Stay

Before leaving His headquarters for Hyderabad, in one of the informal gatherings of those who stayed with Him, Baba made a casual reference to Ghani's Urdu *ghazal* that was sung by the Poona *bhajan* party portraying Ghani's "heartache" following him. The refrain of the *ghazal* was:

> What a sunny day it was!
> What a dreadful night it is now!
> (I hope) God's hand is on the Wheel of (my) fate!

The whole composition, though spiced with humor, expressed Ghani's woeful feelings. In reply to this *ghazal* and perhaps in consideration of his school day friendship, Baba in a sympathetic and witty mood, composed the following poem, addressed to His dear companion, Ghani.

HUNDRED DAYS' SECLUSION

If you are well
If you feel swell,
If you have not gone mad
Or don't say you are sad,

      Have no material loss
      From servant or boss,
      No talk of Old Life
      Or child or wife;

But entertain me
With jokes and poetry,
Will pay both fares
But won't listen to your cares.

      Then come for eight days,
      So Meher Baba says.
      Don't give me pain
      By asking material gain.

Talk of spiritual benefit,
Will give you gober* and shit.
In New Life no responsibility,
Of reward no possibility!

Naturally, Ghani felt highly honored and delighted at this most unexpected invitation from the Compassionate Companion. For an answer he spontaneously wrote the following stanzas and mailed them promptly to Baba. He wrote:

Received your loving letter
I feel awfully better,
Is India getting dry?**
It never looked to me wetter!

---

* *Gober* — cowdung.
** During those years there was a prohibition drive in India.

A thousand thoughts and what not,
It looked almost a boycott!
Twelve months no (w)-ink, no inkpot,
I could not get the upshot

And Jal with dates noting,
Gadekar drowned in doting,
With Pappa seemingly bloating
And Ramjoo meaningly gloating.

This atmosphere was pretty sure
Could not very long endure,
De facto verdict for a cure,
Could not ignore my stand *de jure*.

Accepting all your orders
Will come for dates and numbers,
On mind no madness, murder!*
Be damned the cares and "thunders!"

Hoping there are no blunders,
For ever I remain yours

sd/- Abdul Ghani

After Baba's arrival at Mahabaleshwar, the above stanzas were read out to Him. He seemed pleased with this reply full of humor and in appreciation of Ghani's response, in a jovial mood, Baba dictated the following four lines as a message and confirmation of the call.

After carefully your letter noting,
I feel like going a boating;
If any of my orders you break,
Your body on the Ganges be floating!

---

* About a decade earlier, Ghani, through sheer desperation, had tried to commit suicide and Baba, most unexpectedly, visited his town, Lonavla, and helped him at the right moment.

HUNDRED DAYS' SECLUSION

Later, Ghani visited Mahabaleshwar for a short stay with Baba and it was a period of good relaxation and recreation for both, especially for Ghani.

A Short Visit to Bombay

As it was previously planned, after a little rest Baba agreed to visit Bombay. On the way, at Poona, near the Aranyeshwar Temple, He did a part of His work with the poor by offering monetary help. This sum of money had been offered to Him by Pilamai Irani when Baba was about to begin the New Life. Pilamai was one of Baba's early stalwart disciples who, in spite of great opposition in the 1930s from the Parsee community at Karachi, was the first to make beautiful rings and lockets containing Baba's pictures. People wondered at her conviction in Baba's Divinity as the God-Man. Baba wished to offer this money to seven deserving people who were His Old Life devotees. In addition to this work, at Bombay, He gave seven hundred rupees to two Parsee families.

It was noticed that even in the New Life, Baba's work with the *masts* and the poor proceeded hand in hand. Besides the servant companions (Eruch, Baidul and Gustadjee), Baba had called Adi Jr., Jal S., Padri, Ramjoo and Savak (Kotwal) to travel with Him during the *mast* contacts in Bombay. This work of contacting the God-intoxicated ones did not differ much in its outer features from what has been described in the earlier chapters. As for its spiritual significance, Baba once casually remarked that these contacts with the souls drowned in Divine Love had a 100% bearing on the forthcoming work to be achieved in the hundred days' seclusion which was to begin on February 13, 1951. In Ashiana, Nariman Dadachanji's residence in Bombay, Baba, in the company of His close ones, once conveyed, "It is natural for me in my New Life to feel void of all that it was natural for me to feel in my Old Life." So Ramjoo, the author of *The God-determined Step,* referred to

Baba's role during the New Life as one of a very "extraordinarily ordinary man".

It was about this time, on His return from Bombay, that Baba received a cable from Elizabeth Patterson. It stated that Baba's visit to the West in July, 1951 was not feasible. In answer to this Baba asked Donkin to send the following reply to her, "Baba's plans are changed. Instead of leaving in July, 1951, He will leave in February, 1952. Do not worry and rest assured that Baba wants to come and stay for one year." In Florence Hall, on February 12, Baba had a meeting with His companions and the following decisions were arrived at: from February 12, 1951, the servants were freed from the bindings of the New Life conditions except for a few standing orders, i.e., not to commit any lustful action, not to create circumstances that will invite homage, not to accept money or food from anyone and above all to obey Baba 100%. All the companions were to stay with Baba as His servants till June 10, 1951.

Self-giving Love Accepts Suffering

On February 13, the sacred seclusion began. This phase of work caused great physical and mental strain for Baba. He tried to adjust for His subsequent fatigue by changing His places of work in the Aga Khan bungalow (Florence Hall). Sometimes He stayed in a small cabin or closeted Himself in a specially built hut with a thatched roof. The first forty days, from February 13 to March 24, turned out to be very critical and crucial. Perhaps in order to participate in His spiritual burden, Ali Shah, a *mast* of the fifth plane, was brought from Ahmednagar to Mahabaleshwar. For three weeks (February 15 to March 5), Baba sat for some time each day with Ali Shah who was very co-operative in Baba's inner work. At the beginning of this sublime seclusion, Baba fasted for a week and for the rest of the period He had only one meal a day. The work in the hut seemed very strenuous for Him and whenever He came out

HUNDRED DAYS' SECLUSION

He looked very tired. This was one of the indications of the profundity of His work.

A typical way of working in the hut was that at night when He was all alone by Himself, He spent some hours in complete darkness and some in bright glaring light. Was He dealing with the prevalent forces of darkness and the impending days of spiritual sunshine? Baba never explained the significance of this particular method of work which was adopted only once to accomplish the required spiritual results. And had He conveyed anything I wonder how far it would have been of avail to us! Baba lovers carry the conviction that the depth of Baba's work is unfathomable and love expects no explanations other than those the Divine Beloved gives on His own. To those who stayed with Baba, it was clearly visible that out of unbounded compassion He had to stand great physical strains which made Him extremely helpless.

Kitty Davy who was staying at Mahabaleshwar wrote her impressions about Baba's seclusion as follows:

> I can recall Baba's weak physical condition and supreme state of helplessness during the hundred days' seclusion, yet every evening during that period the *mandali* were called to Baba for recitation of evening prayers in Marathi, Urdu and English. This period was my first experience of seeing Baba so helpless and in such great physical pain.... On one occasion, Dr. Goher, realizing how much Baba was suffering and his state of helplessness and humiliation during this period, gave way to tears. Baba asked her why. She replied through her tears, "Because we have done all we can and that has not helped." Baba replied that it did not help him to see her so upset — that all was as it had been ordained, and our part was to keep cheerful and happy.

In this New Life phase when Baba emphasized his

purely human aspect with all its limitations, it was difficult at times to remember that Baba had also "Eternal Bliss." Perhaps as someone suggested this unlimited Bliss forsakes a Christ when he deliberately out of his compassion and mercy for man takes on the sufferings and the limitations of man and this, though appearing to limit the unlimited, is really fuller proof of the true perfection of a Christ, for it expresses the self-giving love which accepts suffering for a struggling humanity.

Krishna, we read, used to offer prayers and homage to God, worship and serve saints and his own lovers and devotees in all sorts of lowly capacities. Christ asked God to forgive him in order to give the world the example of seeking forgiveness from God, thus assuming a separateness from Him. Baba, in this New Life phase, living life in its different phases, holds up before us all the practical example of repentance, worship, prayer and service.

> "We may not know, we cannot tell
> What pains He had to bear
> But we believe it was for us
> He hung and suffered there."

And we too must believe it!*

Dr. Nilu, one of the companions, was also attending Baba as a physician. One day, he felt very nervous while giving an injection to Baba, who looked extremely tender and utterly helpless. In Nilu's attempt to be overly cautious and careful, the injection needle got twisted. Beads of perspiration crowded Nilu's forehead while Baba, silently writhing in pain, was looking with great compassion and forgiveness at Nilu. Throughout this seclusion the barometer of Baba's health fluctuated

---

* Kitty Davy, *The Awakener*, Vol. VII, No. I, (1960), p. 31.

greatly; the pointer mostly tending towards great physical weakness.

A Step of Revolutionary Change

When the critical period of forty days was over, Baba issued a Statement and after a fortnight it was followed by an Elucidation. The excerpts given below from both the circulars are self-explanatory.

> Out of the hundred days' seclusion that began on 13th February, 1951, the main work was achieved during the first forty days which were very crucial and important. Without the help of God, I could not have gone through this ordeal successfully, considering my usual changing temperament and the physical and mental strain that I suffered during this period. It was as if God wanted to prove His help to me by giving me suffering as well as strength to endure it. I also feel that the prayers and the invocations dictated by me and offered on my behalf by the servants have been accepted by God.
>
> The remaining sixty days are not very difficult for me to live through. With God's help I can adjust the activities and the place of work according to my convenience.... In view of the fact... that my hundred days' seclusion is likely to be accomplished to my entire satisfaction and that I feel God also will be entirely satisfied with it, I have, God knows, the honest conviction that during the period between 10th June and 30th June, 1951, God will, out of His infinite wisdom and grace make me take a Step which will bring about an extraordinary revolutionary change in my life, and in the life of the servants, the Arrangementwallas and the Old Life disciples and all those directly or indirectly connected with me.*

---

* *Circular NL* 25, Statement issued on 1-5-1951.

While elucidating this Step, Baba continued:

I have firm conviction that God is so determined that I shall certainly be made to take the irrevocable Step.... This Step might plunge me into a life older than the Old Life or newer than the New Life; or into a life below both these lives; or into a life above both these lives.... I am also confident that by God's help and by His Will the result of the irrevocable Step which I shall come to know and declare in June, 1951 and which I shall put into execution on 16th October, 1951 will fructify by 16th February, 1952. All this has been put before you plainly and clearly in order that my statement may remove confusion, if any, and give confidence, if none, to you all. Nevertheless I feel, the result of this irrevocable Step that God will bestow in His own ways will in no way depend upon whether one is confused or confident.

The extraordinary that has to happen must happen by God's Will.*

Correspondence Course in the Bible

On May 23, the seclusion was over and the Baba-party was getting ready for a shift to Hyderabad. After this strenuous work of a hundred days, Baba wished to leave Mahabaleshwar for a short period. A change. Before leaving for Hyderabad, Baba consented to visit Poona for a few days. A bungalow in one of the suburbs of Poona was kept at Baba's disposal and also for the *mandali* going with Him. This was a huge unfurnished house in the part known as Wanori. On arrival Baba felt that the house was not suitable for His relaxation and work, especially because of a nearby tannery which filled the surroundings with an awful odor. The men *mandali* went out in search of another house and were

---

* *Circular NL* 25. An Elucidation issued on 1-5-1951.

delighted to find a really ideal place for Baba. This was Guru Prasad. Thus the foundation of Baba's work that He did in Guru Prasad in the 1960s was laid in the New Life.

During Baba's stay at Mahabaleshwar, He had expressed a wish that no one should directly or indirectly try to see Him or write to Him. The Baba people abided literally by His instructions. However, one day there came a visitor, a Roman Catholic priest. He had not come to see Baba about whom he knew nothing, but he wanted to meet Murli Kale, who was one of Baba's New Life companions. During Baba's stay at Satara, Murli, to improve his knowledge of English, had enrolled as a candidate for a correspondence course in the Bible. A novel idea! Every week he received a printed lesson based on the gospels of the apostles. Along with each lesson there would be a questionnaire on that particular part. It was a sort of test to find out how far the pupil had studied and grasped the truths revealed in the New Testament.

From the beginning of this course Murli relied on Eruch's help in writing the answers. Eruch in his teens had studied in a Catholic school at Nagpur. There he attended the scripture classes and studied the New Testament with great interest, so much so that he developed a great love for Jesus the Christ.

In the scripture classes, Eruch would sometimes ask questions about certain incidents in the life of Jesus. The Father would explain the matter well but at times there would arise a question to which he, being unable to answer, would reply, "Sit down, Jessawala. That's a mystery!" When this continued to happen often, Eruch thought, "How nice it would have been if I had been in the company of Jesus! Then everything would have been plain and simple; no mystery!" It was about this time (1930s) that Meher Baba frequently visited Nagpur and stayed in Mary Lodge owned by Behramshah D. Jessawala (Eruch's father) who was a high ranking government officer — the Chief Inspector of Factories and Boilers — for the Central Province and Berar, now the state of Madhya Pradesh. This estate had a big garden with some fruit trees and many potted flower plants.

During Baba's visit, on school days, Eruch would sometimes get into the house by the back (wicket) gate, have a wash, change clothes and leave for the playground to join his friends, while Baba would be strolling near the main gate, occasionally inquiring about Eruch. Gaimai, Eruch's mother, would later say to her son, "Why do you evade Baba's company, Eruch? Do you know who is Meher Baba? He is our Prophet Zoroaster come again!" Eruch would frankly tell his mother what he thought and did. Of course he revered and respected Meher Baba very much. But he had not as much love for Baba as he had for Jesus. His heart silently whispered, "Even if Meher Baba is Zoroaster come again, so what? I love Jesus the Christ. I await His second coming." Thus the *Avatar* of the Age, Meher Baba, was lovingly waiting for Eruch at the main gate, while Eruch with his genuine yearning to be in the company of the Christ was unknowingly evading Him by sneaking through the back gate! What irony! Years later, Eruch had the conviction that the same Ancient One, who had come as Zoroaster, as Jesus and as other *Avatars* in the past, had once again assumed the human form as Meher Baba and he accepted Him as the Lord, the Highest of the High.

Eruch had left Nagpur in 1938 to stay permanently with Baba. Now after twelve years, while he was going through the Bible lessons that Murli received, he was in a way reliving his days at school. His deep interest in the New Testament and love for Jesus were reflected in the answers he framed in reply to the questionnaires. As the weeks passed by successive lessons were received, but with each lesson Murli's enthusiasm diminished, and he started depending entirely on Eruch for the answers. After a month or so, the Baba-party shifted from Satara to Mahabaleshwar where Murli's course concluded and he heaved a sigh of great relief!

According to the convention of the institution, one of the priests in that area was asked to contact Murli and to offer him a special present as his answers were most remarkable. The priest congratulated Murli on his scholarly answers. Murli had never dreamt of such an honor and was completely taken aback. He hurriedly ran to Eurch who was warming water for Baba's bath and said, "You helped me in submitting the answers during the Bible course and now I request you for the last time to relieve me of the subsequent predicament! At present a priest has arrived to offer me a present for the distinction I obtained in the scripture course. But how can I reveal to him the secret of my success?" Eruch did not want to go but sensing Murli's awkward position he decided to accompany him. Eruch was in his *banian** and boxer shorts. During the conversation that ensued, Murli practically said nothing, except "Thank you, sir" when the Father offered him the prize.

The visitor was very much impressed by the way Eruch conducted the talk and felt impelled to ask him, "What are you doing here my son?" "I am serving my Lord," was Eruch's reply. This made him all the more curious to ask Eruch more questions. As Eruch wanted to return soon to his work, lest Baba notice his absence, he gave precise but profound answers. The priest, a thin, middle-aged person, indirectly challenged Eruch on the truth of his statement that he was serving the Lord. He also quoted some references from the Bible asking people to be beware of imposters. Eruch answered, "I am speaking from my personal experience and not from the words stated in any Book or books. Again, how can you prove to me that the One I am serving is not the Lord?" During this talk Eruch, however, did not make even a passing reference either to his own study of the New Testament or to his love for Jesus the Christ when he was studying in the St. Francis De

---

* Undershirt.

Sales High School conducted by the Roman Catholic Mission. The conversation between Eruch and the Father continued and the latter seemed to be more and more receptive to Eruch's words. When he left, what feeling he carried about Meher Baba, the Lord alone knows!

Murli had already sneaked away from the scene. Eruch returned to Baba who did not ask him anything about his absence. After many days when Baba heard the funny incident of Murli's "grand success" and the visit of the priest, Baba beamed with a smile. Maybe it was the reason why He allowed Eruch to have a long talk with the Father. Baba in His infinite patience knew when the seed of His name would germinate in the heart of the priest.

It will, however, be interesting to mention that Murli's casual interest in the Bible was in a way rewarded by Baba in November, 1952 during one of the meetings in the hall at Meherabad. Under Baba's instruction, Murli wore a gown like that of a priest and read the Sermon on the Mount to Baba who solemnly stood before him, holding a cross in His hand.

The hundred days' Seculsion began on February 13, and ended on May 23, 1951. The Great Seculsion in the Blue Bus (June-July 1949) marked the initiation of the New Life, while the present Seclusion irrevocably established the foundation for the next "Step of *Manonash*", the concluding phases of the New Life.

13

Manonash Meeting at Hyderabad

1951 — Part II

The Unexpected Call

BY the first week of June 1951, Baba, the women *mandali* and the servant companions were at Hyderabad. A month earlier, Baba had wished to inform some of His disciples and devotees of the Old Life about a meeting to be held in the last week of June. A special letter of invitation from Baba was sent to selected Baba people. I give below a part of the letter I received:

> To enable you to come within the field limits of my association for the period, I desire you to be present at Hyderabad [Deccan] for three days, 28th to 30th June, 1951. In compliance with this you should be present at Hyderabad for the occasion. If, in spite of your wishing it deeply and your trying for it utmost, due to unavoidable circumstances you are unable to come, do not worry.... You are to come alone.... Send the acknowledgement slip duly filled in and signed whether you will attend.... If you are coming details of when and where to arrive at Hyderabad will be sent to you by Adi during the first week of June.
> — BABA

The letter points out how Baba was perfectly practical in arranging any meeting or program, big or small, to enable His lovers to attend it with a free mind. A few were summoned by Baba for ten days, some for seven days and the rest, by far the largest group, for three days.

At the Mahabaleshwar meeting everyone had the impression that they would never see the Beloved Master in person again. Baba's life and activities whether in the Old or the New Life were simultaneously simple and mystical. Yet whatever He did or said was so perfect that it carried the stamp of finality. Therefore, the only hope of seeing Baba again lay in His perfect unpredictability. In one's life with Baba the unexpected happens only when He leads you beyond all hopes. As one grows in His love, the intellect voluntarily agrees to be subservient to the Divine Will — the natural flow of Life — and then follows the fun of following Baba! Baba, though infinitely slippery, guides each one in learning and relearning the basic requirements of spiritual life — whole-hearted love and unconditional surrender to Him. But this is not an easy lesson!

When I received the earlier circular about "the irrevocable Step" it evoked a considerable concern in me. The intellect tried to interpret, understand and sometimes even rebelled against Baba's mystical statements. But each time, in the end, the storm would subside with the heart reaffirming, "Whatever the Compassionate One does or says is for the ultimate good of all, irrespective of the outer crust, the words." In such a reflective mood I received the unexpected call to be with Baba for three days and it filled my being with joy to its brim.

The rallying point for this meeting was Hyderabad. The northwest part of this extensive city is known as the Jubilee Hills. It's a very clean and quiet locality, with many well-designed bungalows and villas, some with pretty flower beds and good lawns. A palatial building, (H.N.G 2/529), was reserved for the meeting and also as a residence for those who were expected to come for it. Formerly this house was owned by Nawab Ali Nawaz Jung, a very influential person of the State and an architect of some renown. The spacious dining hall, the beautiful terrace, as well as a circular staircase winding round a fountain and other similar amenities which were provided expressed the high artistic caliber of the *Nawab*. As for me, I had never stayed in such a royal residence so the bungalow impressed me greatly. Of course, long stays with Baba in the palatial Guru Prasad came much later.

The Arrangementwallas Arrived

On June 20, the few who were invited by Baba for a stay of ten days arrived at Hyderabad. They were either the Arrangementwallas or the old resident *mandali* members. On the first day of the meeting, as Baba walked up the staircase, He looked radiant as usual but a new slowness in His regal gait was noticeable. It could be assumed that the physical weakness was the result of intense spiritual work. He later conveyed to the visitors that He was suffering from piles and also had gnawing pain near the diaphragm. He had lost His appetite and the very sight of food was nauseating to Him. However, His general health after the strenuous seclusion, He gestured, was good. He then inquired of everyone present about their health and instructed all to be very careful about it during their present stay. He also asked them to forget all their worries and remain cheerful. Normal physical fitness and a free mind were the essential requirements to participate in any Baba gathering.

It was generally observed that prior to such meetings Baba would not be in good health. Was He taking upon Himself the sufferings of those invited and thus warding off the difficulties that the lovers would have encountered in their visit to Him? I have this thought because those who attended such gatherings often wondered how, despite great odds, they had managed to attend the meeting. And by the time Baba's dear ones arrived, He would start regaining His strength and good mood.

In one of the informal sittings with the first batch of visitors, Baba mentioned that before taking the "Step" He wished to be free from any *boja* (lit. burden — physical/mental) before October 1951. As a sequel of this intention, Baba wished to make some basic provisions till February 16, 1952 for the *mandali*. Baba instructed the Arrangementwallas about such provisions. With reference to the *mandali's* spirit of dedication which was without any spiritual or material expectation from Baba, He proudly stated, "Compared with the importance of the day to day carrying out of the Master's orders through thick and thin, even the courage of the martyrs is trivial." On another occasion someone brought up, though inadvertently, the subject of mass *darshan*. In reply to this Baba conveyed, "At first I am going to have *darshan* of [the] Old Meher Baba [State] or go blind. And this seems to me the only remedy for the many problems including the mass *darshan* programs." He also added that *darshan* was worthwhile only if people were truly ready to avail themselves of the opportunity.

This reminds me of Kabir's couplet wherein he succinctly says, "If the Master offers you anything, however insignificant it may be, it is precious like 'milk'; if you ask for something, even anything which you think is the best, and the Master gives it, it is like plain 'water'; and if you force the Master to give you something, it is as bad as extracting 'blood' [of the Master]." If you ever dare to receive the most precious gifts at the hands of the God-Man, surrender to Him totally and voluntarily, and do not ask. He KNOWS best what to give and when to give. True to Baba's words about *darshan* we find that after the period of *manonash* Baba visited the West and some parts of India to give *darshan*.

And He awakened in some the rare spark of His love, a unique gift from the God-Man. And as love is essentially self-communicative, its radiance will continue to enkindle the hearts of others and keep aglow the *Avatar's* work of awakening humanity.

In Baba's Overwhelming Presence

On June 27 the third group of about seventy Baba lovers, from different states of India reached Hyderabad.

MANONASH MEETING AT HYDERABAD

Kalemama, one of the old *mandali* and the father of Murli, one of the New Life companions, came to Kurduwadi, my town, on June 26. We decided to travel together. In those days the trains were overcrowded but because of Kalemama's old age and serene expression the passengers in the overcrowded compartment treated us well and we got sitting accommodations. We had to change trains at Wadi but we missed our connection and instead of arriving at Hyderabad in the morning we didn't get in till late afternoon. Vishnu had come to the station to receive the Baba people. He also arranged for our transport. In the taxis we were driven to the bungalow on the Jubilee Hills. It seemed a lovely place. The flowers in the garden seemed to wave at us but our hearts were eager to greet the Divine Gardener, Baba.

From those who had arrived earlier we learnt that Baba was on the first floor and the new arrivals would be ushered into His presence soon. This made us extremely happy. We met Pendu, the manager, and we were directed to our rooms and beds. I also contacted Adi and paid him seventy-five rupees towards my lodging and boarding arrangements. This prompt payment on arrival was one of the conditions mentioned in the printed letter from Baba. After a quick wash, I rushed near the room where Baba was meeting His dear ones. Within a few minutes I was called in and there was Baba, as beautiful and radiant as ever, His entire form beaming with love. Though in the circular it was clearly mentioned that no one should ask Baba any questions, He, of His own, lovingly gestured if I had to ask Him anything, anything! I kept silent. He continued, "How is your health? Any worry?" "Nothing special, Baba. Sometimes physical weakness wearies me," I replied. With a sympathetic smile He gestured, "Don't worry about it, about anything! Again as long as you are here remain happy and cheerful; do good justice to lunch and supper." And with a twinkle in His eyes He gestured, "Forget about school and family members, but do not forget to be punctual at the meetings!" The interview ended with my intimacy with Baba not just renewed, but invigorated as well. A fresh wave of love refreshed me. I felt my body and mind were geared to a new energy to face life, come what may.

About fifteen of us who arrived in the afternoon got together and we were apprised of the points conveyed by Baba in the earlier part of the day. In the morning, Baba told the gathering that He had to attain "the zenith of strength" at a time when He was at the "zenith of weakness", in an impossibly short period of four months — October 16, 1951 to February 16, 1952 — and as such His life was at stake. To the visitors He conveyed, "You have been called here to bear witness to the Declaration that I am going to make tomorrow, before God." "Witnessing the God-Man's Declaration, what does that mean?" I thought. But in Baba's overwhelming presence such thoughts vanished like mist before the bright sun.

In the evening, Baba left for His residence and we were told that He would be visiting Ali Nawaz's bungalow by 8 a.m. the next morning. We were to get ourselves ready before that time for the meeting. After a sumptuous supper the Baba people lovingly shared many stories of the Master's grace and compassion. Baba lovers from Hamirpur performed a *bhajan* program. Their simple love for Baba impressed me deeply. I was lodged in a billiard room with many pointers lined on the wall. I thought, "We are like the billiard balls rolling on the table depending on the skillful strokes and touches of Baba."

The rather long train journey had tired me but because of the intense inner joy of meeting Baba, I did not sleep well. There were not enough bathrooms to accommodate the number of guests. But everyone, as is the custom among Indians, wished to have a bath before meeting the Beloved Master. In fact, a bath was compulsory only if one had had a wet dream. However, by 4 a.m. most of the people woke up. They were attending to the morning chores, repeating slowly and melodiously the blessed name of Baba. We knew Baba's habit of arriving earlier than the scheduled time. So, by 7 a.m. almost all of us had finished our breakfast. Baba arrived at 7.15 and was busy talking with some of the *mandali* in connection with the three day program. He also met some people from different groups.

Meher Baba's Declaration

On June 28, the momentous meeting was to be held in a special hall on the first floor. As per the instructions, before getting near the hall we washed our hands and faces and we were eagerly waiting in the adjacent rooms for a call. At ten minutes to eight, Baba clapped and we started going into the hall. All squatted on the carpet in the Indian fashion. Baba, with flowing hair, wearing a white *sadra* was sitting in a wooden chair. He inquired of Pendu, Adi and other group heads if all had come in. Then His fingers started moving on the alphabet board. Addressing the gathering He stated, "One thing I can definitely say with all emphasis is that for me, for you all and for those connected with me by February 16, 1952 things won't be as they are now, whether for good or bad, and I feel confident it will be for the best." He continued, "To be honest, in the New Life I never felt so happy as I feel now. And this happiness makes me feel that God wants me to make the Declaration."

Baba casually referred to the hundred days' seclusion and told the gathering how enormously helpless and incredibly nervous He felt in that period. He added, "Last night I hardly slept. All of a sudden at about 3.30 in the morning, it was clearly revealed that God wants me to take the irrevocable Step. Since then I am happy and do not feel nervous at all. I feel deep down in my heart that God will definitely help me to regain the Old Life Meher Baba State by February 16, 1952." Asking us to be very attentive, He gestured, "Be here wholly when you listen to the Declaration." He got up and washed His face and hands in a basin that was placed in a corner. As He occupied His seat He looked very solemn but of course not without the Divine glow about Him.

Before the delivery of the Declaration, Dr. Ghani read out its Corollary — What God Has Determined — to the audience. The important parts are given below:

1. The period required for this inevitable Step will be from October 16, 1951 to February 16, 1952.
2. The Step God wants me to take is one of complete and absolute annihilation. That means, that during this period of mental annihilation, I will, in the natural course of events, be facing physical annihilation as well, without my actually seeking it.
3. Irrespective of what I was, am, and will be, God in His Infinite Justice will see to everything. My strongest and only advice to each one of you is to hold fast to your faith and love — at least in the same proportion as now, if not in greater.
4. I will plunge deeply into the act of Annihilation from October 16.
5. I ask God in all humility to help me achieve the desired end by February 12.
6. In the event of my physical death the Arrangementwallas have to carry out the instructions I have given them.
7. I will be away from Hyderabad from October 16 to February 12, 1952.
8. Anyone who wants to go through this dying process with me can join me, but ... I will have absolutely no responsibility and might have no concern whatever for anyone accompanying me.
9. I order the servants who are with me, to choose between two things; to join me in this hopeless task, or to stay at Hyderabad doing whatever duty I allot to them.
10. From July 1, to February 12, I might be available either to all, to a few, or to none.

MANONASH MEETING AT HYDERABAD

11. Even if there is only one of you accompanying me I shall be quite pleased and satisfied and even if many choose to come with me I will not mind.
12. Also, from amongst those offering to come with me, I will finally decide who is to accompany me, and who is to stay [behind].
13. During this period of annihilation my actions and mode of living will be free from any binding conditions. I might beg for anything, demand anything, accept anything or reject anything, or perhaps I might do none of these things. I will do anything ordinary or extraordinary, good or bad, as the occasion may demand of me, based on the Will of God for this great Annihilation.*

Dr. Ghani also read aloud the Urdu and Hindi translation of the Corollary and Dr. C. D. Deshmukh its Marathi version. After this reading, Baba got up from the chair and gestured for all to stand up. He folded His hands in a devotional manner. Most of the visitors did the same. Baba also closed His eyes. Dr. Donkin on behalf of Baba very solemnly read out the following Declaration:

In the presence of God, and bearing in my heart all the Perfect Ones of all times as witness, I declare that by the help and Will of God, I will definitely take this Step of Annihilation on October 16th of this year. God helped me to do the seclusion work of the 100 days to my entire satisfaction and I feel absolutely confident that God will help me to attain to the Old Life Meher Baba State by 16th February 1952, and to manifest universally.

To those present, Baba gave the following order:

I want everyone of you who is present here as

---

* *Circular NL* 26.

witness to this Declaration, to fast for 24 hours on tea and water, on the 16th of October, beginning from 8 o'clock in the morning of that day.

This profound and sublime Declaration was received in great silence and admiration by the Baba people. Baba, as He took His seat, declared a break of fifteen minutes. Whenever any serious message or discourse was given, Baba would generally order a short recess.

The Discourse on *Manonash*

When we assembled again Baba looked very cheerful and relaxed. He told the gathering that from the middle of October He would not be in Hyderabad for four months. To give all an idea of the magnitude and seriousness of His work that He had to accomplish during those months He spelt on the board, "It would be facing 400 deaths in four months!" He asked the servant companions and all the visitors to seriously and honestly consider if they really felt like going with Him during that period. Baba reminded all that He would bear responsibility towards none. No one who wished to join should expect any material or spiritual benefit from Baba; on the contrary he would have to face sleeplessness, sickness and starvation. One of the old persons asked if there was any age limit in accompanying Baba. With a smile Baba gestured, "No age limit! But for heaven's sake do not say 'yes,' assuming that I may order you to stay behind." Looking at the gathering He added, "Don't fool me and fool yourself. After knowing your decisions I shall decide for each one wishing to join me."

Then Baba commenced dictating from the alphabet board a discourse in English on *Manonash* (annihilation of the mind). It was simultaneously translated into Hindi. A few, including myself, tried to note down Baba's words to the extent that we could. I must state that I am neither a steno nor a typist. But from whatever I scribbled in long hand and with the gaps filled in from my memory I am trying to reproduce the matter in this chapter. I have, however, tried to maintain the sequence in which the discourse was given. Later on, the notes on this discourse were edited, compiled and published in a book, *Meher Baba and the God-determined Step,* by Ramjoo Abdulla. To me this discourse is a superb commentary in simple words on the Sermon given by Baba at Mahabaleshwar.

Baba opened the subject:

> Mind. Mind changes according to the *sanskaras* [impressions] but it is not [basically] transformed. Mind is of the false and it remains false. Being false it can be annihilated. Today you think "I am a man." If your body falls and you get a body of a woman, you will think, "I am a woman." This "I" of being a man or a woman is false and it continues to think so till there is real transformation. Mind is never transformed; Ego is transformed only once. Ego is of the Real and it shall ever remain Real. By Ego, I mean your very Being as *Astitva*. Ego by itself is not false; mind makes one think so. Mind creates worlds, delusions and illusions yet it is never One in itself. Ego [as witness consciousness] is always One in itself. The Real Ego that each of us has is apparently bound up by the mind and makes the Real Ego think of itself as false. Mind makes you think birth and death, happiness and misery are real; and nothing can be more false than this. You are never born but mind gives the impression: "I am this." "I am that." "This is my wife." "This is my child," etc. Mind always keeps you in a tap dance. If you know that you and your wife and your children and all are One, and that you never die, never suffer, what else would there be to know?
>
> So mind which is made up of false impressions makes the Real I think itself false. Mind may make You say, "I am God," but not make you feel, "I am

God." So as long as mind is there, Ego cannot be transformed from its false assumption [attitude] of its Real State. You are really Infinite and Eternal. But you do not feel it. To experience this Original State, mind must go. But who is to destroy mind? The very act of destroying creates impressions and mind gets bound. The magic (*jadu*) of *sanskaras* has bound you so tight and skillfully that the more you try to come out, the more you get bound. The only recourse is that mind has to annihilate itself by itself. So Hafiz says:

Tu khud hijabe khudi, Hafiz, uz miyan burkeez
(Hafiz, remove thyself for thou art the veil.)

But how to remove yourself? The very process of removing creates impressions.

So the Perfect Masters laid down different paths that subsequently direct towards destroying mind, retaining consciousness. These paths are based mainly on action, meditation and love. The Masters knew that actions which have false ego and mind full of impressions as its background, instead of destroying mind, feed it. And there is no escape from action. So some Masters demonstrated the path of "actionless action". The secret lies in performing action in a way, [as if] it had not been done at all. Then what happens — past impressions of actions done get spent up and [as you have no self-interest] no new impressions are formed.

It was lunch time and Baba told the gathering that it was no good in getting on with the discourse (though on *Manonash*) on empty stomachs. We were with Baba for about four hours but we became time conscious only after hearing Baba's remark. In the dining hall the tables were already spread. After a delicious lunch and a little rest we were back in the meeting hall by 2 p.m.

MANONASH MEETING AT HYDERABAD

Decisions about Accompanying Baba

Baba first asked the servant companions about their decisions. He made it clear that if anyone or all of them wished to stay behind, He would provide for each good boarding arrangements plus some pocket money! Baba of Himself asked Vishnu to attend to the lodging and food arrangements of the women staying at Hyderabad. Nilu was sick and so he did not attend this session. Murli decided to stay behind. Donkin very devotedly said, "Baba, my heart will go with you but my body shall stay at Hyderabad." The remaining six servants, Pendu, Gustadjee, Baidul, Eruch, Kaka and Kaikobad, decided to be with Baba.

Then turning to the visitors, Baba asked those to stand up who were willing to go with Him for four months, accepting the conditions laid down by Him. Out of 75 Baba lovers 15 showed their readiness to accompany Baba through thick and thin. They were: Minoo Kharas, Nana Kher, Pankhraj, Goma Ganesh, Sailor Mama, Todi Singh, Kishan Singh, Daulat Singh, Pritam Singh, Gadekar, Babadas, Shripat Sahai, Kain, P. D. Nigam (Pukar) and A. C. S. Chari. The Arrangementwallas were not to consider anything about this subject as they were given certain duties from the beginning of the New Life. Baba concluded, "Today you have decided for yourself; tomorrow I will decide for each of you. As for me, whatever I have already declared is final." Baba continued, "In fact, this New Life [phase] is only for me. I began it on October 16, 1949. Till now, although I am leading the New Life, I have not been able to live it as I wanted to. In the coming period of four months, I want to live the whole of the New Life and end it for me."

Baba looked very happy for the main subject of the meeting was over. He, however, did not wish to continue the discourse on *Manonash*: He desired to complete it the next day. He further suggested, "Now let us not be serious. Tell me some good jokes or humorous stories. Make me laugh and laugh yourself." If I remember correctly I vainly tried to entertain Baba with a joke I had recently read about the "sane sailors". When a large steamer was in mid-ocean these "wise" sailors were ordered to throw a passenger from cabin No. 36, who had recently expired, overboard. In all readiness they went there. Surprisingly enough the man in the cabin said, "But I am alive! Perhaps you got the wrong number." "Who are you?" asked the sailors. "I am a press reporter," the man nervously replied. "We don't believe reporters! They give false news," said the sailors jointly and holding him tightly they threw him overboard! I do not recollect how far I was successful in telling this joke but my diffidence in speech and poor presentation must have amused my friends, I hope. Of course there were some funny stories and jokes in Hindi, Gujarati and English that made Baba and the whole group laugh heartily. As opposed to the solemn morning session the afternoon atmosphere in the hall was one of joviality and light-heartedness. vibrant with Baba's loving presence.

Born Once; Die Once

The next day, June 29, all assembled in the same hall by 8 a.m. Baba had already arrived. He told us that He had not slept well the previous night and so could not make any decision about those to accompany Him during the *Manonash* phase. He added, "As I want to be absolutely free from any kind of interference the selection is difficult. I find servants — Pendu, Eruch, Gustadjee and Baidul — O.K. but, God knows, I have not yet finally decided about them. I had a very restless night and hence I could not take any decision. Now till I decide I cannot sleep! If I feel that even to have one [person] with me is a hindrance, I shall go alone. But again that does not seem possible."

After such casual talk, Baba wished to continue the discourse. He gestured, "This is the last thing I wish to explain in my New Life." But before Baba began the discourse, Ghani directed His attention to the question of "one birth and one death" as believed by Mohammedans and Christians. To enlighten all on this subject Baba replied:

> The real Goal of life is not the death of the ego but the death of the mind. When Mohammed or Jesus or Zoroaster talked of being born once and of dying once, it was of the mind [and not of the body]. When mind dies totally, the false ego becomes Real I [i.e., false ego is completely effaced and Real I manifests]. In reality ego is not born and as such it does not die. Ego [as witness consciousness] is always Real. It is only due to mind that ego acts and feels limited and false. Mind takes the body according to its good and bad impressions. Taking up and giving up of bodies is not the mind or the ego taking birth or dying. Every time when body is discarded, mind survives, impressions remain. These impressions press on mind to spend them by taking another body. So mind takes another body according to the impressions; ego witnesses. And another body and another. When you are in sound sleep, ego, mind and *sanskaras* are there. *Sanskaras* wake up mind. They say, "Go on, spend us." Waking up from the sound sleep is, in a way, an everyday birth for the body. When one body is left, another body comes up though there is a time lag between the giving up of one body and taking up another. Mind exists even when a new body is not given to the ego; it is the mind-state of heaven or hell. But mind has to die while it is in a human body, retaining full consciousness. This is the Goal.

At the close of His reply to Ghani's question, looking at the gathering Baba gestured, "If you can really grasp the central point of what I have been explaining now, it will be easy to follow the rest [of the discourse on *Manonash*]."

The Three Paths

Through simple words Baba further elucidated:

Yesterday, I told you that the Perfect Masters chalked out different paths for the annihilation of mind. Let us commence with the path of action because the main activity of mind through body is of actions. As long as mind is there body is there and actions too are there. Actions leave impressions and impressions feed the mind. So for the false ego to be transformed into Real there is no other remedy than *manonash*. Therefore the Masters wanted actions to be done in a way so that the effect of the impressions becomes impotent, hence no result, no binding. For example, a scorpion generally wags its tail and stings. It is natural for it to sting someone. What is the result? The person suffers. Even if the scorpion's sting is cut off its act of wagging and stinging continues. But as the "thorn" is removed the person concerned does not suffer. So, the Masters thought of the following remedy on actions: act in a way so that the results do not bind and no impressions are created. But for this, the action has to be rendered impotent in the matter of its dangerous results and this is not easy. Why? I will explain.

There are three ways by which the actions done do not bind. One is to act but absolutely without having any self interest. But this selfless action which is referred to as selfless service is almost impossible. Even the feeling of pity for others should not be there. The moment you think that you are serving or uplifting others you get caught and bound. The second way is to dedicate whatever you do to God or to the Perfect Master. This dedication must be constant and continual, without a moment's break. If you are able to do this then actions have no impressions created. But this is very difficult. The third way is to act on the orders of the One whose mind is annihilated and so is free from impressions. If you do whatever He tells you to do, you are not bound. This too is not simple for you must have 100% unflinching faith in the Perfect Master.

The second path is of meditation. Some Masters put forth the way of defeating the mind through mind itself, through meditation* and concentration. When mind is concentrated, its further function is weakened and the *sanskaras* exhaust themselves. Thus the *sanskaras* which are like [earth] worms and which must have execution, eat themselves. But during this process the mind feels frustrated and gets more desperate. Unwanted thoughts, that you never had, assail you and eventually one of the three things happen: 1) you get fed up and you can no

---

* During this meeting Baba did not explain further regarding the path of meditation. But as this subject is of great interest to some seekers of God, I quote below some excerpts from a discourse which Meher Baba gave in later years:

There are various retreats in India where meditation classes are held and different but set techniques of meditation are observed, which, if followed faithfully and for a long time, result in slight occult experiences such as seeing flashes of light, colors, even visions, etc. These occult experiences by themselves are nothing, are in the domain of illusion, and not only have no direct bearing on the incomparable reality of God-Realization, but can actually become a hindrance and obstruction to the aspirant's path to God.

The direct Path to God is the Path of Love. Love is not derived from meditation — it has nothing to do with it. Love is a grace of God. One in many has it, and it is all sufficient. Love does not depend on anything but itself. Love without meditation is enough — meditation without love is not. That is why *Sadgurus* or Perfect Masters do not set meditation for their disciples as a necessary routine. Rather, they stress the aspect of love and selfless service. The masters of the Path, on the other hand, not having reached the Goal themselves, advocate meditation to the aspirants following them.

In the Prem Ashram the boys were touched with the spark of Love.... Then, when the phase of intensive meditation followed (with the resultant flashes of occult experience), the love aspect began gradually to decline. (*The Awakener*, Vol. III, No. 4, p. 31.)

more concentrate; 2) you get sleepy or drowsy; 3) you continue to get more and more bad thoughts. For the very few who persist patiently with a brave heart the result is that the mind is temporarily stopped. Then one experiences ecstasy [*bhav*] but it becomes like a dope to which one gets addicted, or one goes into *samadhi* [trance]. But this is not *manonash*. Thus through concentration, annihilation of mind is not possible.

The third path is of *bhakti* [devotion]. When one is totally devoted to God or the Perfect Master he forgets himself and his mind gets no chance to form new, binding *sanskaras*. The Eternal Beloved is ever present but unless you step out of your old habits how can you aspire to meet Him? So Hafiz says:

Hazoori gar hami khahi
az uoo ghayeb mashow Hafiz
(O Hafiz, if you want the Beloved's Presence, do not absent yourself from Him.)

But even through the path of devotion complete and continual self-forgetfulness is practically impossible. So, no *Manonash*.

At the close of this discourse Baba stated:

The mind's part is to make ego think through body, feel false and experience the *sanskaras*. But when mind sees that the false ego is not ready to accept its dictatorship, then submissive, loose and weak impressions are formed which eventually lead one towards the Goal. Thus either through selfless service or meditation or devotion, though not perfected but if persisted, with 100 percent faithfulness a stage comes when mind is permanently at rest or becomes totally quiet and sees God everywhere [and longs for Union with Him]. Only the Perfect One, who is free, can uproot [annihilate] the minds of others, even of the masses.

MANONASH MEETING AT HYDERABAD

In conclusion Baba continued:

All the paths are meant for *manonash*, to make you feel, "You are God, the Infinite, the Eternal." We are all the same, One God, but we are misled by the besharam [illusive] mind. With the death of mind, ego feels [experiences], "I am God; I have no connection with the body." If this shock [of gnosis] is too strong, the body drops down, otherwise the momentum [of the impressions] keeps the body going for some time and then it is shed. This is the state of a Perfect *Majzoob* [*Majzoobiat*]; mind is not there but Real I and body remain. Few after *manonash* keep their bodies and get minds too, but these minds have "impressionless impressions"; then Real I, Real Mind and Real Body remain. Such a one is a Perfect Master.

When mind dies ego realizes Reality. With *manonash*, dawns the Knowledge. By Knowledge I mean the experience of "I am God State." Then God's Knowledge is yours. God is All-knowing. So in a flash you know Everything; you KNOW that there was/is nothing to know.

When the discourse was over Baba conveyed, "I am absolutely in the New Life and full of weaknesses. To achieve this extremely difficult task of *manonash*, I have four months in hand. It is like a lame person wanting to reach the top of Everest in four months. But I feel 100% confident that God will help me to achieve this. On October 16, when you all fast that day, pray for five minutes from the bottom of your hearts asking God to help me gain this end."

We Thanked God

Baba concluded the discourse and proposed that in the afternoon He would like to have some indoor games. He added, "This will be a sort of relaxation for me and will help me to decide about the persons who should be with me during the *Manonash* period." From this serious subject the minds of all were thus switched to playfulness and fun. Different persons suggested different games and Baba attentively listened and even joked about certain proposals. Unexpectedly He ordered an interval of half an hour. During this period He interviewed one by one all the twenty-one persons who had volunteered to accompany Him. Baba freely dicussed the commitments, liabilities and responsibilities that each one had to shoulder as most of these men were householders. He appreciated the courage and devotion of all and their loving response to His call. Any honest and sincere offer or expression always evoked Baba's admiration. But He comforted them all and asked each one to wait for the opportune moment. When we all gathered in the hall we were told that out of 21 persons, Baba had decided "No" for fifteen.

Pendu, Eruch, Gustadjee and Baidul were to accompany Baba definitely for four months. About Minoo Kharas and Daulat Singh, He was to give His final decision on Sept. 7, 1951. Baba instructed Adi to issue a circular to the Baba people instructing them not to have any correspondence with Baba and not to try to see Him, even if they happened to hear of His whereabouts. The suggestions for games were again invited. Baba, being very practical, directed the discussion to a program of light entertainment, including a fancy dress parade. He, Himself proposed the names of some who were to participate in the program.

After lunch the Hindi group was apprised of the discourse in English on *Manonash* given by Baba in the morning. Pendu was busy having a small stage put up in the hall. Exactly at 3 p.m. the "show" commenced. An atmosphere of joy and lightheartedness prevailed. Dr. Ghani appeared on the stage as a Pathan to loud applause. Savak Kotwal, though in his forties, danced so well that his skilled performance gave Baba the surprise of the day. The last item was a song by

MANONASH MEETING AT HYDERABAD

Mirabai, sung by Rustum Kaka (Hatidaru), with the accompaniment of a harmonium, in a very melodious manner. The refrain of the song was:

Payori mainay Ramaratan dhan payo.
(Verily have I found the most precious pearl — the Divine name of the God-Man, Rama).

As the song proceeded Baba looked very solemn. With a steadfast gaze, He commenced looking outside the window most of the time. This was unusual. It seemed that He was gradually withdrawing Himself from everything about Him. This had its effect on the audience too. Rustum Kaka with eyes closed continued to sing in his warbling, inviting voice.

When the song was over, with a remote glow in His eyes, Baba conveyed, "I have heard this song and some similar songs many times. But today it is something different! The song has evoked 'something' in me and in the presence of God I felt that the work I have undertaken will be done successfully. So let us thank God whole-heartedly." At Baba's indication all the people rose up and thanked God from the bottom of their hearts. It was 4.30 p.m. At the close of the program, Baba gave a locket (with His picture on it) as a present to each one who had tried to entertain Him. The rest of the people felt that they had lost a good opportunity to receive something precious from Baba's hand. Perhaps sensing this feeling, Baba called for some roses and very lovingly gave a petal to one and all. He dictated, "The main program for which I have called you is over. Tomorrow we go out for sightseeing to Osmansagar." Someone suggested that a group photo with Baba be taken; Baba agreed and this made all happy. This was perhaps the first and the last group photo in the New Life. A great treasure! We were to get ready by 7 a.m. the next day.

Grand Game of the God-Man

On June 30, we were in the hall in the morning. Baba had put on a yellowish silk coat over His usual white *sadra*. He had His hair plaited though a few loose strands were still flowing about His earlobes. To me He looked rather slim but very beautiful and powerful too. He dictated from the board, "These two days have been of extreme happiness for me. I hope you too must have shared this happiness. Having made the Declaration in the presence of God and the Perfect Ones of past, present and future and you to witness it, I feel extremely happy. Honestly I feel happy." Baba put the board aside and at His gesture we left the hall for the two buses waiting outside. We reached Osmansagar, a very extensive man-made lake (*sagar* literally means a sea). We walked along the bridge and reached the other end of the garden. A very cool and charming place indeed!

Then we drove to Char Minar (the famous four minarets) and Madina Masjid (mosque). To make us feel more refreshed, Baba asked all to have tea in a good hotel. Then we were taken to Bagh-e-Aam (public gardens). With Baba in our midst we quickly strolled through the garden. Stopping on the way Baba conveyed, "I like Hyderabad for its spiritual atmosphere; specially for its Hindu-Muslim unity in matters spiritual." He also told us that He had not washed His head for the last two months but after our departure, He intended to wash His hair. Some wondered why Baba should tell them about such a personal thing. Was it not a sign of intimacy towards those who had come?

The party returned to Ali Nawaz's bungalow by 10.30 a.m. The photo was taken on the steps of this building. Baba again called us on the first floor and distributed *prasad* packets (sweets) to all. He instructed each one not to open it until one got home. Once there, however, we were permitted to share the contents with our family members and whomsoever we liked. Baba was lavishly showering His love on us all. As He left for lunch, He told us that He would be back again by 2 p.m., and that no one should ask Him any question at the time of farewell. We had our meals and we packed our bedding and bags. We were about to rest but Baba's car rushed up the driveway and within a few minutes we were in His presence. It was again a session of humorous stories and good jokes. By afternoon we collected our small supper cartons. Baba gestured, "Don't waste a single particle from this stuff." *Prasad*, from the abode of the God-Man, is indeed one of the most precious things to receive. With a cheerful face He waved at us and gestured, "Don't worry. Be happy." What a loving parting!

The next morning I reached Kurduwadi. For a number of days the happenings in the hall at Hyderabad often filled my being with a delightful feeling. Thoughts about Baba and His graceful gestures brought me luminous, lively remembrances. Yet, sometimes, a part of my mind would raise questions about the discourse on *Manonash* and especially Baba's New Life — its inauguration and imminent consummation. My heart continued to remain steadfast in His love but the mind would not keep quiet. How can it ever understand the grand game of the God-Man who in fact is leading His own self — in and through us all — beyond births and deaths. The explanation given by Meher Baba linking the reincarnation theory of Hindus with the no rebirth concept of Muslims and Christians was undoubtedly superb and matchless. Till this day, I personally have not come across such simple yet most convincing statements made by anyone on such a paradoxical spiritual subject. Besides, Baba's statement that each time one gets up from sleep it is a new birth in the same body appealed to my heart very much. "What a challenge and an opportunity each day, for a new life!" I thought.

And the New Life? This phase was and still is a divine enigma to me. Can the limited mind ever fathom the Universal Mind? Never. Yet, my monkey mind went on speculating upon this phase. Now, years later I may add that Baba had to become an "extraordinary" ordinary person of the New Life subsequently to declare on September 7, 1953 His status as the Highest of the High (Perfect God: perfect man) which is beyond the phases of the Old and the New Life.

The Declaration of the irrevocable Step of *Manonash* at Hyderabad was an intensely profound event of the New Life.

14

Beginning of the Manonash Phase
1951 — Part III

A Tentative Program

AFTER the momentous meeting held in the last week of June, Baba and those accompanying Him in the New Life continued their stay at Hyderabad. Murli Kale was one of them. One day, however, he expressed a wish that, if Baba had no objection, he would like to complete a full course in homeopathy. Baba readily released Murli from the New Life and sent him back to the Old Life asking him to qualify as a homeopath. Murli later practiced as a doctor in Jabalpur, till he died in 1977. According to Baba's order, on July 10, the servant companions and the women *mandali* fasted for twenty-four hours, beginning at 6 a.m. the same day.

Perhaps this was the year when Baba started giving instructions to His dear ones about observing a fast or silence on this memorable day. In the later years, especially in the 1960s, a regular circular would be issued to Baba people about such observances. In 1968 the option of fasting was not given. Maybe Baba indicated that henceforth His followers should commemorate this day by observing silence. The silent loving remembrance of the Silent One on July 10 is a delightful experience, a spiritual treat, worth trying.

In the second week of August, Baba called Meherjee, Adi, and Adi Jr. (Baba's youngest brother) to Hyderabad for a meeting in which He discussed certain arrangements to be made in the near future. With reference to the immensity of *manonash*, Baba hinted that there was the possibility of His dropping the physical body during this critical phase. He also told them that during the specified period of four months (October 16 through February 16) He would be absolutely free to act as He liked. He would, if He so felt, change any previous plans at any moment. He would exercise absolute freedom from any conventional bindings. During this meeting, He also chalked out a tentative program for the four months which consisted of the following phases:

(1) Baba wanted to spend thirty to forty days on a hill which had a spiritual background. He wanted the hill not to be too close or too far away from the city of Hyderabad. (Baba informed Meherjee and others that He had already approved of such a hill and that preparations had been undertaken to make the place suitable for His stay.) His work on the hill was to be the first phase.

(2) In the second phase Baba planned to march on foot from Hyderabad to Aurangabad. He casually mentioned that during this journey He might don just a loin cloth (*langoti*) or any other dress; He might eat four times a day or fast for days on end. In short He would do whatever God would want Him to do.

(3) The third phase depended on Baba's physical condition. Adi was to find a suitable hill near Ahmednagar or Poona where Baba would be concluding His *manonash* work. Baba also stated that because of the two preceding phases, wherein He would be deeply absorbed in achieving *manonash*, there was the probability that His physical body would be on the verge of being shed. If such a situation would arise, Baba wanted to spend the days till February 16, 1952 at a place associated with His Old Life — Meherazad Hill. In anticipation of such an exigency, He gave certain instructions to Adi and Adi Jr. to consult Sarosh and Padri about repairing the cabins and erecting a tent on the top of that hill.

Such indefiniteness and refusal to commit Himself to a set program was not treated by His close ones as a gap in or lack of knowledge on Baba's part. They were deeply convinced that Baba was setting an example for man, the way he should totally trust, under any and all circumstances, in the Omnipotent Will. Owing to this element of unpredictability, Baba's New Life is regarded by some as a period of utter incomprehensibility; they are not completely wrong. The Divine Life of the *Avatar* is beyond the comprehension of human understanding. In addition, it cannot be denied that the New Life of Meher Baba was an unprecedented phase!

Unexpected Help from Baba's Schoolmate

In the third week of August a circular from Meher Publications brought the following news to Baba people: "Baba never has had and never will have any concern with politics. He, therefore, desires that if any of you do political work you must never involve Him or make use of His name in connection with that work. Baba desires that all His Old Life followers should not give way to the temptations of pursuing selfish ends. [They should] kindle in their hearts the light of love for God." Perhaps by this Baba meant that the real religion of man lies in loving God selflessly.

Here I would like to include an excerpt from Meher Baba's Message on "Religion and Politics" delivered a year or so later, clarifying His approach towards these two much talked of subjects. He stated:

> As the Divine Life embraces in its being One and All including even the members of the animal and vegetable kingdoms, and since from the moment of the attainment of *manonash* [annihilation of the limiting mind], I have attained complete unity with that immeasurable and illimitable Divine Life, I cannot and will not identify myself with any caste, creed, religion or political party. From my point of view, *all religions are great, but God is greater*. In the same way, all political parties are, in their own

way, noble, at least in their consciously accepted objectives. But the claims of the undivided and indivisible life are irresistibly supreme, and, as such, greater than those of any party, howsoever noble.*

The issuing of the previous circular about participation in politics had also a practical reason. In August, 1947, after India's independence from British rule, the Nizam of Hyderabad tried to establish his sovereignty apart from India. Soon a stage was reached where the Indian government had to intervene by declaring a "Police Action" against the Nizam who eventually had to surrender, and Hyderabad state became an integral part of the rest of the nation.** A year had passed by but the communal unrest and political rivalries had not subsided. Movements of people visiting Hyderabad from different parts of India were looked on with apprehension, and Baba's companions, a group belonging to different religions and even nationalities, were sometimes unduly interrogated by the police.

In the earlier meetings with the *mandali*, Baba had hinted that during the *manonash* phase He would exercise absolute freedom from the conventional ways of life. So it was rightly presumed that if such behavior on Baba's part evoked inquisitiveness in people, it would unnecessarily bother Him and might even impede His work. Eruch thought that before the commencement of this phase it was essential to meet the Superintendent of Police and inform him of Baba's activities, especially the proposed march on foot from Hyderabad to Aurangabad, for this division was under his jurisdiction. He also planned to request the authorities to issue a departmental notice informing the police outposts

---

* Meher Baba, *The Fiery Life and Seven Other Messages*, (November 1952).
** In 1951, on the basis of linguistics, Hyderabad State was divided and merged into three existing States; Andhra, Karnatak and Maharashtra.

along this particular route about the movements of Baba and His group.

So one day Eruch visited the Superintendent's office and tried to convince the junior officer to grant him an interview with his superior. He did not reveal his intention except to say that he had to see the Superintendent on some urgent and serious matter. The subinspector in charge reluctantly led Eruch to the chamber of his boss. Mr. Reddy, the Superintendent, seemed to be a fine person. He said to Eruch, "What can I do for you?" Eruch explained, "We are a party of six. My elder brother and one other member of our group observe silence. We intend to go on foot on a pilgrimage from Hyderabad to Aurangabad. During our journey my elder brother, in His own way, wishes to offer some financial help to needy persons. Besides, He wants to pay His respects to the God-intoxicated ones. We are from the Bombay area. In view of the present situation, as a precaution, I request you to inform the police stations on this particular route about our journey so that our intention will not be misunderstood and that we may not unnecessarily be detained anywhere. And sir, if you could give us a letter of introduction we shall be grateful to you."

Mr. Reddy very attentively heard each word but he asked Eruch to wait awhile and he phoned his residence to say that he would soon be returning home with a guest. Eruch thought that Mr. Reddy was preoccupied with some other work. The talk, however, continued and at the end the Superintendent unexpectedly asked Eruch to accompany him to his bungalow. With a feeling of wonder Eruch followed him to the car and in a short time found himself in a well-furnished house. Mr. Reddy asked him to make himself comfortable in the living room and he went inside the house. After about ten minutes a servant brought some refreshments and tea but the host did not return. After a few minutes more of suspense Mr. Reddy entered the room. He looked happy and was holding an old glass photo frame in his hand. In it was a group photo of young students, a cricket team. Pointing at Baba, Mr. Reddy said, "Is M. S. Irani your elder brother? I guess I am right." This was a great surprise to Eruch.

Mr. Reddy explained that he had studied at St. Vincent High School with Baba at Poona and that they had been on the same cricket team. It became clear that Mr. Reddy, as the Superintendent of Police, already knew about Baba's stay in Hyderabad and from Eruch's talk he had definitely concluded that Eruch was referring to his schoolmate, M. S. Irani. Eruch could no longer conceal Baba's identity. After some cordial conversation, he left the house with the assurance that he would get the letter of introduction and also a confirmation that information about Baba's activites would be issued to the police stations on the Hyderabad-Aurangabad highway. When Eruch told Baba about this unexpected response from the Superintendent, Baba looked very pleased. However, because of the New Life conditions the "two good old cricketers" could not meet each other. Within a few days Eruch collected the required certificate without any difficulty from the office. Thus, a friendly gesture from an old schoolmate saved the Baba-party from any type of interrogation from the police in the state of Hyderabad.

It was about this time that another of Baba's schoolmates who was also one of His dearest disciples, Dr. Abdul Ghani Munsiff, breathed his last. On August 20, at about seven in the evening he passed away of a heart attack, in Poona. Baba dictated a special circular about Ghani; a part of it read:

> Of the many things I have had to renounce and to suffer in this New Life, the passing of Ghani is among the greatest.... To me, more than to any of you, Ghani was unique and of all the work that still remains to be done for me by others, there is much that could have been done for me by Ghani and none else. The big head of his was truly a treasure

house in which wisdom and wit were blended to perfection. We were intimate friends since our earliest years, and no one knows better than I how courageous, and how loyal and loving, was his heart. To me, therefore, Ghani is irreplaceable, both as a friend and as a tool for my work.*

Models Safely Reach Khojaguda Hill

Khojaguda Hill is about 15 to 18 kilometers from Hyderabad. On its top there is a *dargah* of Hazrat Baba Fakruddin who lived in the fourteenth century. He was regarded and revered as a great *wali*. At present, although this *dargah* has become a place of yearly pilgrimage, strangely, it has no roof. On inquiry one learns that in the past, quite a few times, the *wali's* admirers contributed to build a roof over the tomb, but every time, within a few days, it was blown off. This led people to conclude that Baba Fakruddin preferred exposure to the heavens for all time. On one of the hill sides there is an old temple of Vishnu, with an image of the god reclining on a big coiled cobra (Shesh), its hood spreading over his head. Another important place close to the *dargah* is a cave about 20′ x 15′. The height from the entrance gradually decreases and the darkness increases as one gets inside. In the interior part there is a ledge which served as a shelf for the models which Baba kept near Him during His special work of *Manonash*.

Baba, on His first visit to the hill instructed the companions to construct two improvised rooms in the premises of the *dargah*. He asked them to keep the three places — the *dargah*, the temple and the cave — clean. Baba wanted to stay here for a fortnight, but the scarcity of water threatened to upset this plan. The companions, while walking about happened to notice a pond of stagnant water. Baba seemed happy to hear

---

* *Circular NL* 30, issued on 1-9-1951.

this. Having regarded this site as an ideal place for His work, He told the companions that they could use the water for all purposes after boiling and filtering it. At the foot of the hill were paddy fields and palm trees, some standing erect while a few grew close to the ground. This hill itself was barren and had no vegetation; it only abounded in big black stones.

Before the inauguration of the *manonash* phase, a month or so earlier, Baba had asked Eruch to get five models: a temple, a mosque, a church, a pagoda and a fire-temple (known as an *agyari*).* These respectively represented five religions of the world: Hinduism, Islam, Christianity, Buddhism and Zoroastrianism. A craftsman from Agra was assigned the job of preparing these models. He, however, expressed his inability to carve an *agyari* — the place of worship for the Zoroastrians or the Parsees — because he had never seen the interior structure of a fire-temple. So Eruch sent him a drawing of a fire urn which is kept in the sanctum of any Parsee place of worship. Accordingly all these models were cut in alabaster. The approximate size of each was about 7″ x 7″ x 7″. Each one could be separated into four or more parts and could easily be fitted on a very thin plate of soft marble. The temple had a small *Shivling* and inside the pagoda was a tiny image of Lord Buddha. When Baba learnt that all the models were obtained intact at Hyderabad from Agra, He looked especially pleased. The companions, however, had no idea of the way Baba was intending to use these models.

On October 13, Baba instructed some of His companions to take the necessary luggage to Khojaguda Hill, along with the box containing the models. They packed and placed every piece carefully in the car and set out. The car stopped at the foot of the hill. Pendu, Gustadjee and Baidul started to walk towards the *dargah* to inspect the site and rooms. Meanwhile,

---

* Lit: Friendship with fire.

BEGINNING OF THE MANONASH PHASE

Eruch parked the car, rolled up the windows, locked the doors and then followed the other companions. He had hardly gone ten to twelve meters when the sound of the moving car made him look back. He was greatly astonished to find that the car had started rolling backwards. He rushed towards the car but it had already started picking up speed, so it was impossible for him to open the locked door and get hold of the steering wheel. He helplessly tried to run alongside the car and slow it down but soon he had to give up for, unbelievably, the car started leaping over rocks and bushes. Fantastic! Sometimes, confronted with an obstacle, the car would stop, back up or turn aside. Extremely quixotic! Eruch had left the car in neutral and had put the emergency brake on. In spite of this the car started "skipping over" slanting toddy palms as if it were possessed by some spirit. This erratic movement of the car could be regarded as symbolic of the frenzied mind, waiting for its annihilation at the end of the *manonash* phase! Eventually, after this incredible display of jumping, the car got stuck in a muddy paddy field.

Pendu and others who were watching this strange phenomenon felt relieved at its expiration. Eruch, however, looked worried, perhaps for the models' safety. He knew that the other pieces of luggage were replaceable but not the alabaster models. These had been designed under Baba's instructions and it was obvious that He definitely wanted them for His work, beginning on October 16. Eruch anxiously got near the car and cautiously opened the door. He was sure that the car had been seriously damaged. He turned the ignition key and the engine started, but it made a frightful noise. With his hands on the steering wheel, Eruch was trying to think of what to do next. Just then a truck, which had brought faggots (fuel) for the Baba-party, arrived. With the help of this truck, they towed the car from the muddy field onto the regular road. Eruch and the driver of the truck inspected the car engine and found that the paddy straw and leaves had gotten into it. When these were removed the engine no longer made a queer noise and despite its mysterious jumps there were no visible signs of damage to the car.

The pieces of luggage along with the box containing the models were carried up the hill. In one of the rooms Eruch, somewhat nervously, opened the box and had another surprise. All the models were perfectly safe!* Not a piece was broken, not even a scratch was noticed on any of them, and all heaved a sigh of relief. Owing to this unforeseen event, the companions were late in getting back to Hyderabad. Baba inquired about the delay. Gustadjee, one of the *mandali*, who was observing silence and had silently witnessed the whole episode, was also a great mime and exquisite story teller. He related the entire episode, Eruch interpreting Gustadjee's gestures. This gave Baba many a hearty chuckle. Nevertheless, He neither expressed any surprise over what had happened nor did He make any passing remark about this mysterious happening, not even in later years.

Second Anniversary of the New Life.

On October 15, Donkin drove Baba to Khojaguda Phahad (hill). Vishnu, Nilu and a *mulla* (a Mohammedan priest) accompanied Baba in the car. The five companions — Gustadjee, Baidul, Pendu, Eruch and Daulat Singh — who were to stay with Baba during the *manonash* phase, had already arrived. Minoo Kharas, who was permitted by Baba to be with Him, could not join the party for reasons of health. It was drizzling and at 3 p.m. Donkin's car, wet with rain, arrived at the foot of the hill. All walked up and after a quiet round of inspection, Baba looked pleased with the arrangements made in the *dargah* of Baba Fakruddin. After a

---

* At present these models are preserved in a glass case in Adi K. Irani's office at Ahmednagar, India.

BEGINNING OF THE MANONASH PHASE

short while the *mulla,* in the presence of Baba and His companions offered the conventional prayers, and those who came with Donkin, except for Baba, returned to Hyderabad.

The next day, October 16, was the second anniversary of Baba's New Life, and it seemed that He wished to plunge deeply into His *manonash* phase — "the abnegation of the personal will in the Divine Volition". This was also a day of great importance to those who had attended the meeting called in June at Hyderabad. The participants were regarded as witnesses to the Declaration made by Baba and they were ordered by Him to fast on October 16 for twenty-four hours on tea and water only. In the premises of the *dargah,* Baba offered five slightly different prayers to God, the Infinite One, who, during the *Avataric* Advents assumed the human forms of Zoroaster, Krishna, Buddha, Jesus and Mohammed. As all the companions were solemnly standing, Baba gestured to Eruch to read the following:

O Ahuramazda! In the name of your Infinite Greatness and in the name of your Beloved Self, Zoroaster, and in the name of all prophets and saints and your lovers, Meher Baba beseeches you to help him to carry out successfully his four months' work beginning from today, the 16th October, 1951, and asks you in all humility to have his desire fulfilled and the ultimate object achieved by 16th February, 1952.

With a few changes in addressing God, the Eternal One, as *Paramatma* or *Allah,* the above quoted prayer was proffered in the names of the Beloved *Avatars* — Krishna and Buddha, Beloved Son Jesus and Beloved Mohammed Mustafa.

On the same day, according to Baba's earlier instructions, five of His dear ones who were in the Old Life were deputed by Him to visit Udwada (Gujarat), Mathura (Uttar Pradesh), Sarnath (Bihar), Goa (near Bombay, M.S.) and Ajmer (Rajasthan). According to the

Indian traditions, these towns respectively represent one of the principal places of worship for the Zoroastrians, the Hindus, the Buddhists (including the Jains), the Christians and the Mohammedans. These are also the centres of immense spiritual importance. The nominated Baba lovers were to visit these places in advance to find one righteous, poor person belonging to the faith, the place of pilgrimage stood for. Baba followers were then asked to request that this person fast on October 16. On this day, after taking a bath the man was to visit that sanctifying abode — an *agyari,* a temple, a pagoda, a church or a mosque — and recite a special prayer previously dictated by Baba. At the end, on Baba's behalf, the nominees were to offer each one of these five persons a hundred and one rupees as *dakshina.**

On this day, in the *dargah* of Baba Fakruddin, Baba went into seclusion at night, till the early hours of the morning, continuously for seven hours. The companions were posted outside, on watch, so that nothing should disturb Baba in His work; only the five models were keeping Baba's company. Thus began the phase of *manonash* in earnest.

Manonash means passing out of the separative self (mind) to abide in God. Baba being the God-Man, whose *manonash* did this phase indicate? He did not explain. With reference to Meher Baba's Advent as the *Avatar,* (the God-Man), Hazrat Babajan, one of Baba's *Sadgurus* (Man-God) used to refer to a Persian couplet meaning:

Of your own, you were free;
Of your own, you allowed yourself to be bound.

And any Baba lover, as an ordinary man, may dare say that Baba, out of His compassion for those who are ordained to be in the orbit of His Love, took on Him-

---

* Cash or kind offered to a person as a mark of respect for discharging spiritual duties.

BEGINNING OF THE MANONASH PHASE

self this additional binding (of *manonash*) so that its consequent consummation could help His dear ones break the shackles of their minds to get closer to Him, in His own time. One has not to forsake one's rationality after coming to Baba. As long as one has a mind one is apt to have views whether he expresses them or not. However, after sincere and honest efforts there comes a blessed moment, when one cheerfully accepts one's inability to understand the hidden meanings behind the actions of the God-Man and one totally gives in. Perhaps with the development of such an attitude Baba lovingly reveals a glimpse of Himself in the heart of such a person that quiets the mind. The more the heart is emptied of dogmatic interpretations, the more it is filled with the light of His renewing Love. Then the apparent contradictions and paradoxes do not bother such a lover. It is love alone that counts.

Baba's visit to the cave on Khojaguda Pahad started on October 18. Eruch carried with him the box of models and according to Baba's instructions arranged them on the ledge inside the cave. The first sitting was of seven hours at a stretch. A day later, in a similar way, Baba spent three hours in Vishnu's temple. In the afternoon He contacted a *mast* named Gulam Hussain. Baba's work in seclusion continued for nine days on this Pahad and He felt satisfied. So He changed His previous plan of staying there for fifteen days and decided to set out on the march on foot. Two routes in India shall especially be remembered by Baba lovers for the Avatar of the Age having journeyed on foot on these roads during His New Life. One is in the north of India — Benares via Sarnath (Bihar) to Najibabad (Uttar Pradesh) — and the other to the south — from Khojaguda Pahad (near Hyderabad. A.P.) to Meherazad Hill via Aurangabad, Khuldabad and Imampur in Maharashtra.

In the afternoon of October 24, Baba with the five companions left the memorable hill of Khojaguda with their bag and baggage. It took Him about a month to reach the most memorable and significant Seclusion Hill at the back of Meherazad. During this journey, depending upon Baba's mood and the urgency of His work, the party sometimes travelled by bus, goods lorry or even a bullock cart. The first halt of this march was at Lingampeta. In a *dak* bungalow the party rested for the night and the march was resumed the next morning. During the first week of tramping, Baba once noticed that dear old Gustadjee looked rather tired. Though he did not complain of any fatigue, Baba, under this pretext, allowed the whole party to avail itself of the opportunity to travel by truck. In fact, it was loaded with so many odd things that the companions had somehow to accommodate themselves on pieces of luggage of various sizes.

At Jogipeta the party got some information about a *mast* of that town and got down. The companions tried to find this person but all their efforts were in vain. At the next stop, Sadashivpeta, Baba was very happy because he contacted a good *mast*. This God-intoxicated soul looked bizarre for his eccentricities had veiled the flame of love that had lit his heart. The party moved on to Chitgop and another "fool of God" named Gopal was contacted. In his divine intoxication, Gopal seemed to flout the laws of hygiene. Love indeed is self-sufficient; it does not depend on anything but itself.

In the Old Life, the *mandali* were not allowed to witness Baba's meetings with the *masts*. With the commencement of Baba's New Life the ban was lifted and the companions could watch the loving responses of the *masts* in the company of their Divine Beloved. The *masts* would often be drawn closer to Baba with sudden affection. Sometimes, overpowered with emotions, they would gaze at Him, beaming with intimacy and inner recognition. Baba's redeeming touch and radiant glances would fill the hearts of the *masts* with rare ecstasy and "blissful agony" which, I presume, later opened wider visions in their states of involved consciousness.

The next stop of the journey was at Humnabad which

is famous for the *samadhi* of Manik Prabhu, a Perfect Master of the nineteenth century. Later, his son and disciple, Manohar, enjoined his followers to bury him alive near the *samadhi* of his dear father and Master. At midday, Baba quietly sat near the *samadhi* of Manohar Prabhu and then the party proceeded to Gulbarga.

A Delightful Diwali Day

On October 29, Baba left Gulbarga for Itgah where He contacted a very lovable *mast*. In the 1940s Baba had twice visited this village. Some years back, this *mast* in his divine exuberance, used to roam about naked; later he was persuaded to wear clothes. He usually stood near a particular well, eating roasted gram "grain by grain". At the time of the first contact, in his innocence, he implored Baba to break His silence, while during the second meeting he offered Baba a cup of tea from which he had some sips. Baba accepted the drink with love. After this third satisfactory meeting, Baba boarded a bus for Gulbarga. But after a short journey He got down and with the three companions walked the distance to the *dak* bungalow at Gulbarga. The fourth companion was asked to follow a bullock cart in which a few belongings of the party were kept. Use of any conveyance or its rejection was totally at Baba's discretion. No one questioned, "Why?" Rather such thoughts were alien to the companions.

The next day Baba visited the distinguished *dargah* of Khwaja Bande Nawaz. Arrangements were made for Him to sit for half an hour quietly in a secluded spot. After this silent sitting, instead of going back to their residence, Baba wished to contact some *masts* who usually roamed about the city. Baidul, who was with Baba, was adept at finding these God-intoxicated souls. With his tenacious memory he could remember the names of the *masts* residing in different parts of India and also the localities where they moved about. So he began to lead Baba to different parts of the city to spot these "men of God". In the morning Baba had entrusted some additional work to Eruch. Side by side with the work of contacting the God-absorbed and the God-communed, Baba also wished to continue His work with the poor in a special way which He had adopted from the New Life. He instructed Eruch to find a few "once rich" middle-class families, irrespective of caste, color and creed, who, owing to some unforeseen calamities, were in dire need of some financial help. Baba wanted to extend some monetary aid to the "heads" of such families.

Eruch who had previous experience with this type of work, set out to meet some social workers in the city and gathered some preliminary information. To verify the facts he started visiting different houses with a few people who volunteered to help him. This activity of Eruch's aroused an uninvited concern in a prominent businessman who happened to be one of the city fathers. Incidentally, it was at this time that the communists were concentrating on a major revolutionary move for the poor, in the adjacent province of Telangana.

The above mentioned businessman belonged to the other political party which had its base in Gulbarga. He assumed Eruch was one of the workers of the Communist Party. He was upset that Eruch seemed to be setting up some sort of poor relief program without consulting him; his political influence was challenged! He phoned police headquarters and suggested an immediate inquiry into the intentions of this stranger visiting the city. A police constable was at once sent to summon Eruch for interrogation.

The constable approached Eruch and asked him to report to the police station. Eruch refused to obey this oral order and continued his work of visiting the houses. When he felt convinced of the information gathered from the social workers, he started instructing the "heads" of the families about the formal procedure that his elder brother would observe while offering the financial help. Then he started for the rest house. While on his way back he met Baba and Baidul. A little later the constable approached Eruch for a second time and in an authoritative tone asked him to present himself before his boss. The Baba-party already had official permission to travel throughout the State as well as credentials from the office of the Superintendent of Police at Hyderabad. So Eruch openly told the policeman, "We are staying in the *dak* bungalow. This is our address. And if your inspector needs any information about us please request him to see us there."

The constable was surprised to receive such an outspoken reply but he had to leave. The party went back to the rest house. It was late afternoon and no one had had his lunch. The walk had been quite exhausting. So the companions preferred to have a bath before the meal. By evening they felt relaxed. But just then a police van drove in. The Deputy Superintendent of Police, who felt rather offended at Eruch's reply had personally come to the *dak* bungalow, perhaps to exercise his authority.

But the moment that he saw Pendu all the misgivings he had had about the Baba-party vanished. He knew Pendu well as one of Meher Baba's closest disciples. Some years earlier he had been working as an inspector of police at Ahmednagar. In the beginning he had suspected that Pendu was a member of one of the leftist groups, for he had seen Pendu in close company with a political leader of Ahmednagar, who worked for the Communist Party. In fact, Pendu's concern in meeting him was in connection with Baba's work for the poor residing in certain villages. Baba wanted to distribute food grains and cloth to the needy villagers. The inspector, after awhile, realized his mistake and felt convinced that Baba's *mandali* were above politics, leading a disciplined and dedicated life under Meher Baba's orders. He apologized to Pendu for his mistrust of him and their relations became very cordial, especially after his having Baba's *darshan*.

Some years passed and on promotion he was stationed at Gulbarga as a Deputy Superintendent of Police. Seeing him Pendu said, "What brought you here? Any inquiry?" And both had a hearty laugh and a warm handshake. In his conversation, he told Pendu about the departmental circular they had received from the Head office at Hyderabad. But in the route stated therein Gulbarga was not included. When he read it he even had thought how nice it would have been of Baba, had He decided to pass by Gulbarga! And he requested, "Can I see Baba, today?" Pendu went inside and explained to Baba the whole affair and it surprised even Pendu that in spite of Baba's New Life conditions, He permitted the police officer to have His *darshan* the next day.

Accordingly, on October 31, which happened to be the second day of *Diwali (Padwa)*, Mr. Ghanti, for that was the name of the police officer, came in the morning with his wife and children. He had brought a big, beautiful garland of scented flowers and a basket of sweets for it was an occasion of great rejoicing for the family. As he did not know about Baba's recent restrictions, he prostrated before Baba and Baba did not object. After some time the family left in a very happy mood. Thus, instead of Eruch reporting at the police station, Baba made the Deputy Superintendent present himself before Him at His residence!

The same day Baba with His companions left for Yadgiri by the morning train at 10.30 a.m. In the afternoon, He walked a distance of about four miles to reach Tumkur to contact Tilgur Swami. Baba had previously met him in July 1944 and May 1949. Years earlier there was a time when the children used to stone the Swami and make fun of him. But soon the people were convinced of his Divinity and the whole village began to revere him. The headman of the Tumkur village built a special room for Tilgur Swami and also a cellar which was to be the resting place of the Swami after the dropping of his body. Baba had earlier revealed

BEGINNING OF THE MANONASH PHASE

to the *mandali* that Tilgur Swami was a *Jivanmukta*, a Perfect One with God consciousness and Creation-consciousness. He was a tall person with a regal face which radiated peace about him. This meeting like the two previous ones was remarkable. As they looked into each other's eyes and perhaps gazed into their infinite depths, the Swami tried to bow down to Baba who gracefully prevented him from doing so. The meaning of the Swami's reverential gesture appears very significant.

Baba, in spite of His innate wisdom of being the Ancient One, had entered the New Life phase of complete helplessness for His *Avataric* work. He had "become" an ordinary man, but Tilgur Swami, a realized soul, having recognized the infinite humility of the *Avatar* in stooping to the level of a common man, could not resist honoring this amazing *Avataric* role by paying obeisance to Him. Thus, in the New Life, Baba established His relationship with ordinary men, with the men of God (*masts*) and also the Perfect Ones, through the *Jivanmukta* of Tumkur. As soon as this perfect meeting was over, Baba briskly walked back to Yadgiri. As the party reached the town it was presented with a delightful sight. The whole town was, as if welcoming Baba, flickering with lights from small earthen lamps placed by the door and courtyards of every house. It was *Padwa*, the second day of *Diwali*, the Festival of Lights. The lights were welcoming the Light!

15

Arriving at the Blessed Consummation

1951 — Part IV

Father Blesses the God-Man!

AFTER offering some financial help in His own unique way to the "heads" of the families selected by Eruch, Baba left Gulbarga for Humnabad. During a short halt in this town, out of His loving concern, He made a specific provision for the essential medical treatment of a poor girl. The itinerary of the New Life provides a good many instances of Baba benevolently helping others, without divulging His identity, one of His ancient habits. The party journeyed by the highway to Tuljapur, famous for the temple of Bhavani Devi, the goddess who is supposed to have offered Shivaji the Great a sword as *prasad* which brought him victory in almost all his battles. During a two day stay at the *dak* bungalow, Baba contacted a few *masts*. In the early morning on November 4, Baba with His companions left Tuljapur on foot for Osmanabad. They had to walk continually for six hours. After a little rest the party proceeded on the journey via Bhir (Bid) and Aurangabad. Baba and the companions reached Khuldabad on November 8.

This small village was Baba's headquarters until November 15. Their quarters, adjacent to the Awalia Masjid, in what is now the VIP guest house, consisted of three rooms. This is regarded as one of the important places connected with Baba's New Life. This little village is rich in spiritual heritage. In fact, during the thirteenth and fourteenth centuries, the area from Daulatabad to Ellora, with Khuldabad in the middle, became

AVATAR MEHER BABA

*With His Four Companions of Manonash Phase
Gustadjee, Baidul, Pendu, and Eruch
February 1952 — Meherazad*

the focus of Sufi culture in the Deccan (the southern part of India), and hundreds of people aspiring for spiritual guidance migrated to this part of the country. By the end of the fourteenth century this region boasted of fourteen hundred tombs, big and small, including those of some great spiritual personages. Amongst these the most important *dargah* at Khuldabad is of Zar Zari Zar Bakhsh, one of the illustrious Sufi Perfect Masters, a pioneer who established himself in this area.

A day after His arrival at Khuldabad, Baba began visiting the different *dargahs* of the saintly personages. On one occasion, He sat all alone by Himself in a cave associated with Zar Zari Zar Bakhsh. He concluded this silent sitting by bathing and giving new clothes to a *mast* of that place. It was in this cave where Sai Baba in one of his earlier lives was observing spiritual austerities under the direct guidance of Zar Zari Zar Bakhsh. Pleased with his love and devotion the Master bestowed on him his Grace which bore fruit after a few lifetimes and Sai Baba became not only God-realized but *Qutub e-Irshad*, the head of the spiritual hierarchy until he handed over the charge to the *Avatar* of the Age, Meher Baba. On November 11, Baba visited Daulatabad which is about 15 kms. to the northwest of Aurangabad.

The next day He went to Ellora (Verul), famous for its caves, carved by Buddhists, Brahmins and Jains. These were carved between the fourth through the thirteenth centuries A.D. They are massive and magnificent, charming and most artistic. Owing to the anonymity of the artists, the spirit of selflessness and perfect dedication to the spiritual ideals shines through every cave. During His visits in later years, Baba seemed specially interested in caves nos. 10 and 16. In all there are 34 caves. The former — no. 10 — is known as Sutar's (Carpenter's) Jhopra where Lord Buddha is represented as Vishwakarma, the personification of creative power. Vishwakarma is also regarded as the "lord of the arts, executor of a thousand handcrafts," including carpentry, Buddha the Perfect Craftsman. Cave no. 16 — the Kailash temple — is truly regarded as one of the world's wonders, a monolithic structure not built but rather carved out of a mountain of rock.

Baba's preference for this day's work was cave no. 32. This cave is known as Indra Sabha (Assembly), wherein the statue of Mahaveer, the founder of Jainism and the twenty-fourth Tirthankar, seated on a lion throne has a place of prominence. Baba sat all alone near the austere image of this Perfect Recluse. The delicate carvings, hewn with consummate skill, are meant to propagate the tenets of the Jains belonging to the *Digambar* (one wearing no clothes, nude) sect that advocate total renunciation, inner and outer. Hence this place might have been one of the ideal seclusion spots for Baba's work during the New Life of "helplessness and absolute renunciation". On the way back to Awalia Masjid, Baba met two spiritually inclined people named Pralhad and Keshav Maharaj.

On November 14, Baba called the *mujawar* (attendant) of Zar Zari Zar Bakhsh's *dargah* to His residence, washed his feet and gave him 21 rupees. Then the Baba-party went to the shrine of the Perfect Master (Bakhsh) where the *mujawar* collected seventy-four people from the Mohammedan community. Baba repeated the usual formalities of washing and drying the feet of all. A special prayer from the Holy Book was recited by the *mujawar* which ended with a chorus blessing from all: "May His [Baba's] spiritual work, whatever it be, get fulfilled. Amen!" Baba then left the *dargah* for the village and went round for *bhiksha* at the doors of five Hindu families. He accepted with love and humility whatever was offered to Him. This begging was followed by serving some poor Hindu villagers in the way He had done with the earlier group that morning. On this day Baba gave over a thousand rupees as *dakshina* to the needy residents of Khuldabad. He begged for food; He distributed the riches; Baba the Beggar, Baba the Bestower!

The next day, November 15, shall be remembered

for two uncommon incidents. In the morning, Baba with His companions left by bus for Aurangabad. As the party arrived Baba had an unusual desire. He asked Eruch whether he would be able to find a venerable Christian Father in Aurangabad who would bless Him! Eruch replied that he would try his best and Baba added, "You will know who he is when you meet him." With this hint they got into a *tonga* and the quest for finding the "blessed bishop" worthy of blessing the God-Man, took them to the churches, quarters and bungalows located throughout the city. Eruch met some priests, but none whom he thought was the one Baba wanted.

However, Eruch's visits to so many different priests aroused the curiosity of the *tongawalla* and he politely asked him, '*Saheb,* whom are you looking for?" Eruch told him that they wanted to meet "old venerable priests". The driver smiled and said, "Had you told me earlier about your intention you would have easily saved much of your time and trouble. I know the place where the old clergymen, priests and ministers live in retirement." And he whipped his horse and headed off in that direction. Soon they arrived. Leaving Baba in the *tonga*, Eruch went inside to inquire. A priest, dressed in a white robe, who was standing on the veranda came towards him and affectionately said, "My son, what do you want?" His loving tone and gracious demeanor made Eruch say spontaneously, "Will you please give blessings to my elder brother? He is waiting outside. Should I call Him in?" "Of course," was the kind reply. The priest was a short but robust person. From his accent Eruch gathered that he was not an Englishman. He was not sure whether this Father was French or Italian but he felt deeply convinced that he was the person Baba was looking for.

He turned round to go to the gate but to his surprise he noticed that Baba had already gotten down from the *tonga* — for the first time during that morning's *tonga* rides — and was gracefully striding towards the stairs leading to the veranda. Coincidentally, there wasn't anyone else there. A perfect Baba timing! Eruch said to Father Berger (that was his last name), "Here is my brother." Baba came up. He reverentially knelt down and touched the Father's feet and lovingly kissed his hand. The Father solemnly and whole-heartedly blessed the Son. A good *Avataric* joke! Baba got up and Eruch thanked the Father on behalf of his brother. Without any further conversation both quickly left the veranda. Father Berger, not knowing what had really happened, addressed Eruch, saying, "Son, don't you want me also to bless you?" "No thanks," replied Eruch and he followed Baba back to the *tonga*. The New Life events are incomprehensible, and infinitely inconceivable is Baba's New Life!

Baba with the companions went to the *dakhma* (the funeral premises of the Parsees, also known as the Tower of Silence). He instructed His men to offer Zoroastrian prayers and He, Himself silently joined them in praying with *kusti*. There He sat for some minutes in a *saghdi* (a place where a dead body of a Zoroastrian is placed before final disposal). On that day Baba seemed to be in a peculiar mood. For immediately after this, He asked the companions to take Him to the Christian cemetery. It was on the outskirts of the city, a far-off quiet place as it should be. Baba wanted to sit inside the graveyard, under a small neem tree, undisturbed by anyone for some time. As usual He posted the companions in different directions on watch so that no one might try to get near or try to look at Baba.

Eruch was asked to stand outside the cemetery by the main gate. It was noon and there was no possibility of anybody visiting the place at such an hour. Thus everything started well but after just a few minutes, as if from nowhere, a long funeral procession was seen approaching the graveyard. The bearers were carrying the coffin, silently followed by the mourners, friends and relatives of the deceased. Eruch was distressed at the thought of these people entering the cemetery for this would disturb Baba in His work. On the spur of the moment, with his unique presence of mind, Eruch had the nerve to go forward to meet the procession. As it came closer he approached those leading it and offered his condolences. In a most natural way he began asking them questions about the sickness and the dependants of the deceased. He did this so naturally that the people voluntarily stopped; the conversation continued and the procession temporarily came to a standstill. Eruch's intention was to while away the time till Baba clapped, the signal that His work was completed. The spirit of obedience to the God-Man does not expect anything for oneself except the pleasure of the Beloved. The *mandali* carried out Baba's orders at any cost, irrespective of other people's comments.

At last, to Eruch's great relief, for this was really a severe trial for him, he heard the clap and at that very moment he abruptly stopped the conversation and hastened to attend to Baba. Those at the tailend of the procession had no idea of what had happened at the front. They wondered why they had stopped when the graveyard was so close. However, they also thought that there must have been a good reason for this delay. Baba had finished His work. All the companions joined Him and the party was ready to leave. Meanwhile the procession picked up where it had left and entered the cemetery. As the coffin passed, Baba gestured, "A fortunate soul, to be blessed with my physical presence just before the gross body is being laid to rest!" The day's work was over. Baba left the graveyard in a very lively mood. During such a mood His strides would be long, His arms would move swiftly and there would be a light jolly feeling about Him.

Incredible Imampur Incident

After the middle of November, Aurangabad was Baba's headquarters. One day after contacting two God-communed souls in the city, Baba, with his companions, left on foot for a place five miles away to contact a *sadhu* and immediately returned to the *dak* bungalow. On November 17, He visited Paithan specially to offer His homage to the *samadhi* of *Sadguru* Eknath Maharaj, of the sixteenth century, one of the most revered Perfect Masters of Maharashtra. All year round thousands of pilgrims visit this sacred place. Shri Janardan Swami was his Master whose *samadhi* is in the Fort at Daulatabad. Shri Janardan outwardly led the life of a perfect householder, inwardly experiencing his Oneness with God. The works of Dnyaneshwar, Eknath, Tukaram and Ramdas, written in the Marathi language, are respected as being as good as the *Vedas* and *Upanishads* by the Marathi speaking people, though in those centuries it was blasphemous to write on spiritual subjects in any other language than Sanskrit. At Paithan, Baba contacted two "fools of God". One of them was a young boy who remained naked throughout the year. Baba fed him with His own hands. A lucky lad!

The next day, Baba went to Jalna for His work with the God-intoxicated souls. One of the *masts* he met had dozens of rings on his fingers, including his thumbs. He was called Chhallewala Baba. (*Chhalla* literally means a ring.) He was a good *mast*. On his insistence Baba agreed to call him to Meherazad in the near future. He was instructed to see Adi at Ahmednagar. Eruch wrote Adi's address on a note and Baba signed it to convince Adi of its authenticity. Baba used to cater to the various whims of the *masts*. Nevertheless, this *mast* never turned up. Baba alone knows why.

On November 19, Baba was at Nanded (Nander). He paid a special visit to the shrine of Guru Gobind Singh, who was the tenth *Guru* of the Sikhs. His great contribution lay in giving his followers the book, *Guru Granthsaheb* (the Guide to God). He was also a militant Master and infused a martial spirit among the Sikhs. To counteract the aggression and harassment by the Moghul rulers, he raised a strong army. But eventually he had to flee to the Deccan Plateau. During his camping at Nanded he was fatally wounded and consequently lay aside his mortal coil. The lineage of *gurus* which commenced with Guru Nanak, the Perfect Master and founder of Sikhism, ended with Guru Gobind Singh. At Nanded a big shrine — *Gurudwara* — has been built in honor of Gobind Singh and the city has become an important place of pilgrimage for the Sikhs. Baba visited the *Gurudwara* to recharge the spiritual atmosphere. He also contacted about eight *masts* of high and low grades in the city. Then the party proceeded by train for Aurangabad.

During this journey one of the companions, Daulat Singh, fell ill. He had very high fever which made him very weak. In view of the forthcoming work of *manonash*, Baba did not feel it practical to keep Daulat Singh with Him any longer in the party's wanderings towards Meherazad Hill. The next day Baba ordered him to return to Bangalore and stay with his family members. Baba told him that he was really pleased with Daulat Singh's resolve to accompany Him; however, without any fault of his, Baba wished to send him back home. Unlike his return from Belgaum, this time the homeward journey of Daulat Singh was not so painful as it was done expressly under Baba's order. Daulat Singh, cheerfully followed Baba's order which pleased the Master Companion very much.

Later, Baba with the four companions, (Pendu, Baidul, Gustadjee and Eruch), reached Toka by a bus. This town is situated on the banks of the sacred Godavari. In the year 1928, Baba, with the *Prem Ashram* boys had stayed here from June through November. The first group of Westerners, including Meredith Starr from England and later a Russian *sadhu*, Christian Leik, had met Baba at Toka. The *mandali* living with Baba in those days liked the premises at Toka so much that they renamed the place New Meherabad. During the New Life the Baba-party did not stay here even for a day. After a simple meal and a little rest they left the town for Ghodegaon.

Here, by chance, the companions saw a truck owned by Sarosh (Irani), one of Baba's closest disciples and a businessman dealing in automobiles at Ahmednagar. The driver knew Baba and the *mandali* very well. After a little discussion with him it was decided that the luggage of the party would be carried in that truck to Imampur, which is about 12 kms. to the east of Meherazad. Baba asked Pendu and Baidul to wait till the loading and unloading of the goods at Ghodegaon was completed, then they were to travel by the truck to Imampur. Baba with Gustadjee and Eruch continued the march on foot. After an hour or so Sarosh's truck caught up with them. It was evening and Baba agreed to journey in the truck to Imampur. The party reached the old *dak* bungalow* by 9 p.m. There was no caretaker there and the place looked deserted. Baba, however, decided to halt there. The short stay in this dilapidated structure will nevertheless be remembered by Baba lovers for a symbolic, indelible event of the New Life.

I wish to relate this exceptionally significant occurrence, as far as I remember, in the words of Eruch who was a party and witness to what happened in that rest house. He once narrated:

> We had come some three hundred miles from Hyderabad via Aurangabad on our way to Meherazad, little knowing that this was the last leg of our New Life wanderings. Our mode of transport was by bullock carts, hitch-hiking in trucks, sometimes journeying by buses but mostly walking the distance along the highway which was then a dirt road full of potholes and dust. The countryside has remained unchanged but the road is paved now.
>
> At around 9 p.m. on 21st November 1951, after a long day we came upon an old dilapidated *dak* bungalow now known as Imampur mosque. Baba de-

---

* At present this building is no longer a rest house. It is now known as a *masjid* or mosque of Imampur.

cided to rest here for the night. I selected one of the rooms for Him, felt around in the dark, cleared a space and dusted the area with a coarse woollen blanket which we used for everything — sleeping, wearing, and as a protection from the sun and rain. Baba's blanket was then spread on the floor and He went to sleep. I was posted by the door as a night watch, just outside the room in which Baba slept. The other three companions (Gustadjee, Pendu, and Baidul), slept below the parapet of the mosque.

After some time the snoring of some of the companions disturbed Baba so much that He had them moved, about a hundred yards over by the main road under a tree. Again, after half an hour or so, Baba clapped. With the aid of matches I was able to see His gestures and interpret their meaning. In the New Life we did not have the luxury of torches or lanterns. Baba gestured, "There is some sort of disturbance inside this room. Find out what it is." I waited and listened for some time and finally heard the sound of fluttering of a bird's wings. I felt around in the dark in the far upper right hand corner of the room from where the sound was coming. I found there a bird's nest. Returning to Baba, I told Him that there was a mother bird nesting in a niche. He gestured that I should throw it out. In the New Life we had to do our best to obey Baba's orders. I approached the nest, wanting to catch the bird—it was a dove. Baba, however, began to clap incessantly which meant to stop everything and come to Him immediately. "Did you throw the bird out?" He asked. "No Baba," I replied. "Good that you didn't." He gestured, and added, "Have you forgotten the order I had given you earlier? This action would have been an expression of cruelty on my part. Why didn't you remind me about it?"* I apologized, "Baba, I com-

---

* In the New Life, Baba told some of His companions to draw His attention to any of His actions if they honestly felt that He

pletely forgot." Baba continued, "Well, anyway it's good that you didn't throw that bird out or it would have ruined the whole New Life career! Now, don't worry about it any more. Go and sit outside and remind me about it tomorrow."

In the morning when all woke up, I got water for Baba to wash His face and hands from a nearby well. There was a small bathroom (a cubicle) adjacent to the room where He had slept. After the wash, He called the rest of the companions and conveyed, "Now listen to Eruch who will tell you what had happened last night." After my narration of the entire story, Baba picked up the thread and repeated, "Eruch, why did you not remind me about being unkind to a dumb creature?" I replied, "That was my mistake, Baba. I thought that I should not argue with you at that time." Baba continued, "But as you had kept quiet and you all being my companions of the New Life, the only thing to rectify such a mistake is to punish myself. Now the only way for me to have the satisfaction of a clear conscience for what had happened last night is for you all to remove your sandals and beat me with them because of my having expressed cruelty to an innocent mother bird that was nesting!"

Well, here was another severe test and the companions had to obey Him. Baba then pinched His own ears and gestured, "We should be kind towards all creatures." That done, He looked quite happy and His look radiated ineffable tenderness all around. Then He rubbed His right hand over His heart region meaning, "I am satisfied." He, however, added, "I am pleased but to crown the whole event, the last thing you all have to do is to spit upon me." And

---

was expressing anger, harshness or cruelty towards any being. They were simultaneously expected to obey Him without questioning, irrespective of the nature of the order, good or bad, ordinary or extraordinary. Thus, in the New Life phase the companions, in a way, had to be in readiness to "stand and sit at one and the same time!"

we did it because Baba was our Master and Companion of the New Life and we had pledged to obey Him implicitly. Thus Baba, for some unfathomable reason which He alone knew, took upon Himself, His own humiliation, at the hands of His own close companions. Maybe, He was setting some sort of guidelines for all to be humble and kind and to respect life in all its aspects. What a profound lesson!

Some incidents in Meher Baba's New Life are most touching and unforgettable. The symbolic saying of the "dove's nest" at Imampur, at an incredible cost to the God-Man, is surely one of them.

Cabins Brought down the Hill

On the morning of November 23 began the last march of the New Life. It was a distance of about twelve kms. from Imampur. Baba, with His four companions, reached the lower Tembi Hill, now known as Seclusion Hill, without passing through the Meherazad estate. A couple of days back the men and women companions from Hyderabad had arrived at Meherazad. They were not permitted to see Baba. Only Mehera and Mani were called to see Him at the foot of the hill. Baba, in His white robe and green turban, looked serenely beautiful. In spite of His extreme physical and spiritual sufferings, Baba would sometimes look very radiant, beaming with a smile. He inquired about their welfare and within a few minutes He left for the hill. After a short distance He turned back and waved at His dear ones, it was a signal for them to return and for Him to speed up His striding to the summit. Across the narrow spine of a ridge, on an oval top of the hill, was Baba's cabin. On the *ashram* side there is no gradual slope but a steep drop.

According to Baba's earlier instructions, Padri had repaired the two cabins and erected a temporary canvas covering, a sort of a tent for the four companions. The arrangements for water and food were well attended to. Baba, however, did not like the proximity of the small tent to the lower cabin where He stayed during the day time and worked in seclusion. So the companions were asked to keep away from the tent for the whole day and occupy it only during the night. After sunset, Baba would retire in the cabin on the top of the hill. At Baba's clap the one on duty had to go up to Him but while getting to the top he had to be careful not to sprain his ankle on the rough ascent.

From the very beginning it seemed that Baba was not fully satisfied with the pitching of the tent. So He called Padri and suggested a few alterations. Whether in the Old or the New Life, with Baba, change was the order of the day, a glimpse of His ever-renewing creativity. From December 8, Baba fasted for four days, taking only water; for the next three days He had only liquid food. During the stay at Hyderabad, Baba's physical suffering was severe. Until the phase of *manonash* ended, He refused to pay any special attention to His physical complaints. The journey on foot, the irregularities in the programs and frequent fasting had an adverse effect on His physical health. During the first week of December, He conveyed to the companions that in view of the final phase of the New Life, beginning on December 16, it was neither suitable nor practical for Him to stay on the hill. He wanted to feel "at home" and yet keep Himself secluded from all the *mandali*. He wanted also to exercise His freedom of movement and actions to the fullest extent. With due consideration to the prevailing circumstances He expressed His readiness to continue the work, down the hill, on the Meherazad premises.

Padri was summoned and was entrusted with the plan of providing Baba with suitable accommodations, with a properly partitioned compound separating the present *mandali* hall from the Blue Bus. It was to be extended to the small building in front, then known as the engine room. The time limit given by Baba to complete the arrangements was December 14. Padri volunteered to finish the work in time, provided the cabins on the hill were immediately dismantled.

Baba suggested that if both the cabins on the hill could be made into only one room, it would be an ideal and perfect set-up for His work. Baba also agreed to Padri's suggestion of staying temporarily in one of the improvised rooms at Meherazad, adjacent to the Blue Bus. To maintain the "link" with the work, Baba had started on the hill, He wished to have a good God-intoxicated soul in a room behind the Blue Bus, and He wanted to serve him daily. By the time the work of demolishing the structures was done, Baidul returned from Thana with a good *mast* named Pathan Baba. Baba came down the hill. Baidul stayed with Baba and also looked after the *mast*. Daily Baba sat for some time with the *mast*. As this occasion turned out to be the concluding *mast* contact in Baba's New Life, I quote below an excerpt from an interview given by Baba in November 1936 which gives a general indication of the nature of His work with the God-intoxicated souls. He stated, "It is a 'game of consciousness.' I direct the spiritual consciousness towards material consciousness by rendering them [the *masts*] physical service, and uplift the material consciousness of others to God-consciousness by my Spiritual guidance. Thus my Infinite Consciousness links the two."*

It may be mentioned here that Baba's first stay in these cabins on the hill began in December 1947. It was for a period of 13 days. The last stay in the same cabins was from November 23, 1951, terminating in the second week of December. Since then the lower Tembi is known as Baba's Seclusion Hill, one of the dearest places to Baba lovers all the world over. Baba's presence and His special work in seclusion on the rocky summit have made this hill wholly holy, to the last piece of its rock.

---

* *The Awakener*, Vol. XVI, No. 2, p. 13.

In spite of the absence of any shelter, Baba asked Gustadjee, Pendu and Eruch to stay on the hill. He added that this would help Him to retain the "link" with the work He would do during the interim period of His stay down the hill. The camping of the companions on the bare top, under the sky, automatically linked them with the sun, moon and the stars! It was very windy and hot in the day, and the nights were very cold. Raising a cot to a slanting position like a low roof of a hut, Gustadjee covered it with a coarse blanket to serve as protection from the sun. At night the temperature would fall considerably, and the companions had to roll themselves in their blankets to ward off the cold. They had to be up there on the hill "sitting doing nothing", one of the disciplines of the New Life!

For the final phase of *manonash*, Baba felt that the nearness of a "pure being"— a *mast* or a saint — would greatly facilitate His work. So, through Adi, letters were sent to some of Baba's dear ones about the possibility of bringing such a person, residing in their respective areas, to Meherazad. Baba was to bear all the expenses. The following were included in the list of "pure beings": Badri Baba of Chandtara, Inayatulla of Mathura, Sobha *mast* of Katni, Merwan Baba of Kolhapur, Batwa Shah of Benares and a few others. Baidul was specially deputed to Tumkur to meet Tilgur Swami, the *Jivanmukta*. Baidul was asked to invite the Swami for a stay with Baba from mid-December to mid-February. In spite of the sincere efforts of one and all, no one succeeded in persuading any of the "pure beings" to go to Meherazad. Absence of such a spiritually advanced person perhaps intensified Baba's helplessness in the conclusive phase of the New Life, initiated on December 16.

True to his words, Padri completed the allotted work in time. He used all the material of the two cabins — asbestos sheets and stone floorings — including a door and two windows to erect a single room on the ground level. On the left hand side there were two shelves, used for keeping the five models. This part of the room, separated by a curtain running across the room, served as Baba's "office" and the other part was His relaxing room. At night He rested in the room in front of this cabin, now occupied by Pendu. On the other side of the partitioned compound stayed Nilu, Vishnu, Kaka and other companions of the New Life. But they were not allowed to meet or even greet the four associates residing on the other side. Food for the Baba-party was brought from Meheru Damania, Eruch's sister, residing nine miles away in Ahmednagar while the kitchen for the other companions was just nine yards away from the partitioned compound! What was outwardly close or convenient had no special preference in the New Life; whatever Baba wanted was implicitly done.

On December 15, Baba's final work began. On Khojaguda Hill, He commenced the *manonash* work, keeping the five models — temple, mosque, church, pagoda and fire-temple — near Him. Whenever He worked these models continued to remain by His side, till the end of this particular phase. The external use of certain things for inner spiritual work, though incomprehensible, is not too uncommon with the Masters. I am reminded of two similar instances from the lives of the Perfect Masters.

Sai Baba for some years used to keep with him, in a small pouch, a few coins of different denominations and during a certain period of his life, standing behind a coarse curtain he everyday used to rub these coins vigorously over one another, so much so that the surface of the coins eventually turned very smooth. The moment anyone peeped in or pushed the curtain aside to approach him, he would immediately stop this game! Another of the Perfect Masters of the nineteenth century named Akkalkot Swami Maharaj would keep by his side small and big measuring bowls containing food grains. His entertainment-work consisted in emptying out and refilling these measures. In relation to the nature of spiritual work the Perfect Masters have used some external media to accomplish the results on the inner planes. Baba, being the *Avatar* of the Age, seemed to have used these models for reviving and recharging the spiritual potentials inherent in different religious practices. The use of the models was one of Baba's mystical ways of working about which I dare not write any further.

Life of Oneness in Manyness

On December 24, a list of 124 "departed ones" who had loved Baba very dearly was read out to Him at a private program that began at 9 in the morning. A couple of days earlier He had given the following dictation, to be read on the occasion.

> Today, December 24, 1951, in this New Life, knowing how unworthy I have been of the devotion, love and service of so many departed ones, I appeal in all humility to the most merciful and gracious God, that He should bestow His grace upon each of these departed ones according to their merits.
>
> As an expression of this homage, and in memory of these dear ones and of many others, now departed who graced my life by their love and service, I shall today make an offering of Rs. 124 to a poor man of worthy character and shall bow down before him.*

The list was read aloud which comprised the names of 87 men and 37 women (total 124). It opened with Baba's dear father, Sheriarjee, followed by His childhood friend, Ghani, ending with Ganu Chambhar (a poor cobbler) and Kashya, a boy servant at Meherabad. The list of women was topped by Baba's dear mother, Shirinmai, succeeded by the western women *mandali* — Nonny Gayley, Nadine Tolstoy and others — as well as

---

* *Circular NL* 33, issued on 25-12-1951.

ARRIVING AT THE BLESSED CONSUMMATION

the faithful servants Shanta and Dhondi. To Baba all those who loved Him and served Him were alike, irrespective of their social status or worldly riches. In the later years, on one occasion, He remarked, "My 'deads' live in me." At another time He stated, "I have only love to give and all I want is love."

Two needy pious people were invited to be present at this program. While bowing down and offering a sum of 124 rupees to one of them, Eruch, on behalf of Baba, invoked the Lord as follows, "O God, by bowing down to this man, I bow down to the departed ones."

Then the next dictation was read. It was in relation to the dedicated life of selfless service led by His disciples and devotees who were alive. It was as follows:

> Today, ... in this New Life, Baba is experiencing an utter hopelessness of spirit, mind and body. He is full of weaknesses and feels himself utterly unworthy of the love, service and devotion of all those both in the East and the West who have placed their loving faith in him.
> ... Baba desires to pay homage to their love, service and devotion by making an offering of Rs. 51 to a poor man of worthy character, by bowing down before him.*

As Baba handed over money to the second man the following invocation was read, "O God, by bowing down to this man, I bow down to these living ones." After offering homage to His dear ones — whether dead or living — Baba asked the worthy guests to leave.

In the third dictation, Baba invoked the help of God for His *manonash* work. All His disciples and devotees who wished to join Him in this act were allowed to do so by whole-heartedly and lovingly repeating any one of the following names of God (according to their religions), for half an hour each day, from December 29,

---
* Ibid.

1951 through February 16, 1952. Parsees were to repeat Ahuramazda; Iranis, Yazdan; Muslims, Allah Hoo; Hindus, Parabrahma; Christians, God the Father, God the Son, God the Holy Ghost; the rest to repeat the name of God, commonly used in their religions. Baba concluded the dictation by stating. "The One Indivisible, Infinite and Eternal God, who is in everything and everyone, ... is being invoked by Baba through His various names to help him through the instrument of His Infinite Power, Love, and Mercy."* With this concluded Baba's unique program of offering homage to His loved ones and of soliciting help of God. What a symbolic expression of the incredible life of Oneness in manyness!

By the way, it may be mentioned here that though in the earlier years Baba sometimes asked His followers to repeat any one of the names of God, after the completion of the *manonash* phase, especially from the late 1950s, He categorically asked those who loved Him and obeyed Him and also those who would want to do so, to remember Him whole-heartedly, as a panacea for all the ills/problems of life, whether material or spiritual. The holy name, Meher Baba, is the legacy of the *Avatar* of the Age to the world in general and to His dear ones in particular. Out of His unlimited compassion for one and all, Meher Baba has occasionally and unreservedly revealed to His followers,

> I am God in human form.... If you make me your real Father, all your problems will become dissolved in the Ocean of my Love.... I like being meditated upon because then I help directly.... If you cannot love me, don't worry, I will be loving you.... If you cannot remember me constantly then repeat my Name before going to sleep and on waking up.... When I drop my body, I shall remain in all who love me.... I am the Ancient One.

---

* Ibid.

ARRIVING AT THE BLESSED CONSUMMATION

This is Meher Baba's clarion call to His followers; it is also an open invitation from the Awakener of hearts to all those who want to know about Him — His Love. Sincerity in repetition is our concern; the melody and "madness" of it is His gift.

Dhuni Lit on January 31

The beginning of the new year, 1952, also turned out to be the concluding period of Baba's New Life. He continued to confine Himself regularly in the *manonash* cabin. This room* was roughly 18' x 9.5' x 8.5' and rested on a wooden framework. It had no real foundation (just like the mind of man). Its walls and roof were made of asbestos sheets which became extremely hot in summer and cold in winter, coincidentally resembling the nature of the mind with its extreme changes in temperament.

During Baba's seclusions, although He appeared inactive, He was intensely busy with His inner spiritual work on different levels of consciousness.

Whenever He would come out of the cabin and rejoin His companions, He would communicate on a variety of subjects (with the exception of spiritual topics), and always with His enormous sense of humor. One day in January, as was His old habit, He casually asked each of the companions his age. Pendu while replying, happened to add that he had only four years left to live. Baba looked amused and asked, "Why?" In reply, Pendu related an incident which had taken place in December, 1926.

In that year, under Baba's instruction, a well was being dug at Meherabad. It was between the road and the railway track (and it is still there). Pendu's duty was to empty the leather bucket that was used to haul out the pieces of hard rock and murram (soft

---

* The room still stands on the Meherazad premises and, after the completion of His *manonash* work, Baba asked Eruch to stay there. It has been Eruch's cabin ever since.

rock) from the bottom of the well. While hauling out the rocks, he had to lean forward to pull up the leather bucket. Sometimes, when he happened to look below, he felt as if the gravitational pull was dragging him down into the darkness of the pit. Occasionally, he was afraid that he might fall in and die. One day when Baba visited the site, Pendu told him about this fear. Baba brushed the subject aside with a casual remark, "Don't fear, Pendu, you won't die for 30 years!" Pendu felt relieved, but whenever Baba asked him his age, he involuntarily recalled Baba's words. The prescribed period was to expire in December, 1956. This was the reason for Pendu's incidental comment while answering Baba's question.

Patiently hearing the whole story, with a swift glance at Pendu, Baba added, "Pendu, you won't die in December, 1956!" But at the same time, He made a sweeping gesture of passing His fingers over His left side. Pendu thought that although the death was averted. Baba's sign might indicate a paralysis of the left side. He, however, did not say anything and Baba switched to another subject.

Nevertheless it should be mentioned here that in December, 1956, Baba met with the second auto accident near Satara (Maharashtra). Nilu, Pendu, Vishnu and Eruch were with Him in the car. Nilu (Dr. Nilkanth) and Pendu were seriously hurt and became unconscious. Nilu died without regaining consciousness. Pendu, as he came back to his senses, found himself in the Civil Hospital at Satara, with a cast around his entire left side, from shoulder to toe. On top of that, because of the injury to his pelvis, his right leg was also placed in a cast. With the slightest movement, Pendu suffered excruciating pain and sometimes even fainted. In a sense, he was dead and yet alive! Thus was Pendu's "sentence of death" reprieved by Baba! I have specially narrated this episode to show that Baba could be mysteriously precise if He wished to be. And also to illustrate how even the casual gesture of the

ARRIVING AT THE BLESSED CONSUMMATION

God-Man has tremendous significance.

On some days after scheduled sittings, Baba would call the companions inside the cabin. He would ask Eruch to read aloud a few passages from some selected books. The five models always remained on the shelf, and no one was allowed to touch them. This was a firm order! Sometimes, Baba Himself would observe the external rituals practised by the followers of different religions. On the last day of this month, January 31, Eruch recalls that Baba made him write some sentences on a slip of paper. Although Eruch does not remember the exact text, he recalls that the gist was: Rites, rituals, and ceremonies of all religions of the world are hereby consumed in the flames. Baba took this note in His hand, silently glanced through the lines, and put it in His pocket. He then instructed Eruch to dig a circular pit behind the *manonash* cabin, before evening. The companions were to collect dry wood, branches, and twigs as fuel for the *dhuni*. Those on the other side of the partitioned compound had no idea of the activities conducted by Baba.

At sundown, with Baba walking in the lead, the companions came to the pit. Baba's face reflected an unspeakable solemnity as He lit the *dhuni*. The smoke slowly rose. After a while, as the flames leapt upwards, Baba stood up; the four companions followed suit. Baba folded His arms, and so did the companions. He took out the same slip of paper that was in His pocket and asked Eruch to read it, "loudly and forcefully". He then took back the note, tore it into pieces and threw them in the flames. At 7 p.m., by the light of the fire, Baba directed Eruch to read His previously dictated message — an invocation/declaration. A part of it is given below:

O Source of Infinite Knowledge, Almighty God! You know that I did all that was humanly possible for me in this ordinary state and I leave the result entirely to Your Will.... From this moment, You must guide me to declare in all truth by the 16th February 1952 what you have decided. From now on I free myself from the external religious ceremonies that I observed during the New Life and the *Manonash* period.*

A holy hush, imbued with an indescribable feeling, fell over them all.

All sat down by the *dhuni* for a second time till the fire died down. Afterwards, Baba, with His own hands, filled two big tins with the *dhuni* ash and the pit was covered. At that time, Baba specifically instructed that "this ash" should not be used by anyone for any purpose whatsoever.

Baba's lighting the *dhuni*, witnessing the rising flames and then glowing embers, offering prayers and lastly, collecting the *dhuni* ash seemed to have a profound significance, especially since this proved to be the concluding act of Baba's New Life.

It is my feeling that through this unique phase of "becoming an ordinary man", the God-Man reached and touched the hearts of His future lovers, in their inner levels of human existence. It is these souls which are now accepting Meher Baba as the Eternal Awakener of "new life". For me to narrate all the incredible stories which justify this supposition would be a large digression at this point. That this is so, however, will in time become clear to all.

Meher Baba's New Life externally began with rain (on October 16), and ended in fire (the *dhuni* on January 31). The whole phase seemed to symbolize fire emerging from water, an age old paradox, and thus an exquisite joke of the God-Man. Perhaps it was in this vein that Meher Baba once stated, "This New Life will live by itself eternally, even if there is no one to live it."

---

* *Circular NL* 34, issued on January 31, 1952.

ARRIVING AT THE BLESSED CONSUMMATION

First Real Birthday

With the cooling of the *dhuni* fire, it seemed that Baba's New Life phase was over. However, a clear announcement of its conclusion was not given for a few days. On February 6, Baba dictated a profound, matchless message which was issued as the first "Life Circular". It combined the characteristics of the three main phases of His *Avataric* mission — the Old Life, the New Life, and the LIFE. I quote below a relevant passage from this particular message, relating to the invocation made by Baba, on January 31. He stated:

> For these last four months, according to ordinary human standards, and by ways and means known to me, I have tried my utmost for the achievement of *Manonash*, and I can say in all truth that I feel satisfied with the work done. This satisfaction is due to the feeling I have, of having regained my 'Old Life Meher Baba state,' yet retaining my 'New Life ordinary state'. I have regained the Knowledge, Strength and Greatness that I had in the Old Life, and retain the ignorance, weaknesses, and humility of the New Life. This union of the 'old and new life states' has given birth to LIFE: Life that is eternally old and new.
> My efforts for *Manonash* have been positive and the result of *Manonash* will be positive. But the actual and concrete manifestation of this result, I leave entirely to the Divine Sanction: where, how, and when the result will be, I leave entirely to the Divine Decree.*

And within a week the *mandali* had one of the most delightful surprises of their life with Baba. It was the celebration of Baba's "First Real Birthday" on February 12, 1952, at Meherazad in a very simple yet

---

* *Life Circular* No. 1, issued on 6-2-1952.

buoyant mood. By this time the partition had been taken down, and the four companions — Gustadjee, Baidul, Pendu, and Eruch — were allowed to greet and meet the rest of the men disciples in Baba's love. Kitty Davy who was staying with the women *mandali* at Meherazad wrote a short, graphic account of this festive occasion:

> As Baba came over to our quarters at 5 a.m. on the morning of February 12th exactly to the minute, bells and gongs were rung, drums beaten and guns fired, and in the midst of all this tumult, the voices of the *mandali* rose clear and loud repeating the different names of God. The evening before, prayers were intoned and the *dhuni* (sacred fire) was lit and kept burning for twenty-four hours. Baba called this day, February 12, 1952, his "first real birthday", the beginning of the period called "Life", and He sent the following message by cable and otherwise to all His devotees:

> GOD'S BLESSINGS AND MY LOVE TO YOU ALL ON THIS, MY FIRST REAL BIRTHDAY.*

On this eventful day Baba, the God-Man, implored God as follows:

> O God! Today being my first real birthday, my heart expresses that the declaration of the "Life" by me was entirely Yours and by Your Will; because nothing happens save by Your Will. ... This Life Eternal will be lived by me in conformity with Your Will and every word of the declaration of the 'Life' will come to pass by your Grace.**

A charmingly paradoxical yet significant statement!

---

* *The Awakener*, Vol. III. No. 4, p. 25.
** *Life Circular* No. 3.

ARRIVING AT THE BLESSED CONSUMMATION

Thus Baba's Old Life and the New Life ended and blended in a graceful manner, and there emerged an everlasting phase which He named as Life Eternal: "Life that is eternally old and new."

Our *new life* in Him

While almost all are puzzled by Baba's New Life, they are also fascinated with it. Baba's New Life has an indescribable charm of its own; there is something gloriously splendid about it, however incomprehensible it may seem. Baba's external activities during this phase— long journeys on foot, at times begging with a begging bowl, wearing a loin cloth and a *kafni*, sweeping out His rooms, washing His clothes, offering prayers and serving the poor — have an austere grandeur about them. In a way, they demonstrate a simple way of living — a life of self-effacement. Was Baba laying the guidelines for a most natural, yet consecrated way of life? In the first discourse published in the *Meher Baba Journal* (November 1938), Meher Baba stated:

> He [*Avatar*] is like a gauge against which man can measure what he is and what he may become. He trues the standard of human values by interpreting them in terms of divinely human life.

This does not mean, however, that one can blindly imitate Baba, or participate in His New Life by merely copying its external aspects. Baba's New Life had a specific context in His *Avataric* mission, and the various external activities were like the scaffoldings erected to accomplish His spiritual work of awakening the heart of humanity. Thus the sublime significance of Baba's New Life is immediately lost if the external activities are given undue importance. However, the New Life as a whole will ever remain as a guiding star for the sincere seeker, but no one can imitate or institutionalize Baba's New Life.

One should very cautiously use the term New Life to describe the change in one's life after coming to Baba, for the term New Life has been consecrated by Baba and has real meaning only in relation to His *Avataric* mission where He, the Emperor (highest-Divinity), became a beggar (lowest-humility) to quicken the lives of all those who are slaves of the world.

Should we attempt to venture on a *new life* based on heresay and a mere intellectual understanding, this would be tantamount to a mimicry of the life of the companions who were with Baba in His New Life. Living with the God-Man was never an easy affair. It was a life which tested ōne's capabilities to the limit and this was especially so during the New Life. The life of the companions who accompanied Baba in this phase can be likened to the ordeal of retaining the freshness of a rose (pure love for the God-Man), while keeping it unscathed by the flames (implicit and instantaneous obedience to the God-Man). What distinguished Baba's companions was not so much that for certain periods they wore *kafnis,* or *langotis,* or begged, or did hard labor but that they constantly lived a life of complete surrender to the God-Man, pledging their lives in obedience to any wish which God in human form might have.

Even while Baba was leading the New Life, there were those who wished to join Him. For them, Baba reissued a statement, first given six months earlier, in which He clearly declared that the New Life would be kept alive by those:

> Who live the life of complete renunciation of false hood, lies, hatred, anger, greed and lust; and who to accomplish all this, do no lustful actions, do no harm to anyone, do no backbiting, do not seek material possessions or power, who accept no homage, neither covet honour nor shun disgrace, and fear no one and nothing; by those, who rely wholly and solely on God, and who love God purely for the sake of

loving, who believe in the lovers of God and in the reality of Manifestation, and yet do not expect any spiritual and material reward; who do nòt let go the hand of Truth, and who, without being upset by calamities, bravely and whole-heartedly face all hardships with 100% cheerfulness, and give no importance to caste, creed and religious ceremonies.
This New Life will live by itself eternally, even if there is no one to live it.*

Herein there is no mention of emulating the external activities which are associated with Baba and the companions in the New Life. This eternal New Life is really the essence of all spiritual life. As such it is a personal intimate relationship with the Benevolent Omnipresence; it becomes defiled by the slightest imitation. It has to have an originality of its own.

This type of *new life* is not meant for the self-cherishers. Unless one sincerely longs to divest oneself from self, the game of keeping company with the God-Man (even in spirit) cannot begin. A true *new life* is the conviction of the *Avatar*'s companionship in all our deeds, words and thoughts. Outward withdrawal is not necessary; one has to renounce the world within one's heart. It is not a question of ignoring or escaping from anything but of facing facts and offering the results totally to the Lord and maintaining a "clean slate."

Baba has on many occasions made it quite explicit, for example, that one should not use drugs like LSD or even marijuana. And He was equally unequivocal that sex outside of marriage was definitely alien to spirituality. It would be the height of hypocrisy for anyone, but especially so for one who claims to love Baba, to try to justify an indulgence in either, in his enthusiastic attempt to lead a *new life*. A *new life*, in fact, is a new way of living. It is an honest, sincere effort to please the God-Man by shedding all of our old selfish attach-

---
* *Circular NL* 17, issued on 11-9-1950.

ments that veil us from our Eternal, most intimate Companion — Baba.

In Baba's New Life there were many instances where the companions and Baba received God's help in the form of coincidences and unexpected occurrences. But these were definitely devoid of any occult or supernatural elements. They were not miracles which Baba performed; He had adopted perfectly the role of an ordinary man, hence it was a natural unfolding of events in response to the *Avatar*'s compassion in stepping down to the level of mankind. Baba once conveyed:

> To guide, instruct and help humanity which is my only mission, I have come down to the level of human understanding and consciousness, and here it is that I am misunderstood. My infinite state of God-consciousness remains unaffected even when I function at the level of normal human consciousness.*

Nothing happens in the life of the God-Man which is out of tune with the Infinite.

The secret of the *new life* is not to strive for anything except to respond continuously to the awakened intuition — the Will of God. Thus, one should not venture on a *new life* guided solely by one's intellectual powers, or detailed study of Baba's New Life, which is inimitable. Hafiz, a Persian Perfect Master, who was Baba's favourite poet, has skillfully explained one of the secrets for anyone's *new life* in a couplet which freely translated means:

> Dear Friend! If you wish to be our classmate, wash away all the leaves of your books (unlearn all that you have learned).
> For my dear, the knowledge (lesson) of Love is not found in books.**

---

* *The Awakener*, Vol. XVI, No. 2, p. 13.
** *Beshooy aurag agar hamdarse mayee
ke elme eshk dar daftar nabasshad.*

ARRIVING AT THE BLESSED CONSUMMATION

Thus my narration of the New Life must end here. However, I am sure that it will be appropriate to conclude this volume with the words of guidance, truth and authority of the God-Man, Meher Baba. In the public programs, when thousands thronged to have Baba's *darshan,* He extended His open, loving invitation to the masses, through the following messages:

I want you to feel that I am one of you.
I am on the level of each one of you.
Make me your constant companion.
Think of me more than you think of your own self.
The more you think of me the more you will realize
My love for you.

To those who responded to His call and came in His close *sahavas,* He would casually convey:

I am the One so many seek and so few find.
No amount of austerity can attain me.
Do not try to understand me. My depth is unfathomable.
Do whole-heartedly whatever I tell you to do:
do not do what I do [Don't imitate my external activities.] If you sincerely follow me — my instructions and teachings — you will feel that I am with you always.

And to the still smaller group who long to surrender their all completely to Him, Meher Baba, out of His unbounded compassion has lovingly revealed:

I am the way; I am the Goal.
I authoritatively say; I am the Ancient One.
If you love me with all your heart,
 then you will be made free eternally.
I am the Ocean of Love;
I am the only Lover;
I am the only Beloved;
I am LOVE.

May Avatar Meher Baba awaken our hearts and bless us with a *new life* of abiding companionship with Him, the Eternal Beloved.

Glossary

arti: A traditional Hindu ceremony performed in the worship of gods by moving a lighted lamp, camphor or joss sticks circularly around the idol. In the case of Meher Baba, His lovers do not necessarily follow this conventional ceremony when the *arti* (song of dedication) is recited or sung.

Avatar, an: An Incarnation manifesting a specific divine quality.

Avatar, the: The Incarnation of God in human form The God-Man, Messiah, Christ.

bairagi: A mendicant with long matted hair and ashes smeared over the body.

bidi: An Indian cigarette.

bhajan: A devotional song, or the singing of devotional songs.

bhakta: A devotee.

bhav: Ecstasy. Form of devotion (in relation to the deity).

bhiksha: Charity, alms. Anything received by one who goes out begging, especially for food.

chapati: Unleavened, flat wheat bread.

chilla-nashini: The undertaking of forty days' austerities.

dal: A common preparation made from any of several types of lentils found in India.

darshan: Formal audience. The appearance of the Master to receive homage and to bestow blessings on devotees, sometimes in the form of *prasad,* q.v.

dharmashala: A free rest house for travelers.

dhoti: A long white cloth worn from the waist and wrapped around the legs.

GLOSSARY

dhuni: A fire, often fueled by faggots, which symbolizes Divine purifying fire.
dnyan: Gnosis, Real Knowledge.

ghazal: A short love poem. An ode. A special poetic composition in Urdu or Persian.

hawa: An aspirant who is not on the Path but is not far from it.

jalali: Glorious. Related to the masculine or outgoing principle. Fiery or hot tempered.
jamali: Beautiful. Related to the feminine or receptive principle. Quiet or mild tempered.
Jivanmukta: A liberated incarnate, a God-Realized One with Creation-consciousness but no specific duty.

kafni: A body length lightweight garment. A long robe.
kambal: A coarse woollen blanket.
karma: The law of action and reaction. Fate. The natural and necessary happenings of one's lifetime, preconditioned by one's past lives.
ki jai: Lit., victory to. Used in the sense of "hail to." Jai in a greeting is used in the sense of calling on the *Avatar,* or in remembrance of the *Avatar,* e.g., "Jai Baba!" "Jai Rama!"
kirtan: The singing of devotional songs, accompanied by music, interspersed with explanations on spiritual subjects.

laddoo: A sweetmeat in the shape of a ball.
langoti: A loin cloth.
lila: The "game" which God plays, which manifests the Universe. The "Divine Sport" of Creation.
lungi: A colored cloth wrapped round the waist, reaching the ankles.

majzoob: One who is absorbed in a plane of involving consciousness.
Majzoob-e-Kamil: One who is God-merged.
majzoobiyat: The state of the God-merged soul of the seventh plane.

mandali: The intimate disciples of a *Sadguru* (Perfect Master), or the *Avatar* (God-Man).
mantra: A sacred name or phrase.
mast: (Pronounced "must") a God-intoxicated man on the Path.
mastani: A God-intoxicated woman.
mela: A fair.

namaskar: Adoration or greeting. A salutation, bow, or obeisance.
Nawab: The title of a Muslim prince.
nazar: Lit., sight. The Master's protective glance or gaze.
nirvana: The first stage of the Real *Fana* — annihilation of the Mind (self).

pan: A masticatory, containing a few spices, wrapped in a betel leaf.
Parabrahma: The Supreme Spirit. God.
prasad: Lit., anything that is first offered to God or the Master and then distributed in His name. A small gift, usually edible, given by the Master as a concrete expression of His love. A gracious gift of the Master.

qawwal: One who sings *ghazals* and *qawwalis.*
qawwali: A special type of singing spiritual songs, usually in Urdu or Persian, intimately addressing the Beloved, sung to spontaneously improvised music.

rava: A sweet dish.

Sadguru: A Perfect Master. A Man-God.
sadhana: A practice, discipline.
sadhu: A pilgrim. An advanced soul. A mendicant.
sadra: A thin ankle length muslin shirt.
sahavas: Lit., close companionship. A gathering held by the Master or held in His honor where His devotees intensely feel His Presence.
sanyasi: One who has renounced the world.

tantric: One who seeks and possesses occult powers.
turiya avastha: The State of Divine Junction.

Bibliography

There are several books by Meher Baba and many on His life and teachings. For convenience, only those from which selections have been taken for this Volume are included in this list.

BOOKS BY MEHER BABA:

Discourses. 6th ed. in 3 vol., San Francisco: Sufism Reoriented, Inc., 1967.
The Everything and The Nothing. hard cover, Meher House Publications (Bombay), for Meher House Publications, Australia, 1976.
God Speaks. 2nd ed. rev. and enl., New York: Dodd, Mead and Co., 1973.
Life at its Best. San Francisco: Sufism Reoriented, Inc., 1957.
Listen Humanity. New York: Colophon Books, Harper and Row, 1971.

BOOKS ABOUT MEHER BABA:

*Circulars NL (New Life) Nos. 1 to 34. Meher Publications, King's Road, Ahmednagar, India.
Glimpses of the God-Man, Meher Baba Vol. I by Bal Natu. Sufism Reoriented, Inc., Walnut Creek, California. 1977.
The God-Man by C. B. Purdom. George Allen and Unwin, 1964. Republished by Sheriar Press, Inc., South Carolina, U.S.A. 1971.
**Meher Baba in The Great Seclusion* by Ramjoo

---

* The above books have been made previously available only to the followers of Meher Baba, but not to the general public.

Abdulla and Dr. C. D. Deshmukh. Meher Publications, Ahmednagar, India. 1949.

Meher Baba and The God-Determined Step by Ramjoo Abdulla. Meher Publications, Ahmednagar, India. 1951.

The New Phase of Meher Baba's Life by Ramjoo Abdulla. Meher Publications, Ahmednagar, India. 1949.

The Wayfarers — Meher Baba with the God-intoxicated (Incorporating: *The Work of Meher Baba with Advanced Souls and Sadhus; The Work of Meher Baba with Advanced Souls, Sadhus, the Mad, and the Poor*) by William Donkin. Sufism Reoriented, Inc. 1969.

OTHER BOOKS:

In Dust I Sing by Francis Brabazon. The Beguine Library, Berkeley, California. 1974.

Stay with God by Francis Brabazon, Garuda Books, Queensland, Australia. 1959. Republished by Meher House Publications (Bombay), India, 1977.

MAGAZINES DEVOTED TO MEHER BABA:

The Awakener. Quarterly, edited by Filis Frederick from 938-18th Street, Hermosa Beach, California, U.S.A.

The Glow. Quarterly, edited by Freiny Nalavala and Naosherwan Anzar. Published from 36 Lytton Road, Dehra Dun, India.

Meher Baba Journal. Published by "Meher Editorial Committee", Ahmednagar, India.

---

* Therefore, the publication of this material in this book is the first-time said information has been made available to the general public.

www.ingramcontent.com/pod-product-compliance
Lightning Source LLC
Chambersburg PA
CBHW020742100426
42735CB00037B/177